Penguin Handbooks

The Penguin Book of Fishing

Ted Lamb was born in Bromley, Kent, in 1944 and educated at
Thornbury Grammar School, Gloucestershire. He sold his first
article on angling when he was thirteen, and from 1966–9
worked as a staff journalist on the *Angling Times*, travelling
widely in the British Isles to fish and interview local anglers. In
1972 he founded Britain's first monthly sea angling magazine,
Sea Angler, now a thriving journal, which he also edited through
its first year. Ted Lamb is a lifelong angler with experience of
coarse, game and sea fishing.

He is married with two young children.

Ted Lamb

THE PENGUIN BOOK OF

Fishing

A complete guide to
freshwater coarse and game fishing,
and sea boat, shore and big-game angling.

Illustrations by Judith Lamb

Penguin Books

Penguin Books Ltd, Harmondsworth,
Middlesex, England
Penguin Books, 625 Madison Avenue,
New York, New York 10022, U.S.A.
Penguin Books Australia Ltd, Ringwood,
Victoria, Australia
Penguin Books Canada Ltd, 2801 John Street,
Markham, Ontario, Canada L3R 1B4
Penguin Books (N.Z.) Ltd, 182–190 Wairau Road,
Auckland 10, New Zealand

First published by Allen Lane 1979
Published in Penguin Books 1980

Made and printed in Great Britain by
Richard Clay (The Chaucer Press) Ltd
Bungay, Suffolk
Set in Monotype Garamond

Contents

List of illustrations

Introduction

To many outsiders the picture often conjured up by the word 'angler' is of a rustic figure, self-absorbed in a green study by some quiet stream, to all appearances immobile in deed, perhaps even in thought . . .

Undeniably, anglers do fish in quiet watermeadows. They – and by 'they' I mean the almost four million people who count fishing with a rod and line as their main pastime – also fish in lakes, torrent rivers, mountain tarns. They fish in the ocean, over reefs and the wrecks of long-lost ships, and they fish from beaches, coastal cliffs and estuary shores . . . in short, wherever there are fish worth catching.

They come from all walks of life, and in the records of past angling achievements you will find listed, kings, peers, clergymen, farm workers, bank managers, mechanics, schoolchildren and nonagenarians. In a curious sort of way all are bound in their sport by a relationship devoid of social distinctions, a brotherhood. To that I must add sisterhood for, long before this age of equality, women participated in angling on an equal footing with men, holding among other distinctions the record for rod-caught salmon (64 lb taken by Miss G. W. Ballantine in 1922) and for mako shark (352 lb taken by Mrs Hetty Eathorne in 1955, superseded by a 500 lb fish taken by Mrs Joyce Yallop in 1971).

Of the fish that this huge body of anglers seeks – even in the watermeadow – just a few are easy to catch. Most are challenging to both ingenuity and skill. Each fish species has a taste for a particular watery environment (slack, flowing, deep, shallow – in varied proportions) and a liking for a particular range of foods. The angler must first of all know where to look for fish, and what to tempt them with. That done, he must learn how to use his tackle to present the bait in the best possible way and in a wide range of water and weather conditions.

But he has more to contend with. Some fish are moderately easy to approach, but most are extremely shy. Some are small, others large, and some (among sea species especially) can only truly be described as 'huge'. Tackle must be balanced carefully; it must be so light that it avoids scaring the quarry, yet it must be strong enough to secure and land the fish.

You can easily see that immobility has little part in these proceedings, and there can be no lack of thought. If the angler does appear self-absorbed, his absorption is an inwardness from which the right actions emerge after a rapid calculation of myriad influences, and after the prompting of a lively imagination which is seeing through the light-reflecting surface of the water to the fish, their minds, and their outlook.

There remains a less-serious charge that angling is a waste of time, a misconception that springs in some measure from the fact that anglers have been known to spend whole days at their pursuit without catching anything, and also from the more curious fact that much of what is caught is returned alive to the water. To understand the subtler rewards of angling you have to look deeper than the belief that the objective is a tasty meal.

To begin with, once the angler has set his cap at a particular quarry and is, as it were, half in his own world and half within the fish's, he is experiencing a delicious thrill of anticipation. I don't, like some, put this down to a latent hunting instinct – I rather make it an abstract thing, somewhere between the hope of winning a game of chess and the delight of exploring an untrodden land.

Small wonder that out of a great deal of literature about anglers and angling, one short philosophical statement has wide appeal. It is a saying attributed (untraceably) to Allah: 'Of man's allotted span, time spent fishing is not deducted.'

There are many reasons why angling is an attractive sport with a wide following. Accessibility is one – few places in Britain are far from fishable water. Angling is not governed by time limits and you can go, fish, pack up and return whenever you wish. You can choose to fish alone or in company.

It is, too, a year-round, all-weather sport. True, there are close seasons – times, enforced by law, when you cannot fish for certain species of freshwater fish. But there are no close seasons for sea fish, and when the freshwater coarse fishing close season begins, the trout close season is just about to end. If you have the taste and the tackle for alternative kinds of fishing when your favourite kind has to stop, you can carry on angling without a break. As to weather, so long as you are well protected against the elements, you can enjoy fishing in midwinter just as much as in the summer. Fishing presents no barriers to youth or old age, and only extremely large sea fish are particularly demanding on strength. And besides all that, the sport is not over-costly; the greatest expense is basic equipment, a rod and reel which, with care, will last a lifetime. Thereafter, trips involve only modest outlays for bait, transport, replacements of small items of tackle, and licences or permits.

Above all, a beginner finds that skill and knowledge are quickly accumulated by fishing as often as possible, and by keeping an ear open for advice from other anglers and taking note of the exchange of information and ideas in angling books and journals. There is always something new to learn, some different approach to an old problem perhaps, or even the emergence of a problem which you never knew existed . . . I always remember Dick Walker, a sage, experienced angler who has the rainbow trout record (18 lb 4 oz, 1976 – unclaimed) and the carp record (44 lb, 1952) under his belt, saying fairly recently that it had been brought to his notice that he could unblock a varnished-over hook eye with the point of another hook. Up to then he had been carrying around a pin for the purpose!

Acquiring rod, reel and tackle and setting out some day in the morning air is a step towards a whole new world; but therein rests a problem in itself – how do you start, where do you start, and what do you need to start angling? I hope this handbook provides the answers, both for beginners and for experienced anglers who would like to encounter a different facet of their sport.

The scope of this book

Catching fish is the essence of angling, and setting about catching fish with some success is the aim of this handbook. 'Success' does take different forms, however. It might mean seeking and capturing a very large fish of a particular species, carp for instance. This is frequently termed 'specimen hunting'. It might mean catching a heavier bag of fish than other participants during a fishing match, or simply being consistently able to catch good bags of varied species without any competitive motive.

Limited space forbids making these distinctions in the main course of the handbook. The approach to match fishing and notes on the sort of dedication required for specimen hunting are included separately, of course, but the general techniques discussed are relevant to all fields. They set out to abolish chance or 'luck' from angling expeditions, replacing them with confidence in tackle and ability – the 'secret bait' of the angler who wins distinctions in matches, specimen fish lists, or in the simpler role of fishing for pleasure alone.

There are many different kinds of rod and line sport fishing. There are differences in tackle, baits and approaches for, firstly, the most obvious division of sea and freshwater angling, and after that there are further differences for the varied species of fish which inhabit both of these worlds. The role of a handbook is to set out these many differences so that they provide a progressive guide for a beginner, who might otherwise find himself presented with a bewildering choice, and to give the more experienced angler a sound reference book.

The handbook is divided into four parts. Part One begins by outlining the path towards taking up angling, with notes about acquiring tackle (and what it should cost), the angling organizations in Britain, and points of law which affect the angler.

This part then goes on to outline the main items of fishing tackle – rods, reels, lines, hooks and so on – and the accessories that complement them. Towards the end, the section concentrates on combining these various items, with instructions on tying knots. It ends with a novel feature – a checklist summarizing all the items required for particular types of fishing and advice on the sort of preparations which lead to efficient angling, increased enjoyment and better catches.

Part Two is concerned with practical angling. It looks first at the make-up of fish, following this with details of the freshwater and sea environments in which they will be sought. It then shows how to use the tackle and baits – noting how to acquire, and in some cases how to breed, baits – and lists the different species which can be caught in British waters, with descriptions of the approach best suited to catching them. This advice is set out under four headings; coarse fishing and game fishing, which are freshwater disciplines (game fish are the important members of the biological family Salmonidae – trout, salmon etc. – and coarse fish are the remaining freshwater species), and sea and big game fishing – 'big game' accounting for the larger sea species such as shark and tunny. Approaches to match fishing and specimen hunting are also discussed.

After these major sections about angling 'at home', Part Three deals briefly with angling abroad, and contains helpful addresses for holiday anglers, and those contemplating longer periods in other countries.

The last part of the handbook gives information about British and international specimen fish records, and how to set about claiming a record. It lists, too, the major angling organizations, river authorities and weather stations – with addresses – as well as many books which will be helpful to anglers.

Throughout the handbook there are line drawings which serve to clarify points in the text. The drawings accompanying the details of fish species in Part Two are a handy quick-guide to species identification.

Part One

1 Beginning to fish

This chapter is intended mainly for beginners, to give them a picture of the various branches of angling, and to help them avoid pitfalls in the choice of tackle. It also suggests sources of advice on fishing in your area. Later in the chapter is a summary of the sort of costs you are likely to face if you take up angling from scratch.

Choice of what sort of angling the beginner should start with is determined to a large extent by the sort of fishing water available locally. A local water is always best for learning basic skills, for the simple reason that it can be visited more frequently than waters further afield. No matter if such a location hasn't the fame in the angling world of, for instance, the Hampshire Avon, or the Eddystone Reef; such spots do not automatically give the beginner the best chance of catching fish.

§1 Sea or freshwater ?

Sea water and freshwater have different physical attributes, and each contains a totally different range of fish species. There are a few species attracted to estuaries, which share some physical aspects of sea and freshwater, and here sea and freshwater techniques and tackle can overlap in a small way. In most other situations there are wide differences in tackle, baits and approach.

§2 Freshwater, coarse and game fishing

Freshwater fishing is divided into two basic disciplines, 'coarse' and 'game' fishing, which separates the members of the salmon family of fishes, regarded as game, much as are grouse in the shooting world, from the twenty or so species of freshwater fish that are worth catching.

By and large, most coarse fishing is 'bait' fishing; that is, fishing with a worm, bread or some other offering on a hook, either suspended from a float, or cast out on floatless, weighted tackle, a technique known as legering. Species such as the roach, which reaches only modest weights, and the carp, which runs to over 30 lb, are normally approached by bait fishing. Predators, such as the pike, a species which reaches prodigious weights, are usually approached with live or dead fish baits, and they will also attack metal spinners which imitate small fish. Fly fishing will also catch some species of coarse fish.

All of the game fish will take lively baits such as worms, but normally the approach to trout, sea-trout and salmon is with artificial flies, lures and spinners which represent insects and small fish. Trout and sea-trout view such imitations as food, although their motive in attacking one might occasionally stem from aggression. The salmon, however, does not feed during its run upstream to spawning grounds, and whatever induces it to consider any of the offerings of an angler is a mystery. There are theories that flies and spinners remind them of food organisms in the North Atlantic feeding grounds, and that this momentarily sparks a feeding instinct, or that they might be purging the water of creatures that could prove a threat to their eggs and offspring. Whatever the reason, salmon do get fairly and squarely hooked, for which anglers can be thankful.

§3 Sea shore, boat, and big-game fishing

Sea fishing creates its own natural divisions. There is, first of all, a marked difference in the sort of tackle needed for fishing from the shore – the most obvious being a rod with some casting capability – to the sort of tackle needed to lower a bait over the side of a deep-sea boat.

The sea fish species encountered by the shore angler are not entirely the same as the species of offshore locations such as reefs, wrecks or open sea. Species attracted to estuaries, such as grey mullet and flounders, are not found in any quantity far out at sea, while some large sharks prefer to stay well out. Of the species which are shared by both these locations, the fish caught from the shore are usually (but not invariably) smaller than those found offshore.

The larger species of sea fish – sharks and rays, conger eels and so on – deserve to be regarded as a separate branch of sea fishing since they call for tackle of a different order of strength from the moderate and small species. 'Moderate' in the scale of sizes of sea fish is somewhat different from the word used in the context of freshwater fishing. Into this range fall ling, which reach 50 lb, and cod, pollack and coalfish, which are somewhat smaller (although commercial boats have landed cod of over 100 lb). The large 'big-game' fishes are normally encountered offshore, although occasionally they can be approached from shore vantage points.

Most sea fish, like coarse fish, are approached by bait fishing, but the bass, for instance, is frequently taken by spinning, while cod, pollack, coalfish and a number of other species will take spinners and lures of various kinds besides accepting bait.

The angling branches we have arrived at are coarse fishing, which consists mainly of bait fishing with float or leger techniques and a small amount of spinning and fly fishing; game fishing, which consists of a small amount only of bait fishing and a large amount of fly fishing and spinning; shore fishing, which includes bait and spinning techniques for a wide range of locations like beaches, rocks, estuaries and so on; sea boat fishing for species running to a moderate size, using either baits or lures; and finally big-game fishing – mainly bait fishing.

Kitting out : Once the choice has been made to start in any of these branches, the first aim is to select suitable rods, reels, lines and end-tackle; but once these have been acquired, a small range of accessories is vital to efficient fishing.

Some implement to assist in landing a fish should be carried by an angler. Small fish can, of course, be swung-in without fear of breaking your line, but bigger fish will not be landed in this fashion without damage to the line and possibly the rod too. Landing implements – such as a long-handled net, or a net on a long cord if you fish some distance from the water on a pier; or a gaff, which is a stout metal hook fastened to a shaft; or a tailer, a wire slip-loop on a shaft – are virtually a 'must' unless you are prepared to plunge into the water and grab the fish by hand.

The next essential is something to recover hooks that have either been swallowed by a fish, or which are lodged in a fish's mouth behind a formidable row of sharp teeth. Disgorging implements can either be a thin steel probe with a forked end, used by the freshwater fisherman, or a pair of long-nosed pliers or artery forceps for bigger fish.

Many other accessories are useful, but not so vital as the landing and disgorging implements for the actual business of fishing. For instance, the coarse fisherman may want to hold onto his catch alive until the end of the day's fishing, in which case he will want a large keep-net which can be immersed in the water. Many branches of fishing will also require rod rests. Finally, suitable containers will be needed for rods, reels, tackle and accessories, together with some sort of holdall suited either to carrying, if you are to move about while you are fishing, or for sitting upon if you will be staying still for long periods.

Confidence in your tackle and bait is a big factor in angling, and so is the ability to make changes of hooks and so on at speed. Much groundwork can be done at home, perhaps on the day before a trip. Checks can be made on the main items of tackle to see that no rod-rings, for instance, are loose, and that the line has not deteriorated since your last trip. Hooks can be ready-tied to traces, finished with loops which make change-overs easy. Floats can be marked with an easily recognizable code, so that you know what sort of counter-weight they will need at a glance. Above all, you should strive to organize your tackle – floats laid out in a float box, for instance, and hooks and other items in appropriate containers – so that you know exactly where they are when you want them. While you are searching for some mislaid piece of tackle the fish of a lifetime could sail past unnoticed, and swim out of your life forever. If parts of your tackle are faulty, you might lose a good fish. Whenever your hook is out of the water, perhaps to tie a knot that could easily have been tied the night before, you stand no chance whatsoever of catching a fish.

Tuition: Although this book strives to impart all the basic skills of angling, you can obtain instruction from other sources. Private schooling in fly fishing for trout and salmon can be traced through tackle dealers or the advertisement columns of angling journals. Tuition in sea and coarse fishing is a little harder to find, but classes are arranged in some areas through the Sports Council, and in Scotland through the Scottish Council for Physical Recreation. Tutors in such courses are vetted in many cases by the National Angling Coaching Scheme, which is organized by the National Anglers' Council (address in Chapter 36).

Choosing tackle: This advice has been given time and time again, but it has by no means stopped people falling into a trap: always avoid a so-called 'beginner's outfit'. Such outfits are, for the most part, inadequate for many tasks, and in any event your rapidly-growing skill will soon make them redundant. It is important to have the real thing so far as rod and reel are concerned, even if it seems that these are difficult to handle in the early days. If somebody is going to buy some tackle, show them this advice. Remember that the most expensive items will last a good many years, and will have a trade-in value if they are well cared for.

Equipment costs: New and perfectly serviceable fishing rods can be obtained for something between £10 and £15. Big beachcasting rods, however, contain a large amount of material and cost a small amount more. The less expensive rods might not look so attractive as hand-finished rods, but they will usually do the same job. You can pick up good secondhand bargains, but these must be examined thoroughly for damage or signs of wear. Minor faults like frayed whippings can be repaired with little trouble and worn rod-rings can be replaced, but you might never find a spare to make good a broken section, and it is not worth buying something so damaged in the hope that you will. If you are happy with your skills of construction you can make your own rod at home, saving a certain amount of cash. The various components and materials are obtainable through dealers, or by post from specialist firms.

A reel, the other major item of expense, ought to be from the middle price range of the selection offered, since you will want it to last. For any beginner I would recommend a fixed-spool reel (small for freshwater fishing, larger for shore fishing) except for deep-sea fishing from a boat, where a multiplier or a big heavy-duty centre-pin reel is more manageable (these terms are explained in Chapter 5). A fixed-spool reel suitable for freshwater fishing will cost about £8, and one for shore fishing between £10 and £15. Multiplier reels for sea boat work begin at around £15, and a centre-pin for the same work costs the same or slightly less. Fly fishermen need a specialized centre-pin reel and a heavy casting line, and both items are surprisingly cheap if you are happy with a basic fly reel and plastic-coated line – around £6 covers them both. Like rods, reels can be bought secondhand. If you buy one in this way, try to get hold of a copy of the manual usually supplied with the new item and follow the instructions for cleaning and overhauling, keeping an eye open for parts that might need replacing – particularly the bale-arm of a fixed-spool reel. Always, without exception, discard whatever line comes with a secondhand reel and replace it with new, because you can never be entirely confident about its quality.

Other long-lasting but cheaper items you will need are a landing net or gaff, perhaps a keep-net, and a basket, box or bag for carrying your tackle. A few pounds will cover them, and it will not cost a great deal to complete your outfit with a line and hooks, flies, lures, spinners, floats, weights and so on, each amounting to only a few pence. Rod rests for shore and fresh-water fishing can be improvised to begin with, and it should be easy to find tins, jars and cigar boxes suitable for carrying bait and small tackle items. Obviously, it is better to start with all-new tackle, but it is often not practical and certainly not essential.

Other expenses: Most sea anglers who fish from the shore do not need to pay anything in the way of dues, although if they fish from privately owned or corporation-owned piers, jetties and wharves, they may be asked to pay a fee for fishing rights. You do not need permission to fish in the open sea, but unless you are lucky enough to own a boat, or are friendly with a boat-owner who will take you out for free trips, you will have to pay for an offshore outing.

For freshwater fishing the picture is somewhat different. In England and Wales, the area in which you fish will be controlled by a water authority which imposes charges known as rod-licence fees, usually covering you for a day, a week, or the entire season. These charges vary from authority to authority, and they vary in amount for coarse and game fishing, and for the length of period covered. You may, for instance, have to pay as little as 50p for a season's coarse fishing – or you might be asked for £1 or more. A rod licence for salmon fishing is at the expensive end of charges, but it can be as low as £2 or less for a season. Trout rod-licence charges usually fall in between these two extremes. For juveniles and pensioners, fees are sometimes reduced.

But, be warned, these statutory charges only allow you to use a rod and line for the purpose of taking fish, and they don't entitle you to actual fishing rights. After acquiring a rod licence you must then track down some free fishing – which still exists as an ancient right in many riverside towns – or you must seek permission from somebody who owns fishing rights. More often than not you will have to pay for such fishing, although these charges are often modest. Many freshwater fishing clubs own fishing rights on a good selection of waters, and it is a good idea to join such an organization. Membership fees average about £2 a season for a full member, with reductions in some cases for pensioners and juveniles.

Outlays of this nature, which are spread over several months, amount to very little cost per trip. Bait and replacement tackle will have to be added on – also the cost of boat charter or boat hire if you are going on the water. Many baits can be collected – worms and other creatures for sea and freshwater fishing – and bread or flour-and-water paste for freshwater fishing can be rifled from the kitchen. You can also breed your own maggots, a popular freshwater bait, and there is advice on this subject later in this handbook. However, if you do not have the opportunity to collect your own baits you will have to buy some. Most tackle dealers carry a range of sea and freshwater baits.

Transport is becoming increasingly expensive and there is a great deal of sense in making up parties of anglers who live fairly close to each other, to share fuel costs for a car or van – not necessarily to fish in company or even at the same places so long as a route covering convenient dropping places and picking-up points is drawn up.

Local advice: A one-inch or half-inch Ordnance Survey map, or in the case of sea fishing an Admiralty chart for your area, will help you to identify the various waters and marks within easy reach of your home. However, you then have to establish who owns the fishing rights if you are to fish in freshwater. An experienced local angler will be your best source of advice, and he may even allow you to accompany him on an angling trip and perhaps borrow a spare set of tackle. Do not, however, pester an angler while he is fishing, for he is unlikely to welcome such intrusion.

Another valuable source of advice is a good fishing-tackle dealer, preferably one who deals in fishing tackle, or perhaps tackle and guns, alone. The staff at tackle counters in big stores may know nothing at all about fishing; the tackle dealer, on the other hand, is likely to be well-versed in local fishing requirements and will not mind taking time over your problems. You are, after all, likely to be a customer of his for a long time. The information you need most is what tackle and baits are best suited to your area, and you should also ask if any regulations govern local fishing.

The officials of fishing clubs will also be helpful to beginners, and some clubs even offer instruction for young members. Membership also puts you in the way of cheap outings, and if the club is for freshwater fishing you will also be entitled to fishing rights on a selection of waters if you join.

Sea fishing charter-boat skippers earn their reputation by finding good marks and advising anglers on how best to fish them, and a beginner can be utterly confident about placing himself in the hands of a good skipper. Many charter boats also carry rods and reels for hire or loan during a fishing trip, so you can often sample boat fishing without having to buy tackle.

I mentioned briefly in the last chapter that there are no general legal restrictions on fishing in the sea. There may, however, be local by-laws which prohibit angling on busy holiday beaches at certain times of the year. Bait digging for marine worms is similarly restricted in some areas. Harbour breakwaters and piers, and other structures which may be privately owned, or owned by local councils, can charge for fishing rights.

In freshwater fisheries you must obtain a water authority rod licence before either fishing in free fisheries, or seeking permission and perhaps paying for the right to fish in water covered by private fishing rights. You should always carry these licences and permits with you when you are fishing so that you can show them to a bailiff if asked. In some areas you may be asked to stop fishing, and even have your tackle temporarily confiscated, if you cannot produce the appropriate pieces of paper on request at the bankside.

Failure to cover yourself with rod licences and permits could lead to your being taken to court on a poaching charge, regardless of whether you are fishing for game or coarse fish. The penalty in many cases is permanent confiscation of tackle besides a fine. Written on rod licences, and in some instances permits, you will generally find two further sets of regulations – close seasons and size limits.

Close seasons: The intention of close seasons is that they shelter fish from the attentions of anglers during spawning periods, but considerable controversy rages over whether or not they accomplish this aim; spawning would appear to fluctuate according to the weather from year to year, while factors such as water temperature can create widely different spawning times for fish of the same species in different waters. Even if they don't truly protect spawning fish, which anyway show little inclination to feed, they do give the water a rest for a period. Without disturbances for a length of time fish can become less wary, while bankside vegetation improves from being untrodden, all of which goes towards making the start of a new fishing season something to look forward to.

There are national statutory close seasons for salmon, trout and coarse fish, laid down by the Salmon and Freshwater Fisheries Act (as amended in 1972 and 1975). These times can, however, be further changed by water authority by-laws, and thus you might find different close seasons in different water authority areas, or even alterations from river to river within one authority's area. The national close seasons are:

> Coarse fish: 15 March–15 June
> Trout: 1 October–Last day of Feb.
> Salmon: 1 November–31 January
>   (all dates inclusive).

The 1975 Act left it up to individual water authorities to make provisions for a close season for rainbow trout, as distinct from native brown trout. It also classified eels as 'freshwater fish' which brought them within the protection of the coarse-fish close season. Formerly, the migratory eel was often left out of close season legislation and could be fished for throughout the year – only where by-laws permit can this now be done.

Frequently you may find that there are by-laws giving separate close seasons for migratory sea-trout. You may also find places where, by by-law, coarse fish close seasons are absent, or waived for a period. In some private enclosed waters statutory close season legislation need not apply.

Size limits: These are to ensure that immature freshwater fish are returned alive to the water to continue growing. Size limits vary from species to species. There are no national guidelines, and instead they are fixed by water authority by-laws, and there can be considerable differences in size limits from authority to authority. In some areas you may be allowed to keep immature fish in a keep-net for release later while in others you can keep only sizeable fish. You may also be allowed to retain a certain number of small fish for use as pike-baits.

As well as there being no charge for fishing in the sea, there are no close seasons or size limits for sea fish. To protect immature sea fish, however, the National Federation of Sea Anglers has drawn up a list of size limits which are enforced during competitions run under the Federation's rules, but which are voluntary outside them.

Other restrictions: You might find by-laws banning the use of certain baits for various species of freshwater fish, and also restrictions on the type of tackle you may use to fish for salmon or trout – bait fishing is often banned in game fisheries, and some are strictly 'fly fishing only'.

Insurance: If you collect a good deal of valuable fishing tackle, it can be worthwhile to insure it against theft, loss or damage other than fair wear and tear. The cost of fishing accidents where a third party is damaged are rare – injury from a flying fishing weight, for instance, or accidentally catching somebody with a hook – but if you do want to cover yourself in this respect cheap policies can be obtained.

Most of Britain's anglers belong to a club or association. There are hundreds of these bodies, some with only a few members and some with thousands; they represent either sea anglers or fresh-water anglers, and occasionally both.

The reason for forming clubs (some of which were established centuries ago) is part economic and part social. In freshwater fishing, rights to fish certain stretches of water are quite expensive. Landlords owning these 'riparian rights', as they are known in law, can and do run their own fisheries, but it is obviously convenient for them to lease the fishing to some other person, or a syndicate or club. Such leases often include the responsibility of maintaining the fishery and restocking it. By 'clubbing' a group of anglers in a village or town can acquire such a lease for a comparatively small amount of money each, and they can also chip in towards its maintainance.

Similarly, sea-fishing clubs have been formed with economics in mind. For instance, the cost of boat hire can be shared for a party of anglers, and so can the cost of a coach trip from an inland town to the coast.

On the social side, clubs provide places where angling friends can meet and exchange ideas, and some well-organized clubs even have their own premises. Others are based in factories or offices, and some in pubs. Annual socials might be held, but clubs form a particularly useful basis for running matches and specimen-fish competitions for prizes and trophies. Within any area boasting several clubs, there is likely to be a good deal of friendly inter-club rivalry, and a league with regular matches might be formed to decide the best club of the year.

Affiliations and national organizations: After club level, larger bodies are encountered in freshwater fishing. These are combinations of smaller clubs, affiliated to a larger body so that a wide choice of water and facilities are open to the combined membership. The Birmingham Anglers' Association and the London Anglers' Association are examples; both have huge memberships and a wide range of fishing waters.

Clubs and the larger associations in Britain are almost all linked to large national or area federations. It is obviously a good thing to have a strong body that can represent collected interests with a united front, not least in the role of a pressure group able to influence the direction of legislation which might affect angling.

The biggest federation representing sea anglers is the National Federation of Sea Anglers (N.F.S.A.) and there are other federations for Welsh, Scottish and Northern sea anglers (the addresses for all the organizations mentioned below are given in Chapter 36). The National Federation of Anglers (N.F.A.) represents freshwater coarse fishermen. Besides their varied duties, the N.F.S.A. and the N.F.A. are perhaps best known for their organizational work in large-scale competitions.

The Salmon and Trout Association is the largest body representing game anglers. Specimen hunters have the National Association of Specimen Groups (N.A.S.G.) as an umbrella for clubs concerned with catching large fish of individual species, such as The Tenchfishers. Single large associations exist for anglers in highly specialized fields – the Shark Angling Club of Great Britain, for example, and the British Conger Club.

As a sort of high-powered clearing house able to make direct representations to the Minister of Sport on all matters of coarse, game and sea fishing, there is the National Anglers' Council (N.A.C.). Delegates from all the major angling organizations help it to function. Finally there is a national organization for fighting pollution cases in or out of court, supported by voluntary contributions from anglers. This is the Anglers' Cooperative Association (A.C.A.).

British anglers are in touch with their continental counterparts chiefly through competitions. The bodies maintaining these links are the Confédération Internationale de la Pêche Sportive (C.I.P.S.) for freshwater fishermen, and the European Federation of Sea Anglers (E.F.S.A.).

The other two organizations of importance to British anglers are those concerned with the ratification and recording of record-weight fish. The British Record (rod-caught) Fish Committee, which is a part of the N.A.C., handles records for British sea and freshwater fishes, while world records for the larger species of sea fish are ratified by the International Game Fish Association (I.G.F.A.) based in Florida.

If you cannot find clubs in your vicinity through a tackle dealer you can send an inquiry (with a stamped addressed envelope) to the N.F.A. or the N.F.S.A., or perhaps one of the Northern, Scottish or Welsh sea angling federations.

Modern tackle : rods

Any attempt to trace the origins of the fishing rod must be based on guesswork rather than fact. Written evidence is scarce and ancient objects made out of wooden materials have long since decomposed. However, bone and metal fishing hooks made several thousands of years ago have survived (some are in the British Museum) showing that the use of a line and baited hook has been one of man's main fish-catching methods from primitive times.

Today, fish are still taken by the same means, but anybody using a line and baited hook alone is hopelessly outclassed by an angler equipped with rod, line, reel and terminal tackle, chosen to match water conditions and the sort of fish being sought. He would also get less pleasure from the exercise. Try fishing without a rod yourself, and you will quickly realize the limitations. You are more or less restricted to fishing 'at your feet', lowering your bait into the water which you hope will hold fish. You also have to exercise extreme stealth so that you do not scare the quarry.

If you tied your line to the end of a longish stick, however, you would find your reach extended. Not only would you be able to explore water further away, but you would also put some distance between yourself and the fish. Although you would have no means of placing the bait far beyond the length of the stick, the improvement on hand-lining would still be considerable. Indeed, rods with a line fixed to the tip are still used today – the freshwater angler's roach pole is an example, as are the long canes used by rock fishermen in some of the Mediterranean countries.

Of course the baited line can be thrown further away with the addition of a weight, but a stick – an extension of the arm – is a much closer contact with the terminal tackle; the tackle-thrower would have to use skill and effort to reach the places where the stick-user simply lowered his bait, and when a fish was hooked, the thrower would find that lessened contact made control over its movements less easy.

Although the earliest rods were probably used simply to extend the fisherman's range, it must have been quickly apparent that they improved the angler's powers in other ways, and that flexible materials made better rods than rigid sticks. Some 'give' in the rod, for instance, absorbed the plunges of a hooked fish, protecting the line from the sort of sudden shock that could snap it; the same give, when the reel came along to make the rod and line an even more formidable fish-getter, also ironed out the snatch of sudden acceleration in casting, which again might break the line or cause the bait to fly off the hook. The important functions of most rods are:

Casting: Throwing weighted tackle beyond the end of the rod is a technique used in float fishing, legering, spinning and fly fishing (in the latter the weight is the heavy fly line and not the terminal tackle). A man's arm is quite strong, but in the act of throwing it moves through a fairly small arc and releases the thrown object at quite a low velocity – it cannot travel far before gravity and air-resistance drag it down.

If you use a rod, moving your arm at the same speed as you would for throwing, the rod-tip – and the bait travelling behind it – swings through a much greater arc and has a much higher velocity (Fig. 1). In practice, with a long rod you need put less effort than you would for throwing into making a long cast.

In the act of making a more powerful cast the flexibility of the rod is a great asset. The arm-action which puts the power into the cast is relatively sudden compared with the smoother acceleration of the rod-tip as the rod compresses into a bend and then straightens out to shoot the tackle forward. Snatch is eliminated.

The longer the rod, in theory, the greater the tip speed – but there are practical limits to the length of rods which can cast efficiently. Most fall between 7 ft and 14 ft (215 – 425 cm) beyond which length they tend to become unwieldy. Long beachcasters and salmon fly rods are designed for double-handed casting and the longest rods of all, roach poles (up to 24 ft – 730 cm – or more), are not used for casting at all. At the other end of the scale

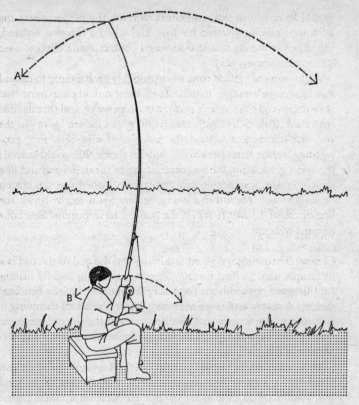

Fig. 1 The arc covered by the rod-tip (A) during casting is much greater than the arc covered by the arm (B) during the same time – the rod-tip is therefore travelling at a higher velocity than the arm.

the deep-sea angler's short boat rod (to 7 ft – 215 cm) is used mainly to lower baits into deep water over the side of a boat.

Controlling tackle: Once a cast has been made and the bait is in the water the angler can manoeuvre his tackle into more favourable positions by altering the angle of pull with the rod – again, longer rods are more useful in this respect than shorter ones.

Striking: When a bait is taken by a fish, there is little chance of the hook penetrating if left to itself unless the fish smashes into it at

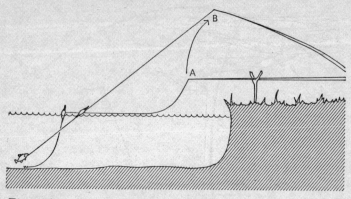

Fig. 2 There are considerable areas of 'slack' in the line when the tackle is at rest (A) but the rod straightens the line to make contact with a fish when a strike is made (B). During fishing, excessive amounts of slack line should always be avoided.

speed. Instead, two other things might happen: the bait can be mouthed and rejected, often very swiftly, or it can be swallowed, where there is a danger that the hook might lodge in the fish's gullet or deeper in the gut. The latter is to be especially avoided, since the fish could suffer great damage: the ideal of all fishing is to make sure that the hook catches on the cartilage around the mouth where it will do little harm. The angler must therefore react to a bite with a smart tug to set the hook home before the bait is swallowed or rejected. The rod enables you to react to a bite with alacrity. When the bait is at some distance from the angler – either deep on the sea bed or across or down the river – the action of the strike cannot reach the hook until slack line has been taken up, and the rod recovers slack line with a single, smooth lift, setting the hook (Fig. 2).

Controlling a hooked fish: All rods fulfil the vital role of a shock-absorber when a fish is hooked. Besides absorbing the shock of the strike, the plunges and tugs of a fish need to be dampened if they are not to break the line. As with the control of tackle, the rod is useful for altering the angle of pull when a fish is being played to steer it out of danger spots such as overhanging bushes (Fig. 3).

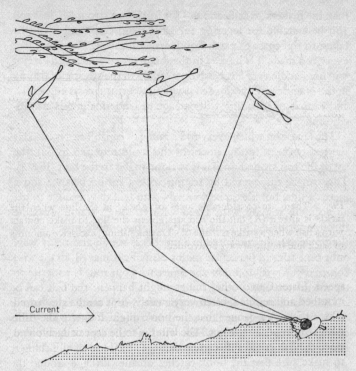

Current →

Fig. 3 Fish are normally played with the rod more or less upright. However, a fish running hard towards a snag can be steered clear by laying the rod to one side, parallel to the water, so that sideways pressure ('sidestrain') is exerted.

All of the above functions are easily learned, and after a little practical fishing the angler is usually oblivious of the fact that he has come to master an efficient tool – the body accepts that it has 'grown' a useful extension and the mind is free to concentrate on choosing terminal tackle and baits and deploying them to the best advantage.

§4 **Different designs**

There is no such thing as a rod capable of use in all types of fishing. Some rods can certainly be put to a wider range of tasks than the makers' specifications – for instance a strongish float rod will be suitable for legering for barbel and carp, and it can be taken to the coast to catch flounders and mullet. However, like every rod made it is limited in the range of weights it can cast; it will not handle very large fish or stand up to the stresses of fishing in the open sea. If overloaded it will not perform casts efficiently, and serious overloading will damage it. Underloading is also inefficient.

The factor on which every rod's range of capabilities is based is the test curve, a measurement of the strain required to pull the tip of the rod around until it is at right angles to the butt (Fig. 4). This can be discovered by testing with a spring balance and a piece of line, but please be warned – you will only be able to get an accurate reading with a rod with 'through action' (flexible throughout its length) and rods which have more give towards the tip need to be measured in a much less rough-and-ready way. Split-cane rods in particular might easily be damaged, so the wise course if you wish to know the figure for your rod, is to write to the manufacturers.

Once you have the test curve you can, with a small calculation, work out the range of line strengths suited to that rod – line strength being the factor which will limit the sort of tackle you can use and the size of fish you seek.

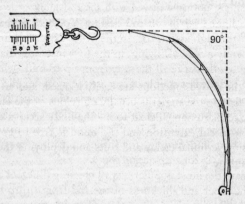

Fig. 4 The test curve (§5) of a fishing rod can be measured with a spring balance, but the method is suitable only for through-action rods.

By multiplying the test-curve figure by 5 you arrive at the 'nucleus' line strength – the ideal line to use, in fact. However, you can now allow 25 per cent variation on the nucleus figure, either way. For instance, a rod with a 1 lb test curve will have a 5 lb nucleus, giving a working range of lines between $3\frac{3}{4}$ lb and $6\frac{1}{4}$ lb. If you keep within this range of lines you can be sure, when you are playing a fish, that so long as there is a constant gentle curve in the rod, the line will not be in danger. If the rod bends beyond the test-curve point, however, the strain on the line increases rapidly and there is no 'reserve' bend in the rod to absorb sudden shocks.

You do not necessarily have to find this information yourself when you buy a rod – the manufacturers' descriptions of various rods will guide you to the sort of tackle you ought to use with them. A rod described as a 'float rod' for instance would normally be suited to light or moderate float tackle in still or moving water, requiring lines of around $2\frac{1}{2}$ lb (nucleus).

There are often more specific guidelines; fly rod manufacturers, for instance, state what size of fly line (a standard scale of fly line sizes and weights has been agreed in the trade) should be used for each model, while for beachcasters there are details of the casting weights (e.g. 3/6 oz; 6/9 oz and so on) suited to each design.

§5   Action and speed

These are linked factors in rod design. You will find rods described as 'through action' or, in the other extreme, 'tip action'. This is merely a way of saying, in the first instance, that the rod flexes in a gentle curve all the way from tip to butt, while in the tip-action rod the last couple of feet are the most flexible, with the rest of the rod becoming progressively stiffer towards the butt (Fig. 5). There are many ways in which differences in action can be obtained, the simplest being the use of different materials – a stiff cane butt and middle, for instance, with a more flexible medium at the tip for a tip-action rod.

Nowadays the most popular way of creating different actions is to alter the taper and thickness of the rod from tip to butt, and with a versatile material such as glass-fibre this can be easily achieved. If you had, for example, a perfectly straight length of glass-fibre tubing, with walls of even thickness throughout, it would

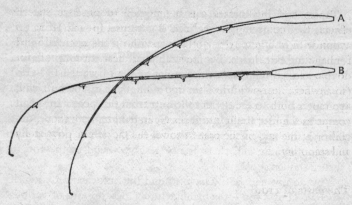

Fig. 5 The through-action (A) bends throughout and under pressure curves from tip to butt. The bend of the tip-action rod (B) is confined to the upper section.

bend into a perfect curve. Introduce a slight taper, however, and the bend would be more marked towards the thinner end, although the curve would still be quite noticeable right through the length. With a severe taper, perhaps only the thin end will bend at all. The curve can be additionally altered by reinforcing the tube wall with extra material.

The reasons for different actions vary; in a float rod, for instance, speed of strike is important because the fish sought are often fast-biting. This is where the 'speed' factor enters the picture – any rod, if raised quickly, will produce a *downward* plunge at the tip. You can test this yourself by 'striking' with the rod tip held six inches or so above water. The time taken for the rod tip to recover and follow through the line of strike can be important, and 'fast action' rods are designed to minimize this by limiting the flexibility to the tip. Such rods will not have the through-action power to handle big fish or cast heavy weights, and they are extra long to assist casting – from 12–14 ft. (365–425 cm). In use, the emphasis is on light, quick handling. For heavier work the sort of rod described as an Avon rod is a better choice. The through action of such a rod provides power to handle big fish and punch out heavier tackle. It can be handled in a more full-blooded way to make up the speed and casting ability of the longer float rod, and therefore need not be so long – around 10 ft (305 cm).

Tapers and thicknesses can be juggled to produce special effects; the 'compound-taper' rod is designed for extra-fast tip action with reserve power, and 'stepped-up' rods are reinforced for handling extra loads. The 'reverse taper' beachcasting rod, for double-handed use, has a thick point at the forward hand-grip (somewhere near a third of the rod's length from the butt end) and tapers both to the tip and the butt from this point. In use, it compresses under strain into an exaggerated longbow shape, uncoiling at the end of the cast to shoot the tackle out powerfully and smoothly.

§6   The parts of a rod

When buying any rod, new or secondhand, it is always advisable to check carefully for damage or faults in any of the parts or fittings. The most likely faults in new rods are damaged or badly-made rings, through which the line has to pass, and unfinished whippings binding various components to the rod. Rings in which a ceramic, glass or mineral lining is cracked, or chromed rings with a rough finish, will quickly damage your line, particularly if it is wound through them under pressure. Unfinished whippings can unwind and shed parts of the rod, and you ought to look especially for small loose ends which might let this happen. Make your inspection in the shop, so that you can point out faults and choose an alternative.

But, in general, most rods from reputable manufacturers will be soundly constructed, and the various components will have been chosen with care. However, the trade does insist on coating many rods with a super-shiny varnish finish to make them attractive to purchasers, and I usually re-varnish freshwater rods with a matt-finish varnish to avoid the 'flash' from shiny surfaces on a sunny day, which can scare fish.

The main rod components vary in shape and dimension according to the type of rod, but their functions are essentially similar – the butt is the handle of the rod, ferrules are joints connecting the various sections, rod rings (line guides) are the eyes through which the line runs, spaced at intervals along the rod, and the reel fitting holds the reel on the butt.

The butt: This varies in length and shape a lot (Fig. 6). In a fly rod

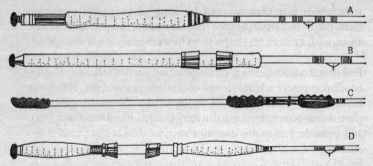

Fig. 6 Various types of rod butt: A – fly rod with cork handle shaped for a good palm grip; B – a coarse-fishing rod with a long cork handle and sliding reel fittings; C – a beachcasting rod with upper and lower handgrips; D – the butt of a boat rod with handgrips each side of the central, reel fitting.

it is comparatively short and shaped to afford a good palm grip, while the reel fitting is at the extreme bottom end. In a boat rod, the handle is a couple of feet long and terminates behind the reel fitting, with a further hand grip added to the fore of the reel fitting. The most widely used material for butts is cork. It provides an excellent grip for most kinds of fishing and is in addition warm to the touch, even in cold and wet weather.

Cork handles should never be varnished, since they would then lose their advantages; if they become dirty or encrusted with fish scales they can be scrubbed gently with a nail brush in warm, soapy water and left to dry naturally – never before the fire, because this could make them split.

Wood is sometimes used as an alternative to cork in sea-boat rods but since it has to be varnished to avoid rotting I don't think it has any advantages – apart from cheapness. Some expensive boat rods have the fore-grip finished with felt or leather, and if you have a wooden-handled rod it is worth your while to buy a scrap of suede for a few pence and cover the fore-grip, using a high-performance glue.

Extra purchase with the hands is often needed with big double-handed beachcasting rods, and often, shaped rubber or plastic grips – the sort of things used for bicycle handlebars – are a better alternative to wood or cork.

By and large big-diameter butts will be more comfortable on

rods which you have to hold for long periods, and extra-thin butts ought to be avoided for this reason. A cramped hand can be an annoyance towards the end of a day's fishing.

Ferrules: To have perfect, unhindered action rods should, ideally, be all one piece, without joins of any kind. However, this is far from practical with long rods which have to be stored and transported (imagine carrying a thirteen-footer onto a crowded bus), and nowadays only the specialist rods of tournament casters are constructed without ferrules. Most rods (depending on overall length) are divided into two or three sections of manageable length. The ferrules (Fig. 7) joining them, since some reinforcing material is generally used, introduce 'dead' or stiff points in the action, and this is especially true of the older metal ferrules used until glass-fibre technology reached its present stage. Hollow glass made alternatives to metal ferrules possible, notably the glass-to-glass join (sometimes described as the ferrule-less join) and the spigot join, in which an internal projection of flexible plastic at the end of one section pushes into the hollow of the other, so that the glass tube-ends fit snugly together. Both these alternatives improve action, although metal ferrules are still used and are perfectly serviceable.

It is worthwhile taking special care to see that ferrules are

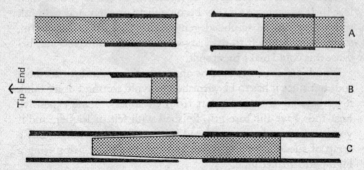

Fig. 7 Types of ferrule (join): A – machined metal ferrule. The female, or butt-end, long metal collar fits over the upper, male ferrule. The glass-to-glass join (B) works in the same way, and the walls of the hollow glass tubes are reinforced with extra materials at the joining point. The spigot join (C) reverses male and female ferrules with a flexible insert over which the upper glass or carbon fibre tube fits.

always clean – metal ferrules in particular are machined to extremely fine limits and any grit will jam them, giving a frustrating experience when you come to pack up. When not in use the hollow part of a ferrule ought to be plugged against dust and grit, and most makers supply cork or rubber stoppers for this purpose. Light oiling is useful with metal ferrules (wax is a better alternative with glass-to-glass and spigots) when you are setting up your rod for a day's fishing, and if you have no oil you can rub the male ferrule through your hair, which will coat it with natural lanolin.

Rod rings: The American term 'line-guides' seems much more apt than our own description of the spaced eyes along the length of a rod through which the line passes; sometimes the rod rings are not 'rings' at all – they can be grooved rollers which turn as the line passes over them, used in heavy-duty sea rods, or they can be a half-loop of wire, the 'snake ring' used for fly rods (Fig. 8).

The numbers of rings and the length of space between them vary from rod to rod – this is shown in the descriptions of rods which follow. The rings at the tip and butt ends normally serve heavier duty than the intermediates, and they are frequently lined

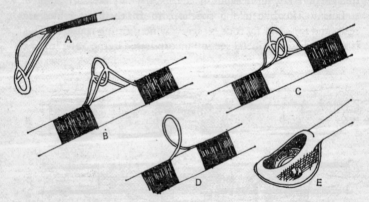

Fig. 8 Types of rod-rings (line-guides): A – a stand-off, tip ring, normally used on float and leger rods, together with stand-off intermediate rings (B). The snake ring (D) is used on some fly rods, while the bridge ring (C) is used on spinning, boat and beachcasting rods, and some fly rods. Roller guide rings, both intermediate and tip (E) are used on heavy-duty boat rods.

with ceramic or mineral eyes (described as 'jewelled' eyes, or sometimes by trade-names such as Syntox and Reglox). In addition the butt ring is frequently large, to accommodate the oscillations of the line as it spins off the reel drum, and the intermediates following become progressively smaller in diameter up to the tip.

It is essential that all parts of the ring in contact with the line are smooth, so that no friction will hinder casting or damage the line – rings that are unlined, or without rollers, are normally made from stainless steel or steel finished with smooth, hard, chrome plating. Rollers might in fact be used for all rings in big-game rods (and they are essential if metal line is used).

In some rods the rings are close to the rod, in others they keep the line well clear. In a fly rod, for instance, it is useful to have the line working with the rod, held close against it. The fine lines used in freshwater float fishing, however, will cling to the rod when they are wet unless held off with high 'stand off' rings.

Reel fitting: The reel is usually fixed to the butt of the rod by two sliding metal collars (or one sliding, one fixed) which are pushed over the sloping seat of the reel to hold it tightly (Fig. 9). In most freshwater rods, light handling means that this pressure alone is sufficient to keep the reel in position, but for the more robust sea rods, and for some fly rods, a 'screw winch' fitting is useful. This is a large-diameter metal section incorporated in the butt; it has a

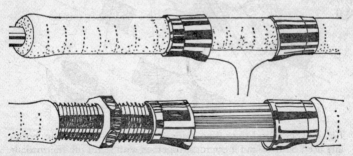

Fig. 9 Reel fittings – the sliding collars (top) are pushed firmly over the reel seat to hold it securely. The lower winch reel fitting has a hexagonal nut on a screw-threaded section which can be tightened to hold the sliding collar over the reel seat.

fixed collar and one slider which is pushed over the reel seat by tightening a large nut which revolves along a screw-threaded part of the section. A second locking-nut is often incorporated.

The positioning of the reel fitting varies with the type of rod; in a freshwater float rod, a fixed-spool reel would normally be sited towards the forward end of the butt, while the reel is fixed to the extreme end of the butt of a fly rod where, since the rod is used mainly in an upright position, its weight is a counterbalance during casting.

§7   Materials

So great has been the acceptance of hollow glass-fibre for rod making in recent years that many traditional materials have been passed over altogether, and the choice of a new rod today is normally between the 'top three' of a range that was once quite wide – hollow glass, solid glass, and built cane (split cane) (Fig. 10). I am confining my main descriptions to these three materials, but I ought first to sketch some of the others.

Greenheart – a rich brown flexible wood – used to be quite widely used in rod making. It could be tapered to fine limits and in medium length rods it provided a nice, robust action. For long rods for float fishing, however, greenheart tended to make a top-

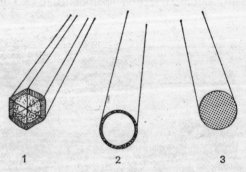

Fig. 10 The three most popular rod materials: Split cane (1), made by glueing long triangular sections of pared cane together to make a hexagonal cross-section; hollow glass (2), which is the lightest and most widely used form of resin-bonded glass fibres; and 'solid' bonded glass (3).

heavy rod since it is a dense, weighty wood. It was, however, suited to the lazier action required of a long salmon fly rod, although such rods tended to be tiring because of their overall weight. There was a much more serious drawback – greenheart would split unexpectedly, no matter how carefully the rod was treated; it might last a season, or a lifetime – this unreliable trait would always be a threat. But fate rather than drawbacks curtailed the use of greenheart, for natural stocks of the wood diminished to the extent that it became costly to obtain.

Lancewood, less reliable than greenheart but similar in appearance, had the additional disadvantage that it could only be obtained in short lengths. It was once widely used as tip-sections for cheap whole-cane rods, but this role was quickly surpassed by the introduction of built cane (below) and solid glass-fibre tips.

Of the whole cane rods, those constructed of a particularly light, straight cane called Spanish reed were excellent, and many would be with us now but for the fact that the cane became scarce. They were, of course, more suited to light freshwater rods and more robust material was used for other purposes.

Another material which was once quite popular – particularly after the last war, when there were many tank-aerials in government surplus stores – was steel tube; this made a fairly light, freshwater rod but damage to any sections could never be properly repaired. Nevertheless I know several anglers who still use them.

Now to built cane. The strongest part of a bamboo cane is its tough outer skin, and the whole-cane rod incorporates much redundant material in the form of the weak, pithy interior. Built cane is made by cutting whole cane into longitudinal strips and scraping off the surplus matter; the strips are then planed so that they are triangular in cross-section and tapered for various parts of the rod (i.e. tip, middle etc.) and glued together with the tough portion outwards to make a hexagonal cross-sectioned rod. With the rubbish pared away, the product is a beautifully light, flexible wand which is extremely strong and adaptable to the whole range of rod patterns. For extra lightness built cane can be made hollow, or it can be double-built for extra strength.

Many anglers still swear by built cane which they reckon to handle more sweetly than the synthetics; in any event a craftsman-made job, which built cane must be, is a much nicer object than a mass-produced one – but therein lies a disadvantage. Craftsmen who can make good built cane rods are scarce, and the process is time consuming. Prices for these rods are therefore higher than for the production-line glass rods and, in addition, the main raw material, tonkin cane, has become difficult to obtain in the sort of quality necessary for rod-making.

Old and well-made built cane rods are still giving good service today – you might well find one in a second-hand shop. The essential thing you must do to keep a cane rod in good condition is examine it thoroughly from time to time, especially near the whippings, to see that the protective varnish coating is not cracked or scratched. If even minute quantities of water penetrate the rod it will be ruined.

The two forms of glass-fibre rods, solid and tubular, are now well entrenched as the leading rod materials; both are fairly cheap to make, and lend themselves well to mass-production techniques. Solid glass is, however, quite heavy, and although it was briefly popular as rod-tip material for freshwater rods before tubular glass came along, it now finds its greatest use in sea rods, particularly boat rods. Some people prefer solid glass to tubular glass as a boat rod because of its 'backbone'; in trying to set a large hook with a big fish at some distance, for instance, the impetus gained by swinging a heavy rod into the strike makes it more forceful than a similar strike with a light, hollow rod. Solid glass is, too, virtually indestructible and you would have to mistreat it severely to damage it.

I would recommend a hollow glass-fibre rod as a 'first rod' throughout the range of rod patterns, although solid glass is a good deal cheaper and might well be considered for boat fishing at sea. Hollow glass will maintain its strength and straightness even after many years of use. It is completely waterproof and cannot be attacked by rot or worm. Lightness and flexibility makes playing a fish an exciting experience, and the only drawback is a degree of fragility. Take care of such a rod, however, and you have a friend for life.

A newcomer to the range of rod materials deserves recording – carbon fibre, occasionally described as 'graphite'. Many rods are now being constructed in this ultra-light material, manufactured on the same hollow-built principle as hollow glass. The carbon fibres – first developed in this country for turbine blades in aircraft technology – are normally mixed with a certain amount of glass-fibre. Their most useful application is in the rods which are either large and fairly heavy – beach-casters, for instance – or rods which are held and flexed over long periods, like fly rods. However, the cost of such rods is very high at the time of going to press, and there is no sign yet of them becoming cheaper.

Selecting your rod
For the sake of convenience, descriptions of rod-patterns have been left aside until the checklists later in this section (Chapter 10).

Reels have to be chosen carefully to match the rod you will be using. Also, it is not a good idea to purchase, say, a multiplier, without learning about the various sorts of this type of reel – you will want the right one for beachcasting, boat fishing and so on.

§8 Centre-pin reels (Fig. 11)

Of the three basic types of reel the centre-pin is the most simple. It is also the first to appear in history, recorded from about the eleventh century in China and from the end of the fifteenth century in England. The construction of a line-holding drum, which revolves on a central spindle, resembles a winch or capstan in miniature. Before any alternatives appeared, centre-pins used to have applications throughout the range of fishing styles, and the float fisherman's ultra-light centre-pin and beachcaster's wooden 'star-back' – a name derived from the pattern of brass reinforce-

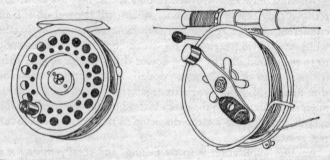

Fig. 11 The two main kinds of modern centre-pin reels (§8). Left is a fly-fishing reel and on the right, is a large sea-boat-fishing reel.

ments on the back plate of the reel – were in widespread use. Most models were free-running, with a ratchet check which could be clicked into action when free-wheeling was unnecessary (the fly-fisherman's reel plays a passive part in casting and has a permanent check so that line will not spin off the drum on its own).

But casting with a centre-pin is not easy to pick up. For beach-casting and other long-casting tasks there is a lot of inertia to overcome to set the big reel in motion, while for the lighter casting weights of the coarse fisherman sufficient line has to be drawn off the reel before the cast is made, or else the reel has to be set spinning with a flick from the angler's finger at the critical stage in the cast, so that it turns-off line to follow the bait. The road to these achievements is paved with tangles, and while many anglers still use the lightweight centre-pin for river fishing, most anglers find the easier-to-use fixed-spool reel a better alternative. However, if trouble is taken to learn the technique of handling a centre-pin for tasks such as trotting, it will be found as useful for tackle control as the fixed-spool reel, and wonderfully direct in handling fish.

There are circumstances when this direct control is not so pleasurable: with the larger deep-sea version of the centre-pin a big conger or skate can give you a muscle-searing experience unless the reel has a lever-operated brake which you can operate independently of finger-pressure on the drum – the normal way of controlling the movements of lesser fish. Without such an aid, if you loose grip on the handle, the reel will set off spinning and you'll probably crack a knuckle or two before you stop it.

Another drawback with centre-pins is that they are slow. You retrieve only one length of line, which will depend on the circumference of the reel drum, each time you turn the handle, while multiplying reels (as the name implies) and fixed-spool reels are geared so that the spool or drum makes several turns for each turn of the handle. Modern centre-pins are therefore slim-drummed, have a cage arrangement to keep the line at the outer circumference of the drum instead of starting from the thin central spindle, and a large diameter to make the line recovery rate greater.

Another application is in fly fishing, and for fly fishing it is difficult to imagine some other type of reel superseding the centre-pin. The need here is for a simple winch, since the role of the reel is not active in casting. To match modern rod-making materials, fly reels have become lighter and lighter.

Exceptionally light fly reels are turned from solid magnesium, a very light metal, but these are enormously expensive. Lower-priced reels are made from various alloys. Extras offered by some fly-reel manufacturers include multiplier-type gearing for fast line retrieve, and even a self-retrieve system. These add expense to the reel of course.

The final modern use for the centre-pin is the big boat-fishing reel, and I think it is most important that some independent braking system such as a lever brake is fitted for the reasons discussed above.

Situations where the centre-pin cannot be recommended, and its rivals are superior, are for distance legering, spinning and beachcasting.

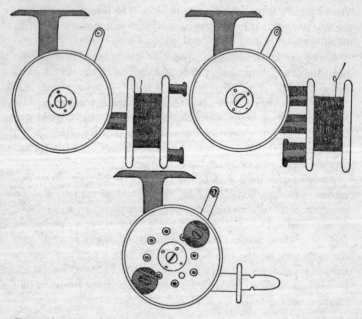

Fig. 12 A centre-pin reel which turns into a fixed-spool casting reel, the Jecta Orlando. The top pictures show how the spool can be reversed for alternate casts so that line-twist is cancelled. Below, the reel becomes a centre-pin for retrieving line.

Before leaving centre-pins, it is worth mentioning that there are 'hybrid' versions, mostly for boat and beach fishing, in which the line-drum can be turned to face the front of the rod so that line spills over the drum-edge on the same principle as the fixed-spool reel, thus making an easier task of casting without the drum spinning. A major drawback of this system is that the line is continually being thrown out with a built-in twist and then recovered on the 'wrong' axis, so that after a time it kinks horribly. The better makes of this type of reel have a reversible drum (Fig. 12) so that alternate casts can be made from each side in turn, and the twist is continuously cancelled.

§9 Fixed-spool reels (Fig. 13)

This reel was invented by A. H. Illingworth in 1905. The drum, or spool, faces along the rod instead of to the side, and does not turn during casting. Instead, a wire loop, which turns about the spool to pay the line back onto it, can be locked aside so that the line simply spills over the spool edge. There is no impetus to overcome, and no spinning spool to get into trouble. And

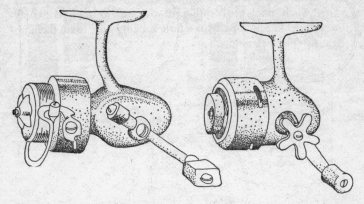

Fig. 13 Two types of fixed-spool reels. The one on the left is the Garcia-Mitchell 300 open-face reel with a flying bale-arm and a clutch operated by a nut on the front of the spool. In the closed-face reel on the right, the Abu 505, the bale retrieve is covered by a protective cowl and the clutch is operated by moving the star-like nut on the handle. Pressure on the frontal button releases the bale, which re-engages automatically when the handle is turned.

because the flying line guide, known as the bale-arm, lays the line back on the same axis, exactly as it spilled from the reel, there is no twist. The spool has an adjustable brake, known as a slipping clutch, which allows line to be pulled off when the strain on the line reaches a particular point, and so as well as providing easier casts the reel can be adjusted to protect fine lines – fixed-spool reels are sometimes called 'threadline reels' for this reason.

The slipping clutch can be adjusted to a point somewhat below the breaking strain of whatever line you use, but it will be better instead to set it so that it gives line once the rod-tip is pulled round to a fighting curve.

A mistake frequently made with the fixed-spool reel is to under-fill the spool with line. The line should be loaded right to the lip of the spool so that, when released, it can spill off easily. As turns of line get lower and lower below the lip, they encounter greater and greater resistance trying to climb over it. Manufacturers have in the past inadvertently encouraged this fault by producing reel spools with line-capacities much higher than is necessary. For instance in most fishing (except perhaps for beach-casting) the number of occasions when you need more than 100 yards of line are scarce. Excess line filling an over-large spool is completely wasted. Such spools are best filled in with cork to leave room only for essential line, and perhaps a little backing line, to fill them up to the lip (Fig. 14).

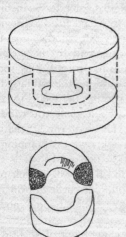

Fig. 14 The wasted line space on over-deep spools can be filled with a cork arbor glued into position, or a length of Terylene line wound tightly into place and sealed with varnish or glue.

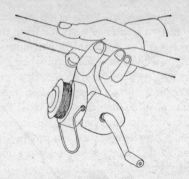

Fig. 15 The fixed-spool reel ready to cast: the bale-arm is open and out of the way, and the line is hooked around the angler's index finger. A turn of the handle re-engages the bale-arm once the cast has been made.

Making a cast with a fixed-spool reel, the angler hooks the line around his finger (Fig. 15) and locks open the bale-arm; at the critical release point in the cast the line is allowed to slip off the finger and the tackle flies out. If the tackle needs to be restricted in flight, or stopped, the finger can be dropped against the front lip of the spool so that the line is hindered from spilling out smoothly. This same hindering action can control the line if the tackle is to be allowed to travel downriver, otherwise the bale-arm can be closed to wait for a bite.

Since the fixed-spool reel is not designed for heavy winching jobs, a certain amount of care needs to be taken in retrieving heavy weights and fish: it would be useless to wind against the weight because you then only add your pull to the weight, operating the slipping-clutch mechanism. Instead, the spool should be stopped with firm finger pressure and the rod raised to pull the weight towards you without turning the reel (Fig. 16). The rod is then dropped towards the weight while you wind in the line gained as the pressure lessens. Then you can lift the rod and gain some more line. This action is known as 'pumping' a fish.

Fixed-spool reels with a cowl around the spool, which prevents line being inadvertently blown off, differ little in principle from the normal open-spool versions, except that some models deprive you of finger-control on the spool. They are normally known as 'closed-face' reels, and the clutch control, instead of

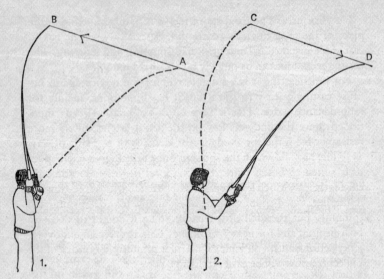

Fig. 16 Stages in 'pumping' to land a fish: 1 – the rod is drawn to the vertical, pulling the weight towards the angler (A – B) while the reel is kept motionless; any attempt to wind will merely operate the reel's slipping clutch. 2 – the rod is dropped back towards the weight (C – D) while the angler winds up the line gained in stage 1. This is repeated until the fish is near enough to be netted.

being on the front of the spool, can be at the rear of the reel or on the handle, while there is a button to engage or release the retrieve mechanism.

The extras that are offered with fixed-spool reels are numerous, the most useful being a toughened section of the bale-arm over which the line runs, or even a tiny roller. Continually drawing line over this point begins to tell after only a short time with cheap reels in which the bale-arm wire is normal strength – the line wears a groove. Besides weakening the bale-arm, this also makes a rough point which will damage your line. For the bigger beach-casting reels, an anti-lash device which prevents the bale-arm being thrown into the 'on' position during a robust cast is a big asset. With smaller fixed-spool reels, to be used with light lines, a fibre brush arrangement at the back of the spool which prevents the line from blowing over into the reel mechanism, is a big help.

Now for uses. The fixed-spool reel is certainly valuable in the place of the river angler's centre-pin, especially when he has to cast some distance for activities like spinning and legering. The casting technique can be quickly picked up by a novice.

For beachcasting it is a suitable reel for the novice again, because casting is easy to learn, but it has limitations, mainly for long-distance work. This is because of the factor already mentioned: once the line gets low on the spool, it encounters more resistance from the spool-edge. And once 60 or so yards of, say, 15 lb line have flown off the spool of one of the bigger fixed-spool reels suited to beach work, the line-level begins to become inefficiently low. Much longer casts will be made with a free-running multiplier. Fixed-spool reels are also suitable for rock fishing and spinning, but they fall down badly when it comes to deep-sea boat fishing, and for heavy work they tend to have an annoying, jerky action and are difficult to manage. A multiplier or one of the big centre-pins will be easier to handle here.

$10   Multiplier reels (Fig. 17)

The origin of this type of reel is more obscure. There were some simple versions about in Britain at around the turn of the century,

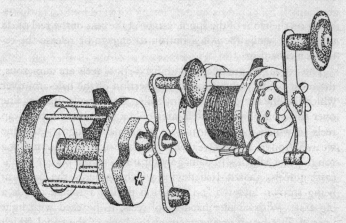

Fig. 17 Types of multiplier reel. Left, is a casting reel with a shallow, wide, light plastic spool. Right, is a boat-fishing reel with a deep, metal spool.

but these disappeared from general use. In America, however, development work continued and now more multipliers are used there than any other types of reel. When some American multipliers started to come on to the market in Britain in the 1920s they were mechanically superb – and horribly expensive. The rest of the world had a lot of technology to catch up on, a task which has now been satisfactorily achieved.

The multiplier is used on top of the rod, with the rod rings uppermost. The line-spool, wide and shallow compared with the deep, narrow centre-pin drum, can be released with a small lever to allow it to free-wheel independent of gears and handle when a cast is to be made.

The cast (Fig. 18) sounds easy in theory, but there are difficulties to overcome. The free spool is stopped securely with the thumb pressing against it until the critical release point in the cast when the thumb is lifted. Light thumb-pressure prevents the reel spinning too quickly while the tackle is flying out, and firmer pressure slows the spool as the tackle slows at the end of its trajectory. When the tackle hits the water (or slightly before), pressure is increased to stop the reel smartly.

The main trouble occurs whenever the reel is turning and pushing out line at a rate faster than the tackle is drawing the line away – the tackle obviously starts off moving fast, and slows gradually throughout its course, losing forward motion abruptly at the end when its impetus is spent. Any loose loops pushed off the reel can catch and rush around the drum, giving you a particularly nasty tangle known as an overrun, or they can knit together and fly off with the line to jam in one of the rod rings. If the weight then still has any distance to travel the line may part. The spools of all multipliers are necessarily strong. Layer after layer of line wound under tension eventually builds up a considerable total pressure on the reel drum, and a weakly-constructed one could easily burst. In a deep-sea boat reel, where the casting role is secondary, this can be accounted for by using metal. But for casting, metal is heavy, which means extra inertia to overcome to start the cast, and once the reel is spinning, a flywheel effect which will be difficult to control. Modern casting multipliers are therefore often fitted with lightweight glass-fibre reinforced plastic spools which have a low inertia and less of the flywheel action of metal spools.

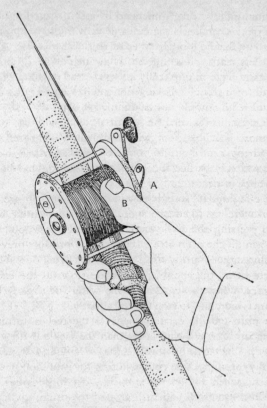

Fig. 18 The multiplier ready for casting – the spool-release lever (A) has been set in the 'off' position and the angler's thumb (B) presses firmly against the free-running drum to prevent it moving.

Such a reel might also have a tension nut which can help to beat overruns if sensibly used. This tightens the bearing in which the free spool turns, and it can be fixed to slow the spool whenever line is not actually being drawn off – obviously it will have to be re-adjusted during fishing if casting weights are changed. For a beginner, it might be best to tighten this nut well up, releasing it gradually as confidence grows.

Other more complex cast-braking systems can be obtained, but while they help beginners, they will not give the really long casts of the free-running spool.

The multiplier's 'drag', operated by a star shaped nut on the spindle of the handle, is the equivalent of the fixed-spool reel's slipping clutch, and it ought to be set in the same way, so that it gives line once the rod is pulled to a fighting curve.

You can obtain multipliers with level-wind devices which flex back and forth to guide line evenly onto the spool – it is important that the line should not be humped at one side of the reel or in the middle, because uneven lengths of line fly off the spool and these can easily knit and tangle. These winding devices do, however, add some resistance to your cast. You can easily learn the trick of pushing the line regularly from side to side of the spool with the ball of your thumb as you reel your tackle in.

Bigger multipliers for deep-sea and big-game fishing may be supplied with lugs to attach a fighting harness, and also a screw-clamp for fixing the reel securely to the rod, backing-up the winch fitting. The main area of fishing in which the multiplier is unsuitable is the long-rod freshwater float and leger range, when relatively light weights are to be cast. Very small multipliers, however, are quite well suited to fairly light spinning for trout, and larger multipliers can be used effectively with salmon and pike spinning rods.

In sea fishing multipliers really come into their own, either fitted with a lightweight spool for beachcasting, or fitted with a large heavy spool for deep-sea and big-game fishing. It is essential that all reels used for sea work are corrosion-proof, not simply corrosion-resistant.

After taking care to match rod and reel, it is worthwhile taking as much trouble over lines and hooks: a line, like a chain, is only as strong as its weakest point and you want to be certain of its limits. Hooks, if they are blunt or unsuited to the bait you are using and the size of fish you are after, will diminish your chances of success. Swivels, for some forms of fishing, are the last factor to prove vital in the important task of securing a fish and bringing it safely back to you. Floats and weights belong to the other, equally important, side of fishing – presenting your bait to the fish, and registering a take (swing tips, quiver tips and bite indicators are also discussed in this chapter).

§11   Lines (Fig. 19)

Perhaps the most important fact to remember about all lines is that their quoted breaking strain diminishes whenever they are knotted – up to thirty per cent, depending on the type of line and the knot used. Regarding the choice between various brands on sale: well-known, regularly advertised makes are less likely to disappoint you, especially when it comes to nylon monofilament, which can vary greatly in reliability and lasting quality.

(a) *Nylon monofilament:* This is the most widely used line in modern angling; it is smooth, making casts easier because of lessened friction on the rod rings, and it is fine compared with plaited and braided lines – this means it has less resistance in moving both through the air and water. It is translucent, therefore difficult to see (or be seen by fish) in water, and it is cheap.

Against this, it is twenty-five per cent weaker than the quoted breaking strain when it is wet, the finer varieties deteriorate

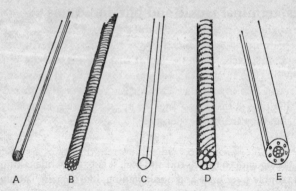

Fig. 19 Cross-sections of lines: A – single-strand, wire line (Monel-metal); B – stranded wire; C – nylon monofilament, normally translucent; D – braided, artificial fibre line, thicker than monofilament of the same strength; E – modern, plastic-coated fly line with a braided core.

quickly when exposed to the ultra-violet rays in sunlight, and it is difficult to knot because of its smooth surface. It is more likely than braided lines to lose strength through bad knotting. Nylon also becomes stiffer as its diameter (strength) increases. Another quality of nylon is that it is elastic. This can help to absorb shocks in striking, but it can hinder making an effective strike with a lot of line out. Pre-stretched nylon line, with the elasticity removed, is useful in some fishing tasks but it needs to be managed carefully – it is thinner than normal nylon, but without the shock-absorbing qualities too harsh a strike will break it.

Except for the fly-fishing lines described later, nylon is used for all types of freshwater fishing, and because of its casting qualities it is ideal for beach fishing. Rivals only get a look in for some boat-fishing tasks, where the stretch factor becomes a disadvantage.

(b)   *Braided lines* (Terylene, Dacron etc.): Take nylon's 25 per cent loss of strength in water, and add to that a further 25 or 30 per cent loss for knotting, and you have a good reason for choosing an alternative line where big sea-fish make line strength critical. Consider also the stretch in several fathoms of nylon – this can mean, first of all, that the pull of a biting fish might not be transmitted back to the angler. It also means that the power of the strike can be absorbed, making it difficult to set the hook.

The gain in using a braided line is reliability, better knotting and lack of stretch, while the loss is that the line is more visible than nylon, also thicker – this can mean that you may have to use heavier weights in some situations than you would with nylon. A further plus is that these lines do not deteriorate so quickly as nylon, but they are more expensive.

(c) *Metal lines:* Steel, for its considerable strength, makes a very fine line, and the double advantage of using it in deep or fast-running water is that less weight is needed to keep it down, and it is virtually stretch-free. It is, of course, essentially a deep-sea line.

The main disadvantage is that minor kinks quite soon lead to a break, and kinking can occur quite easily – the line is heavy and unless the reel is checked carefully when the weight hits the bottom, coils of line will keep running out to pile up on the sea bed. Tangles generally mean the loss of several yards of line, which is expensive, and a beginner will find it better to familiarize himself with cheaper nylon before progressing to steel lines.

Thin steel wire can be dangerous. It should never, never be used for casting, since you could easily slice off a finger trying to brake a fast-spinning spool. Even for letting a weight down through several fathoms of water some precautions are necessary – a stout leather thumb stall will stave off cuts.

This line also has a tendency to retain the shape of the reel spool, and if used on a thin-spindled multiplier it will quickly become too tightly coiled to be of much use – only big-diameter reels of the centre-pin type should be loaded with a steel line. Because it could easily cut through normal, chromed steel rod-rings, a rod with roller guides throughout ought to be used.

(d) *Fly lines:* The purpose of heavy fly lines is to add casting weight to the virtually-weightless flies and lures used in fly fishing – imagine the line as the cord of a long cattle-whip, with the rod as the stock. When the rod is switched, the line unfurls until it stretches full length and deposits the lure on the water. That is a very simplified picture, of course, and fly-casting techniques are described more thoroughly in Chapter 19.

Fly lines used to be made mainly of silk. When each trip was

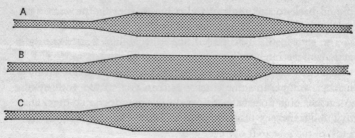

Fig. 20 Exaggerated profiles of fly-line tapers – all have a short length (2 ft) of level line at the tip, and a taper (9 ft) to a level, middle section. A – double taper, with a 70 ft middle section and, at the other end, another 9 ft taper and 2 ft section of level line. B – forward taper, with a 14 ft level section, a short (6 ft) rear taper, and a long section of thin, level line (59 ft). C – single taper, in effect half of a double-taper line (A). Suitable for shooting heads (§11d) if the thick section is trimmed to 18 or so feet.

finished, they had to be carefully dried and re-proofed so that they did not rot. Even with careful treatment, their life was generally not long and nowadays, even though silk is still available, modern plastic-coated lines have largely superseded them. Plastic lines are waterproof, and need only be wiped clean after use. A variety of qualities can be obtained – some float entirely on the water, while others sink quickly to allow the angler to fish a wet fly in deep water. Still others have a tip length of a yard or two which sinks, while the rest of the line floats.

They are sold in a variety of tapers (Fig. 20) usually in 90 ft (27.4 m) lengths. Level lines are cheap, but their use is mainly for wet-fly fishing with the wind behind the angler. Double-taper lines are more popular. Normally only the first 30 or so feet is aerialized, and the idea of the double-taper is that the line can be reversed when one end shows signs of wear.

Forward-taper lines have most of their bulk at the forward end of the line, which helps in casting into the wind, and can also produce longer casts in normal conditions.

A 'shooting head' is frequently used in modern reservoir fishing. This consists of rather less than half of a double-taper line (you could split the cost with a friend and make 2 shooting heads from one line) spliced at the thick end to a 20–30 lb breaking strain nylon backing. In use the angler aerializes the fly line (with some of the nylon off the reel and either floating in the water or on a line raft) and at the end of a powerful forward cast he releases it, so that the light smooth backing is drawn after the fly line to produce a long cast.

A system of coding fly-line specifications has been agreed by the Association of Fishing Tackle Makers (A.F.T.M.) to enable anglers to match lines with their rods (all fly rods should carry an A.F.T.M. number). The number is based on the weight, in grains, of the first 30 ft of line:

No.	Weight	No.	Weight
1	60	7	185
2	80	8	210
3	100	9	240
4	120	10	280
5	140	11	330
6	160	12	380

(These weights can vary within a tolerance of 6 grains for the lighter lines to as much as 12 grains for the heaviest. Lines below No. 4 are rarely used).

A lettering code shows the type of line:

    L = level
  WF = weight forward
  DT = double taper
  ST = shooting taper

These letters precede the A.F.T.M. number:

    F = floating
    S = sinking
    I = intermediate (has to be greased to float)

(e) *Loading line on reel:* Apart from long-distance beachcasting, and sometimes big-game fishing, the number of times that more than 100 yards of line is necessary are few. Very occasionally big fish might draw away more than that length, but believe me, once a fish is as far away as that, even half a mile of line will do you little good – you will have to walk towards the fish, if this is possible, to regain control. When a new reel is bought it is often clear that a great deal of line will be needed to fill it. Nine times out of ten a novice will do just this, purchasing several hundred yards of line, most of which will be wasted and never used. The spools of some fixed-spool reels in particular are much too large.

I recommend that anglers buy 100 yards (150–200 for beach-casters) which should be regarded as the main line, and back this up with 50–100 yards of much stronger line which will outlast several changes of the main line. Any remaining space on a fixed-spool reel should be taken up by a cork arbor, provided by some manufacturers, or you can wind on some hard braided line, tucking the free end under the last few coils and sealing it with two or three coats of waterproof glue – the backing and main line are wound-on on top of this.

How can you judge how much backing you need to fill a reel? Simple. It might take you half an hour, but you won't have to do it again so long as you note the yardages (you can wind on the braided line to fill a fixed-spool reel as an arbor in the same fashion). You will need some sort of large drum to wind line on, or better still a large, dry field. Choose your main line, and tie this loosely onto the empty reel and wind away. When you come to the end, knot it securely to the backing line and wind until the reel is full (or tie in the braided line mentioned above). If you use a drum, you will have to wind all the line off the reel onto it and then rewind this on to a rolled newspaper or another drum in order to get the free end of the backing line coming off first to wind back onto the empty reel. The field is easier – just secure the end of the backing, back-off, and unwind the backing and main line, and then nip back to the end of the backing, tie it on and wind away. Fly lines are bulky, and there is often little room on a fly reel for much backing. Use the above technique to fill one properly. Fly-line backings can be bought, or you can use cheaper braided line of about 25 lb breaking strain. If you are using a shooting head, the first 30 yards of the backing will have to be 20–30 lb breaking strain nylon, joined to the fly line with a needle-knot (the loops on some ready-made shooting heads, when the nylon is knotted-in, are sometimes too bulky to pull through the tip ring of the rod).

(f) *Hook lengths* (traces, leaders, casts): A much finer line than the main line can be incorporated in your tackle to present a less visible link to the hook, but this hook length or cast serves a more important purpose: it will always break before the main line if a fish makes a sudden lunge, or if you have to pull against a snag. The main line is kept intact and you need only tie on another cast and hook to continue fishing. Casts or 'leaders' for fly fishing have to be tapered so that they unfurl at the end of the cast, continuing the action of the fly line.

(g) *Rotten bottom:* This is a weaker section of line joining the weight to the main line, used in areas where there is a high risk of the weight becoming irretrievably snagged – the same principle as hook lengths (above). In such areas it also makes sense to use disposable weights such as stones or rusty nuts and bolts in place of expensive lead weights.

(h) *Wire traces:* With toothed fishes, such as the conger eel in sea fishing and the pike in freshwater fishing, there is a risk of nylon and terylene lines being bitten through or frayed. Wire, either single-strand or braided, is useful in these circumstances – a short length is often all that is needed. You can buy made-up traces or make your own. Plastic-covered wire is best, but expensive.

(i) *Rubbing traces:* Some of the larger rough-skinned sea fish such as sharks might fray nylon by rubbing against the line during a long tussle. To combat this, anything up to 15 ft of rubbing trace is necessary – either wire, or else nylon with a much higher breaking strain than the main line.

(j) *Shock leaders:* In beachcasting situations where a heavy lead weight is to be used with a fairly light line, say a 6 oz weight with a 15 lb breaking-strain line, there is a risk that the snatch of the weight will snap the line during the cast. A length of stronger line from the lead, which gives three or four turns of line around the reel before joining the main line when making ready to cast, guards against a casting break.

(k) *What breaking strain?* Beginners particularly are worried about the strength of line they should choose; the tendency is to pick a line much too strong as a safeguard against lack of skill. One result of this is that heavier weights, floats and so on have to be matched to make the line work properly, and this can mean fewer fish. The main thing to remember is that low-breaking-strain lines are more likely to suffer from your mishandling than from a fish breaking them, and so as skill develops, lower and lower breaking strains can be tried – but don't, at first, go far too high on the strength scale.

As a guideline, for freshwater fishing in the first instance, a 3 lb line will handle roach, rudd, perch, dace, bream to about 4 lb, small chub and crucian carp in still water and rivers with a moderate flow, while a 5 lb-breaking-strain line will handle small barbel, chub, tench and bigger bream. Where flow is exceptionally strong, and in places where you may have to haul fish and tackle through weedy snags to bring them in safely, it will be wise to add an extra pound to the above strengths. Carp fishing, where there is a chance that a very big fish might come along, warrants lines of 12 lb and upwards to begin with, and so does pike fishing. Salmon, exceptionally strong fighters, probably ought not to be approached with lines of less than about 18 lb breaking strain.

Moving to the coast, for estuary and harbour work with mullet and flounders as the quarry, fairly light lines of around 7 lb can be used – but I would not drop below 5 lb. Light rock-fishing can be attempted with lines of around 8 lb where wrasse and small pollack are the quarry, but where there are bigger pollack and bass 12 or 15 lb-breaking-strain lines are more in order. It is probably best to begin beachcasting with a 20 lb-breaking-strain line, which will cast a 4 oz weight tied direct. If you step up the weight to 6 oz, a 25 lb shock leader ought to be used, with stronger leaders for even heavier weights.

A line of 25 lb breaking strain (matched with a 30 lb-line-class rod) is a good 'middleweight' to start with for boat fishing for British species: with it you will not be able to handle exceptionally large fish, and neither will you get full enjoyment from smaller species. After a season you might like to try lighter or heavier tackle.

A fly-fishing beginner will find that a floating fly line serves him best, since it will allow him to fish with dry flies and, with a sinking leader, wet flies to a modest depth. A floating line is easier to aerialize than a sinking one too. Other lines can be bought when casting becomes confident, and when techniques outside the range of floating lines are being explored. The fly line will, of course, be matched to the rod using the A.F.T.M. scale (above).

§12 **Hooks** (Fig. 21)

There are two important considerations when choosing hooks for all kinds of fishing: one is the size of the fish sought, and the other is the size and type of bait – unless the bait is extremely soft, it ought to be secured so that the point and barb of the hook protrude.

The size-scale for freshwater hooks runs from the small 24 (rarely used) to size 1, which is a fairly large hook. From then on, as hooks increase in size, the numbers climb again, and are followed by a nought to distinguish them from the smaller sizes. The small hooks are usually manufactured only in the sizes represented by even numbers, thus: 24, 22, 20, 18, 16 and so on to size 2; while the larger hooks climb 1/0, 2/0, 3/0 and so on up to 12/0.

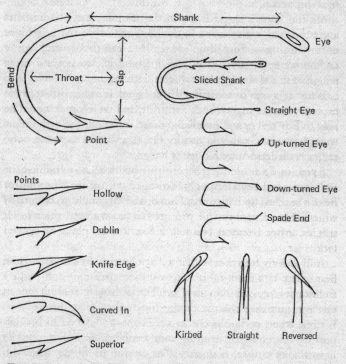

Fig. 21 The parts of a hook, types of hook.

Hooks are manufactured either by shaping fine-gauge wire, or by forging (mainly large sizes) steel. The sizes given above are based on the gape of hooks, which otherwise vary in length and style of shank, shape of bend, and type of point and barb. There are differences in colour, too, particularly since many hooks, other than those of stainless steel, have to have a rust-resistant finish. The choice between these varieties is often a matter of personal preference, but some baits demand that a particular type of hook is used. Casters, for instance – the pupa stage of the maggot – are brittle-shelled with a fluid interior; the use of a thick-sectioned hook would easily burst them and lose their contents, and so a fine-wire hook is a better proposition.

For marine worms, a long-shank is useful; it can be threaded into the body of the worm for a secure hold.

For fly fishing, the length of shank and type of eye (turned-up, straight, and turned-down) vary for different fly patterns. Sometimes the hook's shape helps in the manufacture of a realistic imitation, but it also helps in the presentation of the fly or lure during fishing – a turned-up eye tends to let a dry fly land lightly on the water in advance of the line, and it also holds a short length of line clear of the water after settling.

When it comes to securing fish, the hook is as important as the expensive items such as rods and reels, and therefore it would be silly to buy cheap and unreliable ones – after all, the cash differences between cheap and quality hooks amounts to pence only, except with extra-large big-game hooks.

Even hooks made by reliable firms ought to be examined for sharpness, and any signs of weakness or corrosion. Blunt points can be touched up with a small hone, and this ought to be carried when fishing unless you are prepared to tie on a new, sharp hook whenever one becomes blunted. Hooks should never be carried loose in a tin since they can rattle around and blunt quickly – it is a good idea to keep them either with points inserted in cork, or in a tin filled with foam rubber to stop them drifting, or, if tied-up to casts or traces, in individual small cellophane envelopes (which you can purchase cheaply by the hundred from stamp dealers). Because knotting hooks can be a tricky, or at least time-consuming, job, especially in cold or windy conditions, it is as well to have hooks ready tied to traces before you go fishing. They can then be changed with ease, either by using the loop-to-loop system described in the following chapter on knots, or some other form of attachment to the main line. The variety of sizes you carry on a fishing trip will be governed by the fish you are after and the baits you are using, but you will also find it valuable to have at least half a dozen of each size – you cannot fish confidently if you are down to your last hook, and conscious that you will have to pack up if you loose it.

I have talked so far of single hooks, but there are circumstances when a treble hook is useful (attached to spinners or tube-flies, or for using large fish-baits), and sometimes two hooks joined by a short piece of line will be used as a basis for long fly-type lures or for securing a large bait.

Hooks can be bought ready-tied to casts and traces, but by and large it is cheaper and better (since you can be sure of the strength and quality of line used) to tie your own. It is relatively easy to tie eyed hooks from size 12 onwards, but it becomes progressively harder to thread the eyes of smaller and smaller sizes, and here it is better to use spade-ends which, to my mind, help with bait-presentation on fine nylon. Knots for securing spade-end hooks require a little patience: if you find tying them free-hand too much of a chore, there are knot-tying gadgets on the market to make the task easier. I suggest with these small, freshwater hooks that anything up to a dozen of each size that you will be using are tied at a time, and their numbers made up to this figure whenever hooks are lost on a fishing trip. Shop-tied casts are frequently too short, I find – I prefer 2–3 ft (60–90 cm) lengths mainly because it is helpful to be able to slide small split shot up and down the last couple of feet before the hook. Short, light, nylon lengths also have less stretch between the knots, and are more likely to break under stress.

§13 Swivels (Fig. 22)

Wherever there is a likelihood of the line being twisted, a swivel ought to be incorporated in the tackle. The first, and most obvious, instance where twist is likely is with spinning. Here, even with a swivel, twist will be imparted to the line unless there is some resistance to encourage the swivel to work. Thus leads with a centre of gravity lower than the line between rod-tip and lure, such as the Wye lead, are incorporated in the tackle above the

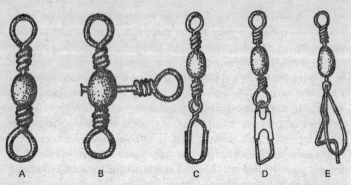

Fig. 22 Types of swivel (§13). A – ordinary barrel swivel; B – 3-way, barrel swivel; C and D – types of link swivel, with small spring clips (useful for attaching lures, traces, leads etc.); E – buckle swivel.

swivel. If no weight is to be used, then an anti-kink vane serves the same purpose.

Some species of fish tend to twist about more than others when they are being played – another reason for a swivel. The eel is one such fish, also the pike to some degree. And wherever live baits are allowed to swim as they will at the end of your tackle, a swivel is again useful.

But it is perhaps in deep-sea fishing more than in any other circumstance that swivels become vital – the fish of rivers and lakes generally keep an even keel because they and the angler are on the same plane, but when you come to bring a fish upwards, often through several fathoms of water, it can twist and turn so freely that a line without a swivel will end up like a corkscrew.

Besides the normal two-way swivel, a three-way swivel is sometimes useful, while a link-swivel, incorporating a small spring clip, is useful for attaching lures, weights and so on.

§14   Floats (Fig. 23)

The range of floats for both sea and freshwater fishing is huge, and there is a tendency to buy, and carry, a large number, many of which are never used. There is no reason to guard against this – indeed, if you make your own floats you can't avoid amassing a collection – but some care in choice before you set out on a trip saves you carrying surplus tackle. It is, however, a very good idea to carry a duplicate of the floats you use most often, so that if one is lost while you are fishing, you can make up an identical tackle rig.

The most useful float patterns are noted in the following chapters on practical fishing, but their main purposes are shared – first as an indicator of what is happening to the tackle below the water, especially fish-takes, second as a means of supporting a bait at whatever depth in the water you choose, and third, carrying a bait along with the current, again at your choice of depth.

Floats are made from a variety of materials, some extremely buoyant, others less so. Different quantities of these materials can be combined for special effects, such as an antenna float with a dense cane tip and buoyant balsa wood body, which makes a sensitive float for fishing in wind – with the body weighted below the water, the fine tip offers little wind resistance, and can be

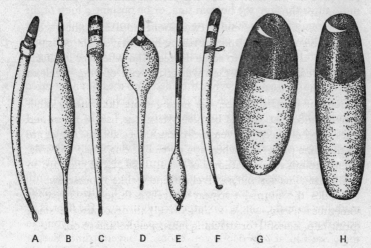

A   B   C   D   E   F   G   H

Fig. 23 A to F are freshwater floats, while G and H are suitable for sea and pike fishing. A – bird quill (goose, crow); B – Avon-type, bodied float, suitable for fishing in moving water; C – stick float (balsa, cane) mainly used in moving water; D – grayling float, suitable for turbulent water; E – antenna float, suitable for still water and some moving-water situations and especially useful in windy conditions; F – quill float with upper and lower line-rings, used as a sliding float in deep water; G – streamlined, pike-livebaiting bung with central line channel; H – sliding 'channel' sea float.

moved by very slight pulls from a fish. Floats should be chosen, during fishing, so that they allow you to use sufficient weight to comfortably reach a particular spot with your cast, and sufficient weight to hold your bait where you want it in prevailing wind and water conditions.

It is a waste of effort to keep striving to cast to a distant spot with a float that is too light; or, for that matter, with a float that you find hard to see when it is in the water. Always keep in mind visibility and ease of casting.

There are various means of attaching floats to the line (Fig. 24) and the most popular ones are 'top-and-bottom', i.e. with the line passing under a rubber band (known as a 'float cap') at the top of the float, and either through a ring or a further band ('double-rubber') at the bottom; and 'bottom-only', either by passing the line through a bottom ring and securing it with small weights pinched on each side of the ring, or by taking the line two or more turns through the bottom ring, or by pushing a loop of the line through the ring and taking it over the top of the float. The 'double rubber' system of top-and-bottom fixing, and the loop method of fixing bottom-only, allow float patterns to be changed without disturbing the rest of the end-tackle. You can also make up a rig with a small link swivel threaded onto the line and secured with a shot each side, which will allow you to clip floats on by the bottom ring and change them with ease.

So much for 'fixed' floats. In deeper water, and occasionally in other circumstances, a 'slider' is more useful. Some of the sea-fishing sliding floats have a channel through the middle for the line to run through, and the float may run freely up the line until restricted by a stop-knot – i.e. a small piece of line tied on to the main line to make a knot too large to pull through the float. The knot does not restrict casting to any great degree, and you can therefore fish at any depth you choose – several times deeper than the length of your rod, in fact. This would be impossible without a slider. Freshwater sliders have either a bottom ring only, or a ring top and bottom (you can use an ordinary float like an antenna as a slider, and also a free-running link-swivel to make floats interchangeable) and they serve the same purpose as the big sea floats.

The aim with all the above floats is to create sensitivity to the take of a fish, but there is a further use with a rather specialized

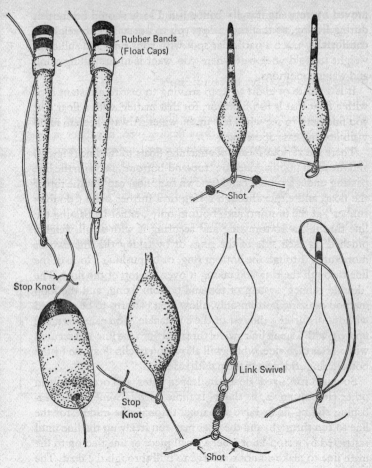

Rubber Bands
(Float Caps)

Stop Knot

Stop
Knot

Shot

Link Swivel

Shot

Fig. 24 Ways of attaching floats.

form of float – the live-bait float. This needs to be sufficiently buoyant to prevent the bait towing it under the surface and registering a false take.

Some very large, old-fashioned cork bungs are sold for this purpose, but to my mind the modern streamlined balsa versions are better – the buoyancy beats the bait fish, but the streamlining helps to allay doubts when a pike takes the bait.

For very big baits, such as a bunch of mackerel for shark, there are no appropriate floats – balloons are sometimes used for this purpose, and streamlined empty plastic detergent bottles are excellent.

§15 Swingtips, quivertips, bite-indicators

These are all basically freshwater aids to detecting bites. The swingtip (Fig.25) is a short arm of fibreglass fixed to the tip of the rod, beyond the tip ring, by a flexible piece of rubber or nylon. It was invented by a Boston tackle dealer, Jack Clayton, and first became popular around the early sixties. It is used with leger tackle and is especially suited to the wide, slow-flowing Fenland waters. In use, the angler casts and allows his leger tackle to settle, tightening the line gently so that the free-swinging tip rests at about 30 degrees from perpendicular. If a fish then takes the bait, pulling the line, the tip will rise; if it pulls the leger

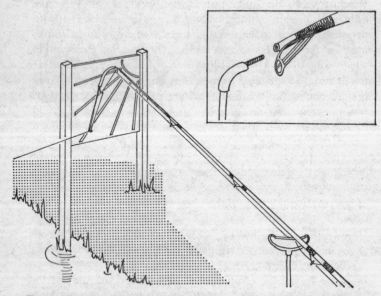

Fig. 25 The swingtip (§15) set for fishing – the clear Perspex shield is scored with radiating lines so that minute movements of the tip show clearly against them. The inset shows a rod-tip ring with a screw-in socket for a swingtip or quivertip.

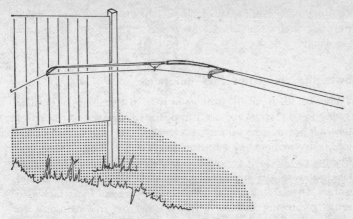

Fig. 26 Quivertip set for fishing. Vertical lines on the shield are the best contrast for the lateral movements of this type of indicator.

weight towards the angler instead, the tip will drop. Often the swingtip is used in conjunction with a Perspex shield scored with dark lines against which the angler can detect very slight movements of the tip. This also serves to shelter the tip from wind in rough conditions. The ideal length for the tip itself is about 12 in (30 cm), and it should have at least one ring close to the rod besides one at the tip. Swingtips are quite versatile, and it is possible to learn to use them in a variety of water conditions and for a wide range of species – they have even been used in sheltered harbours to catch flatfish. Nevertheless, they are best suited to slow-moving water, and in conditions where the swing tip might have to be weighted with lead wire to prevent it being pulled out straight by the flow, a quivertip (Fig. 26) is more useful.

Like the swingtip this is a shaped length of glass-fibre, but it projects stiffly from the rod-tip and does not move freely. A bending point is created close to the rod-tip by filing the glass down to a thin section. As with the swingtip, the angler tightens his line to introduce a bend to the quivertip so that bites register easily.

The butt bite-indicator (Fig. 27) is most useful in extremely windy conditions. The main types consist of a hinged arm with a ring for the line to pass through, and are clipped to the rod between the butt ring and the second rings. This allows the tip of the

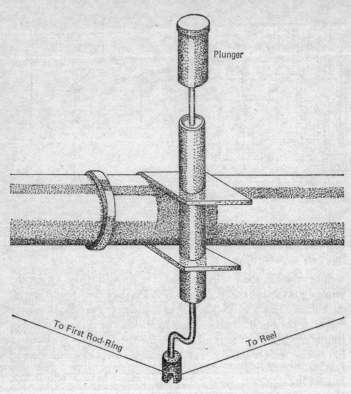

Plunger

To First Rod-Ring

To Reel

Fig. 27 A type of butt bite-indicator. Fish tightening the line will raise the plunger, while slackening line will make the plunger drop.

rod to be pushed under the surface of the water, so that the line is out of the wind, and the rod is set up to point directly at the leger weight. The indicator arm pulls down on the line at the point where the line goes through its ring, so that pulls register by lifting the line or, if the weight is pulled towards the angler by a fish, the slack line allows the arm to drop.

An electronic indicator (Fig. 28) is useful for night freshwater fishing. There are many types about, but they usually consist of a wire arm which rests against the line, and which is connected to a switch so that bites complete an electrical circuit to operate a buzzer or warning light. During daylight a simpler indicator can be made by squeezing a piece of dough or bread onto the line

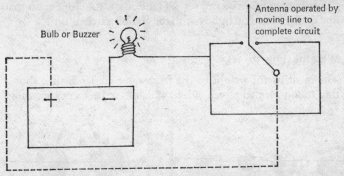

Fig. 28 Simple circuit basis of electric bite indicators.

between butt and second ring, which will be moved by a bite – this can also be used at night with a torchlight shining on the 'bobbin' of dough.

Small clip-on harness bells (Fig. 29) are popular sea fishing bite-detection aids, but you will consistently have better success by watching the rod-tip all the time, and better success still by holding the line lightly to feel for bites. At night, you can illuminate the tip of a beachcasting rod with a small self-contained glow-bulb. Painting the top three or four inches of your rod with luminous or white paint will also make the tip visible in anything but pitch-blackness, when you will probably have a storm lantern to illuminate your tackle anyway.

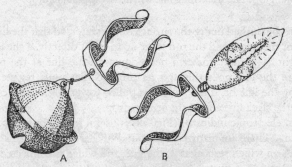

Fig. 29 Bite-detection aids for sea fishing: A – clip-on harness bell; B – clip-on, self-glowing bulb, useful for beach fishing at night, clipped to the upper section of the rod.

For big sea fish, you can set the tension on a multiplier so that line can be pulled off lightly with the audible ratchet 'on'.

§16 Weights (Figs 30, 31)

The most useful weight to the freshwater angler is split shot – tiny round-formed pieces of lead which have been cut something

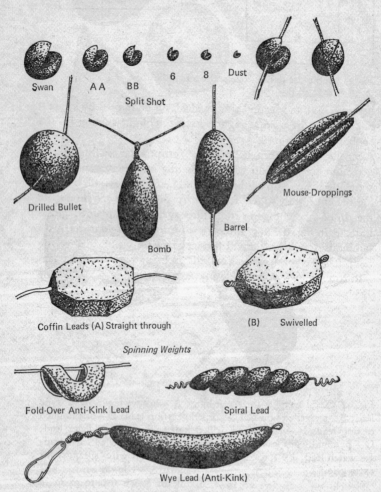

Fig. 30 Freshwater weights (§16).

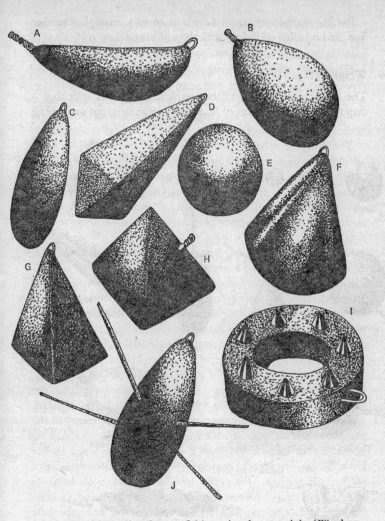

Fig. 31 Useful weights for sea fishing: A – heavyweight 'Wye'-type lead; B – swivelled bomb; C – torpedo casting lead; D – streamlined casting lead; E – large-sized drilled bullet; F – conical leger lead; G – pyramid leger lead; H – Capta, low-profile swivelled leger lead; I – watch lead; J – torpedo casting lead with soft wire 'spraggs' for extra grip.

more than halfway through so that they can be squeezed on to a line. To this end it is imperative that the lead used is really soft, and the trade name 'Dinsmore' springs to mind as the ideal quality. Lead with more temper will need force to be squeezed enough for a proper grip, and once in place will be difficult to slide to another position – an important factor when it comes to bait presentation. Hard shot might also be cut with sharp edges which could part-sever the line.

The range of split shot (the same sizes are applied to bird-shot used in shotgun cartridges) starting with the largest, is:

Swanshot, AAA, BB, No 1, 2, 3 and so on down to No. 8. This last size is generally known as 'dust shot', but you can obtain an even smaller size, known as 'micro-dust', which becomes useful when you want to make minute adjustments to your shotting close to the hook.

Of the above sizes, the best selection to carry is swanshot, AAA, BB, No. 4, 6 and 8, and perhaps micro-dust.

Continental-style elongated split shot, often known by the un-attractive name of 'mouse-droppings', has its converts, although I think that the differences claimed – less water resistance and less visibility – against ordinary round shot are minimal.

With freshwater leger weights, some understanding of the two basic styles of legering, 'straight-through' (running leger) and 'paternoster', gives an insight into the best choice of leads (Fig. 32). In straight-through legering, the line passes through the eye or central drilled hole of the weight before the hook is joined, while paternoster-style rigs have the hook and trace joined to the line above the weight, which terminates the tackle. The Arlesey bomb, a pear-shaped lead with a swivel-eye, developed by Mr Dick Walker, is by far the most widely used lead for both styles of fishing. Of the rest, the coffin lead is somewhat outdated. It offers a great deal of resistance to a taking fish when used straight-through, and its best application is as a paternoster lead (especially with a swivel forced into the line-hole) in fast water, where the current will press flat shapes to the bed. The drilled bullet offers less resistance, and the best use for it is as a rolling leger, allowed to bounce along in the current. Barrel leads will serve the same purpose, but are much more useful as a spinning weight, used in conjunction with an anti-kink vane and swivel. The Wye lead, finally, is designed for spinning and trolling.

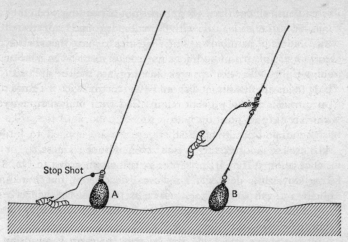

Stop Shot

A

B

Fig. 32 The bomb lead used (A) as a straight-through weight (the line passes through the swivel eye and a stop-shot prevents it from running onto the hook), and as a paternoster weight (B). Here the line is tied directly to the swivel eye and a three-way swivel above the weight allows a trace and hook to be added.

Leger and spinning weights can be improvised with large split shot, and this is also a means of adding weight to a paternoster rig.

The range of leger and spinning weights most useful to the freshwater angler is quite small, from $\frac{1}{4}$ oz to $\frac{1}{2}$ oz (7–14 grammes), and (rarely) $\frac{3}{4}$ oz (21 grammes).

Before leaving freshwater fishing, it is worth mentioning the swim-feeder, which is a leger weight combined with a small cylinder of perforated perspex that can be filled with maggots. The maggots trickle out of the holes while the swim-feeder is in the water, thus groundbaiting the area around the hook. The weight incorporated in the swim-feeder is normally a small strip of sheet lead, but the best sorts of swim-feeder have an additional clip so that other weights can be added if required. They are fitted with a swivel for attachment to the line.

The main requirement of the beachcaster, whose aim is distance casting, is an aerodynamically shaped lead which will fly out with least air resistance. Pear-shaped bombs and torpedo leads are ideal for this purpose, but in circumstances where the tide is likely to push smooth, rounded shapes out of position when they are in the water, leads made with flat sides, or round leads treated with a couple of hard blows with a hammer to make them flatter, are more useful. If this still does not anchor the lead in mud or sand, weights with wire 'spraggs' that dig into the bed are used. The spraggs are flexible, and should pull straight with the strike. You can also obtain a quick-release lead with hinged spraggs which are held in position with a rubber band until the strike pushes the band clear to release them.

Flat, round leads of the 'watch' type are not so suitable for distance casting. They are better for situations where the angler is fishing down into deep water a short distance from the shore – exploiting a sand patch between rocks, for instance. The type with small studs will give a grip on soft sand. They are also useful for fishing in heavy surf.

Conical or pyramid leads are the most popular weights for deep-sea legering, and the modern low-profile pyramid Capta leads are excellent.

For deep-sea trolling, or drifting with artificial lures like the Mevagissey sand-eel, a large lead of the Wye type, or a large barrel lead, is the most suitable weight.

§17   Lead-link booms, paternoster booms (Fig. 33)

Sea fishermen frequently have to change weights to allow for increasing or decreasing tidal flow. Any weight that is therefore fixed directly to the main line with no means of quick-release will force the angler to undo the terminal tackle before changing leads. A large link swivel is quite suitable for this purpose. However, there are other ready-made attachments designed specifically for lead-attachment in running-leger tackles. One is the Kilmore link, which has a large clip for attaching the lead and a large eye, often lined with a ceramic ring to cut down friction-resistance, through which the line runs. Then there is the Clement boom, which consists of a clip, a swivel, and a short wire boom which has two eyes for attaching the line. To my mind both are equally good for deep-sea legering.

Besides attachments for leads, there are quick-release booms for rigging paternoster tackles (i.e. short hook-lengths appended to the main line, with the weight fixed at the extreme end). Of these

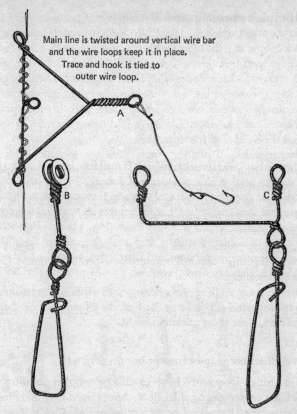

Main line is twisted around vertical wire bar
and the wire loops keep it in place.
Trace and hook is tied to
outer wire loop.

A

B

C

Fig. 33 The sea paternoster boom (A) and two types of sea legering lead attachments – the Kilmore running boom (B) and the Clements boom (C) both of which have eyes for the line to pass through and clips to attach the lead.

the most useful is the wire French boom, which is easily attached by twisting the main line about the base of the triangular section. Other booms are sold, many of them versions of the French boom. Some are made of plastic, but they have less strength than the stainless-steel wire versions.

The 'artificials' are representations of small fish, insects and so on, with an application in many sorts of fishing. The main types of artificials are outlined in this chapter, and they are dealt with more thoroughly, where relevant, in the chapters on practical fishing.

Spoons, spinners and spinning lures (Fig. 34) are designed to revolve or wobble in such a way that they either flash their presence enticingly, or send out distinctive vibrations through the water as they are drawn towards the angler or trailed behind

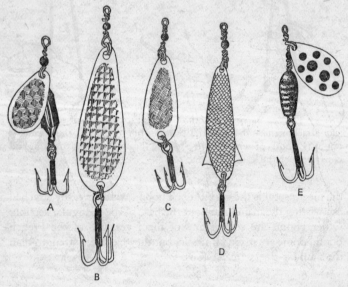

Fig. 34 A selection of spinning lures: A – 'spin-flasha'; B – 'flasha'; C and D – 'Toby' lures; E – Mepps spinner.

a boat. Small spoons are suitable for trout, salmon, sea-trout, chub and perch in freshwater fishing, and the types which seem to be most attractive to salmon are the devon minnow and the wobbling-type spinning lure such as the Abu 'Toby'. Medium and larger spoons are used to attract sea species like the bass, while mackerel are eager takers of any flashy material and have been known to attack screws of silver paper. Pike take a range of spinners from the small to the very large.

Plugs (Fig. 35) are floating or slow-sinking lures, usually finished in bright colours, which have small metal or plastic vanes which make them dive or jig from side to side when drawn through the water. The 'floaters' are particularly useful in weedy pike water since they can be allowed to float over weed patches, and then be made to dive in areas of clear water. They will also take salmon and trout, and many species of sea fish.

Occasionally, more realistic imitations of fish, prawns or small eels are useful, and the artificial rubber or plastic sandeel, particularly the 'Redgill' type, is an extremely good sea bait for bass and pollack, while the artificial prawn is often a good low-

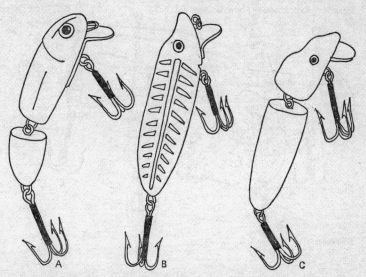

Fig. 35 Three floating/diving plugs – A and C are jointed, B is a single-action plug.

water salmon bait (Fig. 36). Mounts for dead fish baits are fitted with vanes to induce a spin, and can be used for a range of sea and freshwater species.

Pirks and jigs for deep-sea fishing have gained widespread acceptance in very few years, particularly because of their success in catching very big cod. Pirks and jigs (Fig. 37) are self-weighted lures – sometimes weighing 1 lb or more for deep waters with strong currents – which are lowered into the water and worked up and down by the angler to impart a lifelike motion. Pollack and coalfish, besides cod, are attracted to them. There are other types of jigging lures which require additional weights on the

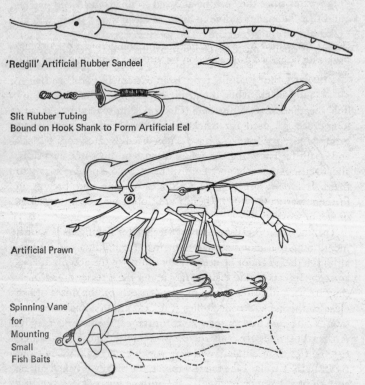

'Redgill' Artificial Rubber Sandeel

Slit Rubber Tubing
Bound on Hook Shank to Form Artificial Eel

Artificial Prawn

Spinning Vane
for
Mounting
Small
Fish Baits

Fig. 36 Artificial eels and prawn are useful for sea fishing, and the spinning vane for small deadbaits is useful for sea, pike and salmon fishing.

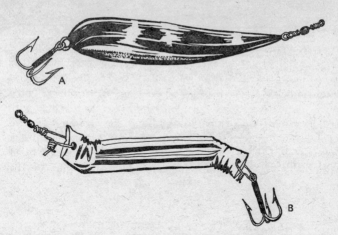

Fig. 37 Two pirks: A – a shiny, metal, shop-bought pirk; B – a home-made pirk fashioned from a section of chromed metal pipe filled with lead.

line – feathers. Sets of feathers (Fig. 38) with several hooks on a long trace are used for mackerel fishing, while large feathers grouped three or four to a trace can be used to catch cod, pollack and coalfish. These feather traces often haul up some surprises, and even conger eels and dogfish have been known to fall to them. It is less rare to take haddock, whiting and bream on feathers, particularly if the hooks are tipped with small offerings of fish or worm bait.

Turning to artificial insects for freshwater fishing, it is worth mentioning that mounts can be obtained for holding real insects, although these cannot be used for fly fishing in the accepted sense since the insects would disintegrate under the stresses of casting – they are used instead to drop or 'dap' insects on the noses of fish close to the bank. Artificial flies (Fig. 39) are in some cases imitations of actual insects such as, for instance, the famous mayfly. Artificial mayflies are constructed from minute pieces of feather, fur and silk to resemble the insects which emerge on many trout rivers in the spring. Like the real insect, the mayfly is fished on the surface of the water, resting on the surface film. This makes it a dry fly, while imitations of underwater creatures – nymphs, for instance, or creepers and chironomids – are fished under the

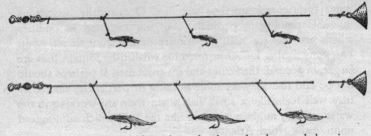

Fig. 38 Feather traces – above is a 3-hook mackerel trace, below is a cod trace made with 3 – 4 in white feathers.

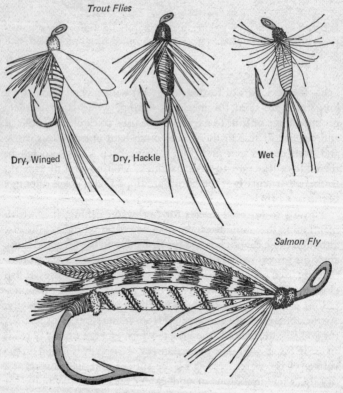

Trout Flies

Dry, Winged Dry, Hackle Wet

Salmon Fly

Fig. 39 Artificial flies.

water surface and are thus wet flies. Occasionally, imitations resemble nothing in particular, but are regarded as oddities which provoke the natural curiosity of the trout or sea-trout. Larger fly fishing lures can resemble small fish. Salmon flies are larger, in general, than trout and sea-trout flies. It perhaps should not be said that they resemble nothing in particular, since they may well seem like a small fish when they are working in the water, or they might even seem like the krill which salmon feed upon in the North Atlantic.

Having amassed all the various components of tackle, the next task is joining them all together – not that this presents a very difficult problem. Many people would have you believe that a vast range of knots should be part of every fisherman's repertoire; instead, the ability to tie a very small range of reliable knots with ease will serve you better – striving to tie a half-remembered knot in wind or poor light will lose much fishing time. When looking at knots it is important also to put them in context, describing their usefulness in various forms of fishing. To avoid duplicating the descriptions, the knots, whippings (Figs. 43–60) and the tying instructions for them follow later in this chapter. First, however, there are a few points to remember.

Joining lines of different diameters, particularly nylon: The only really secure way to join lines of widely differing diameters is to join them loop-to-loop, i.e. with a loop at the fixing point of both lines (Fig. 40). With other forms of knot, such as the blood knot, turns of the finer line will easily slip free of the thicker one. Instead, it will be better to tie-in an intermediate piece of line with a diameter half-way between the two strengths to be joined. With nylon, you can join fine lines with a difference in breaking strain of 2 or 3 lb directly to one another, and with thicker lines you have more tolerance. As an example, if you wanted to join 20 lb line to 10 lb line, an intermediate length of 15 lb would be necessary. But you could join 28 lb line to 20 lb line direct. The difference in diameter is also important when you want to tie a thin line to the eye of a large hook or swivel: a loop will be the best way of connecting the swivel, while with the hook the line should be passed through the eye and whipped to the shank of the hook with a whipping-type knot.

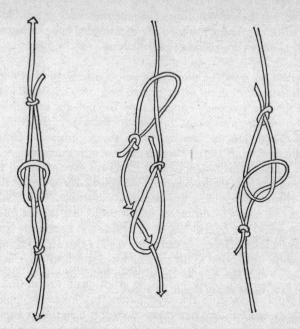

Fig. 40 Loop-to-loop join.

Joining different materials: Some knots are more suited to a particular sort of line than others; clinching and whipping-type knots are best for nylon, because the many turns prevent the knot slipping undone, and also because they do not pinch or abruptly twist the line, which would alter its diameter and lessen its strength.

The textured surface of braided lines such as Terylene will prevent knots from slipping undone so easily, and consequently fewer turns or tucks will be sufficient for a strong hold. For example, a simple overhand loop would need two tucks if tied in nylon, while one tuck will do with Terylene.

Wire does not knot at all in the accepted sense. The end of a wire line or trace should be formed into a loop, made by twisting the line back around itself and whipping tightly with finer wire, or by crimping the loop in place with a small pinched metal tube.

Trouble arises when you come to join these incompatible materials to one another. The loop-to-loop join is always the best method, but 'hybrid' knots are also quite successful – a half-blood knot will secure nylon to a loop of either braided line or wire, and braided line can be fixed in a similar fashion to a wire loop.

Fixing line to a reel: The simplest and most effective way of knotting line to a reel drum or spool is to tie a small overhand loop. Take the line and push a bigger loop through the smaller one (Fig. 41), enlarging it so that it slips over the edge of the drum or spool. Then pull the line tightly so that it grips the central spindle, and wind away. There is only one inherent danger in fixing a line in this fashion – if all the line is ever pulled off the reel by a big fish, the loop around the spindle could slip so that your chance of regaining line becomes impossible. This is very unlikely in most circumstances, but it could just happen in fly fishing where the overall length of fly line and backing is comparatively short. Here, you can either make a clove hitch around the spindle in addition to the slipping loop, which will give extra purchase or, if the spindle has a fixing knurl or a hole drilled through it, make use of this to fix your line.

Keep knots tidy: Overlarge knots and loops might make your line more visible to fish, This is particularly true of fly fishing on a bright day, where anything floating on the surface film casts an

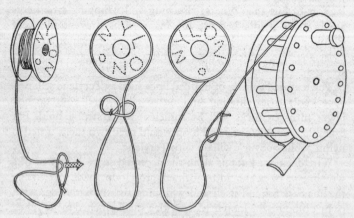

Fig. 41 Tying a small loop to make a large slip-loop for fixing line to reel.

enlarged shadow on the river bed. Big knots can also pick up bits of weed, and can snag bottom obstructions easily. The same is true of untidy knots which have been left with a dangling loose end.

With nylon line, most knots need to have a short loose end to allow for the knot to pull tighter under pressure, but 'short' in this sense means *really* short – about an eighth of an inch. Any surplus should be trimmed.

Knots you don't want: Just as you lose line strength when you intentionally make a knot, so knots that arrive by accident will have the same effect. The 'wind knot' is the particular curse of the fly fisherman – in windy conditions especially, the fly doubles back on the line and ties itself into a neat overhand ('granny') knot. The wind, and small fish which haven't produced a noticeable bite, can also tie these knots in float and leger lines. They should always be unpicked before they pull tight enough to weaken the line. The point of a hook is a good tool for doing this. Nylon line looks a little crumpled after a knot has been unpicked, but if you stretch it with a couple of pulls it becomes straight again.

§18 **Knots for freshwater fishing**

(a) *Float and leger:* With the rod set up, and threaded with line, the float angler should first attach his float (the right way up!) and then think about tying on either the hook, or hook-length plus hook. If the float he is using is not 'fixed', then a shot squeezed onto the line below the float will stop it inadvertently sliding off, if the end of the line is released for any purpose. The same applies to the running leger – lead on the line first, with a shot to retain it, and then the knot for the hook or hook-length.

The most useful way of joining a hook-length to the main line is the loop-to-loop method (Fig. 40), with an overhand loop (double-tucked for nylon) both at the end of the main line, and at the free end of the hook-length. The overhand loop (Fig. 44) is extremely easy to tie, and is versatile. Loop-to-loop is recommended especially because the loops can be slipped undone easily to change to another hook-length. There are alternatives, such as a loop in the main line to which you can attach the free end of the hook-length with a half-blood knot (Fig. 45), or you can use a full-blood knot (Fig. 46). However, these alternatives are less easily tied in a strong wind, for instance, than the overhand loop.

Now for attaching hooks. The purpose of hook-lengths and traces has already been discussed – they provide a 'weak point' where the line will break under extreme stress. The lighter the main line one is using, the more this becomes important. With stronger line used for, say, carp fishing, the hook-length can be dispensed with if you wish, although I don't recommend it. Whether the hook is attached to a hook-length or directly to the main line, the same knots apply.

Two types of hook shank-ending are in general use: the eyed hook, with a small ring at the end of the shank which can be either turned-up, turned-down, or straight, and the spade-end, which has a small flattened 'spade' to prevent a whipping-type knot slipping off the end of the shank. For eyed hooks, the easiest knot is the half-blood (Fig. 45) which is particularly suited to straight eyes. With the turned-up and turned-down eyes a whipping knot, either the Domhof (Fig. 47) or spade-end knots (Figs. 48, 49), tied around the shank after the line has been passed through the eye, attaches the hook much more attractively and, I think, more securely. The Domhof is suitable for the spade-end, although some anglers mistrust it. However, if six turns or so are taken around the shank I feel it perfectly reliable. Both spade-end knots also serve the same purpose. Float anglers who use a sliding float will find the stop knot (Fig. 60) useful.

With the paternoster form of legering, the lead is secured to the extreme end of the main line. The hook-length can be tied to a small swivel, running freely on the line above the weight and 'stopped' at whatever distance from the lead you require by a split shot. This is not, however, a very satisfactory rig and the lead is better fixed to a length of line and free running swivel, with the hook-length joined to the end of the main line – a reverse of the lead and hook positions, in fact. Still another way of making a paternoster rig – and this is where further knots become useful – is to tie the lead to the extreme end of the main line, and to make a loop in the main line some distance above the lead for tying-on the hook-length. An overhand loop can be used for this fixing point, but to my mind the blood loop (Fig. 51) is a tidier and more reliable choice.

(b) *Spinning, livebaiting and deadbaiting:* Most spinning lures, plugs etc. are finished with an eye for attachment to the spinning trace, and (with any eyed piece of tackle in fact) the half-blood is one of the most useful knots that can be learned for this purpose. However, if spinners are to be changed frequently during fishing, the trace is better finished with a link-swivel to make changeovers easy. As with other forms of fishing, it is a good idea to have a quantity of traces made-up before you make an outing, to avoid having to construct them on the bank.

If wire is to be used as the trace material, and this applies especially to pike fishing (livebaiting as well as spinning) then use neatly-whipped loops (Fig. 52) finished with nail varnish (a good, quick-drying sealant) or (if whipped with thin wire) solder. If single or treble hooks are to be attached directly to the trace for livebaiting or deadbaiting, then the Domhof knot will make an emergency fixing in thin multi-strand wire. But it is far better either to whip the wire to the shank, or to loop the wire through the eye of the hook, finishing off with a whipping. Again, it is a good idea to do all of this in advance of fishing.

(c) *Fly fishing:* Up to eight knots at a time can be in use in fly fishing – a knot joining backing to fly line, one joining fly line to leader, one joining cast to leader, two joining the three sections of a tapered cast, and finally three securing a tail fly and two droppers to the cast. Taking these in turn, with the backing join first: the material of the backing is important and the choice lies between dressed silk, linen or terylene lines (all braided) and nylon mono-filament. The nylon line is essential for shooting heads, but it also makes a reasonable backing for a double-taper line. If nylon backing is used, then by far the most useful knot is the needle knot (Fig. 55) – a hole is made in the core of the fly line with a hot needle, and the sharpened end of the nylon is forced into the hole and out through the fly line wall, where it is then made to grip the line with a whipping-type knot. This makes an extremely strong, small, tidy knot which can be pulled through the rod rings with ease. But this is not a suitable knot for the other kinds of multifilament backings. Here I find that actually sewing, and finally binding over a join with fine silk (Fig. 56) is the smoothest and most attractive treatment. The join is then treated with nail varnish to waterproof it and make it extra secure. Moving to the other end of the fly line, where the cast or leader is to be attached: here I think it is essential that a really neat, smooth knot is tied, firstly, so that it can pass through the rod rings with ease, and secondly, so that it has low air-resistance and does not hinder the action of the fly line and cast when they are unfurling.

I also think it is important that 2 ft (60 cm) or so of 12–15 lb (5–7 kg) line is tied permanently to the fly line as a leader. This avoids waste at the end of the fly line – if you had to tie leaders and casts directly to the fly line every time you went fishing, you would wear the end of the tapered section quite quickly and it would be necessary to discard pieces of it every now and then. Fly line is expensive, whereas nylon is not, and so it will not hurt if you lose pieces of the leader.

Although it is possible to whip a small loop in the end of the fly line for attaching such a leader, by far the best knot is the needle knot mentioned above.

Loops are sometimes tied in bought casts, and with a loop in the leader you could attach the cast with the loop-to-loop method, or you could tie the leader to the cast loop with a half-blood knot (or vice versa). However, a neater alternative is a blood knot, which transmits the unfurling action of the line better than loops.

Now the cast. You may buy knotless tapers, which are made of one piece of nylon tapering from a thick 'butt' – the point at which they are attached to leader or fly line – to a fine 'point' at the extreme end. If you tie your own from level sections of nylon – normally three pieces: for example 5 lb (2.2 kg) butt, 4 lb (1.8 kg) middle, and 3½ lb (1.5 kg) point – the blood knot is essential. If you wish to have a cast to which you can attach 'droppers' or extra flies, you can leave one long loose end in each of the two blood knots joining the cast sections.

Finally, attaching the fly or lure: because of the dressings of flies and lures it would be impossible to use the types of knots which whip the line along the shank of the hook. For wet lures dressed on straight-eyed hooks, the ideal knot is the half-blood. The same knot will also give fairly good purchase with other types of fly dressed on turned-up or turned-down eyes. There are drawbacks, however. For instance, with small dry flies the half-blood is large and visible, extending from the 'head' section like an extra-long proboscis. And, generally with small flies again, the hook can swing about loosely on this knot and the fly could be presented at an angle to the line, instead of in-line for ideal presentation. In these circumstances the best knot is the Turle knot (Fig. 50). The line is passed though the eye of the hook to lasso the head of the fly, which therefore cannot swing out of line.

It is worth noting that you can purchase a small nylon link for attaching your fly line to the backing line and to the leader (Fig. 57). I think these are useful as a quick attachment, but for a permanent join the recommended knot is better.

§19   **Knots for sea fishing**

(a)   *Rock, pier and beach fishing:* Although the lines used for these forms of sea fishing are often much heftier than those used for freshwater fishing, the same patterns of knots are adequate. For joining lines, casts and so on, loop-to-loop fixings are ideal, while for fixing eyed items of tackle the half-blood (Fig. 45) is best. The stop knot (Fig. 60) is also useful for a sliding float.

However, there is one area where the blood knot (Fig. 46) is essential for joining two pieces of line – that is joining a shock-leader for beachcasting. This is because the blood knot can be trimmed close so that it is unlikely to catch on any of the rod rings during a cast; there are other knots, but I don't think this one can be beaten.

(b)   *Deep-sea and big-game fishing:* Here again, the most useful knot patterns are overhand loops, blood knot and half-blood (for eyed hooks, lures and swivel-eyes etc.). However, when heavy nylon is used there is a greater tendency for the knot to come undone because of the stiff, springy nature of the line, and it is therefore wise to make extra turns in blood and half-blood knots, tucking the free end for extra security (Fig. 45). With wire line or trace, the whipped or crimped loops (Fig. 54) mentioned above for pike fishing traces should be used.

Bearing in mind the likelihood that there is a greater risk of line twisting in deep-sea and big-game fishing, I prefer to use swivels wherever lines and wire traces, rubbing traces and the like are to be joined. Another good idea to avoid breakages is to protect knots which are likely to be bumped continuously by the sliding eye of a lead or lead link with a short section of rubber tubing (or plastic sheath cut from plastic-covered wire) or a plastic bead (Fig. 42).

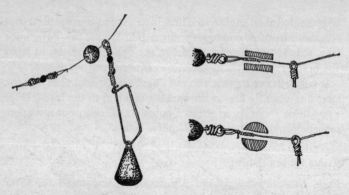

Fig. 42 A plastic bead or a short length of plastic tubing stripped from electric wire protects a knot from being abraded and undone by a sliding lead.

Occasionally, you will want to keep the lead well up on the line above a long, flowing trace, and you can do this with a matchstick hitched onto the line either with a loop-hitch or a clove-hitch (Fig. 58). If the matchstick is weakened by making a small nick in it at the point where the hitch tightens, you can ensure that it breaks when you strike.

With Terylene and other braided lines, it is useful to make a permanent neatly whipped loop at the end of the main line.

§20 Whipping for loops and tackle repairs (Fig. 43)

Whipping is one of the simplest jobs in angling – you simply make turn after turn of the whipping material, be it silk or wire, binding the last five or six turns over a spare loop of line. The end of the whipping is then passed through the loop, which is drawn back under the last turns, and the small free end is pulled tight. With a whipping you can finish off loops in wire or other line, and you can also bind items like a replacement rod-ring to your rod, or a loop to the end of a quill float.

§21 Overhand loop (Fig. 44)

Double line back on itself, turn loop around finger and tuck through. Moisten nylon in mouth before pulling tight. Tuck

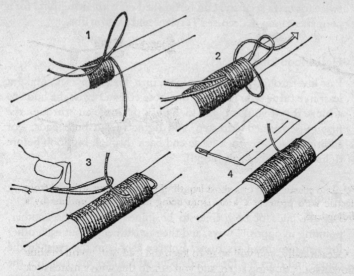

Fig. 43 The whipping finish (§20): 1 – form a loop from a short length of spare line; 2 – bind over the loop with the whipping line or thread for a minimum of six turns and then pass the end of this through the small remaining loop; 3 – grasp loose ends of loop and pull gently out, drawing end of whipping line or thread after it; 4 – tighten and neaten whipping, then varnish, leaving loose end until varnish is dry when it will be stiff and easier to cut off neatly.

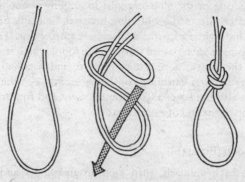

Fig. 44 (§21) Overhand loop (figure-of-eight loop).

twice for extra security. Can be finished off with a whipping for a permanent loop in deep-sea Terylene and Dacron line.

§22 Half-blood knot (Fig. 45)

Pass line through hook-eye or loop, turn it back on itself. Make at least five turns (you can hold the loose end and twist the hook to achieve this if you like) and then push the loose end through the first twist formed. Moisten, and tighten from both ends. For additional security tuck loose end back through big loop before tightening (tucked half-blood).

§23 Blood knot (Fig. 46)

Lay the ends of both lines to be joined against one another, pointing in opposite ways, and then twist them about each other for a minimum of six turns. Enlarge a hole in the twist in the centre and turn the loose ends back, threading one through the hole from one side, and one from the other. Moisten, and tighten

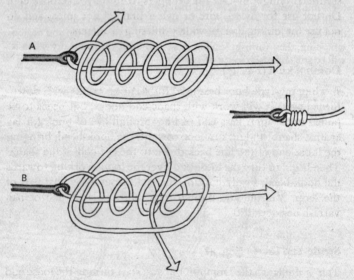

Fig. 45 (§22) The half-blood knot (A) and the tucked half-blood knot (B).

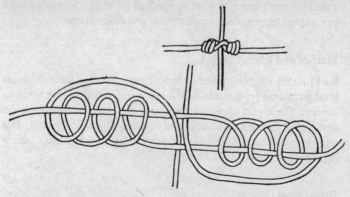

Fig. 46 (§23) The blood knot (cruciform blood knot) for joining two lengths of line, making tapered casts etc. Long loose ends made with this knot can be left in tapered fly casts for tying on droppers.

first by pulling the line on each side of the knot, holding the loose ends securely. Then pull these ends tight. Repeat until knot is secure. If tying a fly-cast for droppers, trim only one loose end. Do not use for nylon–wire or nylon–braided line joins, and do not use for joining lines of widely differing diameters.

§24 **Domhof knot** (Fig. 47)

A whipping-type knot best used for securing hooks with down-turned eyes. It will work with spade-end hooks, but needs to be pulled extra tight. Pass end of line through eye of hook (or lay against shank) and make a loop towards the hook-bend, bringing the loose end of the line back down to the eye end of the shank. Then begin to turn the loose end over the loop, working towards the hook-bend, finally pushing the end through the final part of the loop. Moisten and tighten from both ends. A dab of nail varnish helps security.

§25 **Spade-end knot 1** (Fig. 48)

This is similar to the Domhof, but you start turning the loose end of the line over the loop from the hook-bend end of the shank, working towards the eye or spade-end. The loose end is finally

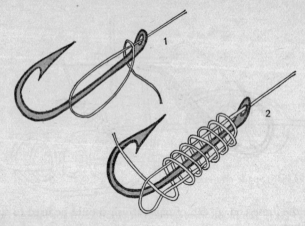

Fig. 47 (§24) Domhof knot.

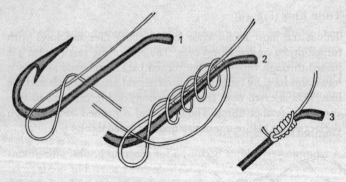

Fig. 48 (§25) Spade-end knot (1).

turned back towards the hook-bend and pushed through the loop before being tightened from both ends (moisten first).

§26 Spade-end knot 2 (Fig. 49)

As an alternative to the spade-end knot above: a large circular loop is laid against the shank of the hook, and the loose end is turned through the loop, binding the inside of it against the shank for six or so turns working towards the hook-bend. Then the knot is moistened and tightened by pulling the main line first,

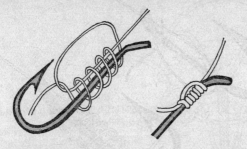

Fig. 49 (§26) Spade-end knot (2).

then the loose end. A dab of nail varnish should be used to seal the knot.

§27 **Turle Knot** (Fig. 50)

This is the most useful knot for attaching flies and lures with turned-down or turned-up eyes. The end of the cast ('point') is passed through the hook-eye, turned back onto itself and made into a slip-loop by tying a single overhand knot back around the line. This is eased over the fly-dressing, taking care not to trap any of the feather fibres. The loose end is pushed back through the large knot before it is moistened and eased tight.

Fig. 50 (§27) Turle knot.

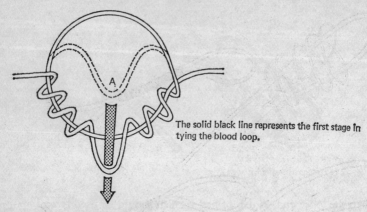

The solid black line represents the first stage in tying the blood loop.

Fig. 51 (§28) Blood loop.

§28   Blood loop (Fig. 51)

This is a means of making a secure loop in traces etc. for attaching a hook length. A large loop is made, with the loose end passed through several times to make a twist at the bottom of the loop. A hole is then enlarged in the middle of the twisted section and the top of the large loop is pushed through. Both ends of the line are pulled while this loop is held tightly between your teeth.

§29   Whipped loops for wire, Terylene (Fig. 52)

There are several ways to make the loops in wire and other materials. Provided the wire is not too thick, a simple overhand loop (above) will do. An alternative is to twist the wire back around itself, and yet another method is laying the end of the wire back along itself, tying an overhand knot to make a slip loop which can be overbound (whipped) with silk or fine wire. Whipping makes a really superb finish of all loops – it provides extra security, too. The same applies to loops in Terylene or Dacron which you want to remain permanent. Whippings should be finished with waterproof glue or nail varnish (silk) or solder (wire).

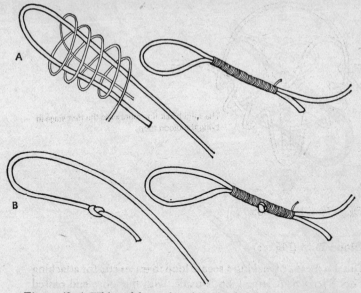

Fig. 52 (§29) Whipped loops in wire, Terylene: A – a simple loop, overbound tightly with silk which should be wound on to cover the loose end and secured with a whip finish (§20) and varnished. B – a loop with a single, overhand knot tied in the wire or line for extra security. The whipping is bound on each side of the knot, and finished as in A above.

§30   **Whipped hooks to wire (Fig. 53)**

The loops directly above can be used to secure hooks to wire, but there are better methods. First, for eyed hooks (which ought to have turned-down or turned-up eyes), pass the wire end through the eye and then tie a single overhand knot around the shank, overwhipping this with silk or fine wire. For double or treble hooks, pass the wire through the eye, around the 'crutch' between the hooks and tie a single overhand knot around the shank before passing the loose end back through the eye in the other direction. Finish off with a whipping around the line and the loose end.

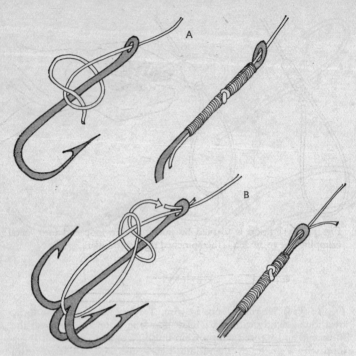

Fig. 53 (§30) A – wire knotted and whipped to shank of a single hook. B – wire knotted to treble hook and whipped.

§31   Crimped loops (Fig. 54)

These are essentially for use with wire, and the metal sleeves used for crimping should just, and only just, accommodate twice the diameter of the wire you will be using. Pass the line through the sleeve, double it back into a loop and pass the free end back through the sleeve in the opposite direction. Leave a small section poking from the end of the sleeve – about an eighth of an inch – before pinching the sleeve tightly. The piece of wire you have left poking out of the sleeve will tell you if the crimp is starting to slip.

§32   Needle knot (Fig. 55)

I have described this as the most useful knot for joining fly lines both to backing and to leader. A warmed needle should be pushed

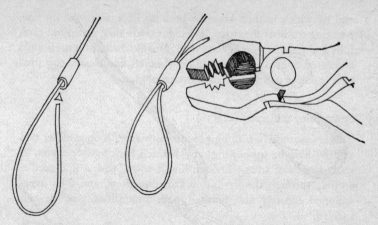

Fig. 54 (§31) Loop is formed by pushing wire loop-end into metal crimping sleeve, which is then pinched tight with pliers.

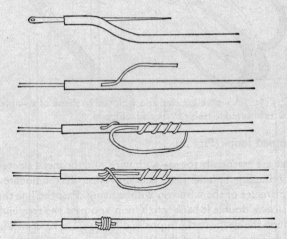

Fig. 55 (§32) Needle knot. Secure with a lick of varnish. Forms a permanent join between fly line and backing or leader.

into the core of the fly line for about half an inch, and then out through the wall of the line. The end of the nylon backing or leader is sharpened to a point with a razor blade and then eased through the hollowed fly line to emerge through the wall. Five or so turns of line are taken along the fly line with the nylon, the end of which is then brought back to lie against the fly line, pointing towards the turns. These turns are then unwound carefully and re-laid over the loose end. Finally, the knot is moistened and eased tight. It should then be trimmed, and treated to a protective dab of nail varnish or waterproof glue.

§33 **Sewn join, whipped** (Fig 56)

This is a method of making a secure permanent loop at either end of a fly line, or for sewing-on a braided backing-line direct. A short length of strong braided line is sewn, with a fine needle, entirely through the fly line in two directions, and then over-whipped securely and finished with waterproof glue or nail varnish.

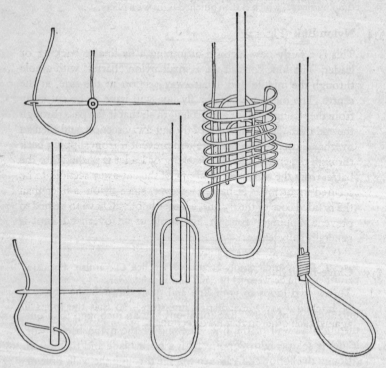

Fig. 56 (§33) Sewn loop for backing end of fly line.

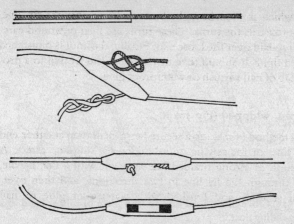

Fig. 57 (§34) Nylon link for joining fly line and backing/leader.

§34 Nylon link (Fig. 57)

This is a fairly new method of joining a fly line to backing or leader. The link consists of a small nylon 'barrel' with a hole through the middle and a cut-away section in the side, at the centre. The outer wall of the fly line will have to be cut away from the strong core for a short length so that it can pass through the end of the barrel and out of the cut-away section, and then an overhand knot tied in the core will prevent it from slipping back through the entry-hole. The backing or leader is pushed into the barrel from the other end, and out of the cut-away section, to be secured in a similar fashion. However, since nylon is finer than the braided core of the fly line, a larger knot will have to be tied to prevent slipping – four or five turns of an overhand knot is generally sufficient.

§35 Clove-hitch (Fig. 58)

Throw two loops in your line and push through the object to be hitched – say a matchstick line-stop – so that the loops lie against each other in reverse directions.

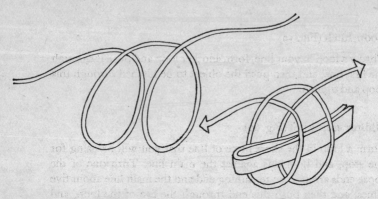

Fig. 58 (§35) Clove-hitch, used here to fix a piece of rubber band as a stop for a sliding float.

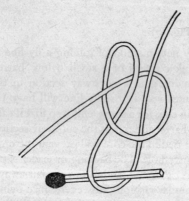

Fig. 59 (§36) Loop-hitch fixing match stick as a lead-stop.

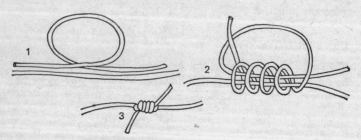

Fig. 60 (§37) Sliding stop-knot.

§36　**Loop-hitch** (Fig. 59)

Throw a loop in your line, form another loop and push it through the first one, and then push the object to be hitched through this loop and tighten.

§37　**Sliding stop-knot** (Fig. 60)

Form a loop in the short piece of line that you will be using for the stop, and hold this against the main line. Turn one of the loose ends around the remaining end and the main line about five times, and then push this end through the eye of the loop, and tighten gently from both ends. Trim loose ends to an eighth or a quarter of an inch (3–6 mm).

It has sometimes been said that a well-equipped angler somewhat resembles a loaded Christmas tree. Although there are circumstances where a large amount of equipment is necessary, the aim should always be towards cutting out inessential gear. By way of illustration, I once knew somebody who always carried all of his rods – sea rods, float rods, fly rods – whenever and wherever he went fishing. To some extent it is wise to cover yourself with alternatives, but to carry this need to such an extreme limit is absurd, particularly if you want to be mobile while you are fishing.

Besides the fish-getting gear of rod, reel, line, hook, weights and floats, or perhaps flies and spinners, there are other pieces of equipment to add to fit you out properly. Some, like landing nets or gaffs and disgorgers, are essential and should never be omitted whenever you pack to go fishing. Others are less essential, but they do add a great deal to your enjoyment – a keepnet, for instance, for the coarse fisherman to save his catch up for release at the end of the day, or perhaps some sort of seating that will make long stays on the riverbank or beach more comfortable. All of the items of equipment mentioned below can be bought at a tackle shop, but some – bait tins, or containers for floats and hooks – can be improvised. Cigar boxes are handy for keeping floats, and many food containers make good bait tins. These will save you some money when you begin fishing.

Landing nets, gaffs, tailers: You can get away with swinging very small fish through the air on the end of the line to land them, but modest-sized and larger fish, which you ought to be prepared for even if you are after smaller game, will need to be helped ashore or into the boat with some sort of landing implement, or else be lifted by hand. While it is quite practical to lift a few species by hand, it is often risky and you stand a fair chance of either losing the fish or falling in the water. Tope can be grasped by the upper tail lobe and the dorsal fin and hoisted inboard; you can grasp trout and even pike across the shoulder just behind the head, and the salmon has a waist or 'wrist' just ahead of the broad tail fin that provides a fair hold if a gaff or net is out of reach.

In general, however, it is wise to carry some landing equipment. A landing net – a largish conical net fixed by the mouth to a round or triangular frame and a shaft to extend the angler's reach – is the most versatile of these (Fig. 61). It can be used for all but very large fish, or fish that might damage netting with their teeth or rough skins. For modest-sized coarse fish, and species such as wrasse and mullet caught from the sea shore, a net with a rim diameter of around 15 in (38 cm) is sufficient, but it must have a long handle – at least 6 ft (1.8 m). The length enables you to reach across bankside vegetation; also, with a shorter handle, you might have to lay your rod well back over your shoulder to draw a fish within range of the net, and a fish with a bit of life left could easily lunge and break the line before you brought the rod back into playing position. Cane net-poles with two sections, or more modern aluminium or tubular-glass poles with two sections, are easier to carry than one-piece poles. The net size and mouth diameter will have to be increased for larger fish.

The fly fisherman, especially if he will be wading, needs a net which he can carry slung over his shoulder on a cord or elastic lanyard, or clipped to his belt. Nets that fold double and lock into the open positions are very good for this purpose. The wading fly fisherman could otherwise carry a net fixed to a 4 or 5 ft shaft with a pointed end for wading in waters with a soft bed. The shaft acts as a staff for feeling your way over the bottom as you make your way out from the bank, and while you are fishing it can be stuck into the mud so that it stands within reach.

Extended reach is less important in deep-sea boat fishing, and because of the greater sizes of fish that can be expected, an altogether stronger net is fixed by the mouth to an iron hoop and stout, short wooden pole. Most good charter boats will carry one or two of these nets. For fishing from piers and other high vantage points where you cannot hope to reach a fish with a net on a

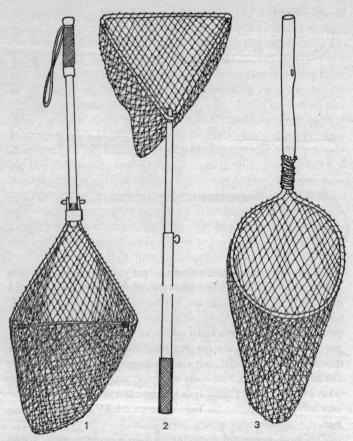

Fig. 61 Landing nets: 1 – folding fly-fisherman's net with elastic lanyard; 2 – extending, coarse fisherman's landing net; 3 – net with large-diameter heavy ring fixed to a stout shaft for sea boat fishing.

handle, a dropnet – a weighted round-rimmed net fixed to a length of strong cord – is essential.

The gaff (Fig. 62) is a large, strong, metal hook fixed to a 4–5 ft pole for freshwater and beach fishing and a somewhat shorter shaft for boat fishing. Gaffs, which might damage fish if they are not handled properly, should be used mainly for fish that are to be killed and kept, and for fish that are extra large. Two or more

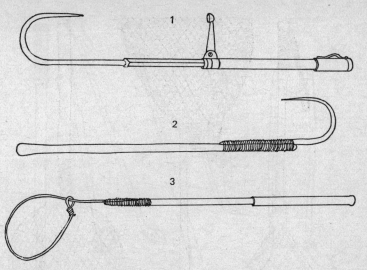

Fig. 62 1 – extending, pike or salmon gaff; 2 – stout, sea gaff with lashed-on head. Point should be protected with a cork. 3 – tailer, a wire noose on a staff.

people each armed with a gaff might be needed to land a big conger eel or shark. Gaffs for anything but boat fishing can be screwed to metal shafts, but since a large conger eel might twist the head off the gaff with a screw-type fitting, a lash-on gaff head with a stout wooden shaft is best for boat fishing. A gaff is more easy to manage than a net for the beach angler fishing in strong surf.

The wrist at the tail of a salmon means that a tailer – a wire slip-loop fixed to the end of a pole – may be used to slip over the tail and tighten for a firm lift (also Fig. 62).

Disgorgers, gags (Fig. 63): It is important to be able to remove hooks that have been swallowed by a fish. The two main types of coarse-fishing disgorger are the thin wire probe with a forked end suitable mainly for situations where you can actually see the hook to be removed, and a slightly thicker probe with a deep groove at the end which can be slipped onto the line and pushed along it to regions deeper in the fish's gullet. Another good disgorging instrument is a pair of artery forceps, obtainable from medical

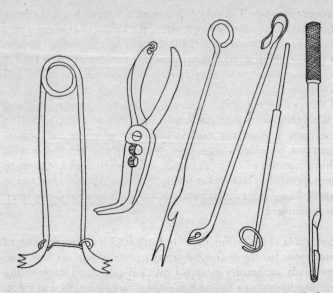

Fig. 63 Left to right: the gag, for keeping open the mouth of a large fish such as the pike (it is humane to bind over the unnecessarily sharp prongs with thick insulation tape); long-nosed pliers which, like artery forceps, are useful for reaching past teeth to remove a hook; a selection of disgorgers, forked and grooved.

stores, which afford a good grip on a hook. They are especially valuable for dealing with a gullet-hooked fish that has a mouthful of very sharp teeth, such as the pike.

With such a fish it is also useful to have something to keep its mouth open while you conduct unhooking operations, not least because you might get a retaliatory bite. The gag, a spring-hinged device made out of stout wire, is designed for this purpose. Gags bought from a tackle dealer do have a major fault – the forked ends of the two arms frequently finish with sharp points which might damage the mouth of the fish. It is humane to bind over these ends with insulation tape or thick plastic tape.

Large pliers are needed to wrest big hooks from the larger sea fish such as sharks, and sometimes it is prudent to cut the trace without attempting to take the hooks out. Pliers with long pipe extensions welded to the grips are especially useful with these big fish.

Keepnet (Fig. 64): The coarse fisherman's keepnet has to be large to be fair to the fish. In recent years, the keepnet has come under scrutiny in directions other than size; wire hoops used to be widely used, but since there was evidence that fish kept in the net could be damaged on these, they have largely been replaced by soft plastic hoops.

Knotted mesh has also been criticized for the same reason, and a fairly recent development in netting, micro-mesh, which has no knottings, is gradually gaining favour over traditional meshes. However, provided a net is large – at least 8 ft (2.4 m) long with a ring diameter of 16 in (40 cm) or above – fish need not come to harm provided the keepnet is not lifted too frequently from the water. Large fish such as pike and carp can be kept safely in an immersed sack.

Bank-sticks, rod-rests (Fig. 65): The bank-stick is a versatile piece of equipment for the coarse fisherman; keepnet mouths, and rod-rest heads, are usually equipped with a standardized screw-fitting for attachment to a bank-stick. Sticks vary in length and thickness, and it is best to carry two or three of varied lengths, avoiding

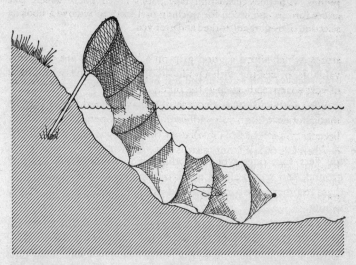

Fig. 64 Keepnet – should be at least eight feet long with soft rings of at least 16 in diameter. Minnow, knotless or micromesh netting is best.

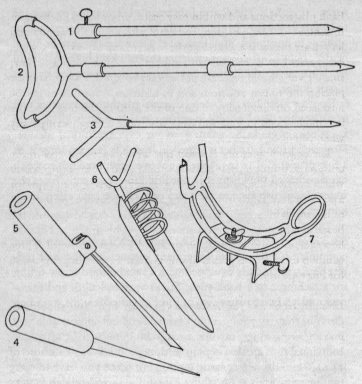

Fig. 65 Freshwater bank stick (1) with thumbscrew grip; extending bank stick (2) with screw-in rod rest head; and thin, forked rod rest (3), less useful than the wide variety. The dig-in socket rod rests (4, 5, 6) are for beach fishing, and the clamp rest (7) is for fixing to a boat gunwale.

the very thin ones which are difficult to draw out of marshy ground, and which afford no grip if the screw-thread attaching them to other accessories is found to be stiff at the end of a day's fishing.

In freshwater fishing it is often essential to have rod-rests which have their own shafts, or rod-rest heads which can be attached to a bank-stick. The float-and-leger fisherman needs a forward rest for his rod jutting over the water (and occasionally a back-rest for the butt of his rod too) so that he can arrange his rod clear of bank obstructions and within easy reach. In order to alter angles to achieve an ideal position, rod-rests with adjustable angles and length are the most useful. For the forward rest especially, a wide, exaggerated fork, padded with rubber or plastic tubing is best; smaller vee-shaped rests are not so easy to aim for when you are placing the rod in position, and in addition, your line might be misplaced on the outside of one of the arms of the fork, and the line might catch on this and foul, instead of lifting cleanly away when you make a strike.

The beach angler needs a rod-rest which keeps his rod in the upright position, so that his line is held clear of breaking waves which might pull his tackle out of place. The best upright rest for a soft beach of sand or mud is one that has a cup for the butt end of the rod with a high, extendable fork. This can be dug into the beach at whatever angle you choose. In pebble and rock beaches, however, a tripod rest with adjustable legs is more useful. Three bamboo canes tied together at one end are a good improvisation for this type of rest.

Holdalls, tackle and bait containers (Figs 66, 67): You should endeavour to carry your gear in a convenient and comfortable way, making sure that you can find most tackle items with little trouble. Individual rods are best kept in sectioned cloth bags or sections of $2\frac{1}{2}$ in (6 cm) diameter plastic piping, but when you have to carry two or more rods on a fishing expedition, a rod-holdall is very useful. There are two types, the first being a tubular canvas bag on the lines of a golf bag, and the second a long roll-up sheet with pockets for rods. Both types have pockets for other items of tackle such as landing-net poles and bank-sticks, and they are fitted with a shoulder strap for carrying. Small pieces of tackle need to be placed in separate containers before considering the main carrying equipment; the coarse fisherman will find a combined float-and-tackle box, with compartments for hooks, shot, leger weights and so on, a big advantage. Failing that, individual boxes, clearly marked with the contents on the outside, can be used. Fly fishermen will need a box with separate small compartments for dry flies which have to be segregated according to type, while for wet flies you can buy small boxes with rows of small clips or a magnetic strip to hold the flies and lures by the hook. Casts can be kept in a multi-pocket wallet for convenience,

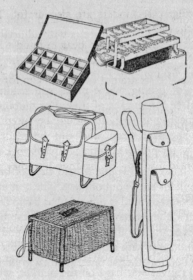

Fig. 66 Lidded compartment fly box for keeping fly selection. Cantilever carry-all with compartment trays, useful for spinning and sea tackle.
Efgeeco canvas seat-holdall.
Wicker basket.
Efgeeco tubular rod-holdall.

Fig. 67 Haversack suitable for fly fishing, spinning, etc.
Plastic paint pot makes a good bait tin.
Plastic washing-up bowl with rim cut off is ideal for mixing ground-bait.

although circular cast-winders are also useful. They hold flies ready-tied to the cast.

The consideration you should bear in mind when choosing a tackle holdall is whether or not you will be moving about while you are fishing. Fly fishing and spinning are essentially mobile forms of fishing, while much bait fishing involves sitting in one place for lengths of time. For mobility, a haversack or satchel-type bag is best. It should be fitted with a broad, comfortable shoulder strap, and can be made of canvas or some other water-proof material. Wickerwork creels used to have widespread use for fly fishing, but they are now fairly uncommon.

For sedentary styles of fishing, I don't think you can beat the large wicker basket, which doubles as a seat (but make a water-proof-covered foam rubber cushion for it unless you want a corrugated posterior at the end of the day). You can of course buy small camp stools, but the seat–carrier is better. There are also metal-framed canvas seat bags on the market, which have most of the benefits of the wicker version. Nevertheless, wicker allows a through airflow, which is important if you are carrying anything damp. Wicker or canvas, make sure that the bag has a broad strap for comfortable carrying.

You can, if carting a lot of gear about, obtain a set of wheels for wicker or canvas baskets, and if you go in for match fishing, which might involve carting about several extra pounds of groundbait, these are well worth considering.

With spinning and sea fishing, the plastic cantilever-type tool box has proved useful for carrying a large range of weights and lures.

Purpose-made bait containers can be bought, but you might find it cheaper at first to improvise with empty food containers. Plastic bait containers, made mainly for maggots, are normally in pint and half-pint sizes (maggots are sold by the pint) and they can also be used for earthworms and marine worms. Another useful bait container, allowing more than a pint of maggots or other bait to be carried, is the type of plastic paint bucket used by decorators, ranging in capacity from 2–4 pts. Holes to allow the bait to breathe will have to be made in the tight-fitting lid. If you wish to carry maggots for loose-feeding when you are either wading or moving up and down the riverbank seeking fish, then a small close-weave cloth bag with a strap to go around your neck is most useful.

The coarse fisherman will often have to use groundbait, usually an admixture of ground-up cereal or breadcrumbs laced with maggots, and in order to mix up on the bank some sort of large waterproof container will be necessary. A canvas bucket is quite useful, although it is difficult to clean off caked breadcrumbs and can easily go mouldy – and the mould will eventually taint any fresh groundbait mixed in the bucket. A better bet is a 2 gallon (9 litre) plastic bucket or washing-up bowl. If you remove the rims, either of these will fit snugly into the bottom of your bag or basket, and they can hold tackle or perhaps dry groundbait to save space.

Waders: In soft-bottomed reservoirs and slow running rivers, ordinary rubber-soled waders are fine, but if slippery rock bottoms are to be encountered, or if the angler fishes in swift streams and rivers, studded soles are essential. Waders that come to thigh level are the type most widely used, and they are adequate for most fishing. Old-fashioned breast waders are banned in some waters nowadays – they are difficult to remove if you fall into the water and can lead to drownings.

While being extremely useful to fly fishermen, waders can also be used in coarse fishing where overgrown banks prove too great a hazard. Waders or sea boots are also very useful for fishing in surf from a beach, where you might be able to add 25 yards (23 m) or more to a cast by wading out before casting.

Odds and ends: A pair of scissors, or a sharp folding or sheathed knife, completes the fishing outfit for most kinds of angling, but there are a number of items which might be useful at times. The coarse fisherman might need to clear his swim of weeds, and a weed-cutter or grapnel tied to a long, strong cord will accomplish this. Sunglasses will protect your eyes from strain in bright weather, and polaroid glasses which cut out surface glare will enable river and lake fishermen to spot fish in clear water. Some form of eye-protection such as sunglasses is also useful to the fly fisherman on gusty days, when casts might accidentally blow across your face. For night fishing, a light is often necessary to enable you to see what you are doing when you are tying knots or

changing bait. Spirit-lamps of various kinds prove more useful
than electric lights, since dry-cell batteries rarely last for a night's
fishing.

An umbrella, large enough to cover you while you sit fishing,
can also be useful for freshwater or beach fishing. Choose one
with an adjustable pole and guy-ropes in case of strong winds.
Wet rags and dry rags are always useful for handling fish and for
cleaning your hands.

The checklists in this chapter by no means exhaust the full range of tackle and accessories which you might find in a shop, but they are nevertheless a sound basis for outfits for the main types of angling, and as such they are fully adequate for anybody taking up angling from scratch. It will be seen that rods and other items of tackle are, in many cases, quite suitable for different types of fishing, and you can explore a range of possibilities opened up by, say, one rod, and a reel with spare spools carrying lines of different strengths.

With sufficient tackle and a small amount of preparation you can approach the water confident in the knowledge that you have completed most of your side of the business of catching fish. Beyond this you need to know the habits and tastes of various fish species, and how best to approach them and use your tackle in varied types of water and weather conditions.

Besides tackle, it is important also to look to your personal comfort. For many types of fishing it will be wise to carry waterproof clothing and footwear, and the boat angler's attention is drawn particularly to the need to take extra-warm clothing on an offshore expedition.

Finally, you might like to weigh your catch – the most useful portable weighing instrument is the spring balance calibrated in fractions of pounds (with alternative metric scales).

§38 Coarse-fishing equipment, bait fishing

Rods: Light float fishing; $11\frac{1}{2}$–13 ft (350–396 cm) tip-action, 3 sections. Rings 10 (average) stand-off; handle $2\frac{1}{2}$ ft with sliding reel fitting. Can also be used for legering with weights up to a maximum of $\frac{1}{2}$ oz (14 g). Use with lines $1\frac{1}{2}$–$3\frac{1}{2}$ lb breaking strain for roach, dace, perch, rudd, bream, small chub and grayling, in water from still to moderate flows. None too suitable for fast, heavy water. Will handle fairly heavy float tackle in still water.

Medium/heavy float fishing, light/medium legering; 10–11 ft (305–335 cm) through-, rather than tip-, action (sometimes described as 'Avon-type' rod). Rings 10, bridge or stand-off; handle and reel fitting as above. Leger-weight maximum 1 oz (28 g). Use with lines 3–7 lb breaking strain for big chub, barbel, tench and small carp, also smaller fish in fast, heavy water. Can be used as a spinning or livebaiting or deadbaiting rod for trout, zander etc., and will handle mullet and flounders in light estuary or harbour fishing.

Carp/medium spinning; 10 ft (305 cm) through-action, 2–3 sections. Up to 10 bridge rings, reel fitting as above. Handles leger and lure weights up to 2 oz (56 g). Use with lines 6 lb and upwards for carp and heavy barbel, small pike, sea-trout and small to medium salmon. Also useful for estuary and harbour fishing, and a very good rock-fishing rod.

Swing-tip legering; $8\frac{1}{2}$–$9\frac{1}{2}$ ft (260–290 cm), through-action, 2 sections. Rings 8–10 stand-off, handle $2\frac{1}{2}$ ft with sliding reel fittings. Tip ring has screw attachment for swing tip, or swing tip is permanently attached. Use with lines $1\frac{1}{2}$–$3\frac{1}{2}$ lb breaking strain and leger weights to $\frac{1}{2}$ oz (14 g) for roach, perch, rudd, dace, bream and small chub in water from still to moderate flow. Especially useful in still or slow-moving water when weather makes long-distance float fishing difficult.

Roach-pole fishing; a much wider range of roach-pole lengths is used on the Continent than the British range. In France in particular, the term might be applied to a rod merely a few feet long. The poles used in Britain are normally very long, from 16–24 ft (488–732 cm) and the most useful size for rivers such as the Thames is 21 ft. They are used for light float fishing with lines from less than 1 lb breaking strain to about $2\frac{1}{2}$ lb, and tackles on which float, hooks and weights are normally pre-tied for quick and easy changing. They have no applications outside this field. Four, five, or more sections of the rod either take apart or telescope inside one another to draw fish close for landing.

Reel: Small, open-face or closed-face, fixed-spool, or large diameter centre-pin (no reel necessary for roach pole).

Line: Nylon, $1\frac{1}{2}$–3 lb breaking strain for fish to 4 lb; $3\frac{1}{2}$–7 lb breaking strain for fish 5–10 lb; 8 lb and upwards for fish above 10 lb. Increase breaking strain for fast or very weedy water. Load spare reel spools with alternative strengths of line to enhance range of fishing capabilities.

Hooks: Selection of hook sizes 20–14 tied to hook lengths finished with a loop, selection of eyed-hooks, sizes 12–6.

Other tackle and accessories: Selection of floats with varied loading capacities and capabilities chosen to cater for close or distant trotting, still, fast and turbulent water, and windy or still conditions (see float fishing, Chapter 15).

Plumet, to find water depth

For roach poles, a selection of ready-tied tackles incorporating float, hook-length, hook and weights, plus rubber thread

Split shot, sizes – swanshot, AAA, BB, Nos 4, 6 and 8, and perhaps micro-dust

Small link swivels for attaching leads, floats

Selection leger weights, $\frac{1}{4}$–$\frac{1}{2}$ oz, perhaps also $\frac{3}{4}$–1 oz (pear-shaped leads with swivel eye are the most useful)

Landing net, long-poled

Disgorger

Scissors/sharp penknife

Keepnet, large (8 ft × 16 in at least)

Rod-rests

Bank-sticks

Containers for bait and small tackle items

Groundbait bucket/bowl

Rags

Bait, groundbait

Permits and rod licences

Lamp if night-fishing

Holdalls for above

§39 Spinning

Rods (see also carp/medium, spinning rod above): Heavy spinning, pike, live/deadbait fishing; 10 ft (305 cm) through-action, 2–3 sections. Screw reel fitting useful. Up to 10 bridge rings, with enlarged butt ring. Handles casting weights to 4 oz. Use with lines 10–15 lb and above for pike, big salmon. A good rock-fishing rod, suitable for biggish fish such as pollack and bass.

Light spinning; 6½–7 ft (200–215 cm) through-action, one-piece or 2 sections. Rings 6–8, screw, reel fitting useful. Handles lure weights up to 1 oz (28 g). Use with light lines, 2–5 lb, spinning for perch, chub and small pike, also trout and sea-trout. Also suitable for small streams, and can be used for worming.

Reel: Small or medium fixed-spool reel, closed face or open face, or small multiplier with light spool

Line: Nylon, 2–5 lb, for perch, chub, heavier for small pike and zander. For large pike, 15–20 lb

Other tackle and accessories: Selection of lures, including plugs, spoons and wobblers
Deadbait spinning flights
Swivels and small link swivels
Selection of anti-kink leads, ¼–2 oz
Anti-kink vanes
Selection of spinning traces, ready-tied, including wire traces for pike
Landing net/gaff
Disgorger and gag
Permits and rod licences
Rags
Holdalls for above, especially haversack for easy carrying

§40 **Pike livebaiting and deadbaiting**

Rods: See rod for heavy spinning/pike livebaiting or deadbaiting, above, or rods used for beach fishing below.

Reels: Small, medium or large fixed spool, or medium light-spooled multiplier.
Lines: Nylon, 8 lb and upwards.

Other tackle and accessories: Selection of wire traces, varied strengths, and made-up livebait tackles
Selection of treble and large single hooks, eyed

Selection drilled bullet/drilled barrel weights
Swivels, including 3-way swivels
Selection of streamlined pike floats
Disgorger and gag
Landing net/gaff
Holdalls for above
Waterproof livebait bucket
Live/deadbait
Permits and rod licences
Rags

Fly fishing for coarse fish: Outfit as below for trout fly fishing.

§41 Preparations for coarse fishing

Oil reel if necessary, following maker's instructions. Check main line and replace if worn (a 2 lb line should be changed every four or five trips; lines of heavier breaking strains do not need to be changed so regularly). Be severe with your float selection for a trip, but try to duplicate the patterns you need most, so that if one is lost you can make up an identical rig. Similarly, if spinning, duplicate favourite lures. Make sure that you have at least six hooks of each size you will be using, and make a note of how many you need to replace to make up this number after fishing. With spinning and livebaiting also make sure that you have several ready-made traces to fall back on.

Strive to make all your tackle easy and swift to change, with loop-to-loop hook-length fastenings for bait fishing, and spring-link fastenings for leads and lures. Easily changed float fastenings are best, e.g. double-rubber.

Mark each float with an easily recognizable, painted, weighting guide, e.g. red dot equals AAA shot, blue dot BB shot, and so on. Mark the contents of all containers clearly on the outside.

You may mix-up your groundbait on the night before fishing so long as you do not have to carry it far. Do not add maggots to wet groundbait until at the waterside, since damp maggots can cling to almost any surface and they will quickly escape to infest your home. If you are using maggot hookbait, select a handful or so and treat them to one of the preparation methods in Chapter 14.

Game-fishing equipment, bait fishing: Equip and prepare as above for coarse-fishing bait styles, or use fly or light spinning rod with float/leger equipment.

Spinning: Equip as above for coarse-fishing spinning styles. Small spoons are especially useful for trout and sea-trout. Salmon favour lures of the Devon minnow type, sprats or minnows mounted on spinning flights, and waggling lures of the 'Toby' type. Also carry artificial prawns for salmon.

§42 **Fly fishing for trout, sea-trout, salmon**

Rods: Light fly fishing; 7–8 ft (215–245 cm) suitable for 4–5 A.F.T.M. lines (sometimes known as a 'brook rod').
Medium fly fishing for larger streams, rivers: 8–9 ft (245–275 cm) for 6–7 A.F.T.M. lines.
Reservoir fly fishing, sea-trout fishing, also suitable for small salmon; up to 10½ ft (320 cm) for 7–8 A.F.T.M. lines (all the above fly rods are through-action following the same basic pattern – 2–3 sections, rings 8–10 snake or bridge, handle 10 in– 1 ft, shaped for palm grip, reel fitting, sliding or screw-winch at extreme, butt end).
Salmon fly fishing: 12½–14 ft (380–425 cm), 3 sections, 10–12 snake or bridge rings, handle 3 ft or more for double-handed grip, reel fittings, sliding or screw-winch. Suitable for 9–10 A.F.T.M. lines.

Reels: Permanent-ratchet reels designed specifically for fly fishing.

Lines: Choice of floating, sinking or sink-tip lines; double-taper, forward-taper, lever, or shooting head. Backing for shooting head should be strong nylon, backing for other lines can be nylon, silk, or braided lines. Leader of 2–3 ft of nylon tied to forward end of fly line saves cutting back damaged fly line after several changes of cast.

Other tackle and accessories: Selection of casts, with or without tails for droppers
Appropriate fly selection for wet- or dry-fly fishing
Folding or staff landing net for trout, sea-trout; tailer or gaff for large salmon

Selection of split shot occasionally useful
Proprietary line flotant
Detergent, to make casts sink
Pads or cotton wool for wiping down line
Scissors
Disgorger/artery forceps – locking artery forceps also make a useful hand-vice for tying flies
Waders
Repair kit for patching damage to rubber waders
Sunglasses
Waterproof container for carrying fish
Permits and rod licences
Haversack/creel

§43 Preparations for game fishing

Prepare for bait fishing and spinning as in coarse fishing above, e.g. duplicate main lures. Check all tackle, oiling reels where necessary. For fly fishing, make special check of knots joining fly line to backing and leader, retying if necessary. Try to make some check on what fly-types are taking at the water if possible. It is advisable to tie flies onto a few casts in advance, wound onto cast-holders. Grease some casts if you think they will be needed. Besides a selection of different types of fly or lure, carry different sizes of individual patterns. Check waders for leaks.

§44 Sea-fishing equipment, shore fishing

Rods: For estuary and harbour fishing, rock fishing and spinning, see rods described as suitable for these purposes in coarse-fishing checklists.

Beachcasting: A variety of patterns for beachcasting rods forces the beginner into what seems a difficult range of choice. The three main types are fast-taper all-glass, reverse-taper all-glass, and tapered glass with a rigid alloy butt. Fortunately all are 'good' once their individual peculiarities of handling are learned, and the choice of any one pattern is therefore not likely to be a mistake. Cost, however, is often a factor in choice, and the basic fast-taper is often the cheapest pattern to buy. There also has to be a further choice of casting-weight capacity, and therefore it is best to know the sort of weights that will be required where the angler is going to do most of his fishing.

Different beaches have different strengths of current, and also varied beds of pebbles, gravel, sand or mud, affording good, moderate or poor grip for the weight, and both these factors influence your choice of weight. By asking anglers who fish regularly at particular beaches – or perhaps by asking a local tackle dealer – you can probably find the most useful weight, and buy your rod accordingly from the range of weight-casting capabilities between 1 and 9 oz. When using weights above the recommended capabilities of your rod, while keeping the same line-strength, it is important to incorporate a shock leader. Beach-casting rods range from $11\frac{1}{2}$–14 ft (350–425 cm) and they are designed for double-handed casting. It is essential that there are good grips at the butt end, for one hand, and above and below the reel-fitting for the other hand. A screw-winch reel-fitting is superior to sliding collars, and an extra-large butt ring ought to be fitted. The rod is also suitable for pike livebaiting and dead-baiting, and for heavy spinning.

Reels: Large fixed-spool with anti-lash device and roller guide on bale-arm, or multiplier with light plastic casting spool.

Line: Nylon, 15 lb and upwards breaking strain.

Other tackle and accessories: Shock leader for use with heavy weights

Selection of made-up traces with hook sizes depending on size of bait to be used

Selection of loose hooks, eyed; also spare line for making up extra traces

Selection of leads, varied weights – streamlined leads are better for casting

Swivels, single and 3-way

French booms

Dig-in or tripod rod-rest

Gaff, disgorger

Heavy spinners and a feather mackerel trace

Tackle containers
Bait containers
Bait
Very sharp knife for cutting bait, line
Seat
Lamp if night fishing
Rags
Holdalls for above

§45 Preparations for beach fishing

Make tackle maintainance and replacement checks. Tie up at least three traces of each kind you will be using, and carry spare line and hooks for making up extra traces. Try to ascertain what state the tide will be in when you arrive at the shore; in general, unless you are familiar with the shore, it will be best to check-over likely fish lies at low water before you start fishing, and spring tides are best for this purpose. If night fishing, always make a daylight recce of the beach. Strive, as in coarse fishing, to make your tackle as easily changeable as possible.

§46 Boat fishing

Rods: For spinning and estuary fishing, see suitable patterns described in selection of coarse-fishing rods, above. The proper, boat fishing rod is 6–7½ ft (183–215 cm), with a handle at least 2 ft long, a forward, screw-winch reel-fitting, and 5–7 rings or rollers. Heavy rods may have a grooved metal fixture at the end of the butt to fit the socket of a butt-pad (groin-protector). Most, modern, boat rods are built to the line-class specifications of the International Game Fishing Association, i.e. they are designed to match lines of certain strengths – 20 lb, 30 lb, and so on. The most useful rod for British waters is the 30 lb line-class, but a 20 lb line-class rod will give more fun with smaller fish species, while if you hunt larger rays, conger and shark, you might consider a 50 lb or even an 80 lb line-class rod. If you use metal lines you will need roller-guides, which are useful with other heavy lines, although some anglers prefer reinforced tunnel guides (except for wire) because small loop-tangles which might form in the line can foul rollers, whereas they will pull through tunnel guides.

Reels: Large metal-spool multiplier, or large centre-pin with braking arrangement.

Lines: Nylon, braided Terylene or Dacron, metal. Breaking strains appropriate to strength of water and size of species sought.

Other tackle and accessories:
Selection of hooks ready-tied to traces
Wire traces for toothed fish
Selection of leads of pyramid or cone type, varied weights
Throwaway weights for rough ground
Kilmore or Clements booms for attaching leads
Selection of swivels – single, 3-way and link-swivels
French booms
Selection of loose, eyed hooks and spare line for tying traces
Pirks, artificial lures
Feather trace for mackerel
Landing net/gaff (supplied aboard all good charter boats)
Leather glove for handling strong line snagged on bottom
Thumb-stall for metal line
Sharp knife
Rags
Holdall for above
Bait (sometimes supplied by skipper)

§47 Preparations for boat fishing

Prepare tackle as above for beach fishing. Make sure that you wear rubber boots or rubber-soled shoes to avoid deck-damage aboard. If chartering, try to arrive ahead of arranged departure time. Check with skipper what mark he is going to fish, and what tackle and bait you might need, by telephoning or writing beforehand. If fishing in your own boat, tell somebody what time you expect to be back in port, or fill in details of your voyage on a form provided by local coastguards (Coastguard 66 scheme) for an emergency check should you become overdue. It is as well to take some precautions against sea-sickness. Carry barley-sugars, or take an anti-sickness pill before setting out. Always take along extra, warm clothing when you go offshore. A light, warm wind on the shore can turn into an icy gale a mile or two off.

§48 Big-game fishing

Rods, tackle and preparations as above for boat fishing, except that rods in 50 lb, 80 lb, or higher line-classes will be used, and lines and so on will be stepped up in strength proportionately. The extras you might need are balloons or suitable containers to make shark floats. You might also consider a groin-protector and a shoulder rod-harness which clips to the reel. Check with charter skipper as for boat fishing.

Part Two

The number of freshwater fish species is small compared with the vast number of species which live in the sea. The freshwater angler can expect to encounter around thirty species, while the sea angler might meet more than a hundred – not counting the many varieties of gobies and other fish too small to be of much interest, or the rarer visitors from warm and cold regions of the ocean.

Life began in the ocean, which means that in pre-history freshwater species invaded rivers and streams from the sea. The difficulties which these species overcame eventually made them distinctly different in appearance and abilities from sea fish. Lack of salt might seem the obvious difference between fresh and sea water, but there is much more to it than that. Freshwater temperatures and chemical and oxygen contents vary widely, not just seasonally but from day to day, and even hour to hour. In the sea, particularly the temperate seas around Britain, these changes are gradual, and so the ancestors of our present-day freshwater fish faced no easy task in establishing themselves. With fish and with many other water animals and plants the difficulties of moving from a fairly stable environment to a very variable one allowed only a few very hardy individuals to make the grade. Although freshwater life is very rich, most of the plants and small creatures that live there have land-based ancestors and have not developed directly from sea life-forms.

If the range of freshwater species is small, then the number of species able to survive in both sea and freshwater environments – the migratory fish – is even smaller, amounting to only a handful. Salmon and eels are perhaps the best known of these highly specialized fish.

§49   Distribution of fish species

Freshwater: The Ice Age and Britain's land bridge to the Continent are largely responsible for inequalities in the distribution of freshwater fish.

Eastern and southern flowing rivers such as the Thames were once part of a vast European river-system, now covered by the Channel and the North Sea, which was largely unaffected by glaciation. These rivers have the greatest range of freshwater species, many of which are absent (unless transplanted by man, sometimes with a good deal of success) in northern and western rivers and lakes, and in Ireland.

Char and whitefish, found only in certain lakes in Scotland, Ireland, northern England and Wales, are possibly landlocked migratory species which once had a much wider distribution in cold regions.

Introductions to the range of British freshwater species have come from many sources. Among the notable aliens is the carp (although some argue that common carp have always been a part of British fauna), which was man's earliest cultivated fish, widely introduced to monastery stew-ponds. Pike-perch, also known as zander, spread rapidly through the linked waterways of East Anglia after being introduced to ponds at Woburn by the Duke of Bedford in 1878. Pike-perch are a European species, but a very similar fish, the North American wall-eye, has also been introduced to ornamental waters in many parts of Britain. Woburn was also the introduction point for the European catfish, or wels, which is now present to varying degrees in the Great Ouse and surrounding area. Among game fish, the North American rainbow trout is extremely popular with trout fishermen and has a wide distribution here.

Sea: The sea temperature rises steadily from spring onwards, reaching a peak in autumn. Warm-water species of fish, and the organisms they feed on also reach their greatest levels at this time. As cold winds and frosts gradually cut the water temperature to its lowest point in March, the warm-water species move south and their place is taken by cold-water species, notably cod. This is, of course, a simplified picture: as any amateur geographer knows, the North Atlantic Drift bathes the westerly coasts of

Britain in winter, and it also occasionally affects temperatures in the Channel and the northern North Sea. More warm-water species reach these westerly shores than reach the east coast beaches, and some extreme westerly points may keep warm-water species well into the winter.

Sea fish also migrate for reasons other than temperature, some seeking shallow water to breed before returning to deep-water feeding grounds and vice versa.

§50   **Evolution**

Land animals developed from early fishes, but long before this branch in the evolutionary tree (represented today by lungfishes) two main groups of fishes had developed – those with skeletons of cartilage (represented by modern sharks and rays) and those with bony skeletons. Before even this took place fish had divided into species with or without jaws: both cartilaginous and bony fish kept their jaws, while the remnants of jawless fish are the parasitic lampreys and hagfish.

Fig. 68 shows this evolutionary tree, from which it is easy to see that modern bony fish – teleosts – are by far the biggest group in the hydrosphere (the term used for all the world's water-masses, sea and freshwater) followed by cartilaginous fish: sharks, dogfish, skates and rays. In fact there are something like 20,000 species of bony fish (only a few of which, of course, are present in waters in and around Britain) and about 550 species of cartilaginous fish.

Apart from this difference in skeletons, both groups of fish have developed separately in other ways. Sharks and rays do not have the scales which most bony fish possess; instead, they often have small tooth-like plates called 'denticles' embedded in their skins, making them rough to the touch. Most bony fish have a swim-bladder, an internal gas-bag that can be inflated or deflated so that the fish can attain neutral buoyancy at whatever level it chooses to stay in water. Besides giving them a graceful freedom of movement, the swim-bladder also enables bony fish to hover. The sharks do not have this buoyancy aid, and in order to stay at a particular level in the water without sinking, they must continually move forward so that the angle of their elevator-like pectoral fins and the down-push from the long upper lobe of the

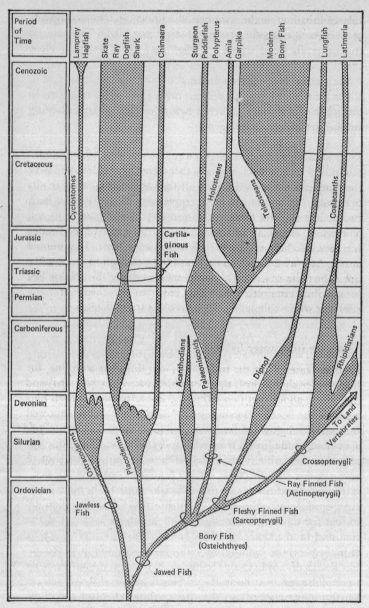

Fig. 68 Fishes' evolution.

tail fin keeps them on the level. The bottom-living skates and rays do not need buoyancy aids.

§51   **Movement**

I used to be quite certain that all fish moved simply by flapping their strong tail fins. In fact this is only true of a few species, mainly oceanic tunnies. These fish have what dynamics experts call an ideal fusiform shape for fast movement in water – a long streamlined body tapering at each end, with the thickest part one third of the way along the fish's length behind the head. The tunny's streamlining comes close to perfection: it has slots to tuck away its pectoral fins when travelling fast, and a special lens covering the eyes so that they do not bulge and set up any water resistance. Their muscles are arranged so that they beat the tail rapidly from side to side to drive their streamlined bulk along. While other fish are streamlined to a degree, they often do not need the speed of the ocean-roaming tunny and there is less emphasis in their make-up on ideal hydrodynamic form. Unlike the tunny, only a part of their motive power comes from the tail; they are able to flex most of their body from side to side, driving themselves forward if the need for speed arises. A broad-sided fish such as the freshwater common bream gets less than half of its forward drive from its tail.

Fish have other fins serving as rudders to adjust trim, to manoeuvre slowly or to stop. The usual arrangement is (Fig. 69) a pair of pectoral fins behind the head, paired pelvic fins on the keel, a single anal fin behind the anus between the pelvic and caudal (tail) fins, and one or more dorsal fins. It is also worth mentioning that sharks and tunnies, while they have each developed along utterly different evolutionary lines, both have small lateral fins or ridges in advance of their tail fins. These 'lateral keels' as they are known used to puzzle scientists until it was discovered that similar structures added to ships' keels in front of their propellers enabled the vessels to turn about in half the space, and in half the time that normal vessels took. It's an interesting example of convergence in evolution between cartilaginous and bony fish.

Flatfish have a distinctive means of propulsion, undulating their broad fin-fringed bodies in a rather serpentine way. Skates

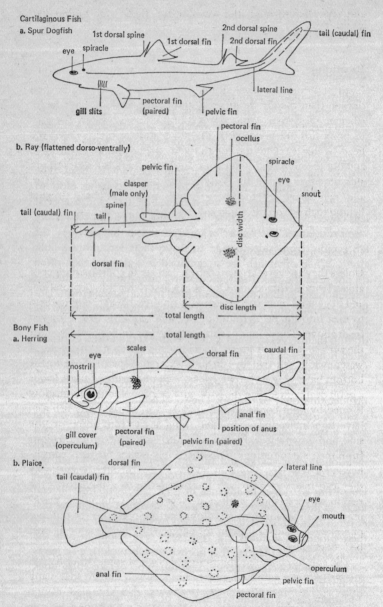

Cartilaginous Fish
a. Spur Dogfish

1st dorsal spine
2nd dorsal spine
2nd dorsal fin
1st dorsal fin
tail (caudal) fin
eye
spiracle
lateral line
gill slits
pectoral fin (paired)
pelvic fin

b. Ray (flattened dorso-ventrally)

pectoral fin
ocellus
pelvic fin
spiracle
eye
clasper (male only)
snout
spine
tail (caudal) fin
tail
disc width
dorsal fin
disc length
total length

Bony Fish
a. Herring

total length
scales
eye
dorsal fin
caudal fin
nostril
anal fin
gill cover (operculum)
pectoral fin (paired)
position of anus
pelvic fin (paired)

b. Plaice

dorsal fin
lateral line
tail (caudal) fin
eye
mouth
anal fin
operculum
pelvic fin
pectoral fin

Fig. 69 Parts of fish.

and rays 'fly' through the water, using their wide bodies like wings.

§52   **Breathing**

Even at saturation level, water contains thirty times less free oxygen than the air we breathe, and so fish have to have large, efficient gill systems exposed to a constant flow of water. The gills of bony fish are underneath the gill plates on each side of the head. Water is taken in through the mouth, passes over the gills, and out through the lifted plates. In sharks there is a series of gill slits on either side of the body behind the head, while in skates and rays there are breathing holes, called spiracles, situated behind each eye on the upper side of the body.

§53   **Coloration and camouflage**

Unless they are very large predators, fish are in constant danger of attack from all directions. One of the first defences is coloration, and in general most species are dark on their backs, helping them to melt into the background of the water and the bed if viewed from above. The colour of this dark shading in fish that live near the surface is blue or green, matching the bluish-green colour of water, while fish that live in mid-water regions or close to the bottom have grey or brown backs. The underside of most fish is a good deal lighter than the back, and this counteracts the shadow formed by light coming from above. Most of the bony fish also have light-reflecting scales, returning light from above to the side, and downwards, besides also mirroring background colour from their surroundings. This effectively makes the fish 'vanish' beyond a few feet of vision, although by turning incautiously they can inadvertently flash their presence to a predator – the reason why a flashing spinner attracts a pike. Camouflage markings, either spots or bars of colour, further break up the outlines of some fish, allowing them to merge with reed beds or against beds of pebbles.

The colour-changing abilities of plaice and some other flatfish are well known, although it is rather less well known that many other species, including many freshwater fish, can also change colour and shade. For instance, if you catch a roach or a rudd at night and are able to examine it under a light, it will be found to be altogether richer and darker in colour than in daylight. Colour cells, which are in the skin of the fish underneath the scales, have relaxed and expanded to smother any star or moon glow that the fish might pick up. During the day these cells are tightly contracted to adjust the fish to daytime colouration. You may test this for yourself by placing a roach or a rudd in a white bucket; after several hours it will have become quite pale. Placed in a dark bucket, or shut off from light, the reverse would happen.

§54   Escape and protection

When frightened, many fish reach terrific speeds from a standing start in fractions of a second. Many of the bony fish have a special nerve cord – a sort of hot line – linking their alarm centres directly to the main motor-muscles. Alarms override all other signals and activate these muscles directly, triggering a panic-dive. The sharks and rays lack this system, and while they can swim quite quickly, their acceleration is slow when they are alarmed.

While some species rely on speed for escape, others protect themselves with defensive spines. Some, like the weever fish which seaside bathers sometimes tread upon, have an additional poison gland under these armaments, and can give a very painful wound. The armour-like scales of fish are also protective, while the mucous covering which many species possess is antiseptic, and shields them from bacterial invasion.

§55   'Sixth'-sense in cyprinids

Biologists have discovered that the cyprinid (carp-related) group of fishes, which make up a large part of Britain's range of fresh water species, have a unique, protective, chemical signalling ability. In the skins of such fish are cells which, when damaged, release traces of chemical into the water. The chemicals, called pheromones, are not received as smells in the normal sense, for they immediately trigger off panic-reactions in a shoal of fish which has, for instance, been attacked by a pike. Moreover, the smell of pike thereafter, even if no further fish are damaged to release pheromones, may trigger the same reaction.

The signalling ability isn't apparent in very young fish, which may be the reason why some shoals of small fish appear to show no fear of pike. It is also reasonable to assume that larger fish showing the same lack of caution belong to a shoal which hasn't before been attacked by a pike.

It is a speculation on my part to suggest that pheromones might be the reason why one can sometimes catch a series of fish, only to have them stop biting until the hook is changed. Could the hook be tainted with pheromones? This particular line of research is very interesting, and I think that in time it will reveal much of value to the angler.

§56 Sight and other senses

Most fish have very good close-range eyesight. The limited light-conducting quality of water, hampered often by suspended silt, prevents them seeing objects clearly at long range. It does not, however, prevent them from detecting sudden movements, or – even in fairly cloudy water – seeing silhouettes of animals or people walking above their skyline, or shadows falling on the water.

In all fishes each eye works independently, although a few fish, pike among them, can temporarily adjust both eyes forward so that they see one picture in very much the same way as we do. This enables them to strike accurately at their prey. With their independently ranging eyes set usually at the widest part of their bodies, fish can see almost all the way about themselves. They are restricted, however, in seeing up and out of the water very clearly. Direct light can only penetrate through the surface of the water to the eye of a fish in a cone of about forty-five degrees; light approaching water at a lower angle will bounce off the surface instead of passing through it. This means that a fish looking upwards will see clearly through a circular patch only (termed a 'window') of the surface, which will vary in size with the depth at which the fish is lying (Fig. 70). If near the surface, the window will be small; if the fish is deep, it will be fairly large. Thus a trout angler using an artificial dry fly, drifting along on the surface of a river, will have to guess the size and position of the trout's window if he wants his offering to be seen.

Not all fish hunt entirely by sight. Sharks and many other fish

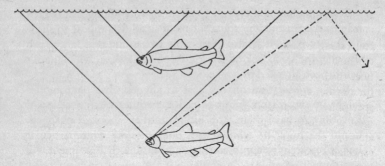

Fig. 70 (§56) Fish's window: fish lying deep can see a wider area of the surface. At greater angles than the 'cone', light is reflected by the water's surface.

track down their prey by smell, using sight at the kill only. Other types of fish have sensory feelers near their mouths to assist in their search for food. Both of these factors are useful at night, when sight does not help a great deal, and since a good many species are nocturnal in their feeding habits, alternative sensory systems to sight are quite widespread.

The other important sensory organ found in fish is the lateral line, which picks up vibrations and fluctuations in current and water pressure. It extends all around the fish, and in the head it is deep-set and connected to the surface by pores. The line is often raised above the radius of the pectoral fins, so that incoming messages are not masked or distorted. Heavy footfalls on the bankside will be recorded by this sensor, so it is always wise to make your approach cautious, especially near shallow, still water. Fish can also hear very well, and sound in fact travels better in water than in air – another good reason for being cautious about advertising your presence.

§57 Species 'fingerprints'

Many species have such distinctive movements and feeding habits that an experienced angler can detect them without actually seeing them. Let me give a few examples: in freshwater fishing, if a maggot comes back which looks as if it has been nipped sharply after a bite has been missed, roach will probably be responsible.

If the maggot looks as if it has been stretched, however, the culprit is more likely to be a bream. In sea angling, it is possible to feel a skate falling across your bait and line, and it will then pause to chew for a while before moving off and swallowing. Much finer distinctions become noticeable after you have been fishing for a while; you can detect differences in the way in which various species pull a float beneath the surface, and you can tell from the fight of an unseen fish what species it is likely to be, with a fair amount of accuracy. Any of these 'fingerprints' which are especially noticeable will be mentioned in the detailed descriptions of fish species later in this section.

Now that the quarry has some flesh-and-bone reality, it is useful to explore the environments in which fish live so that we can sort out the places to find particular species, beginning here with freshwater fish. First, though, there are a few general notes about freshwater locations. When we come to specific water types, the styles of fishing best suited to them will be outlined together with cross-references to these styles in the following chapters on freshwater techniques.

Because we live in a rather rainy group of islands, we have a huge amount of inland fishing water. Some of it, such as the lochs of Scotland, the loughs of Ireland and the lakes of northern England, is in standing bodies. Most, however, is in the form of watercourses – brooks, streams, rivers – which drain the land and deposit excess water in the sea. Still more bodies of freshwater are created by man – storage reservoirs, navigable canals, also drainage channels created to dry out marshy areas such as the Fens and the Somerset Levels.

§58   Present and future

Most people are now well aware of the appalling disregard that we have had in the past for the purity of our rivers and the other types of water mentioned above. Although pollution is being fought, the price of success is eternal vigilance; anglers have at times been lone voices crying for legislation to prevent the sort of shameful state of affairs mentioned by T. T. Macan and E. B. Worthington in *Life in Lakes and Rivers* (Fontana New Naturalist Series, 1972). This is a breakdown of the plant and animal life present for several miles below a sewage outfall on the River Trent. For six miles below the outfall most animals and plants were absent, and sewage fungus was the dominant life form. At eight miles, tubifex worms and algae could survive, and for a further fourteen miles plant and animal life increased very gradually until the pollution could be regarded as 'mild'. Finally, over twenty-six miles from the outfall, the river could be regarded as fairly pure with a reasonably balanced ecology. A river has two banks, and from the angler's point of view over fifty-two miles of fishing had been affected by that outfall.

I'm particularly fond of the story that London apprentices at the end of the eighteenth century frequently complained about an unvaried diet of the plentiful salmon caught from the River Thames; no doubt they would rejoice in the total absence of that species from the river today.

Abstraction, the tapping-off of water from rivers for industrial and domestic purposes, is also detrimental to angling, particularly when water is taken in summer when rivers are usually on the low side already, and might be suffering from low oxygen levels – even if the water eventually returns to the river, most industrial processes de-oxygenate it further. A more reasoned approach to abstraction is beginning to emerge, however, and proposals for creating 'compensation water' could have far-reaching effects on the quality of fishing in the future. The proposals see large holding reservoirs, usually near the headwaters of big rivers, which can be filled with flood water during winter when river levels are high. Come summer and low water, doses of water from the reservoirs can be released to supply abstractors and freshen the river. Such water does not necessarily have to be held in conventional ways; there is also a plan to pipe excess water from rivers like the Hampshire Avon deep into the porous rocks of chalk downs, from where it can be pumped back into the river during dry spells.

There seems little doubt, especially after the drought of 1976, that the overall demand for water in this country will continue to increase, and so more conventional reservoirs will have to be constructed. Altogether, we can expect the amount of fishable water to increase rather than diminish.

§59 Competition for water space

Anglers are not the only water users. A spin-off from wider leisure opportunities has been an increase in boating and activities such as water-skiing. In future these activities must grow apace with angling, and although their followers have not made the best of bedfellows we can be thankful that boatmen have been foremost in reprieving many reaches of derelict canal to our benefit. Anglers must recognize other water users' rights, just as they in turn ought to understand that undue disturbance can destroy an angler's enjoyment. Wider liaison between angling and other watersport clubs might iron out a lot of troubles.

§60 Types of water

Identifying types of freshwater might seem a hazardous business, since no two lengths of river or bodies of standing water are alike in all respects. Nevertheless, it is possible to narrow the field down to seven water-types which will have features that can be recognized in any area. The fishing potential of waters falling in between these main types can be expected to combine their characteristics.

The types are: 1, rivers and streams in mountainous areas; 2, lowland rivers with highland sources; 3, lowland rivers; 4, chalkland rivers; 5, highland lakes and pools; 6, lowland lakes and pools; and 7, canals and drainage channels.

My system of categorizing water can be quarrelled with. It can be quite rightly argued, for instance, that a gravel pit is quite unlike a shallower lake. However, variations in form are discussed more fully under the main sub-headings.

§61 Rivers

There are two main factors which create the differences between the four types of river I have singled out; the first is gradient from source to mouth, and the second is the make-up and chemistry of the land over which they flow.

The first of these factors, gradient, affects the rate of flow and thus governs the nature of the river bed and determines the distribution of plant and animal species, including fish, according to whether they favour fast, medium or slow currents. There is also a difference in the climates of high and low places, and this too can limit or encourage various species. The land over which the river flows determines its character and richness in nutrients which are either carried as silt or dissolved. Water running over hard, rocky areas cannot cut its own course and must follow valleys and faults, while a river running over clays, sand and gravel can cut its own meandering bed. Hard rock is poor gathering ground for nutrients, and waters running through rich, soft lowlands are much more productive in terms of plant and animal life springing from a plentiful supply of minerals.

Gradient and the nature of the land through which a river flows also affect the oxygen content of the water, and its capacity to colour. Oxygen content is high in fast tumbling water, low in still, slow-moving reaches, and thus fish favouring a rich supply of oxygen will shun slow water. Water running on hard rock will pick up little in the way of silt, while clays and various kinds of earth will add their own distinctive colour to a river running through them, particularly in times of flood.

Colour is fairly important to the angler, and merits some discussion. It is quite possible on some days to look at a river and state, 'Looks good today'. Or you might, on the other hand, grimace and say, 'I'll have to work hard to catch much'. There are two kinds of colour, with two different causes. The type favourable to fishing is caused by high water or floods, and it matters not whether it is brown, red or white (depending on the dominant colour of the surrounding soil). Only at the height of a flood, when the water is thick with suspended soil, does angling become difficult. As the flood waters fall, this colour will become less and less noticeable – the river is 'fining down' to use the correct term. Not only is there a plentiful supply of worms and other creatures which have been washed into the river to tempt fish to feed, but also the fish themselves have been fighting strong currents and using up energy reserves and are hungry. A good time to fish.

The other type of colour is caused by the effect of temperature on the minute plant and animal life of a river; as the temperature rises it reaches levels suitable for different species to multiply at their fastest rates. Thus many waters will have a green algal colouration, caused by millions of minuscule plants, in warm, settled weather. The reverse of this, falling temperature, becomes lethal at different levels to the various species. Algal 'bloom' as it is called does not, while temperatures are rising, seem to adversely affect fishing until it becomes very thick. In this event the water will quickly de-oxygenate. The colour caused by these creatures dying in great numbers as the temperature drops, seems to give rise to poor fishing. Dark, inky stains, often accompanied by lumps of dead fungus floating to the surface of the water, are a fairly common occurrence late in the season. It is unlikely that this colouring matter itself upsets fish; they are more likely to feel unhappy about feeding because of the falling temperature. A further detrimental colouring agent is melting snow, which gives water a thick, milky opaqueness.

§62 **Rivers and streams in mountainous areas**

The majority of these rivers in Britain are westerly flowing. They occur in the Scottish Highlands, west Wales, and the moors of the West country. They have only short courses, descending steeply from high ground to flow either into the sea or into a lake. Occasionally they do run for short distances over level valley floors. They are torrential in nature with rapids, chains of pools, and sometimes high waterfalls. Pools at the end of the course can sometimes be quite large. They are quite likely to be affected by snow water in winter.

Behaviour and quality : The water running off high slopes is usually cold, but where there are long stretches exposed to the sun on a warm day, temperature can rise quite quickly. In summer, therefore, the water temperature may fluctuate widely during the day, but it will generally be cold at night. Because water runs quickly from the rocky ground around the source, rain will quickly swell these headstreams. Rapid variations in water level and pace are common. This effect will be noticed in the lower course even if the rain falls only in the hills.

Ecology : In higher reaches there are few nutrients. Because of this, and because of the rapid flow, mosses and liverworts are the main plants. Lower down the course, in more sheltered water, there may be a chance for higher plants like water crowfoot to root and flourish. The main small animals are stone-clinging nymphs, net-spinning caddis, and the freshwater shrimp. In the lower river, depending on how slight the flow becomes and how much nutrient may have been picked up, the ecology might approach low-land standards.

Fish species: Trout are the main species inhabiting mountain headstreams, but they are small and very hardy because of the rigours of the environment, often averaging only six or so to the pound. A small species, the bullhead or miller's thumb, is also sometimes present in these waters. Lower in the river's course where there might be larger pools with an improved nutrient content, larger trout and also grayling can be supported. Salmon find this well-oxygenated water very favourable, and they will penetrate as far as is physically possible in order to breed. Sea-trout and some coarse fish may be present in valley stretches, but many of these waters are outside the distribution range of most coarse-fish species. Perch, however, seem to be fairly widespread.

Fishing methods: The trout angler in the upper reaches has to be mobile. Pools may contain two or three takeable trout, but of these it is usually only possible to take one at a time – scaring the rest. Worm fishing (§195) is a useful method. Fly fishing is rarely practical unless there are broad pools and clear banks. Lower, where pools often are larger, wet-fly fishing (§186) and spinning (§194) are quite practical. Fly fishing and spinning for sea-trout and salmon calls for stronger tackle than that used for trout. Dry-fly fishing may also be possible, particularly in the lower river. If the coarse fish are worth trying, long trotting (§131) is effective, and so might be fixed- and rolling-leger arrangements (§134).

§63   **Lowland rivers with highland sources**

As implied, these are hybrid rivers, but I have singled them out as a separate category because they do have unique properties. Several British rivers fit this description. For the most part they fall to the east of hill and moorland areas. After a torrential course to the foothills they strike fertile valleys and flood plains and have comparatively long courses to the sea. In the north, the Tees is a good example and, moving south, the Severn and Devon's River Exe.

Behaviour and quality: Because hill areas generally suffer greater rainfall than the lowlands, the behaviour of the upper river has a marked effect on the lower course. Such rivers can rise or fall rapidly, regardless of the lowland weather. The temperature fluctuates similarly, with marked influxes of cold water. Because these rivers run into softer, richer materials out of the foothills, they can pick up a considerable load of nutrients. As well as rapid fluctuations in flow and level, they also change colour frequently – occasionally within a matter of hours. In long hot summers the water from the hills continually refreshes these waters, and one of their main features is a cool, bright flow in dry spells.

Ecology: The upland environment has already been discussed, but the lower course of the hybrid river is rich in nutrients, encouraging a greater variety of plant and animal forms. Because of the fluctuations in flow and level, however, water plants preferring more stable conditions, such as the water lily, may not establish themselves. The same is true of some small water creatures such as the water flea.

Fish species: Migratory fish may not be able to penetrate huge distances to the foothills, and so, while the upland reaches are similar to those of purely highland rivers, salmon and sea-trout may be absent. The rivers do tend to be good trout and grayling waters throughout their course, with both these species improving in size as richer land has an effect on the food chain. Minnows and dace seem to be most successful at surviving the fast waters of the foothills, and chub, roach and perch join them at lower levels. But since these rivers often move fast, species less tolerant of heavy flows – carp, tench, rudd – are usually absent. Bream are sometimes able to maintain populations wherever weirs or backwaters can protect them from the heavier spates. Pike are able to thrive in all but the highland reaches. Introduced barbel have established themselves well in this type of water.

Fishing methods: In the upper reaches, fishing methods described above for highland rivers and streams can be followed. In the lower reaches, unless there are distinct pools, it will be easiest to search for salmon with spinning tackle. Wet- and dry-fly fishing for trout and sea-trout is quite practical, also light spinning. Pike also respond to spinning, either with lures or small deadbaits, and you might find sheltered water where livebaiting or legered dead-bait are effective (§149, 150). All the above methods call for a certain amount of mobility, and the angler prepared to cover a lot of water will be more successful than a sedentary one. With other coarse fish too (dace, chub, roach, perch, grayling and barbel where present) it will pay the angler to search out fish, moving on when he feels that particular shoals have been fully exploited. Long trotting (§131) with float tackle is particularly suited to this type of river. Mid-stream swims, and heavy water below weirs and the like, can be covered with a rolling leger or perhaps a stationary one in some conditions (§134). Barbel in particular seem to prefer these fast-water areas. In some places it may be possible to sit down and build up a swim – the best places for doing so are long, even stretches where you might expect fish to be generally distributed.

§64 Lowland rivers

Included in this category are the majority of our lowland rivers such as the Great Ouse, the Thames and the Bristol Avon. Because their gradients, source to mouth, are comparatively gentle, they behave quite differently to the foregoing rivers. Early in their courses they may be fairly swift, but they mature quickly into meandering watercourses which drain huge areas, passing over varied beds of clays, sands and gravels, changing direction and altering in depth and character where they strike different materials. Later in their courses they frequently become quite even in width and depth, and their flow becomes slight. It is in these reaches that the hand of man is usually most evident: weirs and navigable locks are found, and the flow may even be totally controlled by a series of sluices and, finally, a tidal gate (Nene, Welland). This kind of even quality suits such waters to match fishing; there is a fair chance that everybody participating in a match will be pegged in a swim capable of producing fish.

Behaviour and quality: Floods do not build up particularly quickly except in severe conditions; rainwater first has to soak through the land before swelling the river. Once these waters do flood, however, they may stay at high levels for some time – and, of course, they stay coloured by material washed from the land during this time. Even in settled weather, these waters are rarely without some colour; they never attain the clarity of highland waters or chalkland rivers. However, rivers that are controlled by sluices can be artificially lowered during floods – the gates are opened so that excess water runs swiftly away. They may be brought back within their banks very quickly indeed. During summer, with lessened flow, the impounded water in controlled stretches can often be regarded as still water. They do run a high risk of becoming de-oxygenated, and this tendency can be accelerated if weed and algae develop unhindered.

Ecology: As can be expected from the rich terrain these rivers drain, they carry much nutrition. Plants and small food organisms change with the changing pace, and while watercress and water crowfoot may be common in the upper reaches at lower levels their place is taken by burr-reeds and pondweeds. In the medium-pace and slower stretches, water lilies often flourish at the margins, sometimes making dense underwater beds which anglers call 'cabbage patches'. In the slowest water during summer a green alga, blanket weed, may form thick cotton-wool rafts. Unless there is some sort of flow down the centre of the river, these rafts can grow out a considerable distance towards each other from the margins. Insect life is very varied, but the silting of lower levels may not suit caddis and mayfly larvae. Worms, molluscs and crayfish are often abundant.

Fish species: Salmon once thrived in many of these rivers but man-made deterrents, particularly massive pollution and permanent sluice gates, have barred them from reaching the upper levels and clean, silt-free gravel suitable for spawning. Most are now regarded as coarse fisheries, and the upper levels are either trout and grayling waters (where coarse fish are often controlled) or mixed fisheries. Roach, dace, chub, perch and pike are the dominant fish throughout the course, with small fish, such as minnows, gudgeon, loaches, ruffe and bleak, widespread.

In fast, heavy water under weirs and other obstructions, conditions are often suitable for trout and sometimes grayling. These situations are particularly suited to barbel, if present. In slow stretches, deep pools and sheltered bays, there is ample opportunity for still-water species to survive. Carp, tench and rudd are sometimes present, also the bream, which particularly favours controlled rivers.

Fishing methods: Because the character of these rivers is so varied, almost the full range of coarse fishing techniques discussed in the following chapter will be useful at times. Trotting is the most widely used float technique, but there may be opportunities for laying on with float tackle, and also stret-pegging (§131). Of the legering styles, straightforward legering (§134) and swim feeder legering can be tried, including the use of the swing ti (§136) and other bite indicators. Since the trout and grayling waters of the upper reaches resemble the stream stretches of chalkland rivers, the fishing methods for these species are similar to those mentioned under the next heading. For pike, the entire range of spinning, livebaiting and deadbaiting methods can be used (§149–155).

§65 **Chalkland rivers**

The Hampshire Avon is perhaps the best-known chalkland river in England and it is typical of this type of water, springing from the foothills of chalk downs. Very often a feature of the upper reach of the chalk river is that it dries out in summer, which makes it a 'winterbourne'. When the river carries sufficient permanent water it is frequently channelled off into man-made carrier streams, which used to irrigate watermeadows but which are now for the most part disused.

Behaviour and quality: Rain falling on porous rock soaks away quickly from the land surface, but the rock then acts as a sort of reservoir; indeed, it is possible to drill into the saturated rock under chalk hill ranges and tap water directly. This has a peculiar effect on the chalkland river – heavy rain may take weeks or more to percolate through rocks to the watercourse, and even when it does arrive it is released gradually. Consequently such rivers rarely flood, and a drought's effect is similarly delayed by the reserves of water in the rock. Although the fall from source to mouth of these rivers is comparatively slight, they frequently drain huge areas, carrying a great deal of water along fairly straight courses; thus the pace is swift. The water carries most of its nutrients in solution, instead of the insoluble matter carried by other lowland rivers, and it usually appears clear and sparkling.

Ecology: The nutrients of chalk rivers favour plant growth in particular, and this in turn supports a varied range of insects, molluscs and worms. Crayfish are often abundant. Watercress beds are often a feature of the upper river, and this and the burr-reeds and pondweed of the lower reaches all grow very quickly – in parts of the Avon pondweed could easily choke the river if it was not cut regularly. Pondweed tends to grow in long beds, streaming with the current – hence it is widely called 'streamer weed'. While providing excellent cover for fish, it does make angling difficult, and it may be impossible to fish in some stretches until after much of the growth has died away at the end of summer. Because of the rich feed, fish tend to grow and mature quickly.

Fish species: Properly, these waters are mixed fisheries, containing the whole range of freshwater species suited to moderate flows. However, in the upper reaches in particular, stretches are often cleared of coarse fish to allow an artificially high population of trout. Chub, roach, dace, grayling, perch and pike, together with many smaller species, are otherwise present throughout the course. Barbel thrive and often attain great size. Some of these rivers, the Avon in particular, have survived as salmon fisheries. However, the occurrence of carp, tench, rudd and bream is rare because of the swift flow.

Fishing methods: 'Trout stream' is a term which embraces the upper reaches of most lowland rivers, but those of chalkland rivers are especially famous. Here, trout grow quickly on the rich diet, particularly if competition from coarse fish is removed. This is the proper province of the dry-fly angler; quiet watermeadows and carefully tended banks provide the ideal setting for a stealthy approach to rising fish (§188). The dry-fly season runs from March to October, and the imitation fly patterns used follow the natural 'hatches', or emergence from the water-living nymph stage, of different species of insects throughout this period. The most well-known of these hatches is probably that of the mayfly. On these waters wet-fly fishing, i.e. fishing with a sunken imitation fly rather than a floating one, may also be allowed. Delicate fishing with artificial nymphs (§187) is particularly effective.

In the lower course as the river widens, eradication and removal of coarse fish would be quite impractical, and rivers such as the Avon become excellent mixed fisheries, still maintaining populations of trout and grayling besides big, fit coarse fish. The pace, clarity and size of fish in the Avon has led to a style of long trotting named after the river (§131). A high-buoyancy float and fairly strong tackle is cast to run down between beds of streamer weed at distances which obscure the angler's presence from the fish. Legering with a through or paternoster leger style (§134) can be effective in some stretches, particularly late in the year when there is less weed to hazard the operation. Swim-feeder legering can also be very effective. In the wider reaches salmon anglers will find spinning (§180) the best method for covering a large amount of water. Pike run big in the Avon and other chalkland waters: for these, spinning is the most useful method, and sink-and-draw deadbait fishing (§151) is also worthwhile. Trotted livebaits (§149) are also used.

§66 Still waters

Some special problems of standing water deserve mention before specific types are described.

Fish behaviour: Imagine yourself as a fish in a fast-flowing river – whatever comes along in the way of food must be grabbed, you must be an opportunist. The faster the water, the more this applies. In still water, however, there is time to be selective, and time to be cautious about particles of food which behave unnaturally. For the angler, this often means that finer tackle has to be used in still water, and fortunately fine tackle is less likely to come to grief in still water than in running water.

Summer thermocline effect (Fig. 71): Although this factor is by no means general, it ought to be suspected in any fairly large body of still water with the exception of very shallow lakes, canals and small drainage channels. When the upper water in a lake is heated in the summer, it radiates heat only very gradually to the layers of water beneath. As summer progresses, a distinct layer of warm

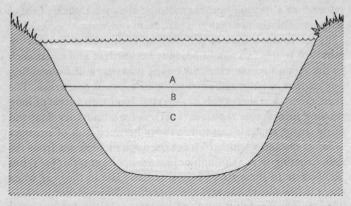

Fig. 71 (§66) Thermocline effect: A – layer of warm water (Epilimnion); B – zone of rapid temperature change (Thermocline); C – cold water (Hypolimnion).

water forms and 'floats' on the colder water beneath. Because both levels of water have different densities they cease to intermix, and until heat is lost at the end of summer when gales again mix both levels, the upper water (epilimnion) is separated from the lower level (hypolimnion) by a zone of rapid temperature change (thermocline). The warm water may extend as much as ten metres from the surface, but it is often much less. In it one can expect to find most of the fish, plants and animals present in the lake, since the water beneath is cold and cannot have its oxygen refreshed by wave action at the surface. Because of the cold, unattractive deeps, it will be impractical to bottom-fish at a great depth where the thermocline effect is present.

The effect of wind (Fig. 72): Another property of the thermocline – the area between cold and warm water – is that it tilts away from the direction of the wind, and there is therefore usually a deeper body of warm, oxygenated water at the exposed end of a lake when the wind is blowing. Wind-drift will also congregate surface insects and flies that have fallen into the water, at the exposed end of the lake; as long as the difficulties of fishing into the wind can be overcome, it is logical to fish in this region.

In Britain there is hardly ever no wind at all, and thus our 'still' waters are constantly in motion. Whether or not there is a thermo-

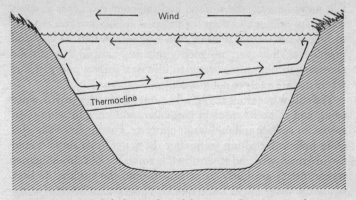

Fig. 72 (§66) Wind-drift circulates lake water. In summer, the water returns to the surface after skating over the thermocline, which tilts under the effect.

cline, there will certainly at times be a surface drift in the direction of the wind. This will push normal float tackle or a floating fly line out of position, and the angler will have to use wind and drift cheating techniques to overcome it. On some occasions, however, this drift can be used to advantage.

Water quality and productivity: As with rivers, the quality and ecology of still waters vary greatly according to the nutrients they receive either from a running source, or by seepage from the surrounding land. Mountain lakes are therefore less productive, in terms of individual size and overall numbers of fish, than lowland lakes fed by streams or drainage from surrounding rich ground.

Finding fish: Unless water is exceptionally clear, the still-water angler may have difficulties in finding likely spots to fish. The first task is to locate swims of a depth unlikely to be affected by the thermocline effect (summer only) and which seem to provide ideal conditions for supporting food organisms. Visible weedbeds are a guide, and because these also provide refuge for small fish, they are also good areas to hunt predators such as pike, perch and trout. Where no weed can be found, the contours of the land about the lake can indicate how gradually or how swiftly the land falls away beneath the surface, and thus one can guess at spots which are neither too deep for practical fishing nor too shallow to hold a reasonable head of fish. For such waters as clay and gravel pits, however, no such guidelines exist and it will be necessary to plumb the water to discover shelves and plateaux where fish are likely to congregate.

The still-water trout angler is less restricted in his search, since trout, and rainbow trout in particular, will hunt in wide open spaces for surface and mid-water creatures. Fishing from a boat is quite practical, drifting to quarter the water. The shore-bound fly fisherman will find it worthwhile to search out promontaries where insects are likely to be blown onto the surface, or bays where the water might warm quickly to produce a hatch of water flies. He will certainly find wading an advantage, to extend his casting range.

On very large lakes it is often advisable to seek local information on the best spots to fish at particular times and, if fly fishing, to inquire about the best patterns of artificial flies, since hatches vary from water to water.

If the coarse angler finds weed too thick for bank fishing, he might like to drag a clearing; the disturbance of doing so often attracts species like tench and bream.

§67 Lakes and pools in mountainous areas

As in the rivers of high ground, the lakes and pools in highland areas are likely to be poor in nutrients and the dominant fish are small trout, occasionally char. The larger bodies of water might have small numbers of bigger fish, and there is always the chance of a few trout turning cannibal and growing very big indeed. It is a red-letter day if one of these is hooked – even more so if it is landed! Unlike the mountain streams, there is no drawback of close banks to prevent fly fishing, normally with a team of small-pattern loch flies (§189). Spinning with a Devon minnow or some other small lure (§194) will also take fish – and is, of course, more likely to attract one of the big cannibals.

§68 Lowland lakes and pools

A great variety of lowland still waters exists, but in general all are more productive because of a richer source of nutrients than highland waters. The main types of lowland water can be separated and examined in more detail; first, the large lochs of Scotland and Ireland. All are trout fisheries, and besides having the capacity to produce bigger trout, there may again be the chance of some very big cannibals. Scottish and Irish lochs may hold salmon and perhaps sea-trout if they are part of a river-system. Some of the Scottish lochs and almost all of the Irish big waters hold pike, and these fish can run to a very great size. Other coarse fish are less evident in Scotland, but Ireland has many very good coarse fishing waters – huge shoals of big bream inhabit most of them, also rudd, perch, and occasionally tench. The carp is rare in Ireland, and so is the roach. Because these waters are so large, local advice will have to be sought to establish where the main shoals can be expected to be stationed at various times of the year. For trout fishing, fly and spinning tackle can be used, both from the bank and from a boat. Trolling (§158) is an excellent method of covering a large amount of water – a useful method for trout and pike. Livebaiting (§149) and deadbait methods (§150) will also be useful for pike. The coarse fish can also be tackled from shore or boat. Fishing from the shore might necessitate long-range float legering (§140) or other legering methods (§134).

Reservoirs, another type of very large lowland water, are different again. A good many of them have been developed as trout fisheries (for example Grafham Water in Huntingdon, and the Chew, Blagdon and Barrow reservoirs near Bristol). Bank and boat fishing (fly only) in such waters is extremely popular. Still water dry-fly fishing methods (§189) are quite productive at times, but wet-fly fishing is generally best. To fish from the bank, strongish fly-fishing tackle capable of throwing long lines is used, with techniques and lures suited to floating, sink-tip and sinking-fly lines.

Not all reservoirs are trout fisheries; some are mixed fisheries, others pike fisheries (Cheddar Reservoir) or coarse fisheries. The various still water float fishing methods (§130) and perhaps float legering (§140) and other forms of legering (§134) are useful. These techniques can also be applied to other bodies of still water which have been developed as coarse fisheries – the natural lakes of water-holding clay land, and man-made ornamental lakes. Gravel and clay pits pose perhaps the greatest difficulties to the angler, since it may take several exploratory visits to find productive swims. Often it will be necessary to fish in deep water, seeking ledges and underwater plateaux where fish might congregate above the hypolimnion. Here a sliding float can be useful. Where pike are present, the range of pike-fishing techniques can be tried (§149–158).

§69 Canals and drainage channels

It is hardly surprising that canals and drainage channels are very good coarse fisheries, both from the point of view that they hold good stocks of fish, and that they have clear banks – often a towpath – giving ease of access. Both types of water are artificially refreshed, the canals (unless disused) by 'tapping' additional water from streams, rivers or standby reservoirs to maintain depth, and the drains by the regular pumping of excess water from level to level (some of the Fen drains are in fact called 'levels'). Their flow cannot be regarded as constant, since locks interrupt water movement in canals, and the pumping in Fen waters may only happen once a day, or even once a week. Nevertheless, a fairly regular change of water takes place, and thus nutrients are evenly distributed throughout canals and drains.

Because the water is shallow and is warmed through quickly by the sun, weed growth is often exceptional. It has to be regularly cut so that the waterway is not choked, unless boat traffic is heavy enough to keep a clearway.

Colour varies in canals with the amount of boat traffic, which stirs up sediment, and the amount of washings from the bank during rain. With drains, those less frequently pumped tend to be clearest, except in winter when large amounts of land washings enter them.

Anglers have problems with these shallow and comparatively narrow types of water, the main one being concealment from the fish. The angler has to make himself as inconspicuous as possible, either by fishing in front of a suitable background or by putting some distance between the fish and himself. If the latter, he will fish to the far bank of the canal or drain, or along it (to the downstream side if there is any flow). Light tackle is usually necessary to avoid splashy disturbances when casting to the fish, and light tackle also helps the bait to fall lightly and naturally through the water. Among the physical problems the angler might have to overcome are wind and surface drift – you can probably imagine the effect of a strong wind blowing along perhaps a mile of straight, exposed water; it usually skates along. Thus forms of laying on (§130) for bottom-feeding fish, so that the bait is not dragged away, and the use of wind- and drift-cheating floats is most useful. Legering may be advisable when conditions are severe.

On very calm days when the water is clear, very light tackle indeed will have to be used, and a slow-sinking bait is particularly effective for rudd, roach and sometimes bream. When the water runs, if locks are opened or if pumping begins, it may be necessary to alter to a trotting rig (§131) or fasten more securely on the bed with leger tackle.

Pike in these waters often run big. They will respond to spinning, and because of weed a plug is often the best kind of lure to use (§156). They can also be caught on live and dead fish baits (§149, 150).

It is often quite easy to find fish in canals and drains by seeking bubbles, which might denote a shoal of bream or tench, or other disturbances and patches of heavily coloured water where fish might have stirred up bottom sediment.

In one shallow stretch of canal near Bridgwater in Somerset I've even seen a big bow-wave preceding a shoal of bream. If you do find fish that are on the move, try to steal ahead of them well away from the water's edge, and put some groundbait in their path to stop them.

Canals and drains might occasionally hold species which favour running water besides all of the normal still-water species – parts of the Kennet and Avon which runs in the West country contain trout and grayling, and even occasional barbel. Normally, though, in any of the still waters mentioned above, dace, barbel, grayling and bleak are likely to be absent. Chub thrive in some still waters, but cannot establish themselves in others.

13 Coarse fish

The smallest fish encountered in Britain (discounting the fry of bigger species) is the stickleback, and the largest that can be caught on rod and line is the salmon. Pike and carp, however, attain great weights. While our smaller species – those which rarely reach more than a few grammes in weight – do not provide any sport, they are on occasions useful for bait.

In general the young fish of any species are the most numerous and the most easy to catch – caution grows and appetite diminishes as a fish ages. By predation and natural wastage, shoals become smaller and smaller from the time they are hatched. By the time individuals are old, large fish, half a dozen might remain out of an original hatch of thousands. In many instances such large fish become solitary in habit and difficult to catch.

During each year, mature fish are at their weightiest just before spawning (late winter, spring, early summer). During spawning, their condition takes a dive and the mortality rate for most species is high.

Survivors move into the summer period of rich feeding, regaining weight and health. Thus you can expect the heaviest and fittest fish at the end of winter, before spawning, and in the early autumn. During the cold months of winter some species become torpid and will fast. Mild conditions, however, may encourage them to wake and feed. Chub, roach, trout, grayling and pike are quite active in cold weather.

§70 **Barbel**
Barbus barbus

A muscular, thick-shouldered fish, guaranteed to provide thrills on medium-to-heavy tackle. It has four sensory barbels on the lips of its large, downward facing mouth. Back colour is bronze or greeny bronze, shading gradually to cream or white on the belly. Barbel are shoal fish, growing to around 6 kg (13.2 lb) in Britain. They like clean water, usually selecting fast, deep runs between weed beds or the heavy water beneath a weir, where they will feed in the rough water.

Late summer is usually accepted as being the best time to fish for barbel, but it is significant that many game anglers have hooked barbel in excess of the British record weight (including fish of 17 lb 14 oz and 16 lb 1 oz) during the close season for coarse fish, some of them on a spinner. A beautiful fish of 14 lb 5 oz was caught in the River Ure in Yorkshire in the middle of the 1976 coarse-fishing close season by an angler worming for trout, and this, like many other close-season fish, was in shallow water and was probably close to spawning. Concentration on shallow-water barbel at the beginning and end of the season might well produce some very good fish.

Natural foods of the barbel are mussels, snails, worms, plant particles and sometimes small fish. Worms, bread, sausage meat and cheese have all accounted for good fish, and maggots, boiled grain and hempseed will also be taken.

Legering with a large bait, or trailing a large bait along the bottom on heavyish float tackle is recommended. Lighter tackle must be used with caution and is not advisable until the end of summer when weed beds are dying away. Groundbaiting is useful to attract and hold a shoal, or you might like to use a swimfeeder leger arrangement.

The fish fights strongly, making powerful runs and sometimes 'going solid' under weed beds or in heavy currents where water pressure helps it to stay fast on the bottom. With light tackle, this can lead to a protracted battle. Barbel tend to use up all their energy before they are landed, and will often need to be nursed to recovery by being held head-to-current for some time before you can safely release them.

Once confined only to a few rivers, notably the Thames and the Hampshire Avon, barbel have been transplanted in recent years to northern waters, the River Severn and the Bristol Avon, where they have done exceptionally well and large shoals are established.

The barbel's flesh is unpalatable and the hard roe of the female is poisonous.

§71 **Bleak** (willow-blade)
Alburnus alburnus

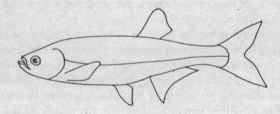

A very active surface feeder, the bleak often shoals in vast numbers and almost anything thrown into the water will be investigated. It is a small fish, usually not growing to more than about 10 cm (4 in), with silvery sides, a green back, and a protruding lower lip which enables it to sip food in the surface film. It is useful as a bait fish, and as a make-weight in fishing matches if better fish are absent.

It prefers small, lively baits such as maggots on hook sizes 16–18, fished with surface float tackle – small worms, fragments of bread and tiny pieces of paste may also be used. To save changing baits frequently a dodge used by some fishermen is to fasten a small piece of light-coloured leather to the hook in place of a maggot – this will not disintegrate even after several fish have been caught and can be cast time and time again to a shoal, in combination with loose-fed maggots to keep them interested. In a match, it takes many, many bleak to make up a decent aggregate weight, and speed in catching them is vital. Some match anglers will fish with a barbless hook (the barbs of most hooks can be pinched flat with a pair of pliers) so that no time is lost unhooking their bleak.

The species is generally not found in rivers north of the Tees and it is rare in Wales and the West country.

Although bleak are occasionally present in still waters, their main habitat is running water.

§72   **Common bream** (bronze bream)
Abramis brama

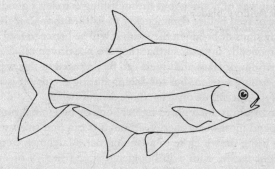

The hunched shoulder and deep, flat-sided body of the bream is unmistakeable, although colouration varies with locality from handsome bronze to grey or even black on the back, and white, pink or cream on the underside. In favourable situations large shoals of like-sized bream move and graze in company, often following a set patrol around a lake bed or up and down a river. Although generally considered to be a fish of slow or still water, the bream can be quite happy in swift flows so long as there is access to resting areas of slack water. They are widely distributed in England, but rare north of Loch Lomond, in Wales, and in the south-west peninsula. In Ireland they are widespread – huge shoals inhabit loughs, rivers and canals.

Lake and river bream feed throughout summer, and although noticeably more active in marginal areas at night and throughout dawn and dusk, feeding is often continued during the day, usually in deep water. Warm, sultry days at the end of summer are especially favourable for bream fishing. While lake fish will become torpid and fast during cold winters, bream in rivers stay more active and will feed with relish if mild weather raises temperatures. During floods, the best place to find them will be backwaters and slack pools out of the main current.

Plant debris, small water creatures such as the freshwater shrimp, and snails and molluscs form the bream's natural diet. Maggots are the most widely used bait, but bread is usually a good early-season bait (flake, paste) while worms are very telling in the winter. Casters, bloodworms, stewed grain and pieces of freshwater mussel will also be taken. Groundbaiting should be heavy to hold the attentions of a good shoal, and undoubtably the best way of going about bream fishing is to lay a good, dense carpet of feed before commencing to fish – although if there are already signs of bream in the swim it will be better to feed lightly and frequently instead, so that they are not driven off. Swims at the margins of lakes and rivers can be prepared in this way for a night-fishing session, but for fishing during the day it is usually better to concentrate on deep, more distant swims.

The bream is not a noted fighter; one or two initial runs seem to expend most of its energy although it can find small reserves when being drawn close to a landing net. Matchmen frequently use light tackle, with 1 lb hooklengths and size 18 or even 20 hooks for quite substantial fish of $1\frac{1}{2}$–3 lb, although for pleasure fishing you will find that hook sizes 10, 12 or 14 (maggots) or 8 and 10 (bread baits) will lose you less fish, even if you don't get the bite-rate you would expect with finer tackle. Light tackle should not be used in fast flows where big bream can 'kite', turning broadside against the flow so that the push of the water helps them to strain against the line. Laying on with float tackle, and legering in deeper, more distant swims are the best methods for still- and slow-moving-water bream fishing, but river bream will take trotted baits either just tripping or slowly dragging along the bottom. They will also occasionally take baits 'on the drop'.

Bream normally grow to about 5 kg (11 lb) although bigger specimens have been taken, usually from large, deep lakes and reservoirs. Small bream are sometimes referred to as 'skimmers', for they can be quickly drawn to the surface and skated ashore across the water surface, flat on their sides. The species is able to hybridize with roach and rudd.

Shoaling fish frequently come to the surface and roll before feeding. Other give-away signs of a shoal are copious bubbles stirred from the bottom and, in canals and drains, stretches of muddied water. Maggots mouthed by bream and rejected have a drawn-out sucked appearance – baits that have been tampered with should be replaced immediately. Traces of mucus adhering to your line is another pointer to bream.

§73 **Silver bream** (white bream)
Blicca bioernka

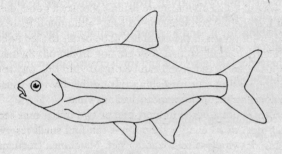

As its name implies this fish has a silvery appearance. A reddish tinge to the fins often helps to distinguish it from the common bream, although bream-roach hybrids can have similar colouration. Small common bream, which are silvery, are frequently labelled silver bream – you must expect to be disappointed if you think you have caught a specimen silver bream.

Its habits are similar to the common bream, and it responds to the same fishing methods. It runs a good deal smaller, though, and a 1 kg (2.2 lb) specimen is a good fish. It is also less widely distributed than the common bream, appearing in a few East Anglian rivers and some ornamental waters.

§74 **Burbot**
Lota lota

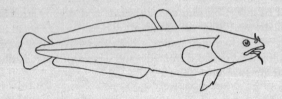

The only freshwater representative of the cod family in Britain, the burbot resembles a small ling and has a very limited distribution in eastern-flowing rivers from Durham down to the Great Ouse. It has become so rare in recent years that there is an amnesty on fishing for it, and any burbot caught accidentally should immediately be returned to the water undamaged. The fish, a bottom feeder taking worms and small crustaceans, is most active in cold weather.

§75 **Carp** (common carp, mirror and leather carp)
Cyprinus carpio

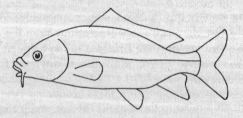

The carp probably creates more specimen-hunting addicts than any other species, and although fishing for them can mean waiting long hours through a warm summer night, the reward of a very big specimen more than justifies the time outlay. The common variety possesses large, regular, bronze scales, but there are numerous ornamental forms such as the leather carp, with scales almost entirely absent, and the mirror carp which has a row of large irregular scales along the lateral line and the ridge of the back. All varieties have small sensory barbels positioned at each side of the mouth.

The fish is tolerant of high water temperatures and in recent years carp populations have built up around the warm water of power-station outlets on some rivers (Nene, Trent), although mud-bottomed lakes and pools which have plenty of shallow water for the carp to breed in are the 'traditional' carp waters. Many slow-moving rivers, and lay-bys and backwaters in faster rivers also produce occasional good fish. Matches on the lower Nene, for instance, have been won by a big carp picking up a bream angler's bait. You can expect the fish to move into shallow water in warm conditions, coming close to the margins and feeding more readily at night. During winter, warm weather may induce carp to feed, but they are usually fished for only until the first autumn frosts begin to knock back water temperature (the true addict can then turn attention to the power-station outlets where warm temperatures are maintained).

Carp tend to be solitary in habit except when spawning. Their natural foods are vegetable matter, small bottom-living creatures, snails, mussels and tiny larvae sifted from the bottom mud. Bread and worms are popular baits, but maggots, par-boiled potatoes, sausage meat and a catholic range of other materials can be used. Normally one would expect to use a large bait, partly because of the need to discourage lesser fish. When introducing a bait new to the water, such as potatoes, it is advisable to scatter a few samples into the swim you will be using over a few weeks, if possible, so that the carp are educated to the bait's food value. Floating baits such as a cube of breadcrust will also be taken by surface-feeding carp.

Night fishing is undoubtedly more rewarding than daytime fishing; at night, freelined or legered baits are used, also floating crust, while during the day a float can be used in addition to these methods. Hook sizes 6 and 8 are widely used because of the big baits and because of the need for a secure hold with big, strong fish. Powerful, long runs can be expected when a good carp is hooked, and it might take anything up to half an hour to land one even with 8 lb line and a powerful rod.

Carp often advertise their presence by stirring up clouds of bubbles from muddy lake beds. During the night, they occasionally roll on the surface in open water and even leap out to crash back with a resounding splash – an activity I have heard described as sounding like a cow falling into the lake. They might also be heard sucking snails and insects from marginal reeds and surface plants.

§76 **Catfish** (wels)
Silurus glanis

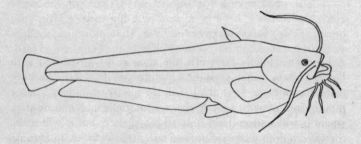

A native of the Rhine and rivers flowing into the Caspian, Baltic, and Black seas, the wels was introduced to Woburn and has spread to the Ouse and linked waters. It may also be found in ornamental park lakes, and wherever these are connected with waterways they might be expected to have spread to some degree.

It is a rather ugly dark-skinned, wide-mouthed fish, with long sensory barbels sprouting from upper and lower lips. Rather unsophisticated in its feeding habits, it takes fish, small birds and mammals, and will eat all kinds of carrion. It is most active at dusk and dawn, feeding more readily in the summer. The best fishing methods are legering with small, live or dead fish or lobworms, or freelining with dead fish. Strong tackle, with hooks around size 6 (or small treble hooks) and lines around the 10 lb mark, is recommended; catfish to 15 kg (33 lb) have been taken in Britain, but in their native waters they grow to 60 kg or more.

§77 Chub
Leuciscus cephalus

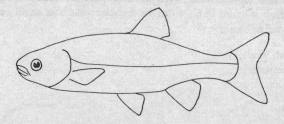

A handsome solidly built fish, the chub is bronze-backed with lighter, brassy flanks shading to whitish undersides, and large mature specimens have thick whitish lips surrounding a large mouth. In summer it usually chooses locations under shade trees where it will station itself close to the surface, but it will make forays into deep water swims and fast shallow water. In autumn and winter it is much more wide-ranging, while in spring, before spawning takes place, large shoals will often congregate near shallow water.

In large waters such as the Severn, chub often form very large shoals, while on smaller waters smaller populations, from two or three fish up to a dozen or so, keep company in fairly restricted territories. Their taste covers a wide range, and they can take a big bait – large worms, bread baits, maggots, wasp grubs, crayfish and (perhaps most popular) cheese have all accounted for good fish. Shoals will occasionally go pack-hunting for minnows, and spinning with small lures and float fishing or legering with small livebaits are useful methods. Chub will rise to floating flies, and they seem to be relatively unchoosy (unlike the trout) in this respect, quite often going for any large, showy artificial pattern which doesn't match the natural insects on the water. With baits, float or leger methods can be used, also floating crust in favourable circumstances. Fish of 2 kg (4.4 lb) or more are strong fighters, and lines below 3 lb breaking strain are not recommended. Hooks from size 10–6 give the sort of security needed, matched to the size of the bait. With large baits, it is best to ignore dithers, plucks and draws until a firm take develops.

Chub don't create the sort of disturbances which give away bottom-feeding fish, but they do make rather untidy rises when surface feeding. Shoals of small fish leaping from the surface can mean that either chub, perch or small pike are minnowing, and the chub is quite likely to make a splashy slash at small surface fish such as bleak.

§78 **Crucian carp**
Carassius carassius

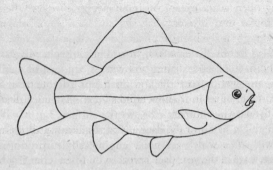

An introduced fish with quite a wide distribution in ornamental pools. It grows to about 2 kg (4.4 lb) and can be distinguished from the common carp by the fact that it has no barbels. Maggots and breadbaits fished on the bottom are effective, and the fish are good sport on light, float tackle. In common with the tench, crucian carp are capable of surviving buried in mud if a pond dries in hot weather.

§79 **Dace**
Leuciscus leuciscus

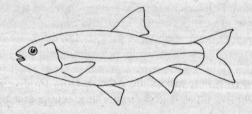

While not attaining any great size (in 1976 the record stood at 1 lb 4 oz 4 dr – 574 g) the dace is a dashing fighter with a greenish back and silvery flanks. The fins are coral pink, sometimes reddish. Small chub and dace are sometimes confused but the fringes of the dace's dorsal and anal fins are concave, while those of the chub are convex. Dace are widespread in England but uncommon in Scotland, western Wales, Devon and Cornwall. In Ireland, introduced dace are spreading through the Blackwater, Fairywater, and Erne river systems.

Dace are shoaling, surface-feeding fish, of running water, inhabiting open water except on intensely bright days when they might move into broken shallows and rapids, or under tree shade. Maggot is the best bait, fished on light, surface, float tackle with 16–18 hooks. Caterpillars, worms and insects will also take fish. The dace of open water will accept dry flies of any small pattern, and wet-fly patterns and nymphs on light, trout tackle can be used to effect in shallow rapid swims – a delightful style of fishing for dace in summer.

Following a hatch of fly, dace are unmistakeable, dimpling the water with rises which are noisy and splashy in proportion to their size. Late in the year dace revert to mid-water feeding before cold weather drives them to fast.

§80 **Eel** (yellow eel, silver eel. Small fish: whips, bootlaces)
Anguilla anguilla

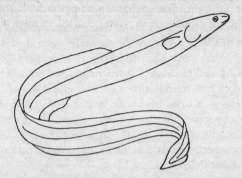

The eel travels here across the Atlantic from the Sargasso Sea region, developing as it goes from a tiny, transparent larva to a small dark elver a few inches long, at which stage it enters fresh-water. After a long life in rivers and lakes, mature fish leave for the sea, but it is by no means established that these adults ever survive the return journey to the Sargasso – research seems to suggest the eels in our waters are spawned by mature fish from the eastern seaboard of America and are transported here by the Gulf Stream, and that eels leaving Europe might well perish long before their objectives are secured. Whatever is the case, the tiny eels penetrate all linked waterways soon after arrival here, and can even negotiate wet ditches and land drains to landlocked lakes. While they are growing to maturity they are dark brown or olive on their backs, with yellow or off-white undersides. Prior to migrating to the sea, which might be anything up to ten years after arrival, they become silvery and adapt in other ways for life in the ocean. At this point (when they are known as 'silver eels' to estuary and sea fishermen) they are commercially valuable, and they are trapped in quantity as table fish.

In both development stages the eel feeds avidly on a wide range of baits, but is especially drawn to worms and small, live or dead fish. They are notably active at dusk and during the night, although they will feed through the day, save in bright conditions, in fairly shallow water. Legering is the best method, although freelining may be used in still water. The bigger the bait used, the more it becomes important to let an eel run with the bait so that it can be taken well into the mouth – eels rarely let go providing no undue resistance from the line is felt, and it is best to arrange a bobbin of dough on the line, as a bite indicator, with the reel bale-arm left off, to let line run out freely when a run develops.

Eels up to about 4 kg (8.8 lb) are taken on rod and line but much bigger fish have been found in commercial catches. The fish fights by making short, sharp rushes, taking every opportunity to dive into mud bottoms or around sunken obstructions (where it can gain a fast hold with its strong tail), and it can also tug fiercely by swimming backwards. Where big eels are known to be present, lines of 6 lb are the lightest recommended, with a swivel to protect against line twist and a wire or stout nylon trace to combat sharp teeth.

The eel is also noted for its slime – the mucous covering is particularly thick and tacky – and its ability to twist back and wrap its tail about its body and anything else within range. A wet cloth is necessary to hold one firmly for unhooking, and with a large fish it is useful to have somebody to help you with this operation. If bungled, it can be a very messy job.

Giveaway signs of eels are disturbed muddy areas of water, numbers of small fry fish moving to the surface of the water, and bubbles – particularly sudden upwellings of bubbles caused by the eel striking blindly into bottom mud after spotting some movement.

§81 **Grayling** (umber)
Thymallus thymallus

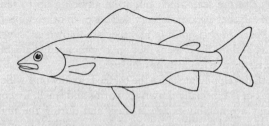

One of the prettiest, and certainly the most distinctive, fresh-water fish, the grayling is a relative of the trout, occasionally encouraged in game waters, occasionally persecuted because it provides competition for the trout's food. It has a large, sail-like dorsal fin, behind which is a secondary small adipose fin (characteristic of Salmonid fishes), and neat rows of small green-blue to silver scales which are sometimes lightly spotted with black. Distribution is mainly confined to England, but it has been introduced elsewhere. It is a shoaling fish, preferring clean streams with moderate depth and medium to strong flows, and it is frequently found in association with trout, although its range does not extend as far upstream as the trout's. It is an active feeder on insects and small creatures from middle depths to the bottom, but it will sometimes take food from the top of the water.

Light to medium weight trotting tackle is best, with worm or maggot bait fished off the bottom. A big fish must be allowed to have its head in the sort of jagging, dashing fight that the grayling puts up, since its mouth is soft and the security of the hook is always in jeopardy. Trout fly-fishing tackle with wet- and, occasionally, dry-fly patterns will also take grayling. Nymphs are particularly good. Grayling grow to around 2 kg (4.4 lb) in Britain.

§82 **Gudgeon**
Gobio gobio

The gudgeon resembles a small barbel. It grows to about 4 in (10 cm) and has two barbels, speckled fins, and a regular row of fingerprint-size smudge marks along the flanks.

The beds of the rivers and lakes which the gudgeon inhabits are patrolled by large, territorial shoals. It is a greedy feeder, and will worry large baits intended for better fish. It can be caught by bottom fishing using light, float or leger, tackle and worm or maggot baits. Small gudgeon can make fairly good baits for perch, eels, chub and pike, but they are not so attractive as, say, the minnow or a small roach.

§83 **Minnow** (penk)
Phoxinus phoxinus

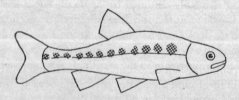

Like the gudgeon, not a fish for sport, but it does make a fine bait for many species. It is found in most of England and Wales, becoming rare north into Scotland and in higher river reaches everywhere. Although it has not been common in Ireland, growing populations are present now in many areas. It feeds greedily and can be caught using a small hook with maggot bait, but it is more conveniently obtained with a baited trap or a net.

§84 **Orfe**
Leuciscus idus

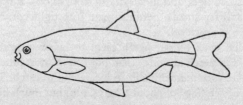

The dace-like orfe has been introduced to many ornamental pools from sources in Europe, where it is quite common. A rarer, golden, ornamental form may be found in some waters. Orfe are bottom feeders, usually caught on light, float tackle with maggots, worms or bread.

§85 **Perch**
Perca fluviatilis

Found throughout Britain except in the extreme north of Scotland and high-ground areas, the perch is a very distinctive fish with a dark green back and bronze flanks crossed with bold, vertical dark bars. The fins on the underside are red or orange and the tail is usually a deeper red, while on the back is a large, sharp-spined, erectile dorsal fin, often distinguished with a single, large, purple spot, behind which is a smaller, softer fin. It is happy in still or running water.

Young fish are particularly greedy, taking a wide range of materials but showing a preference for worms, maggots and small fish. They show little caution and will even tug furiously away at baits on heavy tackle intended for bigger fish.

There is a marked tendency for mature fish to become single-minded fish hunters, and shoals of fish from 12 oz—2 lb will harry minnow and fry shoals, herding them into tight corners where they are easy to pick off.

Strangely, even bigger perch seem to become quite solitary in habit – big perch are rarer than big fish of most other species, and they are extremely difficult to locate and to catch. There is a rod and line 'ceiling' of about 2 kg (4.4 lb) but much bigger fish have been caught in netting operations. There is obviously room here for somebody to make a name for themselves by concentrating on the secretive habits of big perch.

The small to medium fish can be taken on float-fished worm and maggot baits, and a bait held off the bottom produces the best results. Perch will also take spinners and other lures such as plugs (1½ to 3 in being the most useful size), small livebaits, and deadbaits such as minnows and bleak fished in a lively manner with a spinning flight or by the sink-and-draw method.

Perch may be encountered almost anywhere on a water, but they show a marked preference for such natural holts as the tangled, submerged roots of bankside trees, and also man-made structures such as bridge piers and piling, jetty supports, and submerged junk of all kinds. Fry or minnows 'exploding' in terror from the water surface often indicates marauding perch.

§86 **Pike** (luce. Young fish: jack)
Esox lucius

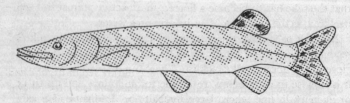

Found throughout the British Isles in all kinds of still and running water, this is our biggest coarse fish and in most seasons specimens of 10 kg and more are taken. Colouration varies with location from brown to leaf- or bottle-green, and most fish are mottled or barred with lighter patches of colour for camouflage. The duck-bill mouth of the pike is crammed with hundreds of tiny, very sharp, backward-sloping teeth. It seeks its prey (fish, small water-birds and mammals) by stalking slowly through summer weed beds or lying in ambush, and in winter it usually harries shoal fish in open water – attendant pike to a shoal of roach, for instance, might amount to tens of fish. It will also take carrion.

In summer, float-fished or legered fish baits (live or dead) are best fished in, or close to, weed. Spinning with spoons, wobblers, lures and plugs (2 to 4 in being the most useful range) should, for the same reasons, be conducted close to weed, rather than in the open water away from the river or lake's bank. The floating plug is especially useful in this respect, enabling you to keep the hooks clear of snags. Winter livebaiting and deadbaiting, spinning and trolling, can search more open water, but it does pay to find the depth at which the main shoals of small fish are swimming, establishing a contour line below which it will be impractical to fish. On big, open waters it will pay to hunt down an actual shoal of small fish (a boat is very useful) so that you can be fairly sure of attracting attendant pike.

Winter pike-fishing is generally accepted to be better than summer fishing, and October–March used to be a more rigidly observed pike season (pike fishing is still disallowed on some club waters until October). The easy pickings of summer, the fry shoals, perish with the first cold nips, leaving only the hardiest and smartest of their numbers to survive to build future breeding stocks; hibernating summer species are out of harm's way; the weed, natural cover for a hunter, is dead – and all of this means that the pike has to become a fiercer, more active animal to keep itself fed, as the winter tightens its grip on a water.

In order to combat the cutting and fraying effect of the pike's teeth either a wire or a stout nylon trace ought to be incorporated close to the hook in pike tackles. Where big fish can be expected, it is unwise to drop below 10 lb line for spinning, and up to 15 or even 18 lb line where large livebaits or deadbaits such as a whole herring are used.

Actively-hunting pike show little caution, and will strike at anything that moves – I've found quite small pike with trout of the same size locked in their jaws, dying because their teeth would not allow them to drop the hopelessly large prey. Scattering shoals of fish, or single fish leaping in panic from the water, will often betray pike. It is also worth concentrating on areas – submerged tree roots, lily pad patches – which are patently avoided by ducks and other water creatures.

§87 **Pike-perch** (I zander, II wall-eye)
I *Stizostedian lucioperca*, II *S. vitreum*

Both introduced fish, the zander is a European species while the wall-eye has origins in the New World. They are so similar that they might as well be regarded as a single species by the angler. They resemble an elongated perch, possessing two dorsal fins, the first of which is armed with sharp spines. A toothed mouth leaves a characteristic vee-shaped pinch on a rejected bait fish.

Fishing methods are the same tactics employed for perch, although wall-eye and zander will also take small, dead fish on leger tackle. They seem less inclined than the perch to chase a bait with any enthusiasm, and anchored live- and deadbaits are generally superior to spinning.

Zander in the Relief Channel of the Great Ouse (a water that has had fairly recent introductions of zander, now breeding rapidly) have grown in excess of 5 kg (11 lb).

§88 Roach
Rutilus rutilus

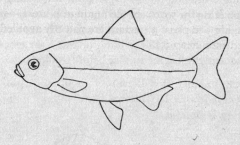

Without a doubt the most popular quarry of English coarse fishermen, the roach is wide-ranging in habit, happy in flowing or still, deep or shallow, water. Well-coloured specimens have blue-green backs, handsome, mirrored flanks and red fins. They are rarer in West country waters than in the rest of England, and hard to find in west Wales or north of Loch Lomond in Scotland. After being introduced to Ireland, they are spreading through the river systems of the Erne, Fairywater, and the Cork Blackwater.

Roach feed most actively in summer, but provide many winter red-letter days, particularly in running waters. It is significant that most of the biggest roach have been taken in still water, especially large waters such as reservoirs and gravel pits. A specimen of 1 kg (2.2 lb) is an extremely good fish, however, and many rivers and other waters hold fish of this stamp.

They feed on plant matter and water animals, occasionally taking flies from the water surface – light fly fishing is telling at times. The usual method, however, is float fishing (trotting or slow-sinking baits) with the lightest possible tackle allowed by conditions – the fish is a very shy biter. Legering will tell in winter, though. Although maggots are widely used, hemp is a particularly good alternative, and boiled grains, tares, bread, worms and wild berries will also be taken.

The biggest fish tend to be bottom rooters, and laying on with float or leger tackle is the best way to seek them. It is worth recording that one or two roach often mature with a big bream shoal, adopting the bream's behaviour and feeding tastes – a roach that thinks it is a bream, in fact. These often grow to be very large fish. The species can hybridize with the bream and rudd.

Groundbaiting for roach should not be as heavy as groundbaiting for bream – the best attractant is small offerings of hookbait introduced frequently while fishing, or else light cloud baiting. Roach frequently roll at the surface before feeding.

§89　Rudd
Scardinius erythropthalmus

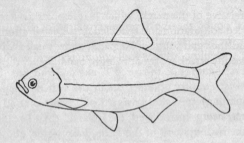

A relative of the roach, widespread throughout Ireland and England where it prefers ponds and lakes or slow-moving waters. Rudd grow slightly larger than roach, and they have bright gold or bronze flanks and scarlet fins. They are active surface-feeders in summer.

Light float-fishing with surface tackle and a small slow-sinking bait such as a maggot or a fragment of bread, especially in or near rushes where the rudd shoal to feed on insects, is the best method, although big specimens are sometimes contacted by bottom-fishing, more often at dusk or in darkness.

Loose-fed hook-bait offerings, or cloud bait can be used, or one can float pieces of crust into the swim so that they disintegrate slowly to release food particles.

Shoals can often be spotted on a still day, making small dimpled rises, while big solitary fish sometimes cruise around with their noses out of the water on a summer evening, picking off moths, grasshoppers and so on.

§90 **Ruffe** (pope)
Gymnocephalus cernua

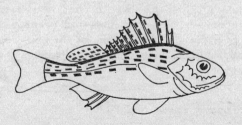

A small relative of the perch, which it resembles save for brown-ish, mottled colouration and speckled fins. Distribution is limited to the Midlands and south of England, and a small area of Wales. It will greedily attack worm or maggot baits.

§91 **Smelt** (sparling)
Osmerus eperlanus

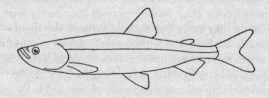

Found in river mouths along the east coast of England and Scotland and in Ireland (notably the Shannon), the smelt rarely travels far from salt water. It resembles a small, silvery herring and grows to about 20 cm (8 in). Smelt are greedy feeders, accepting worms and small spinners.

§92 Tench
Tinca tinca

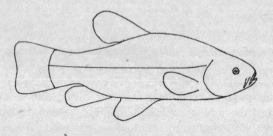

A very popular and distinctive summer fish, the tench is an active bottom-feeder, preferring still or slow-moving water with a muddy bottom. It is a handsome olive green, shading to buttercup yellow on the underside, and the eyes are bright red. There are small rudimentary barbels at the corners of the mouth, and the male fish have larger, spoon-shaped pectoral fins than the females. A rare, introduced form, the golden tench, can be caught in some ornamental waters.

They are most active at dawn and dusk, and, although daytime cloud can prolong their feeding period, they rarely take in the middle of the day or in the darkest parts of the night – dawn fishing is usually best, and with the early dawns of summer this makes a pre-work, tench-fishing session quite practical. Normally, one would try to arrive at the swim in darkness, baiting the swim and tackling-up in anticipation of first light. By groundbaiting, large shoals may be attracted and big bags are often taken in a few hours. Strongish float-fishing tackle is best (3 lb line for clear water, but 5 or even 6 lb line for waters which are very weedy and which hold big tench). Good baits are worms, bread, maggots and fragments of swan-mussel, and bulky, heavy groundbait can be used – sometimes congealed blood, obtainable from slaughterhouses, is stirred into the groundbait to make it extra attractive.

When tench arrive in a swim, the surface is covered with tiny pin-prick bubbles – a characteristic of tench alone, possibly caused by bottom mud being stirred in the mouth of the fish so that marsh gas is released through the fish's gills. When hooked, the tench gives a very good account of itself, fighting strongly, with powerful, short runs, to gain access to weed or snags. Strangely, whenever a piece of weed becomes stuck on the line in front of the fish's nose, it ceases to fight altogether. Tench which do gain their objective often become very firmly stuck – another reason for strong lines, as the fish has to be hauled bodily free.

In late summer, tench shoals tend to break up, and individual fish hunt through shallow, weedy water. At this time, small baits such as a couple of maggots on a 16 hook are better than the quite large baits that can be used earlier in the season; since the weeds are soft and dying, lighter tackle is more practical.

Although they may move about in winter, particularly in rivers when they are disturbed by floods, tench are generally inactive from autumn to spring. June and July are the best months.

§93 **Whitefish**
Coregonus species

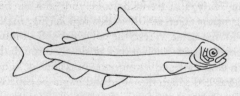

These are sometimes known as 'freshwater herring'. They are confined to a few northern English, Scottish, Irish and Welsh lakes. They have slightly different appearances according to their water of origin, and varieties are gwyniad, pollan, powan and vendace. They are normally plankton feeders, but have been taken on worm, maggot and artificial flies.

§94 **Small fish, rarities**

The stickleback (usually the three-spined variety, *Gasterosteus aculeatus*, although there is a nine-spined species and a fifteen-spined marine form) is widespread in Britain, where it is most active in warm weather. It stays in bank crevices in winter, where it can be winkled out if needed for bait – trout find them very attractive. Loaches make a fairly good bait, and they are sometimes caught on maggot bait. They resemble gudgeon, but they are altogether longer, more sinuous fish. The stone loach (*Noemacheilus barbatulus*) is the most widespread. The bullhead, or miller's thumb (*Cottus gobio*) is sometimes caught on small baits, and may often be the only species accompanying trout in the fast, high reaches of streams. As its name suggests, it has a broad, flattened head and a thin body. It makes a good trout bait. Among imports which have gained a small foothold in some parts of Britain the best-known is probably the goldfish, *Carassius auratus*, which can grow to 1 kg in favourable conditions. The large-mouthed black bass (*Micropterus salmoides*), a North American fish slightly resembling the perch, has become localized in parts of Dorset and Surrey, and the small, iridescent bitterling (*Rhodeus sericeus*) has been introduced in some parts – it is quite common in Europe, and has the interesting habit of laying its eggs in the shell of a living swan-mussel.

The armour-plated sturgeon (*Acipenser sturio*) which migrates to rivers from the sea to breed, has only rarely been found in British waters, notably the Severn. There are no verified accounts of it being taken on rod and line – it attains weights far in excess of most freshwater gear, specimens reaching 50 kg and more. There is evidence that the smaller sterlet (*Acipenser ruthenus*) is thriving after being introduced to the Tyne–Tees systems.

See also, under 'sea fish', the following species which spend limited time in rivers and brackish coastal waters: bass, flounder, grey mullet, allis and twaite shad.

The ubiquitous maggot (or 'gentle') is by far the most popular coarse-fishing bait. Thousands of gallons are sold every week, and maggot-production for anglers is fast approaching a major industry.

Despite this popularity, it is a big mistake to rely always on maggots; there are many occasions when some other baits, such as bread or worms, will do as well or better. I always try to carry at least three different kinds of bait (not always including maggots) so that if sport is slow, or if small fish pester one particular bait, I can offer an alternative – sometimes making a world of difference to results.

When you are after big fish, it is generally best to use a big bait. Besides avoiding the attention of lesser fish, this enables you to use a larger hook for greater security.

You will also find a seasonal influence on what baits fish will take best: for the roach, for instance, bread and maggots are good early in the season, and later, when ripe grain and fruit such as elderberries might be expected to find their way naturally into the water, soft-boiled grain, hempseed and ripe berries are readily taken. Come winter, the higher water levels will be washing more soil creatures into the river and the worm becomes the best bait for many species besides the roach.

§95   **Keeping bait clean**

It is advisable to keep your bait as clean and as wholesomely attractive as possible. A can of high-smelling maggots, some of them dead, squirming in sweaty, greasy wood shavings, will doom you to poor sport – the ammonia stench is far from attractive to humans, let alone fish with their ultra-sensitive sense of smell.

Adverse taints can also be transmitted to bait via your hands – particularly to hook baits. Tobacco and reel oil are both deterrent smells, and if you smoke or if your reel is leaking oil you should think of rinsing your hands before you handle bait.

§96 Arranging baits on hooks

Only with extremely soft baits – over-ripe berries for example – can you afford to bury the point of your hook. With all other baits you should try to make sure that the point of your hook emerges from the bait, so that your chances of hooking a fish are increased. Remember that a fish cannot possibly know what a hook is – any visible part is merely some foreign object adhering to the bait.

§97 Maggots

The ordinary, large, white maggot sold by most tackle dealers is the larva of the bluebottle – they are known as 'hookers' in the Midlands and north of England, and either as 'gentles' or plain ordinary 'maggots' in the southern part of the country. Sometimes they are stained a variety of colours by the use of chrysoidine dyes, or they may be tinted a handsome burnished yellow by the addition of anatto (the vegetable dye used to colour butter) to their feed. Yellow colouring seems to attract bream; reds and greens, on the other hand, make good roach maggots.

Commercial breeders (if you're squeamish, skip this bit) allow bluebottles to 'blow' – i.e., lay eggs – on trays of offal, condemned meat or stale fish, in closed, rigorously disinfected rooms. In warm weather these eggs hatch in a couple of days (artificial heating can accelerate hatching) and the tiny maggots emerge to feed greedily. In a few days they go through skin changes and become quite plump. At this stage, while there is food left for them, anatto may be added to dye them yellow – it takes a day or so for the colouring to get into their systems. When they reach a good size the maggots may be suspended on a grid above tubs of clean bran or sawdust, so that they drop from the remains of the feed, or they may be riddled out of the food scraps mechanically. The bran or sawdust scrubs them clean of grease and, since they cannot digest such matter, they begin to scour, losing the black oblong patch which you can see through their skins – this is food being digested in the maggots' gut.

Before they are thoroughly scoured (since complete scouring will encourage pupation) they are riddled from the now-dirty bran or sawdust into new, clean material and sent off to tackle dealers. Chrysoidine dyes may be added at any of the late production stages.

Left to themselves, the maggots would then continue scouring and begin to turn into 'casters', the paper-cased, soft interior, pupal stage of the fly's development: in warm weather, this will take only a matter of days, but this stage is retarded by cold weather and most tackle dealers now keep their maggots in refrigerated displays.

If you want to produce maggots yourself, you will have to begin about ten days before the date at which you want to use them. Purchase some offal or stale fish (you'll get a pint or more of maggots from about 3 lb of flesh) and leave it outside somewhere for one and a half days at the most in normal weather – if it is left longer and gets overblown, you will merely get a lot of small maggots. It is best then to parcel the whole lot in newspaper which will keep in the heat and keep out the light (maggots shrink away from light) and then place the parcel in an old biscuit-tin which has two or so inches of bran in the bottom (make sure that rain will not get into the tin). It is unlikely that you will get pure 'hookers' from your venture, and your maggots will usually contain many small 'pinkies' – the pink-tinged larva of the green-bottle fly. After six days (longer in cold weather) you can inspect your maggots, and if they are big enough for bait you can shake or riddle the remainder from what is left of the feed into the bran in the tin.

Before you go fishing you can clean your maggots again, this time by emptying the entire batch, bran and all, into a smaller container which has about three inches of either bran, sawdust or dry groundbait in the bottom. Leave this in the light, and allow an hour for the maggots to work down into the clean material (don't, under any circumstances, stir or shake the container to mix the levels) and then gently discard from the top until you strike the clean material – the number of maggots you lose with the debris will be negligible. This is also an excellent method for retrieving live maggots from a batch that has become sweaty and dirty. You can now put the cleaned maggots into your bait container, and if you want to keep them for some days you can put them in the bottom of a refrigerator (providing the rest of the family allows this). You can, of course, dye your maggots (many dealers sell dyes and anatto paste) in just the same way as commercial producers.

Once you have your clean maggots, it is useful to select some for hook bait as distinct from those which you will be using in groundbait or as loose feed, in order to give them a little special treatment. The actual number of maggots you will use as hookbait is very small – rarely more than a hundred and fifty or so (amounting to a large handful). These will fit comfortably into a well-scrubbed 2 oz tobacco tin in which air holes have been made. Many fish prefer lively, polished maggots, and to achieve this I transfer a handful to a small tin lined with some dry, nongreasy, coarse groundbait, where they stay overnight before I go fishing. The result is a particularly attractive, wiry maggot, ideal for trotting for such species as roach. For bream, and other bottom-feeders which have time to pick up and mouth baits before moving off with them, I like a soft, sweet maggot. I select a handful of maggots as before, but this time only a matter of a couple of hours before fishing. They are introduced to the tin along with a slice of fresh bread which has been moistened with a little milk into which a small amount of honey has been stirred. Care must be taken to keep the lid on these moist maggots while fishing – once damp, they can cling to almost any surface and escape.

It is also worth mentioning that fish-fed maggots are softer and more buoyant than maggots reared on denser animal and bird meat.

Pinkies: As I mentioned above, these small pink maggots are the larvae of the greenbottle fly. They are excellent groundbait maggots, and used in conjunction with larger hook maggots they hold the fish while the bigger maggot stands out as a bonus offering. Pinkies may also be used on hooks from size 18 to 20 or smaller, and on some occasions are taken in preference to larger maggots – it is a good idea to switch from pinkies to hookers and vice versa while you are fishing. Pinkies are the best escapers I know, and it is essential to make sure that their tin is securely lidded all the time they are kept indoors.

Squatts: These are the tiny, yellowish larvae of the small housefly, and whereas the flies seem plentiful, producing their maggots in any quantity is tricky and best left to the commercial men. The little squatts, like pinkies, are normally used for groundbaiting, while larger maggots are used for hook-baits. They are especially attractive to bream, probably because they are so small that they take all the fish's concentration. Usually, they are added to carpeting, cereal groundbait. Occasionally they can be tried as hook-bait, although a very small hook – size 20 or smaller – has to be used. Avoid using squatts on fast-flowing waters, since they will quickly be swept away and wasted – and they may take your fish away with them. They are usually delivered in red sand which must be riddled off before you use them.

Gozzers: These count among the many varieties of 'special' maggots bred by enthusiasts on the Midland and Northern open match circuits. All specials are bluebottle maggots, but the sorts of material used to feed maggots give them qualities of density, softness and so on. Sometimes they are treated to honey or sugar in their feed. The ideal gozzer is short, plump, white and soft, and a pigeon breast usually makes maggots of this sort. The bluebottle fly lays its eggs in semi-darkness, and so to get a selective blow for breeding gozzers, the food used to attract the flies should be placed in a biscuit tin with a few pence-sized holes punched in the lid – this can be left in the garden. Gozzers are especially useful for bream fishing.

Presentation: Although maggots are fairly tough-skinned, their innards are tightly packed and a hook carelessly inserted in most parts of their bodies is likely to burst them; the hook point should be nicked lightly under the skin and out again through the tough fringe of the blunt end, near the two black breathing-spiracle spots (Fig. 73). How many maggots you use depends largely on the size of your hook; single maggots may be used from size 16 to 20 and so may double maggots, but smaller hooks will only hold one. Sizes bigger than 16 can take two or three maggots, going up to as many as half a dozen for size 8 hooks. I think it is

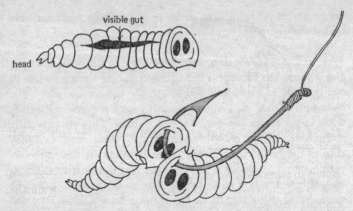

Fig. 73 (§97) Nick maggots through the fringe of skin surrounding the posterior end.

better to think of using some other bait when you get above size 8 hooks – maggots crammed on the thicker-gauge wire of big hooks tend to drown quickly. Sometimes you will find that paired maggots on a hook spin rapidly as you draw them through the water, eventually twisting your line. If you use one large and one small maggot rather than two of equal size you can eliminate this.

Besides being attractive to roach and bream, maggots will take dace, chub, rudd, tench, small perch and eels. They are not so attractive to bigger perch or zander, and while large carp will often take a bunch of maggots, a bait which allows you to use a large hook is a better bet.

§98 Casters

The chrysalis stage of the maggot has been used for bait for a long time – they are attractive to roach, rudd, bream, dace and chub – but it was not until the 1960s that the knack of producing them in commercial quantities was discovered. Up to that time, the few 'casters' that were used were those picked from maggots as they 'turned' or pupated; these will sink in the water for about one day, after which they darken from a rich, red colour to near black, and will float. However, it was found that if casters are deprived of air and kept cool, the floating stage can be held off. Thus, it was possible to hold a stock of arrested-development

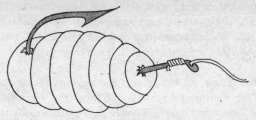

Fig. 74 (§98) Insert hook at end of caster and turn carefully to make point emerge through side without bursting brittle shell.

casters in sealed polythene bags in a cool fridge, and dealers were able to sell them by the pint – the sort of quantity which allowed casters to be used as groundbait as well as hook-bait.

Fish tackle casters in a different way to maggots; the maggot will be swallowed whole, while the caster is crushed, its juices are sucked out, and the shell is rejected. The best way of putting a caster on your hook is to insert the point at the blunt end, gently easing it around and out of the caster's side (Fig. 74). Fine-wire, size 16 or 18 hooks should be used to avoid smashing the caster. You can expect quick bites, and you should inspect your caster after an unsuccessful strike to make sure that it is intact and has not been 'shelled'.

Casters may be added to groundbait or loose-fed – but try to make sure that your groundbait casters are all at the same stage of development or they will sink at different rates and spread your fish too widely through the swim. For hook baits, however, don't avoid using the casters which have blackened to the floating stage; once the weight of your hook is added to a floater, it will sink, and although to us the blackened form seems less attractive than the handsome orange sinkers, the fish don't seem to mind at all. It pays to ring the changes, alternating between floaters and sinkers. Incidentally, you can separate your floaters by filling your bait container with water so that they can be scooped off by hand – the remaining sinkers should be drained or they will drown and become sour.

§99 **Worms**

All of the commonly found earthworms are good freshwater baits; the smaller ones, such as the redworm, are excellent for roach, rudd, dace and bream, while the larger lobworm will take big perch, chub, tench, carp and barbel. By bunching several worms on a hook it is possible to make a large bait, while pieces of large worms can be used for small fish (Fig. 75).

Lobworms: These are the largest earthworms found in Britain. Like other worms, they are found near the surface in damp weather, burrowing deeper if it is dry. They frequently rise to the surface of the soil at night (after dew has fallen in dry weather) and besides digging them up, it is possible to hunt them in the dark with a flashlight, seizing the exposed part of the worm and drawing it gently from the soil. Lawns are the best place to hunt them in the dark, and it is possible to pick up a couple of hundred in a few hours' work if conditions are right. You can keep the worms you have gathered in a tub filled with peat or leafmould, and this is a good idea, especially when the weather is extra dry and the ground is too hard for digging. It is also useful to have a handy stock through the winter – frost, snow and so on will make digging difficult. With lobs, I like to use a large hook and I snick them through just once, usually in the tough, egg-bearing clitellum, which is the elongated collar which sometimes straddles the worm's middle. Worms without a clitellum are referred to as 'maidens' and they have just shed their egg-case – at one time

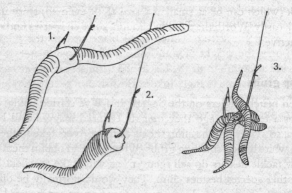

Fig. 75 (§99) Lobworms can be used individually for large fish (1) or broken into smaller pieces (2). Small worms should be used singly on small hooks, or bunched on larger ones (3).

anglers used to believe that these made better baits than ordinary worms, but there is no evidence to support this.

Redworms: These glossy red worms grow to about three inches in length and they make excellent baits for a wide range of fresh-water species. They are found in concentrations of rotting vege-table material such as compost heaps and piles of dead leaves, and also in maturing manure.

Brandling: Like the redworm, the brandling is found in rotting material. It is easily distinguished by the bright yellow bands between the segments, and when handled it gives off a slightly offensive odour – but this doesn't deter fish, and the brandling is a good bait for chub, grayling and trout.

Stone worm: This is the smallest worm that can be found in the garden. Greyish and purple-veined, it is tough and wiry on a hook and makes an excellent chub and roach bait. It is normally found in hard-packed ground, often lying under stones. Unlike the other earthworms, it doesn't actively try to escape when dis-covered.

Marsh worm: This is a small brittle worm, rarely growing above one and a half inches which inhabits the mud at the margins of ponds and ditches – its colour ranges from purple to bright red, and it is semi-transparent. Care must be used in putting it on a hook (which can be as small as a size 18 or even 20) since it will break easily. Worth the trouble, though, since all species find them attractive.

§100 **Wasp grubs**

When match anglers on the Severn and Wye started using wasp grubs a few years ago they quickly eclipsed maggot and bread users, so avidly did the chub shoals of these rivers take to the big, soft, white honey-smelling grubs. When you can obtain them (and a few tackle dealers do sell them) these will make excellent baits for other species besides chub. They would normally be offered singly on a size 12 hook, or two or more grubs can be used with larger hook sizes. I've never collected wasp grubs first-hand – wasps have such nasty personalities. Collecting involves gassing a nest – usually in a dry bank – with cyanide powder and hot water. The nest is then left for a day or more until all the wasps might be expected to be dead, and then the paper-case nest sections holding the grubs can be safely dug up.

§101 **Bloodworms and jokers**

These are the totally aquatic larvae of the midge and the gnat; the bloodworm (midge) growing to an inch, and the joker somewhat less. Bloodworms are hook baits for use on ultra-fine tackle with hooks of size 20 or smaller, while the smaller joker, too fragile to be hooked, is generally used as groundbait. Both inhabit the same sort of locale – slightly stagnant, shallow water, where they live in the bottom mud. Both usually have a part of their bodies emerging from the mud in order to breathe, but when disturbed they behave quite differently – the bloodworm sinks and tries to bury itself, while the joker flexes itself rapidly, jiggling away from the source of disturbance.

To collect bloodworms and jokers you will need a strip of thin metal, a foot to eighteen inches long, two inches wide, and one sixteenth of an inch thick, fastened to the end of a five-foot pole (Fig. 76). This is drawn through the upper surface of mud in stagnant water, and the bloodworms and jokers will be picked up on the leading edge of the blade. They should be placed in damp newspaper, and later transferred to slightly damp peat (in the

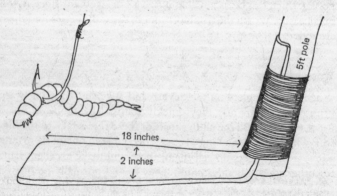

Fig. 76 (§101) Blade of thin metal drawn through mud in stagnant water collects bloodworms.

newspaper they will gather together in a tight knot, but when placed in peat they separate). Bloodworms and jokers will keep in a cool fridge for about six days.

§101 **Bread**

Bread, white or brown, fresh or stale, can always be put to good use as a bait. As an inert bait, it appeals less to predatory fish such as perch and eels than the more lively baits.

Flake: Bread flake is simply a ragged piece of the interior of a loaf, pinched or torn out in whatever size or shape is required. It can be held on a hook by pinching it about the shank of the hook so that the point and barb emerge, or pressed to consolidate one part of the bait so that the hook point can be pushed through (Fig. 77) which I find a superior method. A small thumb-and-finger pinch of flake can be used for roach and bream on hooks as small as size 16, while larger chunks on hooks up to size 6 can be used for barbel, big chub, tench and carp.

Bread paste: Stale loaves make the best paste. The crust should be removed, and the remainder soaked thoroughly in a bowl of water. When soaked through, this is lifted out, and all the excess

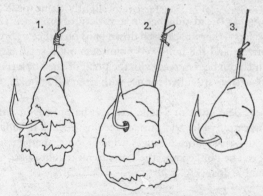

Fig. 77 (§102) 1 – bread flake (soft, new bread) squeezed around hook shank to secure; 2 – flake again, but here a pinch is made to consolidate the bread and the hook is passed through; 3 – bread paste moulded around hook shank leaving point showing.

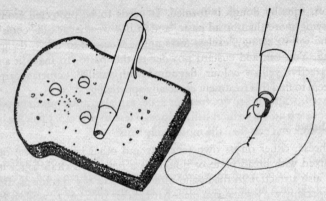

Fig. 78 (§102) The pen-shaped bread punch is used to cut neat, small discs from sliced bread – remove bait from hollow cutting-head with point of hook. Interchangeable cutting-heads for varying sizes of bait are available.

moisture is gently squeezed away. Finally, it is kneeded into a soft, open paste – not too much working, or it will form a hard paste which might mask the point of your hook when you strike. It should be kept in a damp cloth to prevent the outside drying into a hard crust. Paste is attractive to the same species as flake, and it tends to stay on the hook longer without disintegrating.

Punched bread: Bread punches in a variety of sizes are sold by tackle dealers – they are pressed down hard on a slice of bread on a flat surface, and the hollowed point cuts out a small circlet of bread which can be removed with the point of the hook (Fig. 78). The normal sizes are suited for use with size 18–12 hooks.

Bread crust: The crust of a stale loaf can be pre-cut in whatever size suits carp, rudd and surface-feeding roach. If sufficiently large, it can be cast short distances, while if longer range is needed the crust can be dunked into the water to make it heavier, or used with a bubble float (Fig. 79).

§103 Dough

Flour-and-water dough makes a good substitute for bread paste. Flour should be put in a basin, with water added gradually until a soft, squashy dough is formed. It needs to be protected from drying more than bread paste, and in hot weather it can 'cook' and form a stringy, useless mess unless wrapped in thick, damp rag. You can add custard powder to this paste, to make it an attractive yellow colour, flavoured with vanilla – crucian carp seem to find this treatment especially appetizing.

§104 Cheese

Cheese, either on its own (cheddar and other hard cheeses) or mixed with bread paste or dough, is a renowned chub bait – it is also attractive to roach and often produces big specimens. Be especially wary when you place hard cheese on a hook; while it is soft enough to be moulded around the shank before you cast, it quickly becomes rock-hard when it is immersed in water. Do make sure that the point and barb emerge through the bait.

§105 Hempseed

Nobody knows exactly what makes hempseed such an attractive bait; the wilder theories are that the fish become 'hooked' on the drug marijuana, which is derived from the plant into which the seed eventually grows – but none of the active drug is present in the seed. Another theory is that the seeds resemble tiny mussels,

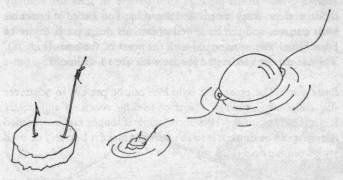

Fig. 79 Bread crust with crumb attached makes a good floating bait – push hook through tough crust so that point emerges. For extra casting weight dunk crust in water before casting, or use with partially filled transparent plastic bubble float.

or even fish spawn, and this seems altogether more likely. However, roach do appear to go wild for hempseed and this has even led to it being banned on some waters, on the grounds that it is unfair to anglers using other baits. I think this is an extreme action, because I have often used hemp merely as a groundbait while baiting with maggots, bread or worms, with excellent results.

Hempseed is hard and dry when it is purchased from tackle dealers or (as bird-seed) from pet shops. To make it usable as a bait it must be boiled until soft, and there are several ways of doing this. The most widely used method is to bring the seeds to the boil with a generous covering of water, afterwards allowing them to simmer until they split and the soft interior is visible. However, this can take hours if the seeds are very dry, and a better method is to soak the seeds in cold water overnight before boiling them, cutting the cooking time considerably. Another way of preparing the seed is to place eight ounces or so in a Thermos flask the night before fishing after first boiling them briskly for twenty minutes, making sure that they are covered with hot liquid, coming to within an inch of the Thermos stopper. The stopper is screwed in, and the seeds cook gently through the night.

Your hook (sizes 14–18) should be pushed through the outer husk, so that the point and barb emerge through the split (Fig. 80).

Since these seeds resemble split shot, you may have trouble with fish attacking your shot rather than the hook bait, giving false bites. The continental-style, elongated, 'mouse-dropping' weights can be used as a substitute for shot to avoid this, but I

Fig. 80 (§105) Hempseed grains, like barley (§107) are stewed until soft and splitting. Push hooks through so that point emerges from soft interior.

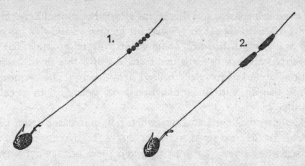

Fig. 81 (§105) When using the small, round, dark hempseeds, there is a danger of fish attacking normal, split shot which they mistake for seeds – combat this with close-spaced tiny dust shot (1) or the 'mouse-dropping' type elongated weight (2).

have found it adequate to string together dust shot in a chain which in no way resembles hempseed (Fig. 81).

Barbel, chub, dace, bream and rudd, besides roach, have all been taken on hempseed.

§106 Tares

These are larger seeds than hempseed, and they are sold in pet shops as pigeon-feed. They need boiling to make them soft, as with hemp, and can be used on their own or as a hook bait when groundbaiting with hemp or vice versa. They are widely used for roach, particularly on the River Trent, but they will take many other species.

§107 Wheat, barley, malt

Wheat and barley (either whole, or the 'pearl' variety) make excellent late-summer baits when boiled soft. Malt, which is barley that has been allowed to sprout and ferment, is normally soft enough to use without boiling. With all grains, I like to nick the point of the hook through the end of the grain so that the point comes through the split (Fig. 80). They are normally used for roach, but will take many other species.

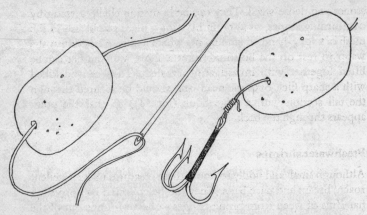

Fig. 82 (§108) When using parboiled potatoes as a carp bait, thread line through with a large needle and then attach treble or large single hook. Draw hook into potato, which should be soft enough to split on striking.

§108 Potatoes

Parboiled potatoes, cooled when the skin splits but before the flesh is very soft (about fifteen minutes' cooking) have been used to great effect for carp on waters where other baits are pestered by small fish. The carp have to be educated to their food-value by liberal handouts spread over several weeks. Pigeon-egg size potatoes are quite easily gobbled by big carp, and the best hooks to use are small trebles – a baiting needle is useful for threading the bait onto the line before attaching the hook (Fig. 82).

§109 Elderberries, blackberries

When both of these wild fruits are ripe they will take roach and chub, particularly in the vicinity of an elderberry bush or blackberry vine overhanging the water. Use individual berries on 16–18 hooks.

§110 Crayfish

This freshwater relative of the lobster is a superb chub bait, particularly in daytime when crayfish normally hide away under stones and dense weed. They can be hunted in shallow water by overturning stones, or at night by tying a piece of old fish to the mesh of a long-handled landing net which is then pushed into the water to rest on the bottom – after a short wait the net can be lifted together with investigating crayfish. They can be killed with a sharp flick over the head, and should be secured through the tail section with a large hook (Fig. 83) so that the point appears through the back.

§111 Freshwater shrimps

Although small and fiddly to hook, these creatures make excellent roach, bream and dace baits. They can be collected by uprooting handfuls of weed from brook fringes – shake shrimps out of the weed onto a newspaper – or caught with a child's shrimping net drawn through weed. They can be kept in a jar or tin, half filled with water and weed, and are surprisingly good at surviving for a long time.

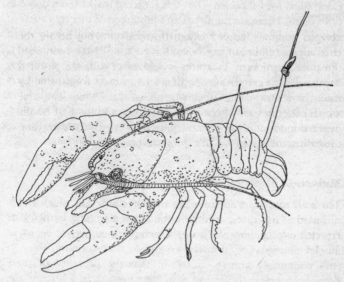

Fig. 83 (§110) Kill crayfish before hooking through tail segments.

§112 Elvers

When these small, dark larvae of the freshwater eel enter certain rivers, such as the Severn, from the sea, they can turn the water almost black – thousands of little bodies pressing into freshwater. Fish find them easy game, and while it would be unlikely that your bait would be taken amidst such plenty, you can transport them to areas where they might not be so concentrated. Many species will find them attractive, notably chub. Although I have never done so, I do not see why elvers should not be frozen while they are plentiful and used much in the same way as the sea fisherman's sandeels.

§113 Caterpillars, slugs etc

One of the reasons that maggots, bread and so on are popular baits is because they are readily and abundantly available; no commercial enterprise, so far as I know, is producing slugs or caterpillars for fishermen – but this far from marks them down as poor baits. There are hundreds and hundreds of different sorts of creepies and crawlies of all colours and shapes, and I have often tried chance finds on my hook with varied success. Similarly, there are many water creatures – caddis larvae, beetle grubs and so on – which are always worth a try if you find them. Anglers rarely hunt now for the docken grub – a small white beetle larva which eats the root of the dock plant – but anglers of an older generation found them extremely useful. If you have the time and the patience it is well worth exploring these possibilities.

§114 Mussels

There are five or six species of freshwater mussel, all of which are included in fish diets, especially the tench, carp and barbel. The largest mussel, *Anodonta cygnea*, is commonly known as the swan mussel, and it is found mainly in still or slow-running water. It isn't commonly known, however, that the presence of these mussels is a clear indication that there are fish in a water – the young, free swimming stage has to latch onto a 'host' fish in order to survive, and later in life it stops being a parasite and drops to the bottom to lead an independent life. The swan

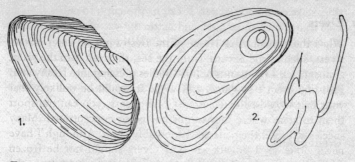

Fig. 84 (§114) 1 – swan mussel; 2 – pearl mussel. The soft interior is removed with a sharp knife for hook-bait.

mussel, with brown, corrugated, hinged shells lined with bright mother-of-pearl, grows to about six inches, sometimes more. It can be found in lakes and in the margins of slower rivers, where it can be gathered with a rake or, in shallows, picked up by hand. A knife is needed to force apart the shells, and to cut the flesh from the inside. This can be presented on a size 6 hook (Fig. 84) for tench, barbel and carp, and smaller fragments will catch roach, rudd and crucian carp. Chopped mussel can be added to ground-bait, especially if whole mussels are being used as hook bait, and it is a good idea to add some smashed shell fragments to ground-bait as an extra attractor.

Another distinctive mussel is the pearl mussel, which has a darker and more kidney-shaped shell than the swan mussel, and which lives in faster-flowing water, favouring neutral and acid (soft) water areas rather than the alkali waters which the swan mussel prefers. This animal can occasionally produce small pearls in the mantle, a fact which the Romans were well aware of – they transferred specimens to a large number of British waters where they were previously absent. They should be treated in exactly the same way as swan mussel for hook bait and groundbait.

§115 Meats

In recent years cooked and raw meats have been used with some success for chub, barbel and carp. Raw sausage-meat is excellent, although it tends to disintegrate quickly in strong flows – tinned luncheon-meat, which is tougher because it is prepared with gelatine, stays on a hook better. It can be pre-cut into cubes (half an inch to one inch square, depending on the size of the fish you are after) and a small amount should be added to groundbait, if used as hook bait.

Bacon (and bacon rind), either raw or cooked, has taken many good barbel, particularly in the lower Thames, and it is also a very good chub bait.

§116 Groundbaits

Quantities: As a general rule you will use less groundbait on a pleasure fishing outing than you would for a match; in a match all other anglers will be groundbaiting against you, and you will want to be sure that you have sufficient at least to equal them – even if, as is sometimes the case, it will pay you to groundbait more lightly than the bombardment that is going on around you. Having said that, let me make it quite clear that you need to groundbait heavily or lightly according to the fish species you are after: heavy-feeders are bream, tench, barbel and chub (big carp don't often feed in a shoal, and consequently you wouldn't need to groundbait for them on a large scale). Roach, rudd and dace respond to light, loose feeding or cloud groundbait. You also need to take into account the length of time you will be fishing – while ten pounds or so of coarse groundbait (dry weight) will be sufficient to hold a large shoal of bream for four or so hours' fishing, you will need a much greater quantity for an all-day or all-night session.

The recipes below all add up to around twelve pounds of groundbait, a happy medium between the quantities required for pleasure and match fishing – you can add or subtract materials *pro rata* for greater or lesser amounts.

Breadcrumb base: Dried crumbs are sold by many tackle dealers, usually in coarse, medium and fine grades – another source is your own kitchen, where saved up crusts and other stale bread can be 'bisked' in the oven and ground in a domestic mincer, then sieved with garden equipment for grades. Bakers sometimes sell off stale bread very cheaply. Crumbs can be used on their own, using the fine grade for cloud. However, you will see that I have advised additional ingredients and various treatments to improve on the crumb base, and they can make a good deal of difference to results. Whether cloud or bottom groundbait, you should aim to get as much hook bait (or pinkies, squatts etc.) as possible bound into the bas . Never add maggots anywhere but on the bankside, though, or you will find them crawling away. If you are using bread bait, then you should not add any other baits to the base.

Colour: I find it a mistake to use pure white groundbait, mainly because fish are unsettled swimming over a very light patch on a dark river or lake bed. I try to get as much brown bread as possible into my groundbait, and any white that I use I first bake to a golden colour in my oven – this removes any grease that might make the individual grains float besides toning down the groundbait colour.

Pre-treatment of base: Whether cloud or bottom groundbait, it pays to soak seventy-five per cent of the amount you will use, overnight – using the remainder as a stiffening agent in the morning before you go fishing, or on the bankside. Even with very fine crumbs you will find that some particles swell to quite a large size, and so if you make your base into a sort of porridge you can remove large pieces and any lumps.

§117 Cloud

Commercial brands of cloud groundbait are made with crumbs and small quantities of silver sand, which encourages the bread particles to separate once they enter the water. I don't like the use of sand, which I feel might be 'inhaled' by fish and could damage their delicate gills. A substitute, equally as good, is fine ground rice added at the waterside to a soaked, crumb base. It pays to pre-soak your crumbs (keeping aside twenty-five per cent for stiffening) and pass them through a fine sieve to make sure that there are no lumps:

10 lb fine breadcrumbs (dry)
$1\frac{1}{2}$–2 lb fine ground rice
Liberal quantity of hookbait samples
2 or 3 dessert-spoons full of soft brown sugar (optional – see optional additives below)

Method: Soak 7 lb groundbait base (adding crumbs to water). Add rice and other ingredients at bankside to form crumbly mixture which can be packed into loose balls with light hand pressure. Use for rudd, roach and dace in still and slow-moving water.

§118 Medium

This is what I would describe as 'regular' grade groundbait, which can be used hard-packed for flowing water or loose-packed so that it will break up on contact with the surface in still and slow-flowing water:

7 lb medium crumbs
3–5 lb fine crumbs
Liberal hookbait samples
Optional additives

Method: Soak the medium crumbs only, adding them to water in a bowl, pouring off any surplus after a couple of hours. Add fine crumbs, hookbait and additives at waterside. Use for all bait-taking species.

§119 Heavy

Heavyweight groundbait should only be used for creating a bottom carpet. The 'bulk' can be chosen from a variety of materials such as soaked stale bread (broken up by hand, with the crusts removed – they will otherwise float to the surface), bran (which provides a good deal of bulk for little weight – or cost!), coarse-grade breadcrumbs, or fine chicken meal.

7 lb bulk (see above)
5 lb medium breadcrumbs
Liberal hook bait

Method: Soak base, adding crumbs at bankside.
Use for tench and bream especially in still water.

§120 Additives

From time to time anglers have fads about 'special' ingredients which are infallible fish-attractors. Aniseed used to be one such, but it is now not very widely used. I prefer not to add anything to my baits, with a couple of exceptions. One is sugar – I think this appeals to bream and carp in particular, but I do use it sparingly in all groundbaits. The other is mud – the sort of fine, dark silt which makes a long-lasting stain when you disturb the bottom of a river or lake near the bank. I find it very useful to add this to my groundbait when the water is clear – I believe fish are drawn to bottom disturbances where ooze-living creatures might be exposed, and they will often swim a considerable distance to investigate a mud-taint. Also, once inside the mud-cloud they are less cautious than they would be in open, clear water.

If you want to try aniseed, or fennel and caraway which have similar scents, you can buy essence forms or boil the actual seeds, adding the water, with the seeds strained-off, to your soaking groundbait.

'Coarse fishing' is a blanket term – one that embraces many facets
of angling. The approaches which one would use for, say, the
roach, a shy, retiring creature which lives on worms, vegetable
matter and insects, and the pike, a bold predator and often a
scavenger, are quite different – nevertheless one can 'float fish' for
either species, offering a worm or a maggot in the case of the
roach, and either a live or dead fish for the pike (on markedly
stronger tackle, of course).

To avoid confusion it is best to begin by looking at the techniques which are useful to anglers seeking either bait-taking
species or predators, the main one being casting. Next, the main
bait-fishing methods – float fishing, legering – can be explained
separately before looking finally at spinning, livebaiting and
deadbaiting for predatory and scavenging fish. When you reach
the descriptions of livebaiting and deadbaiting you can hark back
to the principles governing float fishing and legering which apply
even to these larger baits.

§121 Have an objective

It helps always to aim for a particular objective when you set out
to fish; this might be to catch a big roach, a heavy bag of bream,
or a large pike – it really doesn't matter, so long as you plan
around your aims and avoid arriving at the water at a loss as to
what you are after. You might change your options later in the
day, especially if you notice that some other species is offering
a better chance of sport. Try to keep these options open by
carrying a wide enough selection of tackle and bait to make at
least one change of mind – say from float fishing to legering – a
real possibility. The alternative, if you have struck poor sport

even though well-prepared for a particular species, is to change swims until you find a good pocket of whatever fish you are after.

§122 Approaching the water

Eagerness increases as you near the bankside of a river, canal or lake, and the temptation to rush through the preliminaries of settling yourself into a swim and setting up your tackle is strong. Keenness is forgivable, yet a clumsy and hurried approach to the waterside might not easily win the affections of the fish you hope to catch.

Try, if you are fishing from the bank, to approach with caution. Select a swim with an eye to your own comfort as much as for the likely fish-lies within reach. By this I do not mean a well-worn and obviously popular swim: keep an eye open for sites which might have been overlooked by other anglers, yet which present no obvious disadvantages. Fish are quite likely to be suspicious in the area of a well-used swim, and you will gain an advantage by tackling them from areas which they do not expect to be occupied.

If you know exactly where you are going to fish, keep disturbances to a minimum by staying well away from the bank until you draw level with your spot, and then creep towards it, keeping your footfalls as light as possible. If you are fishing from a punt or a boat, board carefully, taking care not to drop anything or scuff the bottom boards. Row or pole to your swim with the minimum of hurry and commotion.

The next task is setting up your tackle, but before you do so you might like to consider groundbaiting.

§123 Groundbaiting

While many anglers prefer to groundbait immediately before fishing, some like to wait and try for whatever fish are already in their swim in order to gauge how heavily or how lightly they should feed them to keep them interested – the rule of groundbaiting, which means offering bait to hold fish in your swim, is that you should never feed so heartily that you satiate the appetites of your fish.

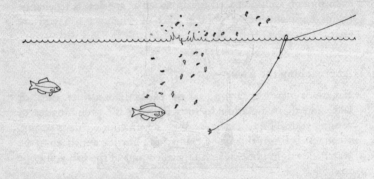

Fig. 85 Loose-fed maggots hold fish in the swim so long as the 'little and often' rule is kept.

With some species of fish this rule allows you to be quite liberal – bream and tench can often clean up a good deal of groundbait without losing their appetites. Other species such as the roach will respond better to frequent, small offerings of maggots or some other bait. If you are fishing for predators, there is no reason why you should not groundbait to draw small fish into your swim.

The main types of groundbaiting are loose-feeding – frequent small offerings of whatever bait you are using on your hook – and groundbaiting proper, with samples of hook bait added to a quantity of soaked cereal crumbs which will either crumble on contact with the water and create a slow-sinking cloud, or sink to the bottom to break up gradually, releasing fragments of bait. Some recipes for groundbaits are given in Chapter 14.

Loose-feeding: 'Little and often' is the rule with loose-feeding (Fig. 85). Your aim is to attract fish in the first instance, and then perhaps to draw them closer and closer to you with tiny amounts of bait. Half a dozen maggots at a time, or as many grains of hempseed, barley or whatever other bait you are using, will generally be sufficient unless the shoal you attract is very large. You should

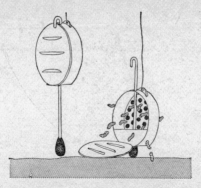

Fig. 86 The bait-dropper is a small box which can be attached to the end of the line – it is filled with maggots or other bait, closed, and secured with a small weighted plunger which releases the lid and scatters the bait on contact with the bottom of the swim.

keep amounts like this going into the water every few minutes, perhaps between every cast. Small baits such as maggots or grains cannot of course be thrown any great distance without a strong wind behind you, and if you wish to loose-feed a distant swim, you might consider using a catapult. Try to avoid scattering loose-feed in a wide area; keep it falling in a close pattern around your float, in still water, or at the same distance from the bank as your float if fishing in flowing water. The bait-dropper (Fig. 86) is useful for loose-feeding in deep swims.

Cloud baiting: By wrapping samples of your hook offering in a soaked, cereal base you can form easily thrown balls to reach a fair distance out. The cloud-type cereal base (§117) should be fine-ground but not binding, or if you wish you can use coarser material so long as it is well-saturated. The idea is to get the groundbait balls to break as they hit the water surface (Fig. 87), forming a cloud of suspended particles containing pieces of more substantial bait. Replenish this cloud as it settles to the bottom or moves away downriver.

Groundbaiting for bottom-feeders: In this instance you want to create a carpet of cereal and bait offerings (Fig. 88) to keep a shoal of fish feeding in your swim (§118, 119). In still water, you can

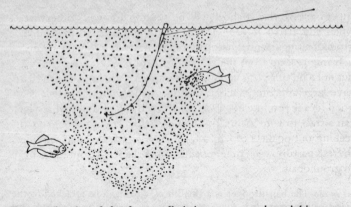

Fig. 87 The aim of cloud groundbait is to create a slow-sinking area of fine particles which keep the fish occupied hunting through the murk for larger good particles.

Fig. 88 Heavier groundbait is used to make a fish-holding food carpet on the bed of the river or lake.

pack balls of groundbait loosely so that they break on contact with the water and fall to the bottom. In flowing water, however, the faster the current, the tighter you must pack the balls to get them quickly to the bottom – if they break in mid-water they may well be swept away, taking your shoal with them.

Pre-baiting: For some species of fish, notably tench, bream and carp, you can often bait for several days in advance of a fishing trip to ensure that a shoal will be waiting for you; otherwise, when you arrive at your fishing venue you start from scratch, groundbaiting in anticipation of a shoal moving into your swim.

It might seem from the above that groundbaiting is essential, but not a bit of it. It is certainly advisable for the sorts of fish that have large appetites, such as bream, and I think also that it is a good idea if you intend to sit in one place and find out what you can attract to your swim. But you can, also, cover some ground seeking out pockets of fish and catching a few of them, moving to fresh pastures each time sport becomes slack, without resorting to groundbait.

§124 Efficient layout

If you are going to fish in one spot for any length of time, much depends on having everything you need immediately to hand (Fig. 89). Arrange your seat with a clear view of the swim, site

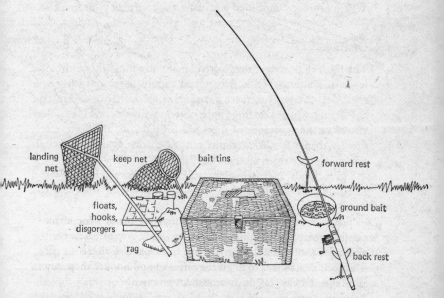

landing net keep net bait tins forward rest

floats, hooks, disgorgers ground bait

rag back rest

Fig. 89 (§124) A good layout of tackle on the bank saves you hunting around for vital equipment – keep everything in reach from a seated position.

your rod-rests, and then thread up your rod and decide on the appropriate end-tackle. Place it aside in the rod-rests and arrange your tackle and bait containers around you (remembering that maggots and worms need to be kept in shade) so that they can be reached without stretching. Make particularly sure that your disgorger is easy to find – I usually stick mine upright in the ground to one side. If you are moving about, you might like to string your disgorger on a cord around your neck, or keep it in a particular pocket; you might also like to hold your bait in a pouch which you can sling around your neck.

Always set up your landing net before you begin fishing – if you catch a good fish you might find it impossible to put your net together while you are playing it. You can use the landing net to hold down or push aside bankside vegetation if this impairs your view of the swim, but do make sure that the handle is always in reach. You can also fix a bank-stick to your keepnet if you are using one – you do not need to put it into the water at this stage, but having it ready will save time when you catch a fish. With all this accomplished you can make ready for your first cast.

§125 Casting

The most important thing to remember about casting with float, leger or spinning tackle is that you should never have to use a great deal of energy to reach a required spot. Distance depends on the weight you are casting; light objects will not travel far unless you have the assistance of the wind behind you, and so to reach further than a few rod-lengths out, or to cast against the wind, you will have to step up the weight.

Three kinds of casting are suitable for most coarse-fishing situations: the forward-swing cast, the side-swing cast, and the overhead cast.

The side-swing cast (Fig. 90) is mainly suitable for shallow depths when float fishing, since your hook might catch on the ground when you hold the rod out to one side if there are more than four or five feet of line between float and hook. For spinners and leger tackle you do not need to worry about this problem. Assuming that you are right handed, you should be holding the rod with the right hand grasping the butt of the rod either above, or just forward of, the reel, with your index finger crooked about

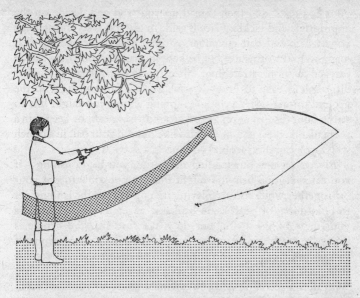

Fig. 90 Side-swing cast – the rod is first held parallel to the bank, and then swung gently out to the fore, where the line is released. A good cast to use under overhanging branches.

the line and the bale-arm of the reel open. Your forearm should rest along the remainder of the butt, and the rod can either be held fully out to your right, parallel to the water, or across your body pointing to the left. The rod is then swung steadily, but not forcefully, to point to the front, and the line is released from your crooked finger as the tackle begins to swing out across the water. Any attempt to force this type of cast will result in loss of accuracy, and it is mainly suitable for casting short distances from banks that are not too overgrown.

The forward-swing cast (Fig. 91) is suitable for deeper water if you are float fishing. The rod is held close to your body, pointing upwards into the air at about thirty degrees from the horizontal, with the tackle hanging in front of you. Your hand and arm should be in position as before, with the reel bale-arm open. Let the tackle swing slightly towards you by raising the rod a little, and then lower the tip, pushing forwards and upwards with your casting arm to impel the tackle forward. Release the line as the

Fig. 91 Forward swing – begin with rod held high (top) then dip and thrust forward and up at the same time to impel tackle outwards. Useful where short distances only are necessary, and where vegetation makes a side-swing cast impossible.

tackle swings forward. Again, this is not a suitable cast for achieving distance, although it is more useful than the side-swing for casting from a snaggy overgrown bank, or through restricted gaps between reeds.

The overhead cast (Fig. 92) is suitable for both sitting and standing; it can be a one-handed cast for short range work or, if you use two hands, you can reach greater distances or cast against the wind. You may, if you wish, use float-fishing tackle with lengths of line between float and hook as long, or longer, than the length of your rod, but should there be any sort of snag on the bank behind you it will be better to use a sliding float instead. With long distances between float and hook, you will first have to flick float, line and hook onto the water in front of you, preparatory to drawing it into the air to stream out behind you before making the forward flick. Otherwise, begin the cast with the leger weight, float or spinner about ten inches from the tip of the rod.

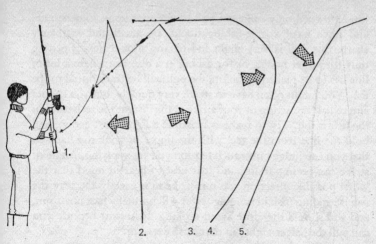

Fig. 92 Overhead cast – begin (1) with rod upright, swing it slightly backwards (2) and begin drive forward as the tackle swings behind. Release line as rod, under pressure, comes well to the fore, and follow through with rod pointing at the tackle as it flies through the air.

Hold the rod pointing in the air in front of you at about thirty degrees from the horizontal. Grasp the butt, with forearm lying against the lower part, as in the casts above, and a finger crooked about the line. If you are making a strong cast, grasp or restrain the extreme end of the butt with your other hand. Draw the rod back over your shoulder, allowing the tackle to swing behind you, and then push the rod firmly forwards and release the line as the tackle swings to the fore. Line the direction of your forward swing with the spot to which you wish to cast, and if there are side winds alter this angle slightly into the wind to allow for your tackle being blown off course.

The easiest mistake to make with the cast is allowing the rod to slope backwards too far when you take it over your shoulder – a shade behind the vertical is sufficient.

§126 Striking

Over-forceful striking is a common fault, and beginners especially are prone to smashing their line on the strike or, perhaps worse, yanking the fish bodily out of the water or pulling off a piece of lip. You need only sufficient pull to get your hook to penetrate, and since most coarse-fishing hooks are small and extremely sharp, this pull is very slight indeed and should be stepped up only for larger hooks, or for fishing at a distance where a lot of line has to be picked up before the pull will be transmitted to the fish. You might often have to strike very quickly, but you should aim to halt the action of your strike at the instant the resistance of the fish is felt. Try to make your strike a light wrist-action, and hold the line from the reel with the finger of your rod-hand so that you can judge how much tension you are applying. Angle of strike can be important, and it is best to bear in mind that the worst possible direction you can strike in is exactly the way the fish is heading (fish in running water will normally face upstream, and you should therefore avoid striking upstream) because you can pull the bait straight out of the fish's mouth.

§127 Playing a fish

Small fish well below the breaking strain of your line may be bullied ashore easily, but a large fish needs careful handling. Your first objective is to draw it away from the shoal, so that other fish are not panicked. Quite often, the fish will rush off on its own anyway, but thereafter try your utmost to stop it running back to the region of the shoal. These initial rushes are frequently the strongest runs a hooked fish will make, and they should always be given their head provided they are not running into obvious dangers such as tree roots or weedbeds. If they are, the most effective control is to lay the rod parallel to the water and pull sideways, urging the head away from the snag. However, if the fish is in clear water and well away from the shoal, it should be played with the rod held upright, so that the curving rod is absorbing the force of tugs. Never, never let the line fall slack; if you do, the hook hold may loosen. Your reel-tension should be set so that it gives line whenever the rod is pulled beyond its most efficient curve (normally when the tip is pulled round at ninety degrees from the butt), but reel-tension can frequently change under pressure, and you should keep an eye on the rod-tip and untighten the reel-tension nut if line is not being given quickly

Fig. 93 (§127) Netting a fish – the landing net should be submerged and the fish drawn over it. Then you can raise net to secure the fish.

enough. As the fish tires, you can tighten the tension nut and bring it under stronger and stronger control.

Be extra careful, however – and prepare to give line – when you are bringing a fish you believe to be well-tired to the bank for netting. Quite often it will shy when it sees the net, or you, and will find a reserve of strength for another run.

Normally, a fish comes to the surface and rolls over when it has tired, and it is an easy matter to push the landing net (or gaff) under the water (Fig. 93), draw the fish over it, and pull it ashore (don't lift, landing nets are not designed to stand this).

In fast water, however, if a fish tires well-out in the river, it may surface and be swept downstream before you can draw it to the bank. It will be useless to try to coax it back upstream to you, and you will have to follow it downstream – bank growth permitting – drawing it gently ashore to your net as you go.

§128 Handling fish

Be kind to your fish once it is on the bank. Handle it with wet hands, or a wet rag, so that you do not dislodge scales or wipe off any of its mucus covering, and strive to get it into a keepnet or back into the water as quickly as possible. If you wish to weigh it with a spring balance, unscrew the net part of your landing net and put the fish into it, fastening the hook of the balance onto the net rim (Fig. 94). When you put the fish back, you can deduct the weight of the net from the overall figure you have obtained. Never, never place the balance hook under the fish's chin or behind its gill covers.

A word about keepnets: place them, wherever possible, in deep water, and, in a river, try to arrange them so that some current flows through them. On bright, hot days, the net should be sited in a shady position, or pushed under the shelter of lily pads.

Don't ever return fish by throwing them back into the water. If you are using a keepnet, push the open mouth under the surface and up-end it so that the fish roll gently back. Very large fish which have become extremely tired may have to be held for a while, head to current, until they become strong enough to swim off.

Fig. 94 (§128) Fish should not be weighed by suspending them from the hook of a spring balance – weigh them in your landing net or keepnet instead, afterwards deducting the weight of the net from the total.

§129 **Float fishing**

Visually, float fishing is a most exciting form of angling, and in running water there is the additional pleasure of controlling the movements of a float, guiding it and your tackle towards likely fish lies.

There seems, however, to be a bewildering range of floats, and in order to understand which pattern you should choose to fish a particular place and combat the prevailing conditions, it is useful to break the subject down.

The first consideration is the amount of weight you wish the float to carry in order to cast to your spot; besides casting weight, you also have to use weight to take your bait quickly down to the levels you want to fish. By and large, the weights most often used in float fishing are split shot (§16), in the range of sizes recommended in the checklists in the previous section. Thus, 'shotting' is the term generally used to describe the addition of weights to a float-fishing tackle-rig. When you have determined the shotting to suit your location, this will show what size of float you should be using – depending, of course, on the buoyancy of the material from which your float is made. Because floats are made from a variety of materials with differing buoyancies, it is best to think of size in terms of shotting capacity (i.e. overall buoyancy) rather than actual dimensions, since a four-inch float made of balsa wood can carry far more shot than a float of the same size made from denser cane.

The next consideration is the shape of float which will behave best in your swim, taking its distance, depth, and the weather into account. Here, it is fair to say that there are only three, basic patterns from which all float designs have grown (Fig. 98) and a beginner should equip himself with a small selection of each of these patterns before exploring variations in design – the selection will cover him or her adequately for most water and weather conditions. For methods of attaching floats to line, see Chapter 6 (§14).

Shotting for casting: Remember that you want to accomplish casts with minimal effort, and that besides choosing sufficient weight to reach a particular distance, you also have to make sure that it will 'cock' the float – i.e. weight the float so that only the bite-registering tip will show above the surface of the water. For fishing close at hand in still water you need very little weight – sufficient to sink your bait and perhaps hold it in place on the bottom – and you can therefore use small, low-buoyancy floats and concentrate on arranging your shot purely for bait presentation. When you step up float size, to carry more shot to assist casting, it is necessary to bunch together the heavier shot so that their combined impetus overcomes the weight of the float, and any other weights (bait included), drawing them through the air with ease. Spacing these shot would prevent a long cast; individual shot do not have the concentrated impetus of bunched, or 'bulk shot' to use the proper term. They are likely to pull against each other in the air, and could well lead to tangles.

Ideally, bulk shot should be added to the line immediately below the float, since this is the heaviest and bulkiest object which the shot have to lead through the air. But there are other considerations, and you might have to place your bulk shot halfway between float and hook, or even fairly close to the hook, for purposes of bait presentation.

Shotting for presentation: In still water it is usually possible to fish with the bulk casting-shot immediately below the float, and a small amount of extra weight to take the bait quickly to the depth you are fishing at. If you are fishing on the bottom, you might find that surface drift or wind drags your tackle out of position, and you will then have to concentrate more weight towards the hook to hold it in place (Fig. 95).

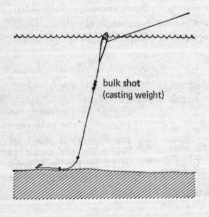

bulk shot
(casting weight)

Fig. 95 In still water it is usually possible to place the main shot directly under the float.

In moving water, the current will easily push along light shot, and will have less effect on the denser, large or bunched shot. You want your bait to reach fishing depth before it travels too far downriver, and if you have bulk shot on your tackle for casting you can move it closer to the hook to accomplish this – the faster the water, the further down it should go (Fig. 96). If you are not casting, of course, you can space out all your shot along the line between float and hook to produce a gentle curve with hook preceding float. Again, the faster the water, the more you will need to concentrate weight close to the hook.

The moving-water shotting arrangements above are for presenting the bait in the normal 'trotting' position, i.e. bait preceding float downriver. If you wish your bait to drag along the bottom instead, with the float preceding the bait, you will have to make the line between your float and the bottom-most shot longer than the depth of the swim (Fig. 97).

Float types (Fig. 98): The first of the three basic float patterns is the quill, i.e. a feather quill fished with the thick-end up and the thin-end down in the water. Its parallel is the 'stick' float, a slim piece of balsa, or some other wood, tapering from a wide section at, or near the top, to a thin lower section. These floats are more buoyant at the top than at their thin lower sections, and they are therefore suitable for moving water where turbulence tends to pull downwards on the tackle. However, since this type of float has a small surface area, making it easy to pull sideways through

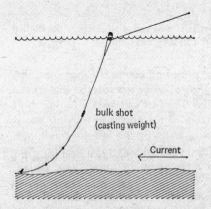

bulk shot
(casting weight)

Current

Fig. 96 In a current, the placing of the bulk casting shot lower down the line helps the tackle to sink quickly and saves the bait from being swept upwards.

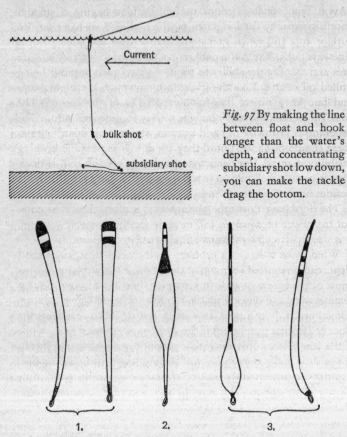

Fig. 97 By making the line between float and hook longer than the water's depth, and concentrating subsidiary shot low down, you can make the tackle drag the bottom.

Fig. 98 Three basic float designs: 1 quill and stick floats; 2 the bodied or Avon float; 3 antenna float and reversed quill.

the water, it could easily be pulled off course if fished some distance out across a river, tending to move towards the angler even with slight checks on the line. They are suitable for fishing short distances out and downstream of the angler in moving water. They can also be used for still-water fishing in calm conditions. These floats are normally fixed top-and-bottom to the line. They should be shotted until all but the barest tip necessary for visibility shows above the water.

For trotting further out, or well across a river, the bodied or

'Avon type' float is more useful. Besides having a greater shotting capacity for longer casts, the bodied float has a largish surface area and much greater resistance than the stick float to sideways pulls. The Avon pattern can be fluted to increase surface area and amplify the ability to travel on a set path without being pulled off course. Like the stick float, however, the higher top-end buoyancy resists the downward pulls of turbulence. The thin, tip section above the body is merely for bite indication. The fastening is normally top and bottom, as for stick floats. Again, these should be shotted until they are as low as possible keeping visibility in mind. For deep water, a sliding version of this float-type is useful; it should have a ring or eye at the top of the body besides one at the bottom end.

The third basic float-type, the antenna, is often chosen to combat the effects of wind on still or slow-moving waters, although it is also a particularly sensitive float to use in calm conditions.

Wind alone is less of a problem than surface-drift, since most floats can be shotted so low that their profile above water escapes most of the effects of a blow. However, in still and slow-moving waters, wind can quickly set the top few inches of water moving, sometimes at quite a pace. In a river, this drift can accelerate the float faster than the current if the wind blows downstream, while if the wind blows upstream and does not produce a marked drift, it can slow down the top layer of surface water, pushing the float against the current and checking the tackle so that it moves only slowly downstream. The antenna is a bodied float with a long, thin tip section. The body is shotted well below the surface area, leaving only the thin tip emerging through the drift area and out into the wind. Being thin, there is less surface area in the tip for the wind or drift to get a hold and your tackle can be held in place more easily.

Antennas are usually fished bottom-end only, and there are sliding versions with a ring or eye at the bottom for the line to pass through. They can, however, be fished top-and-bottom as a trotting float in moving water, and the float design referred to as a 'waggler' is an ordinary antenna fished in this manner – the tip tends to wag from side to side as the line is checked. It is normally quite difficult to trot with an antenna float fastened at the bottom only, since very slight checks on the line will tug against the bottom of the float and submerge it, registering a false bite. With currents any faster than a gentle draw, antennas are best used as wagglers.

The reversed quill, i.e. a feather quill fished with the thin-end up and the thick-end low in the water, also serves the same purpose as the antenna. Reversed quills make light, sensitive floats which are particularly suitable for fishing canals and drainage channels.

Ironing out problems: You may well run into a couple of snags which are quite easily treated. If you are fishing with a fairly heavy antenna float and a light line, especially at distance, there may be a danger of smashing the line as you strike against the weight of the float; similarly, you may find yourself having to strike very hard in order to shift the float before the effects of your strike are transmitted to the hook. In these circumstances, fasten your float by passing the line once through the bottom ring only, and allow it to slide freely on a six-or-seven-inch section of line, between two firmly fastened, small split shot (Fig. 99). When you strike, the energy of your pull will pass through your float rather than against it.

Float creep is a major menace with top-and-bottom fastened floats, either double-rubber or rubber and ring. Each strike tends to nudge the float nearer and nearer the hook. This is easily remedied by nipping a small split shot onto the line immediately below the bottom rubber or ring of the float (Fig. 100).

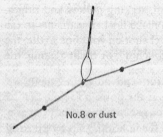

No.8 or dust

Fig. 99 Spaced shot either side of float-eye allow you to strike 'through' the float.

Finding the depth of your swim: Even if you wish to fish well-clear of the bottom of a river or lake, it is useful to explore the depth of your swim to discover banks and gulleys which might attract fish. In running water, knowledge of the nature of the river bed

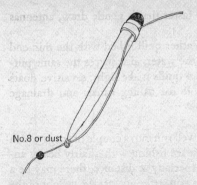

No.8 or dust

Fig. 100 A small shot pinched onto the line just under a quill or stick float stops it creeping down the line when you strike hard or retrieve quickly.

becomes more important, since besides finding likely fish-holding features you will want your tackle to travel safely away from prominent ridges or weedbeds on which it might snag (by checking your float you can make the tackle lift upwards over such snags – see Fig. 113). It is possible, in most instances, to make a general guess at the depth of your swim and set your float accordingly, moving the float up the line if it does not seem to touch bottom, or down if it fails to cock because some of the leads are lying on the bottom. However a quicker and more accurate way of finding depth is to attach a plummet lead to your hook (Fig. 101). An alternative to a plummet is a swanshot lightly squeezed onto your hook. The weighty plummet or swanshot falls swiftly to the bottom, and it will not take many minutes to adjust your float to the overall depth of the swim, or to explore it for a considerable way downstream, seeking gulleys and ridges. Once you have done this, you can make final adjustments to the float's position and arrange the lower shot on your line so that the bait will be presented above, just touching, or trailing along, the bottom.

§130 **Float methods for still water**

So far, I have set one side of the scene leading up to practical fishing, and it is now necessary to add the vital ingredients of water and fish. I'll begin with a fairly typical lake. The main, bait-taking species I would expect it to hold would be bream, perch, roach, rudd, tench, carp and perhaps crucian carp.

I would expect bream, tench, carp and crucian carp to feed

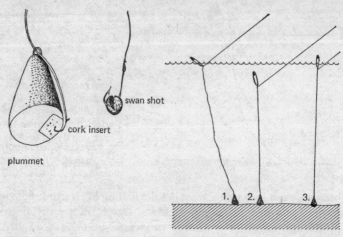

Fig. 101 The plummet is a conical lead with a cork insert for attaching the hook. In use (1) too much line between float and hook will stop the float cocking and too little (2) will sink the float immediately. In 3, the hook will just touch bottom when the float is loaded to cock.

mainly on the bottom, perch and roach either at mid-water or on the bottom, and rudd mainly at the top of the water. However, angling is full of surprises and you shouldn't be disconcerted if these species behave out of character from time to time.

Tackling the bottom-feeders first: all the species mentioned above are fairly heavy feeders and, having chosen your swim, some groundbait will be an advantage. I would normally look for a swim with a depth of about seven feet a few rod-lengths out, one that doesn't shallow too much near to the bank. The sort of bottom features I would like to find with a plummet search, would be the edge of a shelf with water dropping away to deep levels, or some sort of depression a foot or so deeper than the rest of the swim. I would place the groundbait on the edge (but never *over* such a ledge), or into the depression, aiming to make a patch on the bottom a couple of yards square.

My choice of float would be determined by the conditions; in a fairly sheltered bay, for instance, I could use an ordinary quill float. Fishing from a more exposed bank, where wind and drift would push a quill float out of position, I would use an antenna. The tackle arrangement, however, would be the same for either

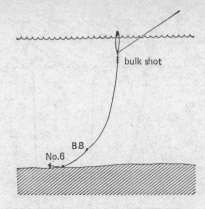

Fig. 102 (§130) Laying-on rig – expect lift bites or submerging float (still water).

float (Fig. 102). This style is known as 'laying on', i.e. the baited hook lies on the bottom, with at least one shot anchoring the float. The distance of the line between float and bottom shot is greater than the depth of the swim and, with the rod placed in the rests, the float is gently wound back towards the bank until the line follows a straight path from rod-tip to hook, and is under tension, so that the slightest pull will dislodge the lower shot resting on the bottom. Thus, if the bait is pulled away from the angler by a taking fish, the float will submerge, while if the bait is lifted, releasing the tension on the lower shot, more of the float will emerge through the surface ('lift bite').

To shot for more purposeful lift bites, move enough weight down to the position of the bottom shot to pull down an inch or more of float. When these weights are raised as a fish takes the bait, the float should react by lifting well out of the water (Fig. 103).

I always try to have a 'tail' – the length of line between the bottom shot and hook – of at least two feet when fishing on the bottom in still water. This ensures that the fish can pick up the bait and move freely for a short distance before it feels the resistance of the shot and float. However, if you find that fish are behaving shyly, you have the choice of making the tail longer to give them more freedom, or shorter, so that bites are registered more quickly. You would expect to strike more quickly with a short tail, giving the fish less chance to drop the bait.

For mid-water feeders, mainly roach, perch, and occasionally

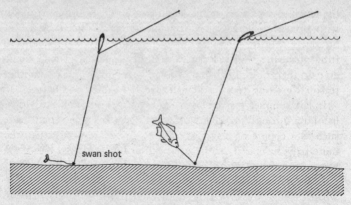

Fig. 103 Still-water, lift-bite rig – as fish picks up bait float will rise.

rudd, the weather again influences the choice of float. Establishing swim depth is important, since it is best to aim for the bait to sink slowly and come to rest on, or very near, the bottom. If the fish are feeding fairly close to the bottom, your shot can be arranged so that the bait is taken swiftly to this region (Fig. 104). Once the bottom shot has come to rest, the tail (three feet or more), which is unweighted, allows the bait to sink slowly through the feeding area. With cloud groundbaiting, one occasionally finds that fish spread upwards through the cloud and might be expected to take a bait before it reaches even halfway to the bottom. In this instance it is useful to strive to fish 'on the drop', i.e. to space out your shot so that as each one swings into position under the float, the float sinks a little (Fig. 105). Note the time it takes for each shot to come to rest, by counting between each interval, and strike at any interruption in the pattern which might mean that a fish has taken the bait and is preventing one of the shot from sinking.

Surface-feeders like the rudd require very little lead on the line; in fact an ideal arrangement is to fish with a self-weighted float, or a normal float with the cocking shot bunched immediately underneath it, and a tail of two to four feet which allows the baited hook to sink slowly and naturally through the water.

Cloud baiting rather than bottom-blanketing groundbait is best for the above two methods, and it may even be better in some instances merely to loose feed. One method occasionally

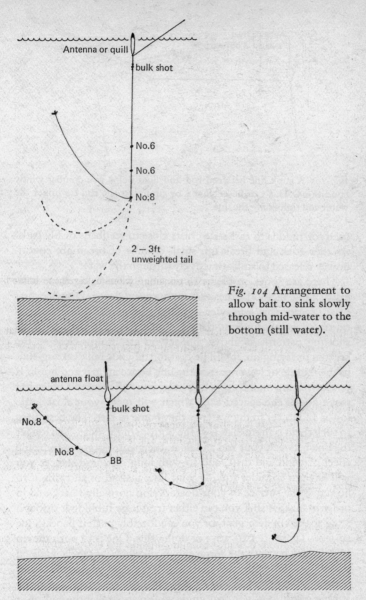

Antenna or quill

bulk shot

No.6

No.6

No.8

2 – 3ft
unweighted tail

Fig. 104 Arrangement to
allow bait to sink slowly
through mid-water to the
bottom (still water).

antenna float

bulk shot

No.8

No.8

BB

Fig. 105 Arrangement for fishing 'on the drop'. Float sinks progressively as shots swing into place and settle under float.

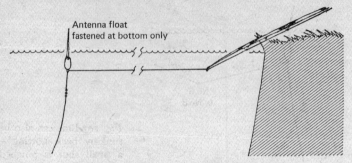

Antenna float
fastened at bottom only

Fig. 106 A sunk line between rod and float helps you combat windy conditions. This can be achieved by plunging the rod-tip under the water and tightening the line.

used for rudd is to cast stale crusts close to reedbeds or lily pads. As they soak and break up, small crumbs of bread are continuously released to sink attractively through the water.

There are some problems to consider when using these basically simple methods; these are distance and depth. Distance, first of all, means that a heavier float must be used, with some concentrated weight to assist casting. You can keep to the same basic shotting patterns as above, but if you are fishing close to the bottom or laying on, it will be best to add your bulk casting-shot to the middle or lower part of the line between float and hook. If you are fishing on the drop, however, you will want this bulk shot to be above the spaced shot which will make your float settle lower and lower in the water as they come to rest. The best place to tuck them is immediately at the bottom of the float. The longer the line between your rod and float, the greater is going to be the effect of wind and drift, and so with long casting-distances you will have to consider sinking your line, instead of allowing it to lie across the surface to your float. Nylon normally floats, and in order to make it sink you can either treat it by rubbing it through a rag soaked in detergent, or you can forcibly push it beneath the surface. There are two ways of doing this. One is to push the tip of your rod beneath the surface immediately your tackle lands on the water, tightening up the line to the float under the water before pulling the rod out to place it in the rod-rest – in really stormy conditions, you may angle your rests so that the rod-tip is held under the water while you are fishing (Fig. 106). The other

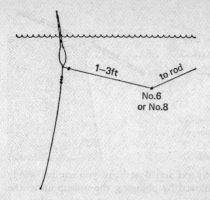

Fig. 107 Line can also be sunk by 'back shotting' – a small shot is pinched onto the line 1–3 ft above the float.

way of sinking the line is to add a small shot above the float (Fig. 107), as much as a yard above in some instances. Again, you can help the line to sink quickly by holding the rod-tip under the water as you tighten up to the float. This method is known as 'back shotting'.

With depths exceeding ten or so feet, it is probably best to resort to a sliding float. I usually find that it is best to shot for a swim of about a six foot depth (Fig. 108) before sliding the stop-knot to the required position of the sliding float. You can thus shot for any of the effects described above, remembering that if you don't allow the line to run out freely from the reel until your sliding float has settled, it will creep towards you and may draw clear of your groundbaited area. If you are fishing on the drop with a slider, it is best to use a float with a fairly large eye since the shot might otherwise settle before the float has crept up the line to the stop knot.

Exactly the same methods of float fishing can be used on other forms of still water, such as canals, drainage channels, and controlled rivers when the flow is stopped. With canals and drains one usually has to think on a smaller scale, using light floats, such as the reversed quill, and fishing to the far bank with light groundbaiting or loose feeding. Wind and drift will often have to be combatted, and one can either back-shot or sink the line as in the larger still waters. On clear water in bright weather, it might be necessary to fish very finely indeed, and bloodworm fishing with floats no bigger than a matchstick is sometimes practised in

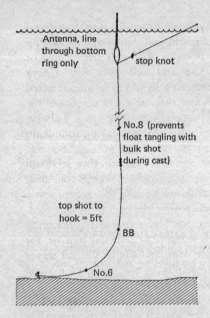

Antenna, line
through bottom
ring only

stop knot

No.8 (prevents
float tangling with
bulk shot
during cast)

top shot to
hook = 5ft

BB

No.6

Fig. 108 For deep swims, it is best to allow the float to slide to a stopknot – fixed floats for great depths are difficult to cast.

canal-matches in the north, when a collection of tiny fish amounting to aggregate weights of only a few ounces might win the day.

§131 Float fishing in running water

Carp, tench and rudd are often absent in running water, while the most noticeable additions to fish species are barbel, chub and gudgeon, which would normally be sought on the bottom (the chub, though, is fairly free-ranging and often moves to the surface to feed on insects); grayling, an active mid-water feeder; and dace and bleak, which feed at the surface unless cold weather drives them deep. Roach and perch vary their feeding between bottom and mid-water locations, while the bream, which tends to be absent in very swift water, is often more inclined to feed off the bottom than it is in still water.

Groundbaiting for these fish ought to bear some relation to their behaviour. Surface feeders, for instance, are not likely to respond to cereal groundbait-balls which sink swiftly out of sight, and the same applies in some measure to mid-water feeders. I say 'in some measure' because it is sometimes possible to draw mid-water feeders to the bottom by heavy groundbaiting, but if you do not want to run the risk of scaring off your fish and wasting groundbait, it is best to think in terms of either loose-feeding or cloud groundbaiting for surface and mid-water fish. Heavy groundbaiting for bottom feeders usually has to be administered more frequently in running water than in still water, since the current will continually move particles out of the swim. I always like to look for some bottom feature that will hold groundbait, like a patch of stones or a submerged weedbed.

Whether bottom, mid-water, or surface fishing, your feed will be trickling downstream and by 'trotting' – allowing your float and tackle to move downstream at the pace of the current – you can present your bait as just one more piece of this moving feed. The alternatives are laying on, for bottom feeders, presenting your bait as a piece of feed that is trapped on the bottom, or, for mid-water feeders, holding back your float so that the bait waves attractively in the current, hopefully in the midst of a shoal which you have kept in position by loose feeding.

To consider trotting first of all: for surface feeders, once a bait has sunk three or four feet into the water it is lost to them, and it is best to arrange your shot on a three-to-four-foot length of line, float to hook, so that the bait is taken just below the surface (Fig. 109). Just under half of this line is unweighted, and the bait therefore falls at a natural pace through the water, coming to rest eventually just within the fishes' interest-range. This rig may be twitched during its passage downstream so that the bait is brought to the surface again. For small streams, and swims close to the angler's bank, the stick float or quill, shotted so that the merest tip shows, is ideal. In shallow, fast water, such as rapids or the race below a weir, it is advisable to use a heavier-bodied float,

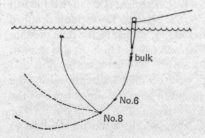

bulk

No.6

No.8

Fig. 109 (§131) Surface trotting rig (running water).

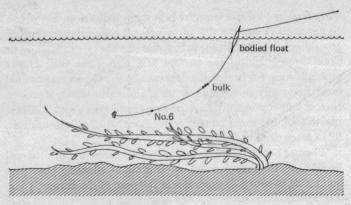

Fig. 110 Rig for fast, shallow water.

shot closer to the float, and hold the tackle back so that the bait precedes it at slight depth (Fig. 110).

Trotting arrangements for mid-water feeders require stick or quill floats for fishing close to your own bank, and bodied floats for fishing further out across larger rivers. The same applies to arrangements for bottom feeders, and the shotting patterns for mid-water and bottom trotting are similar. Close in, you do not need concentrated casting-weight and you can therefore space your shot to produce a gentle curve in the line between float and hook, with the bait well in advance of the float's progress down the river (Fig. 96). For fishing further out, the casting weight can be added to the line mid-way between float and hook, or closer to the hook if the pace of the current is fast.

Now let's look at trotting in some varied situations, first of all, a fairly average swim close to the bank, with about eight feet of water and a level bed with just a few humps and small weedbeds to interrupt the passage of the bait. The float is set so that the bait travels in advance, just tripping the bottom. The tackle is dropped into the water upstream of the angler, so that by the time the shot have sunk and settled, the float is in front of him. At this stage in the trot, the angler should keep the line between his float and rod-tip as straight as possible, lifting it off the water by raising the rod, and swinging the rod round to keep it pointed towards the float as it begins to travel downstream. The rod-tip can then be dropped gradually to lay more line on the water for the float to

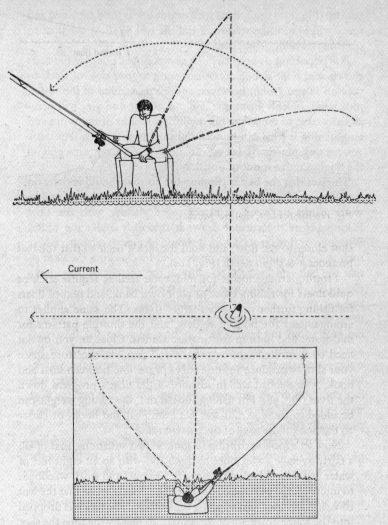

Fig. 111 Follow float with rod, keeping in constant close contact with the float by raising rod as it passes in front.

take up (Fig. 111) until, finally, all of this line is fully extended and more will have to be released from the reel to allow the float to continue travelling downstream.

It is important to keep the line as straight as possible between rod-tip and float since you do not want a great deal of slack to take up as you strike; however, surface movement of the water, plus wind, quickly bows the line out of true and you will occasionally have to mend the line by lifting it clear of the water and taughtening it (this can be accomplished with a quick flick once you are well practised), taking care not to exert too great a pull on the float to move it out of position (Fig. 112).

The fact that the bait is tripping the bottom should register on the float, producing occasional vibrations. Snagging, on underwater banks or weed, registers more visibly, with the float halting before the current draws it smoothly under the water. With two or three trots down, it should be easy to establish where such snags lie, and they can be avoided by checking the float so that the bait and lower tackle lifts in the current to pass above them (Fig. 113). Once the float reaches the end of the swim, perhaps twenty or thirty yards downriver, you can do one of three things. You can strike, on the off-chance that some fish has just taken the bait. You can hold-back on the float momentarily, so that the bait raises and waves attractively in the water – sometimes a very useful way of producing a take. Otherwise, you can begin to draw your tackle back, trying to keep surface commotion to a minimum. I always like to first pull the float well into the side before reeling back, so that the tackle isn't continually passing the wrong way over the fishing area.

Then you can begin the whole process again, normally adding groundbait or loose feed either to precede or to just follow the float downriver. Just as you cast the float upstream so that you get the tackle to settle in front of or just below you, so you should throw your feed upstream so that it reaches the fishing-level in the same place.

If four or five trots prove fruitless, you can begin actively to search out your fish by arranging the shotting and float so that the bait is either travelling clear of the bottom, or is dragging along the bottom at a slower pace than the current – to accomplish the latter, you will want to have at least one small shot tripping the bed. You might also like to try checking the float at

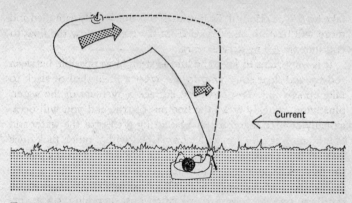

Fig. 112 When trotting, line is quickly bowed by current, impeding contact with float. Straighten line by flicking rod upstream ('mending') without disturbing path of float.

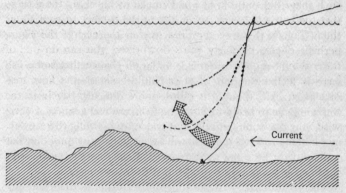

Fig. 113 Checking a trotting float makes the end-tackle rise in the water – this can be useful for avoiding bottom obstructions or searching for mid-water fish.

short intervals throughout a couple of trots, so that the bait rises and falls through the swim. If your fish are feeding at mid-water, rather than on the bottom, you will contact one sooner or later by doing this. If you establish that they are at mid-water, you can then arrange your tackle so that the bait is presented there too.

Similar tactics can be used on small rivers which, incidentally,

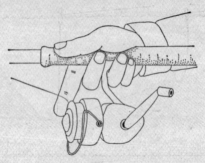

Fig. 114 Keep fixed-spool reel bale-arm off when trotting, allowing line to trickle out under control of the forefinger. Snap finger down smartly to trap line when striking, afterwards engaging the bale-arm as quickly as possible.

should never be despised or overlooked in favour of large waters, since they frequently hold good stocks of big fish – water size bears no real relation to the quality of the fishing, save that you will often have to use extra caution in your approach to the waterside to avoid scaring fish.

To trot the middle, or far side, of larger rivers with some pace, there is little alteration in your bait presentation. Control of float and tackle, though, is a little more difficult. For instance, you will have to begin feeding line from the reel as soon as your tackle hits the water, and the best way of doing this with a fixed-spool reel is to keep the bale-arm open, with your finger on the outer rim of the spool to restrain the line from paying out too quickly (Fig. 114). By using a bodied float, you will find that you are able to hold back to make your tackle rise in the water without pulling the float too far off course. You should strive to search through your swim as you would when close-in trotting. At distance, though, you will have to strike more forcibly when a fish takes.

In slower waters, trotting at distance becomes a little more easy, and the use of light tackle is much more of a possibility. I am thinking of such waters as the lower Nene, a good bream water, where it is often possible to use antenna floats, fixed bottom-end only, or perhaps fished top-and-bottom as a waggler, to trot well-out into a deep channel three-quarters of the way across the river from the north bank. Fig. 115 shows a useful rig for this sort

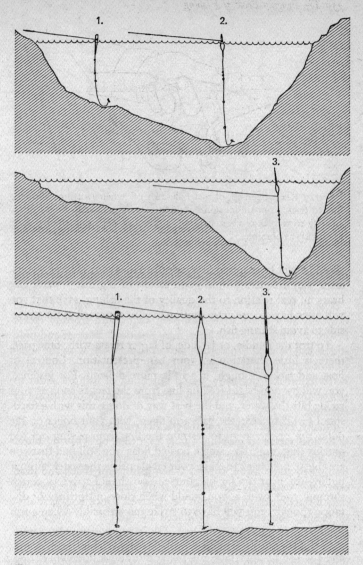

Fig. 115 Trotting rigs for different purposes: 1 – stick float rig for close and moderately close range in medium to fast flows. There is no need for shot to be bunched for casting weight; 2 – bodied float for long-trotting and fishing well out, medium to fast flows; 3 – peacock-tipped antenna rig for fishing at long range on wide, slow-moving waters.

Fig. 116 Treat any untoward movements of the float – rising, leaning, sinking, pausing – as a bite when trotting.

of water. In windy weather, the line should be sunk to avoid the effect of drift.

The slider comes into its own for really deep water. I would normally shot as for a six-foot-deep swim with trotting tackle before moving the stop-knot into position. Bottom-end-only sliders can be used for trotting slower waters, but with the addition of some pace, floats with top-and-bottom sliding rings give better control. I normally would not think of using a slider to trot at any distance on fastish water, and would resort instead to legering.

Finally, before looking at the trickier problems of holding on with float tackle in moving water, a word about trotting bites. The ideal bite, with the float stabbing under the water and continuing to zoom away, is rare. When fishing for roach and dace especially, extremely fast bites, perhaps depressing the float-tip only a fraction of an inch, can be expected. Once you have distinguished the vibrations produced by the bait or lower shot coming into contact with the bed of the river, you can also detect other 'odd' movements which probably signal a bite, such as the float leaning to one side or the other, or rising slightly in the water, or perhaps just pausing slightly (Fig. 116). You should react with a strike.

The main problem of trying to get tackle to hold on the bottom in moving water is that the float will be dragged under by flow. In slow-moving water, this is obviously less of a problem than in medium- and fast-flowing rivers. Using the lower Nene as an example again, it is possible to hold on when the flow is slight with antenna-type floats (wind and drift are an added influence to combat) in which the antenna is made of very buoyant material such as peacock quill. The amount of weight used to anchor the float (Fig. 117) can be as low as one BB shot, but as flow increases more and more shot will have to be added to hold on.

A similar rig can be used to fish just into faster water from a slack bay or inlet, with the float fished well over depth and drawn back into the slack area.

In still faster flows, holding on in this fashion becomes impractical unless a float fixed top-and-bottom is used and the tackle is casted below, and perhaps slightly out from, the angler's own bank (Fig. 118). If the water close to the angler's bank is fairly slack, it will be possible to fish over depth and cast quite far out, drawing the float towards the bank to avoid the pull of the current. Fishing in this fashion, with the tackle held downstream of the angler, is known as 'stret-pegging', or 'straight-pegging'.

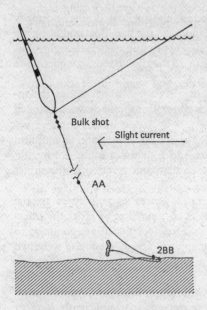

Bulk shot

Slight current

AA

2BB

Fig. 117 It is possible to hold bottom at distance in slight flows with a buoyant, peacock-tipped antenna, fastened bottom only or top-and-bottom. The float should be set well over depth and extra weight concentrated low-down as an anchor.

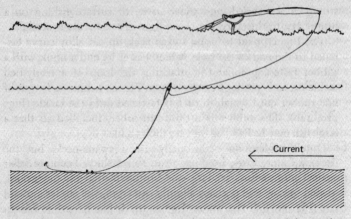

Current →

Fig. 118 Stret-pegging, or holding on near your own bank in moving water. Float must be fixed top-and-bottom.

§132 Using the roach pole

The pole is used almost exclusively for float fishing, normally trotting. It is a fixed-line method, i.e. the line, float and hook are fastened to the tip of the rod, and although often thought of as useful for small fish only, it can, in the right hands, conquer quite large specimens.

In recent years, pole fishing has come much under the influence of Continental styles, since Europeans have developed pole fishing to a fine art.

The aim of pole fishing is to have a huge extension of your arm – as long as twenty-five feet and sometimes more – hovering immediately above the float, so that your reaction to the shyest bites can be instantaneous.

By far the most prominent influences on pole styles are the Dutch and the French, but let us look first of all at the interchangeable tackles used in pole fishing, which are common to both. Pole anglers may carry up to 200 ready-made and weighted float-tackles, with the floats pre-set for bottom, mid-water or surface fishing. The length of the tackles is either short, so that the tip of the pole will be close to the float and the pole will have to be unshipped or telescoped to retrieve fish, or sufficiently long to allow small fish to be swung to hand by raising the pole. Line strengths are varied, and those used for surface fishing on a bright day, for instance, may be as light as 8 oz breaking strain.

The French tend to use a swans-neck tip, an alloy curve fastened to the end of the pole, which has at its end a hook with a rubber fastening-collar for attaching the loop of a ready-tied tackle or, as is more often the case in French fishing, a length of fine rubber cord which in turn is fastened onto the tackle (Figs 119, 120). The rubber is a shock-absorber, included so that a large fish may be handled on very light tackle.

Dutch anglers do occasionally use a swans-neck, but the fastening more often used is a ring, or rubber restraining collar at the tip of the pole, through which the line passes, and a hook further down the pole over which the loop of the ready-tied tackle is slipped. This allows the length of line between pole-tip and float to be altered by revolving the pole so that line is wound onto it.

Pole anglers trot in just the same fashion as ordinary float anglers, with the exception that the line between pole and float is kept taut, and nearly always off the water. The length of trot is curtailed once this line is extended, but a twenty-five-foot rod is capable of covering a considerable arc of water provided the tackle is dropped into the river upstream of the angler and followed round with the pole until it points downstream (Fig. 121).

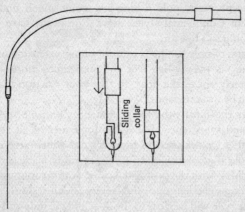

Fig. 119 The swan's-neck attachment for roach-pole tips (§132). Inset shows how loop of line or elastic is secured by sliding collar.

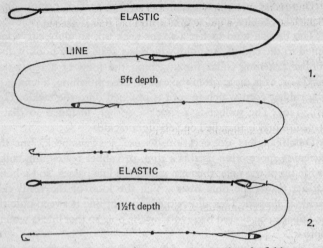

Fig. *120* Ready-tied ('furnished') lines for roach-pole fishing: 1 – a bottom-trotting rig for 5 ft deep swim; 2 – a bleak-fishing rig for surface-trotting.

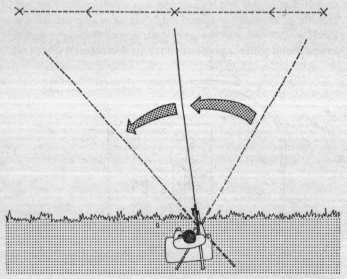

Fig. *121* As in trotting with a conventional rod, the roach pole follows the float around, keeping in close contact. The long, counterbalanced butt makes handling easy.

There is no such thing as a proper strike with pole fishing; with such close contact, a quick, gentle lift is all that is needed.

Float fishing

Legering, that is, fishing with a line weighted on the bottom, is the most versatile and popular form of fishing without a float. Freelining without either float or weight can be useful in certain circumstances, mainly in still or slack water since any flow means that your bait can move at the will of the current and the line beneath the surface can billow out so that effective control of the bait is lost. With a great deal of slack line, bites might not be transmitted easily and your strike may be ineffectual. It is possible, though, to trot floating baits, such as a piece of dry crust, as you would a float in moving water, and in still water, freelined, floating baits are useful for carp and big rudd, particularly at night.

§133 **Freelining**

The arrangement shown in Fig. 122 is useful for most still-water bottom feeders, provided the weight of the bait – a lump of bread paste, for instance – provides an anchor to allow the line to be tightened. In absolutely still conditions, it is possible to detect bites by making the line between rod-tip and bait a little slack, and watching the point at which it enters the water – should the line begin to tighten more, or to fall slacker, the bait will probably have been taken. Another way to detect bites is to counterbalance a piece of paste or bread on the line between the reel and the first rod-ring (Fig. 123) so that a take will either raise or lower it. If you want to keep the reel bale-arm open, and you may if you are fishing for carp and wish to let the fish run with the bait before making a strike, you will have to place such a counterbalance-detector under the reel (Fig. 124) so that line will not spill off the spool rim until the line is pulled. You might also

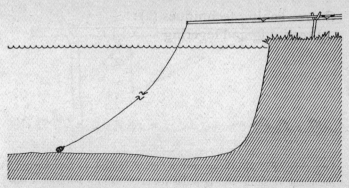

Fig. 122 (§133) In still conditions it is possible to freeline baits such as paste, tightening the line gently so that pulls on the bait will be noticeable.

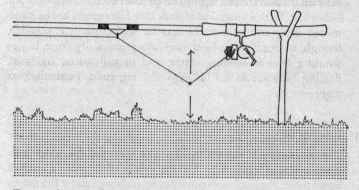

Fig. 123 A piece of paste squeezed onto the line between reel and first ring as a legering indicator will betray pulls or slack-line bites – the reel bale-arm should be closed.

consider using an electronic bite-indicator with this rig, especially if you are fishing at night.

In recent years, the floating bait (Fig. 125) has proved an excellent method for carp. Left to itself, the floating bait will of course move wherever the wind or surface drift takes it, unless the day (or night) is very still. It will probably be to your advantage to allow a floating crust to drift until it rests against a reed bed or some lily pads, since this is where surface-feeding fish

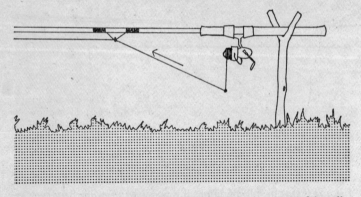

Fig. 124 If you wish to allow line to run out freely when a fish pulls, yet keep a paste bobbin indicator, you can leave the reel bale-arm off and position the paste under the reel spool. Paste bobbin indicators can be hung inside a bucket to shelter them from wind.

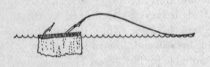

Fig. 125 Freelined floating crust is useful for species such as carp and rudd in still water, but it is at the mercy of surface drift.

will search for floating food. If you do need your floating bait held in a particular spot, you will have to add some weight to the line to anchor it (Fig. 126).

§134 Legering

Only fairly recently has legering achieved the status of a method in its own right; it used always to be an alternative to float fishing when adverse conditions (such as a heavy flood) prevented float control, or was used strictly in areas where float fishing was impractical, such as the fast and turbulent water underneath weirs. The biggest strides in the development of legering have been the invention of bite-indicators (§15) such as the swing tip and quiver tip – these make legering as useful as the float in a wide range of circumstances.

As with float fishing, it is possible to break up the subject of

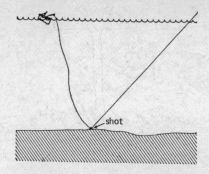

Fig. 126 You can anchor floating crust in shallow water by fixing a shot at slightly more than the depth of water above the hook.

legering, for the sake of clarity. The first thing to consider is the amount of weight that is to be used, followed by the choice of whether to make up a running rig, where the line passes through the leger weight (or a swivel attached to it) before the hook is attached, or to make up a paternoster rig with the hook and trace attached by some means to the line above the leger weight. The choice of bite-indicating methods is largely determined by the circumstances in which you are fishing, swing tipping for instance being especially suitable for still and slow-running water, and rod-tip fishing being more suitable for fast water.

In preparing to fish a swim with leger tackle, you can ground-bait (§123) much as you would for float fishing, i.e. with fairly heavy bottom-feed for species with large appetites, and loose feed (thrown well upstream so that it reaches the bottom where your lead lies) for less greedy fish or for shallow water where heavy baiting will create too much disturbance. Remember though that you are primarily after bottom feeders, for which cloud bait will be ineffectual.

You should try to make your groundbait cover a patch a few yards square, and replenish it as you would for float fishing. If you use a swimfeeder (Fig. 127) you will not need any additional groundbait.

When you are casting leger tackle some distance in deepish water where there is no point of reference, such as a visible weed-bed, to judge the distance of your cast, you may have difficulty in judging whether or not your lead is reaching the same spot with every cast. Initially, of course, you can cast to the disturbance caused by your groundbait, but thereafter you have no 'marker'.

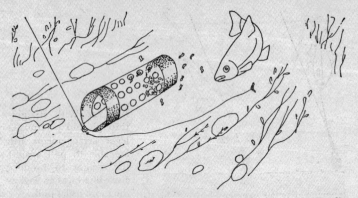

Fig. 127 (§134) The swimfeeder rests on the bottom, gradually dispensing maggots or other bait to attract fish to your baited hook.

A simple remedy to this problem is a piece of cotton thread, tied to the line between the reel and the first rod-ring after the first cast is made. Using this as a guide, you can make a slightly longer cast than the first one, and draw your weight back until the cotton comes to the same place between reel and ring. After a little practice you should get the hang of casting to the right spot every time.

The only circumstance where legering is not advisable (apart from the obvious difficulties of fishing over dense weed beds) is when a flood is carrying a lot of weed, dead leaves or other floating debris. This will quickly build up as it catches on your line, making fishing very difficult indeed. Small, occasional pieces of weed can sometimes be encouraged to break away from a leger line if you give the rod a sharp twitch, but with large amounts suspended in or floating on the water it will be better to use float tackle.

Amount of lead: You need more lead to cast a long distance than you need for close-in legering, but apart from casting you will also have to judge the amount of lead needed to hold bottom if you are fishing in running water. Besides having to hold itself in position without being pushed downstream, your lead has to be an anchor against the current pushing on your line. The longer the amount of line in the water, the greater the surface area that will be exposed to this push.

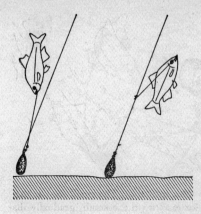

Fig. 128 With straight-through and paternoster leger arrangements fish are able to pull against the weight to produce slack-line bites as well as the more usual pulls.

The surface areas of lines also increase with diameter (i.e. strength) and heavy lines therefore need more anchorage than light ones.

When you take all these factors into consideration, it is easy to assume that an extra-heavy lead will steer you clear of problems. This is far from true; you want just sufficient lead to hold bottom and not even a minute amount more. This is because there are several occasions when a fish pulls directly against the lead rather than pulling the line to signal a bite to you (Fig. 128) and, if the weight is over-heavy, the bait will probably be rejected. With a lighter weight, the fish will be able to move away freely, and while it might soon reject the bait because of the resistance it feels, it will at least have made the line fall slack to signal the take to you.

For this reason, I believe it is best to begin legering by using leger weights made up from split shot (Fig. 129). You can thus add or subtract shot as necessary until you find the ideal balance. Later, experience will tell you if it is practical to use say a ¼ oz or ½ oz leger weight proper.

Type of lead: Split-shot leger weights can be made up either for straight-through or paternoster legering styles. Of the leger weights proper, the three most useful patterns are the swivel-eyed bomb (Arlesey bomb), the drilled bullet, and the coffin lead. Split-shot weights are ideal for holding bottom in flowing water. The drilled bullet, however, is more suited to rolling-leger methods where it is normally used as a straight-through weight.

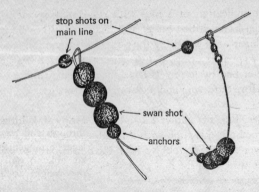

Fig. 129 Leger tackles made up with split shot. The small shot at the end of the weight anchors the large shot on the small piece of line, stopping them from flying off when you cast.

The bomb can be used either straight-through or as a paternoster lead, and its shape makes it fairly stable in running water. The coffin is out of fashion as a straight-through lead, since it can settle on the bottom, at an angle to your main line, setting up a resistance which might impede the transmission of a bite. Its flat shape, however, is very useful for holding bottom in very fast flows, and for this purpose it is best used as a paternoster lead after it has been adapted by fixing a swivel into one end.

Straight through: Fig. 130 shows a typical straight-through rig, with a BB split shot as a stop. To my mind this is suitable mainly for hunting big fish – the paternoster provides a much more

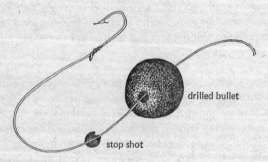

Fig. 130 Simple straight-through rolling leger.

sensitive indication of a bite with small, shy species. The rig illustrated has a drilled bullet as a weight, and can be used as a rolling leger – the weight of the bullet is low enough to allow the current to push it along, and the angler can search a large area of clear river bed by letting the weight and bait trundle some distance before retrieving and recasting as in trotting.

Link leger: Fig. 131 shows a swivel and spring link added to the above method, this time with a bomb as the weight. Note that whichever way the weight lands on the bottom, the swivels allow better contact with the bait once the line is pulled straight. This rig is also more suitable than the ordinary straight-through leger for fishing on soft mud – the weight in the straight-through rig can sink into the mud, burying the line, but with the little distance between the main line and the weight afforded by the link, the line is kept above the mud.

Paternoster: The three rigs shown in Fig. 132 all have different purposes. Rig A is the standard, paternoster rig I use for most circumstances; the lead is connected to a length of line which is knotted into the main line some distance above the hook-length. In rig B a swivel is added to the line connecting the lead, and there is a small, stop shot above the hook-length. This allows you to alter the length of the line between swivel and hook to whatever distance you require, merely by re-siting the shot. Rig C, on the

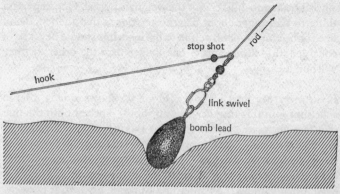

Fig. 131 Link leger.

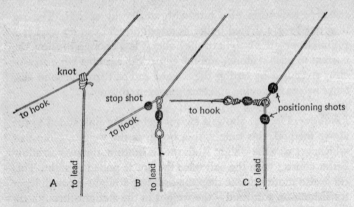

Fig. 132 Ways of fixing a paternoster tackle: A – fixed paternoster which cannot be altered; B – here, the hook-length may be altered by sliding the shot; C – the height of the hook length above the lead can be adjusted.

other hand, has a fixed-length piece of line, with a swivel, attaching the hook, while the main line goes direct to the weight. The position of the hook-length can then be altered by re-siting two small positioning-shots. With these variations you will be able to arrange your tackle so that the bait is above weedbeds or snags, either by tying rig A so that the line linking the lead is much longer than the hook-length, by shortening the hook-length in rig B, or by sliding the hook-length well up the line in rig C. All of these rigs are also suitable for fishing over soft mud, since it makes no difference if the weight is buried. One important thing to remember about paternoster rigs is that the lengths of line connecting hook or weight to the main line should never be of equal length – always make one longer than the other, or they will tangle easily.

Fixed leger: My final leger-rig (Fig. 133) shows simply a large split shot – in this instance a swan shot – pinched onto the line two feet above the hook. In using this rig, which I've found especially suitable for fishing just over the near bank-shelf of rivers such as the Thames, you cast into the main current and draw the shot back until it is resting at the bottom of the shelf edge, usually under the shelter of a bankside lily bed. It is essential to hold the rod, drawing the line back gently with your free

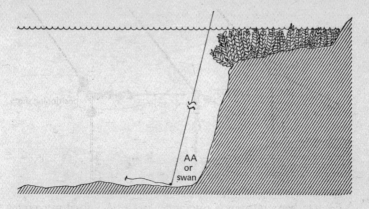

Fig. 133 Simple shot leger for close-in fishing.

hand until you can feel it tightening against the shot. Hold it until you can feel the shot being moved by a taking fish.

§135 Rod-tip legering

The tip section of most coarse-fishing rods make fairly sensitive bite-indicators for fishing in running water; in still and slow-moving water it is better to use either a bobbin of paste, as described above for freelining (Fig. 123) or the swingtip. To use the rod-tip, it is best to begin by arranging your seat and rod-rests so that you are facing downstream and with an appreciable angle between the way your rod is pointing (if you are fishing across the river) and the spot where your leger weight will rest (Fig. 134). This angle should never be acute. After casting, some time should be allowed for the lead to sink unhindered to the bottom before you begin to tighten the line. Tighten up gently, so that your rod-tip is pulled slightly out of true (Fig. 135). Never tighten so that the tip of the rod is pulled into a very noticeable curve, nor leave the line so slack that the rod stays perfectly straight and true. The reason for this is that the resistance of your rod-tip will increase, the greater the curve you make, and you will thus be losing sensitivity, while if you allow the rod to be straight and a fish moves the weight towards you rather than pulling directly against the tip, you won't notice the line slackening.

You will notice that a curve is naturally induced by the current

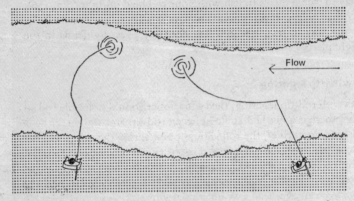

Fig. 134 (§135) When legering, don't angle rod too acutely away from lead, and remember that flow will bow your line.

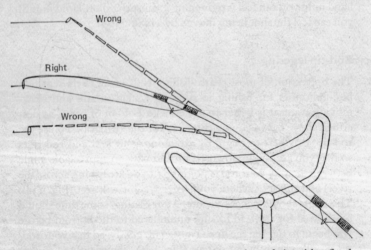

Fig. 135 (§135) Don't tighten too severely on the rod-tip with a fixed-leger, or leave the tip too slack – it should be under slight pressure only so that slack-line bites and pulls will register.

in anything greater than a gentle flow, and so the greater the flow, the less you will have to tighten the line. If the flow is exceptionally fast, in waters such as the tidal Bure for instance, when the tide is running, the tip of your rod might be pulled into an impossibly tight curve and its sensitivity severely reduced. The only way to tackle this is to fish with your rod held upright (Fig. 136), so that only a small amount of line is affected by the flow – a tiring way to fish, but one that certainly pays dividends in the right place.

§136 Swingtip legering

As with rod-tip legering, the swingtipper should point his rod so that there is a marked angle between rod-tip and weight; if he is fishing downriver, the rod should point across the river, while if he is fishing straight-out from his position, it will be best to point the rod downriver (Fig. 134). The cast is complicated by the free-swinging tip, and it is best to make a gentle swing, halfway between an overhead cast and a sideswing, trying to lob the tackle rather than trying to force it out over the water. The line is prone to tangle about the tip during casting, and a forced cast can lead

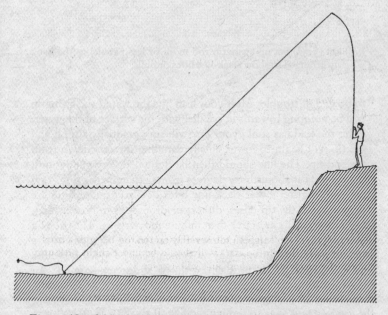

Fig. 136 'Sea fishing' with the rod held high pays off in strong flows – less line in the water means less pressure on the line, making it easier both to hold the tackle in place and to detect bites.

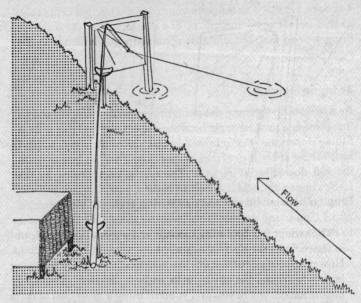

Fig. 137 (§136) Set up swingtip rod more or less parallel to the bank with tip arranged to show slack-line bites or pulls.

to no end of trouble. After your lead hits the water, the swingtip will be pointing towards it, parallel with the surface of the water. After the lead has sunk, your line will sink gradually after it and the tip will begin to lower, finally dangling directly down from the rod-tip. The line should then be tightened very gently until the tip rests at about thirty degrees from perpendicular (Fig. 137) and will register either slack-line bites or direct pulls. Bites are noticeable as the tip raises, dithers or drops – as in float fishing, bold direct pulls are rarer than minute movements. The use of a marked Perspex 'target' allows the tip to be aligned with a scored mark, so that very tiny movements can be spotted, besides conquering a major problem with swingtipping – wind. An angler fishing across a river, with his rod pointing downstream, can avoid an upstream wind by tucking his tip in the shelter of the near side of his target, while if the wind blows from the other direction he can drop the swingtip on the far side of the target (Fig. 138).

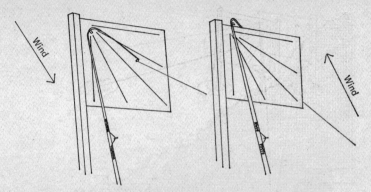

Fig. 138 The shield/target is used to shelter the tip against wind.

The swingtip is best suited to still or slow-moving water, and in faster flows the tip will be pulled out straight by the current. However, you can combat this in some circumstances by wrapping lead wire around the swingtip to make it heavier, although in circumstances where you find yourself using a great deal of extra lead, the quivertip, or perhaps rod-tip legering, is a better choice. Swingtips are also unsuited to very deep water, since it may be impossible to make an angle between the tip and the lead.

§137 Quivertip legering

The lessons above apply equally to the use of the quivertip, which is in effect a super-sensitive rod-tip. Targets are sometimes used in combination with the quivertip, and perpendicular markings are better than the radiating scores used on the swing-tip target (Fig. 139). In general, the quivertip is suitable for faster-flowing water; it is also quite practical to use one in deep water.

§138 Using a butt indicator

Although quite a sensitive bite-detector for calm days, the butt bite-indicator is especially suitable for rough weather, when swing-tipping, quiver-tipping or rod-tip legering is difficult. Unlike these other methods, the rod-tip should be pointed directly at the leger weight, so that the line runs in an absolutely straight path to the indicator. If there are large waves, or if strong drift

Fig. 139 (§137) The quivertip set for fishing – parallel lines are best on target.

billows the line out of true, it is best to angle the rod so that up to a couple of feet of the tip are submerged (Fig. 140) out of harm's way.

§139 Spring dodger

The spring dodger is simply a piece of springy wire (many shapes have been developed) on which the line is passed around (beyond the rod-tip) after the cast (Fig. 141). When the lead has settled, the line is tightened gently until the wire is under tension and will show slack-line bites and pulls.

§140 Float legering

The combination of float fishing and legering is useful mainly for fishing wide, still or slow-moving waters, or very deep swims. The float is essentially a slider, allowed to run freely on the line to a stop-knot fixed well above the water depth or, occasionally – if it is very still – allowed complete freedom with no stop, in which case the friction of the line in the float-ring provides sufficient

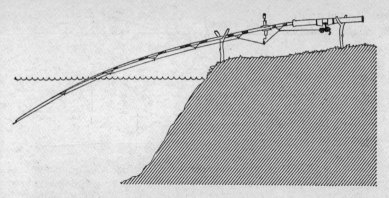

Fig. 140 (§138) Butt bite-indicator set with rod-tip submerged to combat rough conditions.

hold for the float to cock when the line is tightened. Fig. 142 shows a rig that may be used for a wide swim, such as, for instance, the wider parts of the Welland, while Fig. 143 shows a rig for a deep-water swim, such as a reservoir with steep sides. Note that placing the rod-tip under the water surface will aid the friction on the float ring to make it cock without a stop-knot (this method is occasionally called 'bobbing'). The terminal tackle can either be arranged as a paternoster rig, or as a straight-through leger rig – I find the former best, although it is a matter of personal preference. The size of the float does not bear any relation to

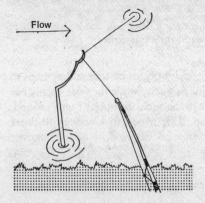

Flow →

Fig. 141 (§139) A type of spring dodger – a wire indicator – set in the water beyond the rod-tip.

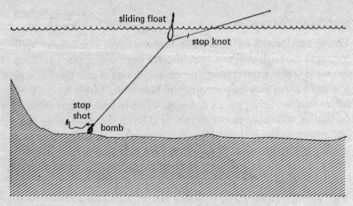

Fig. 142 (§140) Float-leger arrangement for a **wide river**.

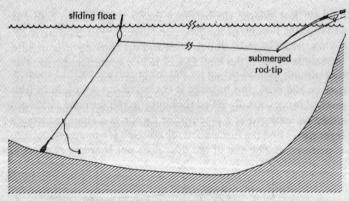

Fig. 143 Float-leger arrangement for a deep, still-water swim – there is no need for a stop-knot if the rod-tip is submerged.

the amount of lead used: the weight is for casting and perhaps to ensure that the end-tackle sinks swiftly, while the float simply has to be buoyant enough to rise to the surface and stay there, cocked, once the line is tightened up. This means that very small floats can be used in still conditions, while slight flow or surface drift will demand more buoyancy.

§141 Searching your swim

The groundbaited swim is your fish attractor, but it may well transpire that fish will not 'sit' directly over the carpet you have prepared – this applies much more in running water than in still water. In flow, fish may congregate below the carpet to pick off pieces that are being swept to them, while in still water bream in particular will make runs to grab food from the edge of the carpet, avoiding the main patch out of suspicion. It does pay to cast outside your carpet now and then, and it is also a good idea to over-cast the carpet and draw the bait gently back with occasional small twitches – the movement can make your bait stand out among the stationary pieces (Fig. 144).

§142 Leger bites 'on the drop'

As with float fishing, the bait may frequently be taken before it settles to the bottom of the swim, and detecting such occurrences is a matter of concentration. With rod-tip legering it is usually impossible to tell if the settling bait is being interfered with, but the swingtip, quivertip and butt bite-indicator are more sensitive and can be used to fish purposely 'on the drop'. The best way to do this is with a count; as the lead sinks, followed by the line, the indicators will slowly settle after them, after which you would

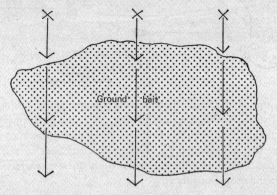

Fig. 144 (§141) Baited leger tackle twitched across groundbaited area is sometimes more attractive to fish than a stationary bait.

normally tighten the line to set the indicators to the fishing position. If you count through this period you know how long it should take for the lead and line to settle, but if the dropping bait is being held by a fish it will take longer for your indicator to fall, which your count will betray.

§143 Line bites

Fish bumping into, or swimming underneath the line will register on the swingtip, quivertip and butt bite-indicator: the bumps will make the indicators move sharply, and if a fish swims under the line, the indicator will lift more smoothly as the line scrapes over the fish's back. It takes concentration and experience to separate line bites from a proper take, but most leger anglers learn to recognize these false takes. The main circumstances in which line bites are likely to arise is when a large concentration

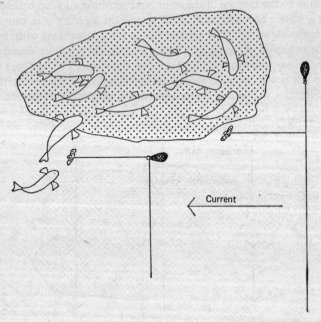

Current

Fig. 145 (§143) With fish concentrated on groundbait, place tackle above or to nearside of groundbait to avoid false bites ('line bites').

of fish have their heads down, feeding steadily on a groundbaited patch – if the line is running through the shoal, it is inevitable that fish will hit it. As well as it being a waste of time to strike, which will mean often that you will 'foulhook' fish through their fins or elsewhere. If you find yourself being troubled by line bites, it is logical to fish to the nearside of your groundbait patch, or, in running water, to fish upstream of the groundbait, with a long tail which will take the bait into the feeding area (Fig. 145).

§144 Striking when legering

Wherever practical, it is best to strike with the rod held low, sweeping sideways as if you are trying to pull the line through a thin tube of water; if you strike upwards you are lifting the line edge-on and you will be combatting greater resistance. The exception to this rule is when you are fishing downstream, where a low-angle strike might simply pull the bait from the fish's mouth.

Freelining, legering

Quick cross-reference guide

17 Coarse-fishing techniques (3):
Livebaiting and deadbaiting, spinning
and plug fishing

Predators and scavengers play a vital role in a fishery. The predators single out weak and sickly fish and ensure that large hatches of fry are decimated before they can reach maturity and overcrowd the water – a state of affairs that can result in the whole fish population becoming stunted. The scavengers clean up fish which have died as a result of injury, old age or sickness, and they thus keep the water in a clean condition.

§145 Predatory fish

Besides pike and perch, the best known of the predators, chub will often take small fish baits and spinners, and so will all the game fish. Eels and catfish, less free-ranging in their hunting habits, will take well-anchored livebaits but are rarely hooked on spinners. It is also worth mentioning that roach, barbel and even tench have been taken on small livebaits, spinners, and fly-fishing lures which imitate fish. The zander (pike-perch) is a fairly recent addition to Britain's list of predators.

§146 Scavengers

Eels and catfish are noted scavengers, feeding on a wide range of carrion besides dead fish. Pike will readily take dead fish baits, and so will the zander, but chub and perch seem more attracted to lively baits – as are the game fish.

Predators and scavengers do not invariably turn their attentions to fish of other species. Many are cannibalistic, particularly the pike and the trout.

§147 **Bait fish**

Pike are capable of taking very large baits, from 6–12 oz and sometimes bigger, while the catfish can take baits to 8 oz with ease. For the other predators, the normal size of baits would range from a few grammes to about 4 oz. This does not mean that pike and catfish will not take small baits – they are even caught on small worm and maggot baits when they're in the mood.

As a general rule, the larger the fish bait you use, the longer you will have to wait for a fish of sufficient calibre to take it.

Before looking at the species best suited for baits, a word about keeping live fish. All fish need plenty of room in well oxygenated water, and they should never be crowded into a small bucket and kept overnight. Unless you have facilities for keeping them, such as an old bath (or even the family bath), catch your livebait immediately before you set out after predators. A dozen four-inch roach is quite a crowd in a two-gallon bucket, and so change the water regularly to keep up the oxygen level through the day. Species such as bleak and dace are particularly delicate in this respect, and they really need running water – a keepnet is a better alternative to a bucket.

It is also a good idea, to avoid transferring disease from one water to another, to use livebaits caught only in the water you will be fishing. As well as diseases, you can spread parasites such as the fish louse, *Argulus foliaceus*, to waters where they might be absent. Also make sure that local fishery by-laws allow you to keep undersize fish.

Sticklebacks: These make excellent baits for perch and chub (also big trout). They can be caught with a shrimping net in most ponds and streams, or with the minnow trap (see below).

Minnows: The best bait for perch, chub and trout, fished live or dead on a spinning flight. They will also take zander. Legered dead minnows are good eel baits and can be caught, like the stickleback, in a shrimping net or a baited trap (Fig. 146).

Bullheads and loaches: When obtainable (you will have to search hard for them under stones in shallow, clean rivers) these make good chub and trout baits.

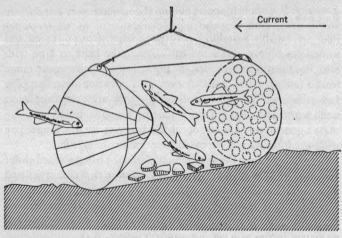

Fig. 146 Baited funnel-trap for minnows.

Ruffe and small perch: Will be taken by pike, but are not recommended where there are alternatives.

Rudd: An excellent pike-bait, normally float fished live, near the surface, because, from habit, rudd try to stay close to the surface.

Bleak, dace: Again, these are properly surface baits if used live. Dead bleak and dace, legered, will take pike, zander, perch and chub. They are both rather delicate, and a better alternative to using them as livebait is to fish them dead on a spinning flight (§153).

Roach: This is the most widely used livebait, suitable for surface or bottom rigs, float or leger. Roach up to 2 oz will take large chub and perch. For pike, roach of 2–12 oz can be used, alive or dead. Zander will take live or dead roach up to about 4 oz, while big catfish can ingest quite large specimens of half a pound or so. Also suitable for use on a spinning flight.

Bream: Appealing mainly to the pike, which is well able to cope with their large, flat-sided shape, bream make good, long-living livebaits, particularly for fishing on the bottom in deep water.

Sprats: A few sea fish, sprats among them, make very good fresh-water baits, and they are particularly useful in winter when tempting small freshwater fish is difficult using rod and line. Try to buy sprats, herrings and mackerel that are really fresh, other-wise they will tend to become so soft that they will not stay on your hooks for long. Frozen fish go soft particularly quickly. Legered sprats will take eels, catfish, zander and pike, and they will also take perch, chub and game fish when used on a spinning flight or fished in one of the lively methods such as sink-and-draw described below.

Herrings: Fresh herrings can be used as freelined or legered baits for pike, and the smaller specimens make good sink-and-draw baits.

Mackerel: Like herrings and sprats, these are good substitutes when freshwater bait-fish are scarce or unobtainable.

§148 Tackle for fish baits

The main tackle requirements for the methods that follow are outlined in the checklists in Chapter 10, but it is worth re-stating a few points.

Rod requirements: Besides using a rod of sufficient strength to master the size of fish you are after, you will have to take into account the weight of the bait you will be casting. While you are able to use small baits such as minnows, for chub, perch and small zander on float fishing and leger rods, you will want something stouter to deal with bigger baits for larger, stronger fish such as catfish or big pike.

The sea fisherman's beachcasting rod (§44) is the really suitable design for big baits and big fish. Purpose-made, pike, livebaiting rods (about the same stamp as a strong carp rod) are an alterna-tive, but the extra length of the beachcaster is really valuable at times. Beach-fishing, multiplier reels are also an advantage, allowing long casts. Carp rods are suitable for big eels, also zan-der to a fair size – in Britain, at least, this species is a poor fighter. Line strength should be suited to the size of your quarry, but con-sider using an extra-strong shock leader (§11j) for casting big baits.

Need for swivels: For livebaiting rigs, swivels are essential, otherwise free-swimming baits will quickly kink a line. Baits on spinning mounts deserve swivels and an anti-kink vane, and deadbaits that are frequently drawn through the water, as in the sink-and-draw method, should also have a swivel incorporated in the line to avoid twist.

For either livebaiting or deadbaiting, pike demand a wire trace (§11h), or a length of stout nylon, close to the hooks, to prevent fraying on sharp teeth. This also applies to fishing for large eels and catfish.

§149 Livebaiting

The principle behind livebaiting, whether using large or small bait-fish for modest or large predators, is that your bait will stand out as either a weak or sickly fish, for some reason unable to follow characteristic behaviour, or a fish that is so preoccupied that it will be fair game to a stealthy approach.

The least cruel, and often the most effective method to tether livebaits is with a single, large hook, or a treble, hooked through the lip only (Fig. 147). Baits hooked like this are frequently re-

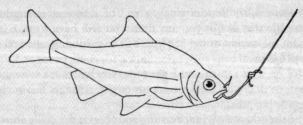

Fig. 147 (§149) Lip-hooked livebait.

leased when you strike, and many must live to fight another day. Large baits, however, do require some extra security when you fasten them, to avoid them flying off the hooks when you cast, and they also need to be 'covered' more fully with more than one hook so that you can be sure that a pike or whatever fish takes them has at least one hook in its mouth. The snap-tackle (Fig. 148) is a wire trace with one or two trebles allowed to slide fairly

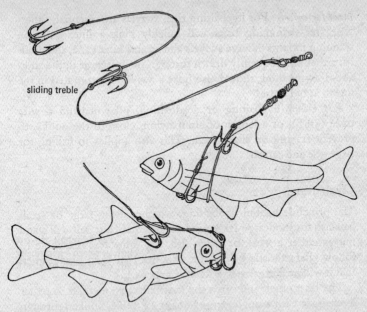

Fig. 148 The snap-tackle and its uses.

freely along it, and one terminal treble. It can be used to straddle the bait, thereby holding it very firmly indeed, or you can hook the terminal treble through the lip, and the remaining trebles into the bait's back.

Hooking a fish in this way goes against the grain with many people, me included, and so wherever possible the single, lip-hooked bait is used in preference to the snap-tackle. Don't throw your snap-tackles away, however: they are valuable for use with deadbaits.

Livebaits may be used on float or leger tackle, but it is not a good idea to freeline them – you will have little idea of where they are moving under the water, and a fish could easily gorge them before you get an inkling of the take.

Fig. 149 shows the basic livebait tackle, in this instance a rig baited with a minnow for perch, chub or zander, suitable for trotting in rivers up to medium pace, or for surface or mid-water fishing in lakes, canals and so on, when you do not have to worry

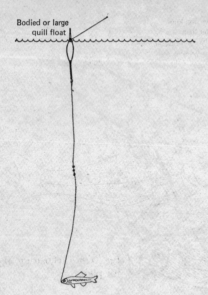

Bodied or large quill float

Fig. 149 Livebait rig for chub or perch – a minnow bait, on size 10 or size 8 hook.

too much about the bait wandering and dragging the float after it. Fig. 150 shows the equivalent tackle for pike, this time with a pilot float free to slide to a stop knot on the line some distance above the bait-supporting fixed float. The pike usually holds its prey crosswise when it first grabs, and it will then swim either to a holt, or into deep open water where the prey cannot make a dash for it, where it turns it head-on to swallow it. The pilot float enables the angler to tell where the pike has halted even if the main float is held beneath the surface, and he can time his strike for the moment the bait has been turned and is about to be swallowed with lip-hooked baits, especially large ones, this is most important. Note that in both rigs the weight is a drilled bullet stopped by a small shot. This is because strung-out split shot are a tangle-hazard when the bait is swimming freely about them.

If you wish your bait to stay within a restricted area in lakes or rivers, then you will have to use a float-leger arrangement or simply leger your livebait. The terminal tackle for the float-leger rig can be straight-through (Fig. 151), but this is prone to tangles and a paternoster rig (Fig. 152) is better. This one incorporates a three-way swivel.

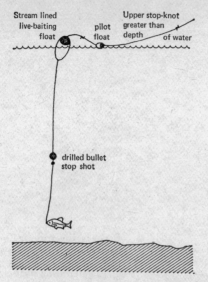

Fig. 150 Livebaiting rig for pike.

The paternoster also makes a better livebaiting leger rig (Fig. 153) than a straight-through leger for pike; for smaller fish, however, such as chub and perch, a minnow may be used on straight-through tackle. The swivel-eyed bomb is the best weight, less prone to tangling than a coffin lead.

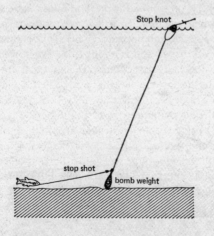

Fig. 151 Straight-through float-leger rig.

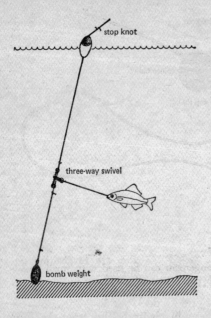

Fig. 152 Paternoster float-leger rig for pike.

A stop shot can be included some distance above the weight, besides the one below – this is to stop your bait fish drawing too much line through the eye of the weight. You can also fish a minnow on the rolling leger, arrangement shown in Fig. 154.

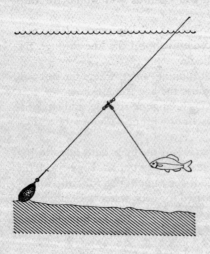

Fig. 153 The three-way swivel also makes a paternoster livebait legering rig.

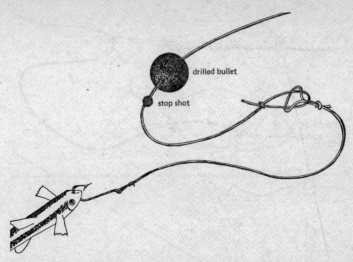

Fig. 154 The rolling-leger arrangement can be used with small live-baits such as minnows, for chub, perch, zander and trout.

§150 Deadbaiting

Unlike livebaits, it is quite feasible to freeline with a deadbait; after casting, the line may be tightened until the resistance of the bait is felt, and then you can pinch a piece of bread onto the line, leaving the bale-arm of the reel open as you would for carp (§133).

Deadbaits are best lip-hooked, or used in reverse (Fig. 155) which calls for a baiting needle to thread the line through the bait before fastening on the hook.

Freelining is impractical in running water, where the bait will be washed downstream. Because the bait is inert, however, it is unlikely that you will have much tangling trouble, and straight-through legering is quite practical, with or without a float (Fig. 156).

A trotted deadbait is effective in medium- and fast-flowing water for perch and chub – the movement imparts some life to the bait. The rig in this instance is the same rig as for trotted live-baits. A sliding float may be used for deep water with either live or deadbaits.

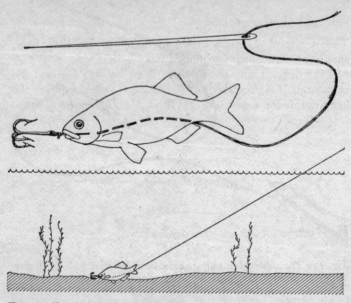

Fig. 155 (§150) A baiting needle is used to thread line through dead-bait from vent to mouth, and hook is then attached. It is quite feasible to freeline a deadbait in still water (bottom).

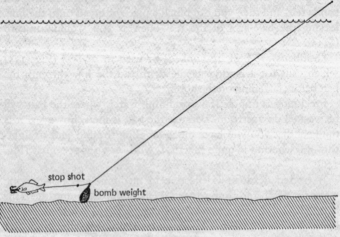

Fig. 156 Weight will be needed when fishing with a deadbait in running water.

§151 Sink-and-draw deadbaiting

This is a method which strives to make the deadbait 'live', simulating the actions of an injured fish.

It can be used with all fish baits, from the very small to the extra-large. It is necessary to rig the bait so that it faces up the line towards the angler (Fig. 157) and a baiting needle is useful

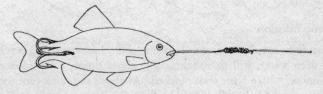

Fig. 157 Fixing for sink-and-draw deadbait.

for this purpose. The line should be threaded through the mouth and out of the anal region, where the hook is affixed. An alternative to threaded baits is the use of a snap-tackle, with the top hook on the trace either lip-hooking the bait, or fastened through the tough gill cover. I also like to weight the head of the fish to make the action more attractive, and a drilled bullet stopped on the bait's nose with a small shot is the best way of doing this (the weight may, if you wish, be forced into the bait's mouth).

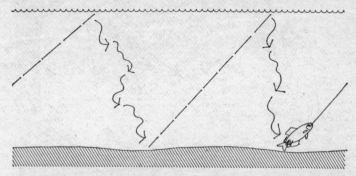

Fig. 158 (§151) A deadbait 'right way round' drawn to the surface and allowed to flutter to the bottom is a good method for most predators ('sink-and-draw').

The bait is cast out, allowed to sink, and then drawn to the surface with an attractive flutter. When close to the surface, reeling should be stopped so that the bait flutters to the bottom, after which it is again drawn upwards, and this is repeated until the bait is retrieved (Fig. 158). Keep your rod low during the later stages of the retrieve so that the bait is in the water until the very last minute – a following fish will often strike when it sees that its prey is reaching the security of the bank.

§152 Drop minnow

This is an extremely useful deadbait method for chub and perch in deep water, still or running. The rig is simply a lip-hooked minnow, with a large shot pinched just above the hook (not too far up or the bait will double back on the line and tangle). The rig cannot be used at distance, or the action will be destroyed – it should be used mainly for close-by swims in water with steeply

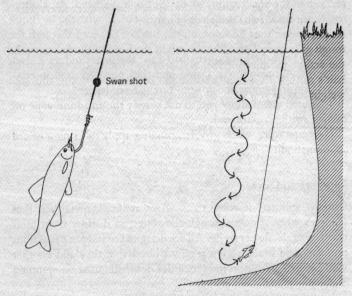

Swan shot

Fig. 159 (§152) A lip-hooked dead minnow weighted by a large split shot and dropped into deep holes, where it will flutter to the bottom, is a good method for perch ('drop-minnow').

shelving banks, or in the sort of deep holes frequently found in rivers to the side of weir races. Simply drop the bait over the edge of the bank or hole, with the reel bale-arm open, and allow it to flutter freely to the bottom. Then withdraw it slowly, allowing it to flutter as in sink-and-draw fishing, and repeat (Fig. 159).

§153 Deadbait spinning flights

Spinning flights can be bought for all sizes of bait fish. They are simply a set of angled vanes (Fig. 160) which are hinged and have

Fig. 160 (§153) The spinning flight makes a deadbait revolve attractively when it is drawn through the water.

'jaws' to hold the head of the bait fish; the vanes induce a spin when drawn through the water, and thus must be used in conjunction with swivels and an anti-kink vane or lead.

Weighted vanes allow you to use simply the anti-kink vane on the line, with no extra lead.

The same rules which govern spinning apply to using a baited spinning flight.

§154 Spinners and lures

Usually 'spinner' is taken to mean an artificial, metal bait that revolves when drawn through the water, as distinct from lures which waggle, flutter or jig. All are designed to imitate the actions of a fish, and besides giving off visible flashes they add another vital factor – vibration (this includes deadbaits used on spinning flights).

Vibrations are a valuable attractor, and they mean that you can tempt fish in coloured, murky water or in poor light conditions.

Whether spinners or lures are used, line-twist will have to be guarded against by using an anti-kink vane or lead. Rigs for pike also need a wire trace.

Colour of lure or spinner: Most lures are coloured either bright silver or bronze, with various pieces of paintwork and trimmings in a variety of colours. The main overall colour is the most important, and it is easy to assume that bright finishes should be used in dull weather, to increase visibility, and duller finishes will be better in bright weather. In fact, the reverse seems to be generally true: in murk or poor light, dull colours are intensified while bright finishes are merely obscured, and in bright weather silvery finishes seem to be best-noticed. Red is widely used for paintwork and trimmings such as a ruffe of wool tassel on the 'tail' treble of a spinner or lure. Some bait fish do have red fins, but I think the 'extras' on most spinners and lures catch more anglers than they do fish.

§155 Spinning

While you wind evenly to retrieve a spinner, lure, or deadbait, you make it appear very ordinary; the secret of successful spinning is to vary the rate of retrieve so that the frequency of visual and vibrationary signals is constantly changing – exactly the signals a predator would expect from an injured, sick or frightened fish which would be easy game.

You can amplify the erratic behaviour of your spinner by moving your rod to the right or left so that you keep making it change course (Fig. 161) and by varying speed of retrieve.

In still water and rivers which have a moderate pace, spinning is a matter of cast and retrieve, but in fast water the current will work a lure or spinner for you. By casting across the stream, and moving a few yards between every cast, it is possible to cover a great deal of water (Fig. 162) with the working lure swinging

Fig. *161* Alter speed and angle of retrieve when spinning, creating an erratic path and attractive, varied, vibration patterns.

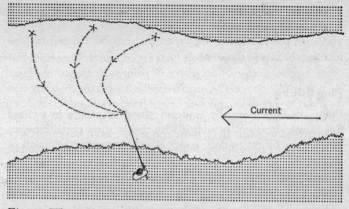

Fig. 162 When spinning in running water, the current pushing on the line will give action to the spinner by pulling it in towards the angler's bank – a slow retrieve is called for since fast reeling will make the spinner travel too quickly across the river.

in a curve towards your bank with each cast. In other situations it is best to fully exploit a swim before moving on, by making successive casts in a fan shape (Fig. 163).

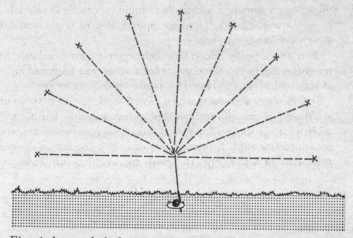

Fig. 163 A great deal of water can be covered from one spot by casting in a fan-like pattern. Cast close to the bank on either side as well as straight out, since the bank is a likely place for predators to be lying.

To keep your spinner or lure working deep in the water, hold your rod-tip close to the water surface when you retrieve – if you wish the spinner to rise, then you can lift the rod-tip and increase the rate of retrieve.

§156 Plug fishing

Plugs are lures normally made of wood or plastic in stylized fish-forms, occasionally jointed with two or three parts. Finishes range from bright to dull, and it is wise to carry a selection of patterns.

Floating plugs are designed to work on the water's surface, imitating a fish that cannot submerge. You should make them fuss

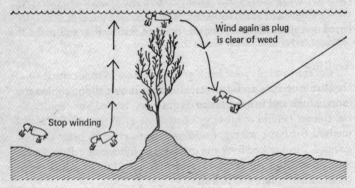

Fig. 164 (§156) The floating/diving plug's action can be varied by altering the rate of retrieve. It can be made to 'climb' over weedbeds.

across the water, altering course frequently and pausing for short periods. These are ideal lures for very weedy water.

Floating/diving plugs are floating lures with an angled scoop at the forward end, which will make them dive when retrieved – the scoop may be adjustable, so that the lure can be made to dive steeply if required. The lure imitates a fish struggling to dive, and it will rise to the surface whenever you stop winding in. By varying retrieve rate (Fig. 164) you can make the floater/diver follow a staggering up and down path in the water. Like the floater, this is a good lure for weedy water – you can exploit patches of open water in between weed beds by making the lure dive, allowing it to surface near the weed bed so that it can be drawn gently over the top without snagging.

Sinking plugs are normally used in deep water; most are designed to jig erratically from side to side rather than dive. After casting, allow them time to sink to whatever depth you choose before beginning the retrieve.

§157 Other lures

Pike and perch have been taken on mackerel and cod feathers, but this is rather an unsporting approach. Among the useful extras anglers might add to their spinning tackle are imitation mice and frogs, based on the floating plug, and rubber fish, painted in realistic colours. Many coarse-fish species are taken on the fly-fisherman's imitation fish such as the polystickle, a fly-lure based on the stickleback, but this is another subject entirely.

§158 Trolling

Deadbaits on sink-and-draw tackle and spinning flights, spinners, lures, plugs and other imitations may be 'trolled' or 'trailed' – i.e. drawn behind a moving boat. This is an especially useful method for large waters, enabling you to cover a great deal of ground. Lip-hooked livebaits may also be used, and a deep-water, livebait trolling rig (Fig. 165) as well as spinners fished deep, should incorporate a Wye lead.

Normally the boat would be rowed gently, with occasional

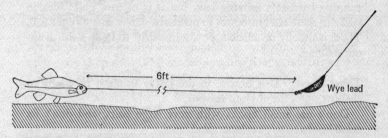

Fig. 165 (§158) The Wye lead makes a trolling rig for livebait or dead-bait to be trailed behind a boat – a good method for covering a large amount of water.

spurts of speed. It is best to fish with two people in the boat, one rowing and one keeping an eye on the rods, but if you do troll alone it is wise to make a lanyard of stout cord to tie your rod to a rowlock – an unattended rod might be pulled over the side before you can ship the oars and grab it.

Drift is normally too slow to make a spinner work efficiently, but it is often sufficient for livebait fishing. The water can be quartered by rowing into the wind and then drifting back with the blow, moving further along the lake or loch each time you return to begin a new drift.

You can troll from a motorized boat providing it will idle along at realistic speeds – I prefer rowing-boats because they cause less disturbance.

Striking with live/deadbaits, spinners, lures: With livebaiting and deadbaiting you should strike hard if:
(a) You have a large float, which has to be shifted before the power of the strike is transmitted to the hooks.
(b) You are using large hooks which require extra power to make them penetrate.
(c) You have a large bait which will absorb much of the power of the strike.

It is wise to follow this up with a further, hard strike, once you have tightened your contact with the hooked fish, to make certain that the hooks hold. Your line should be of sufficient strength to cope with this treatment, and the rod should have enough 'backbone' for a powerful strike.

In spinning and trolling, fish frequently hook themselves by running hard at a moving bait, but it is often a good idea to strike in these circumstances to make absolutely sure of your fish. There is usually insufficient power in a drift to hook a fish without striking.

Things to avoid: It is unwise to use heavy spinners in weedy or shallow water for obvious reasons.

Don't use small hooks with very large baits, and don't fix small hooks to large spinners and lures.

Don't strive to cast broad, lightweight spoons into the wind; ten to one they will double back and snag your line (when a spoon does this it is said to have 'oystered').

Following fish : Do try to keep live/deadbaits and all spinners in the water until the last possible moment when you are bringing them in – fish will often follow them right to the bank before taking. If you notice a following fish, increase the retrieve-rate rather than slackening speed – the fear that the prey is escaping often encourages a following fish to strike.

Livebaiting, deadbaiting, spinning
Quick cross reference guide

Lines, §11a, 11f, 11h.
Hooks, §12.
Swivels, §13.
Floats, §14.
Weights, §16.
Knots, §18b.
Rods, tackle checklist, §39.
Preparations, §41.
Freshwater environments, §58–69.
Species: catfish, §76; chub, §77; eel, §80; perch, §85; pike, §86; pike-perch, §87 (see also game fish, §160–165).

The cost of fishing is an important consideration for game anglers; the noted waters for trout, salmon and sea-trout fishing, in England in particular, are, in the main, privately owned and expensive to fish – there are waiting lists for some English game-fishing clubs that hold water, and syndicate-owned fisheries are practically out of reach, unless you are lucky enough to be asked along as a member's guest.

Nevertheless, away from the more exclusive water, good game fishing can be obtained, as the suggestions below indicate.

§159   Where to go for game fishing

Trout: The English reservoirs are undoubtably the best trout fisheries within the pocket of most anglers; charges for a day's fishing can be as low as 50p and most of the large, popular waters can be fished for less than £3. You will need rod licences besides your fishing permit. Weekly reservoir-permits are a good bet for a holiday, while if you live close to a reservoir a season permit can be a good investment. Club waters on less famous rivers than, for instance, the Test, are good value – this is the best way of seeking river fishing for trout.

Outside the Midlands and south of England the position on fishing charges improves considerably. In Wales and parts of the West country trout fishing can be obtained fairly cheaply, while in Scotland and much of Ireland most trout fishing is free of charge. You do have to seek permission to fish from landowners, though.

Salmon and sea-trout: As for trout, the further you move away from areas where game fishing is heavily preserved, the better prices become. Undoubtedly the best value comes from hotel waters, which are often excellent fisheries with modest charges – many are regularly advertised in angling journals, some on quite famous rivers. It is sometimes possible to fish such waters as a non-resident at the hotel, but you should establish this before-hand to avoid disappointment. In some holiday areas it is possible to obtain visitor's tickets very cheaply from local angling clubs, and this is well worth investigation, particularly outside the main holiday season.

§160 Salmon
Salmo salar

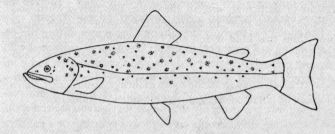

Much has been written about the salmon's interesting life and about its anomalous behaviour towards fishermen's lures in fresh-water spawning runs – a period of its life in which no food what-soever is taken into the fish's gut. It is best to consider the species from two angles; first, from the biologist's standpoint, and second from the angler's point of view.

After hatching from their eggs in the upper reaches of streams and rivers, the tiny salmon feed on their yolk sacs for about three weeks, during which stage they are known as alevin. After this they are known as parr, and they begin to spread throughout the river, feeding on small water creatures, eventually growing to around 15 cm (6 in) over a period of one to two years. While at the parr stage, the young salmon have a row of eight to eleven blackish smudge-marks along each flank, but as they prepare for their passage to the sea these markings disappear and the fish take on a silvery appearance, dropping downriver to congregate in great numbers in tidal water. This is known as the smolt stage. After acclimatizing to salt water, they set out on a perilous journey to the rich, sea feeding-grounds west of Greenland. They may stay here for periods as small as six months or as long as five years (reaching weights of up to 20 kg, although most are much smaller) before setting off for the return journey to the river where they started life. The mature salmon move up to their spawning grounds, overcoming weirs and obstacles *en route*, male and female fish becoming heavy with milt and spawn respectively. The male tends to become redder the longer it stays in the river, and it also develops a hooked lower jaw, or 'kype'. Once in the spawning grounds the female digs a depression, known as a 'redd', in the gravel and then lays eggs which the male fertilizes. After spawning, the fish lose condition rapidly and are known as 'kelts'; only very few – more females than males – survive the journey back to the sea to regain condition and spawn again.

The angler has to study the salmon's behaviour during run-up to spawning in a great deal of detail; no angler is concerned with catching them during their early parr and smolt stages, and if inadvertently hooked at these stages they should be returned carefully to the water. Kelts are caught just as much as are prespawning fish, but generally the longer they stay in the river, the less interesting they become either from a sporting or a culinary viewpoint. A fresh-run fish, not long out of the sea, is the best possible quarry – some fish which have run hard and fast up the river may still have sea-lice adhering to them.

The times at which salmon enter freshwater to begin their runs vary from river to river. In the Welsh Dee for example, the main run begins in April; in the River Camel, Cornwall, July and August see the most fish, and in the River Coquet in the north of England, the run starts in September. For the sake of clarity I have to give a 'typical' seasonal pattern below, but your attention is drawn to the charts showing the best times to fish for salmon and sea-trout, compiled by *Where to Fish*, later in this chapter – the main English, Welsh, Scottish and Irish waters are covered.

In our typical water, a run of salmon enters the lower river in early spring, establishing shoals which can be quite large in pools above the tidal reach. Although at this time of year there is usually plenty of water in the river, temperatures are low and salmon appear inactive and reluctant to move upriver with any enthusiasm. Temperature has been linked a good deal with salmon behaviour, but more of this later – for the moment our early salmon are lying deep, generally out of the main press of the current, and their actions are sleepy.

A water temperature of 42 degrees Fahrenheit has been put forward by some experts as the figure at which these early fish become more active and start to move, pool by pool, towards their objectives. Whatever is the case, in the later part of the run the early salmon 'wake up' although their progress upriver is cautious and they might lie in small shoals in the larger pools for days at a time. Late arrivals show less caution, moving quickly through the lower reaches, sometimes overtaking the earlier fish.

This is important from the angler's point of view because there are now two 'types' of salmon in the river; some lying deep and occasionally moving slowly upstream, and others on the move with few halts. Salmon on the move swim through the upper layers of the river, rarely sinking into the deeper pools. They might occasionally make head-and-tail rises (resembling a porpoise) or show other signs of exuberance.

Moving into summer, and higher temperatures, the distinctions between the two types fade, and smaller groups of salmon press forward when the water conditions are favourable – there must obviously be sufficient water for travelling, and drought hinders the run, while floods encourage movement. During the periods when salmon are 'locked' in their pools, they will take up stations where flow delivers necessary amounts of oxygen without demanding too much energy; if the water becomes stale in the bottom level of deep pools, they will move to mid-water, while if floods fill pools with silt-laden water they will move even nearer to the surface, where cleaner water is present. Characteristic behaviour in this period seems to be some sort of displacement activity, and many a time I've watched fish holding station for long periods, then suddenly making a quick, energetic tour of the pool before returning to station. Signs of excessive exuberance have generally died out by now.

As the males become redder and spawning nears, displays resembling bad temper are often apparent; males might be particularly aggressive towards other males, while females examine areas in a preoccupied way as if eyeing them up as possible redds. Finally, late in the summer when rains freshen the river again, there may be a new run of fresh fish behaving something like the late arrivals in the spring run, pressing rapidly for spawning areas and porpoising and playing on the way. Again, there are two 'types' of salmon in the river.

Taking the views of many salmon anglers into account, it would seem that there is not just a single motive which prompts the salmon to take a fly, a spinner, a bunch of worms or a prawn – there are instead several motives prompted by the salmon's state of mind at various stages in the season.

I don't want this to sound categorical; it is merely surmise backed up by my observations, which are scant in number, and the more reliable observations of anglers whom I regard as far more experienced salmon men than me, many of whom will say that attempts to boil salmon fishing down to an exact science are foolhardy even after a lifetime's experience. Briefly, the earliest fish might not have adjusted their metabolism sufficiently to ignore food-resembling organisms which come very close to them (remembering their sleepy state). These fish tend to take slowly and deliberately, and a large lure moving very slowly does seem to pay at this time. When the fish begin to move, especially the later arrivals, play cannot be ruled out as a motive for 'nipping' objects moving across their path. In the summertime, when fish spend long times in the same pool, displacement activity can be suggested as likely, while in the final near-mating stage aggression, on the part of the males, and house-tidying, on the part of the females, might be responsible for takes – plus play, of course, for the late-run fish. As I said, I can't corroborate these views, which are rejected by as many people as are prepared to accept them. In the final analysis they do not matter: salmon take flies and spinners and will continue to do so.

Now for fishing methods: I've mentioned worms and prawns (which can be real, or plastic imitations) which are often regarded as last resorts when fly fishing or spinning fails to produce results. Spinning is a good means of covering a large area of water, although methods differ greatly from spinning for coarse fish or trout and it is necessary to take heed of the notes on game-fishing methods in the following chapter. The traditional fly-fishing method is fishing with a sinking line, ideal for covering pools for early salmon and summer fish. However, travelling fish and salmon lying high in the water (after a spate for instance) are likely to respond to the floating-line ('greased-line') method, a relatively recent development in salmon-fishing styles. Salmon do undoubtedly take dry flies, but dry-fly fishing for salmon is generally not practised in Britain. American anglers have developed dry-fly fishing to an art, but they often have the benefit of well-stocked waters with huge runs of salmon.

It is also important to link size and colour of artificials used to catch salmon with the stage of the season and the conditions of the day. Many anglers actually link the size of spinner or fly directly to the temperature, and bearing in mind the 42-degree water temperature which spurs salmon to move upriver, this seems logical. Incidentally, it is interesting that 42 degrees Fahrenheit is the biological 'trigger' which sets all plant-life growing, in water as well as on land.

§161 **Sea-trout** (sewin, peel)
Salmo trutta

This is the migratory form of the brown trout. It spends the greater part of its life in the sea in coastal areas, returning to rivers to breed. It normally grows heavier than the brown trout because of its richer food supplies, and it becomes altogether more silvery in appearance.

The fish is taken on wet and dry fly, or by spinning and bait fishing with worms (banned on some waters). Sea-trout are noticeably more active at dusk, and night-fishing is practised in some parts of the country using large moth-like, artificial, fly patterns. There is evidence that the sea-trout occasionally fast, much as the salmon, during their run upriver; this seems to be true mainly of winter fish, since summer fish do take food into their guts. The times at which they visit noted sea-trout waters appear with the lists for salmon at the end of this chapter.

§162 **Brown trout**
Salmo trutta

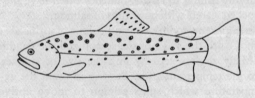

Without doubt the most popular British game fish, the brown trout is present in most waters with high oxygen-contents. Besides torrential streams and large lakes, it will also occur where the water of slow, less well-oxygenated rivers is quickened and tumbled by weirs and other obstructions. The species has been transplanted successfully to many parts of the world.

The trout of high, acid-water regions are small, wiry fish, while those of softer, low-ground regions grow to larger sizes. A few may live long enough to become very large cannibals, occasionally reaching 10 kg or more. Chalk streams seem to provide the best environment of all, and the trout of rivers in the south of England, for instance, grow quickly to about 2 kg (4.4 lb).

Brown trout are individualistic, choosing a feeding territory which they will guard against usurpers. Their diet varies with the changing life of the river throughout the season, and they are at various times preoccupied with bottom-living creatures, nymphs (the swimming larvae of up-wing flies) and hatching or dying surface-borne flies. In general (but by no means invariably), they are single-minded about the particular species of fly they are taking, which they judge by colour, behaviour and size – the angler has to go some way towards matching, some or all of, these factors in order to tempt them with an artificial fly. Besides insects, brown trout will hunt minnows and the small fry of other species, and they can be taken on spinners or the larger fly-fishing lures tied to imitate small fish. They will also take baits such as maggot and worm readily, but on many waters a 'fly-only' rule applies.

Trout survive for about eight years. During breeding, they will sometimes run upriver like the related salmon and the sea-trout, and lake fish often invade the feeder-streams to breed.

§163 Rainbow trout
Salmo gairdneri

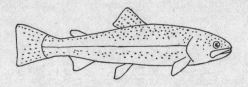

This is a quick-growing trout introduced from America which has been used to stock many British fisheries, besides being a popular fish for commercial rearing. The rainbow can be easily distinguished from the brown trout by the irridescent pinkish stripes running along the flanks, and by the profuse spotting on fins and tail (absent in the brown trout).

Normally, it attains weights of 2 kg, or more, in about three years, rarely surviving longer than five years altogether. However, there is a 'giant' race of these trout, which have been developed by commercial breeders and introduced to some fisheries. Specimens of 8 kg and more have been taken.

Rainbows tend to have much more roving habits than the brown trout, rarely sticking to a particular station for long. They are also more chummy, and ranging packs of rainbows, hunting together, are a common sight to reservoir fishermen. If the species is introduced to a river fishery without any means of restricting them to particular lengths, many will disappear up- or down-river.

Broadly, the rainbow responds to the same fishing methods as the brown trout, although its roving behaviour does mean that an angler may root himself in one spot with a reasonable expectation that a good fish will move within casting range.

§164 **Speckled trout**
Salvelinus fontinalis

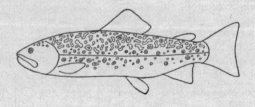

A North American char-like fish which has been introduced to some English and Scottish waters, although it is far from common. It has a mottled pattern on its back and a general scattering of smallish red spots. Fishing methods as for trout and char (below).

§165 **Char**
Salvelinus species

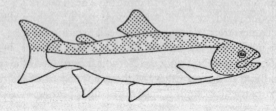

Char are found only in a few, deep, cold-water lakes in Britain. Fish found in different lakes often display different outward characteristics, and in Windermere there are even two separate populations which stay apart and even spawn at different times. These trout-related fish can be taken on bait or fly, and they often feed at great depths. They rarely grow very large. Specimens are often highly coloured with profuse spotting.

§166 **Salmon and sea-trout runs**

The following tables are only an indication of the periods which are locally accepted as being the best times to fish for salmon and sea-trout; 'best times' do not mean the only times, and besides there being a chance of late or early fish outside these times, the runs themselves may be influenced from year to year by the weather and state of the rivers.

	SALMON		SEA TROUT	
River	Lower reaches	Upper reaches	Lower reaches	Upper reaches
Avon (Devon)	Feb, Mar and Sept	Feb, Mar and Sept	June to Aug	June to Aug
Avon (Hampshire)	March to June	—	June and July	—
Camel	July and Aug	July and Aug	July and Aug	July and Aug
Coquet	Sept and Oct	Sept and Oct	Sept and Oct	Sept and Oct
Dart	April and May	May to Sept	July to Sept	July to Sept
Derwent (Cumbria)	June to Oct	August to Oct	June to Sept	June to Sept
Duddon	June to Oct	June to Oct	July and Aug	July and Aug
Eden	Jan to May	Jan to May	May to Sept	May to Sept
Esk (Border)	Feb to May	Feb to May	May to Sept	May to Sept
Exe	Feb to April	March to Sept	—	—
Fowey	July and Aug	July and Aug	July and Aug	July and Aug
Frome (Dorset)	May	May	June and July	June and July
Hodder	Aug and Sept	Aug and Sept	July to Sept	July to Sept
Itchen	Mid-April to mid-July	—	June and July	—
Kent	March, May and October	October	July and Aug	July and Aug
Leven	June to Oct	June to Oct	July and Aug	July and Aug
Lune	Feb to June	May to Oct	June to Sept	June to Sept
Piddle	May	May	June and July	June and July
Plym	A few summer fish	A few summer fish	July and Aug	July and Aug
Ribble	April to Sept (middle reaches)	July and Sept	June to Sept (middle reaches)	July to Sept
Severn	March to May	May and June	—	—
Stour	March to June	—	June and July	—
Tamar	May and June	Aug and Sept	July and Aug	July and Aug
Tavy	May and June	Aug and Sept	July and Aug	July and Aug
Taw	March and April	March and April	June to Sept	June to Sept
Teign	March and April	—	June to Sept	June to Sept
Test	Mid-April to mid-June	—	June and July	—
Torridge	Mar and April	Mar and April	June to Sept	June to Sept
Wye	March to June	Sept to Oct	—	—
Yealm	A few summer fish	A few summer fish	July and Aug	July and Aug

SCOTLAND

River	SALMON		SEA TROUT	
	Lower reaches	Upper reaches	Lower reaches	Upper reaches
Annan	April to July	April to July	April to July	April to July
Awe	Late June to Aug	Late June to Aug	May to Aug	May to Aug
Beauly	April, May, July	July to Oct	April, May, July	July to Oct
Brora	Mar, April and Aug and Sept	April to June	May, June and Sept	June and July
Dee	Feb to April	April to June	June and July	—
Deveron	April and May	April and May	June and July	June and July
Doon	Sept and Oct	Sept and Oct	Sept and Oct	Sept and Oct
Esk (North)	March, April and Oct			
Esk (South)	Feb to April	April onwards	June onwards	July onwards
Ewe	Mar and April	Mar and April	July to Oct	July to Oct
Findhorn	—	April to May	—	April and May
Forth	—	Feb to April	—	May and June
Garry (Inverness)	April to June	April to June	—	—
Moriston	Aug and Sept	Aug and Sept	—	—
Ness	July to Sept	July to Sept	—	—
Nith	April to July	April to July	April to July	April to July
Orchy	April and May, Sept and Oct	July	—	—
Oykel	April and May	July onwards	July onwards	July onwards
Spey	Mar to May	April to June	Mar to May	April to June
Stinchar	July to Sept	July to Sept	July to Sept	July to Sept
Tay	Jan to April and Sept and Oct	Jan to April and Sept and Oct	Aug to Oct	Aug to Oct
Thurso	Mar to June, Sept and Oct	Mar to June, Sept and Oct	—	—
Tweed	Feb to April	Mid-April to mid-June	Mid-July to late August	Mid-July to late August
Ugie	June to Oct	June to Oct	June to Oct	June to Oct
Ythan	—	—	June to Oct	June to Oct

WALES

River	SALMON		SEA TROUT	
	Lower reaches	Upper reaches	Lower reaches	Upper reaches
Conway	April to July	April to July	June onwards	June onwards
Clwyd	March to Aug	—	May to Oct	Sept and Oct
Dee (Welsh)	March to July	May to Oct	—	—
Dovey	June onwards	Aug onwards	June onwards	Aug onwards
Glaslyn	Late July and August	Late July and August	Late July and August	Late July and August
Lledr	April to July	April to July	June onwards	June onwards
Mawddach	April, Sept and Oct	April, Sept and Oct	June to Sept	June to Sept
Teifi	April and May	June onwards	July onwards	—
Towy	May and June	July onwards	June onwards	July onwards
Usk	April to June	Sept and Oct	Aug and Sept	Aug and Sept

ULSTER

River	SALMON		SEA TROUT	
	Lower reaches	Upper reaches	Lower reaches	Upper reaches
Bann	Aug and Sept	—	Aug and Sept	—
Finn	April and May	April and May	June onwards	June onwards
Foyle and tributaries (excluding Finn)	June onwards	June onwards	June onwards	June onwards
Faughan	June onwards	June onwards	June onwards	June onwards
Roe	June onwards	June onwards	June onwards	June onwards

EIRE

River	SALMON		SEA TROUT	
	Lower reaches	Upper reaches	Lower reaches	Upper reaches
Ballynahinch	Feb to May and mid-June and July	Feb to May and mid-June and July	July to Oct	July to Oct
Bandon	Feb to April	April to June	Feb to April	April to June
Barrow	April to June	April to June	—	—
Blackwater	March and April	March and April	June onwards	June onwards
Boyne	Feb to April	Feb to April	June onwards	June onwards
Bundrowes	June and July	June and July	July and Aug	July and Aug
Burrieshoole	May and June	May and June	July to Sept	July to Sept
Caragh	Feb to April	Feb to April	July onwards	July onwards
Cashla	June to Oct	June to Oct	June to Oct	June to Oct
Clare-Galway	April and May	April and May	June onwards	June onwards
Corrib	April and May	April and May	June onwards	June onwards
Clady	April and May	April and May	Aug and Sept	Aug and Sept
Erne	June and July	June and July	July and Aug	July and Aug
Erriff	April to June	April to June	July to Oct	July to Oct
Feale	March to mid-May	March to mid-May	June onwards	June onwards
Gweebarra	April and May	April and May	Late June to Sept	Late June to Sept
Laune	Jan to May	Jan to May	April to Sept	April to Sept
Lee	Feb and Mar	April and May	Feb and March	April and May
Leannan	Feb to May	Feb to May	June onwards	June onwards
Liffey	Jan to May	—	—	—
Maine	April to June	April to June	Aug and Sept	Aug and Sept
Moy	Feb to May and Sept and Oct	Feb to May and Sept and Oct	June onwards	June onwards
Newport	April to Sept	April to Sept	July to Sept	July to Sept
Owenduff	April to Sept	April to Sept	Late June onwards	Late June onwards
Owenea	April to Sept	April to Sept	July to Sept	July to Sept
Owengarve	July to Sept	July to Sept	July to Sept	July to Sept
Owengowla	—	—	June to Oct	June to Oct
Owenmore	April and May	April and May	Mid-June to Sept	Mid-June to Sept
Shannon	Feb to April	—	—	—
Slaney	Feb to May	Feb to May	June to Aug	June to Aug
Sligo	April and May	April and May	—	—
Waterville	Feb to April	Feb to April	July to Oct	July to Oct

Reproduced by kind permission of *Where to Fish.*

Most game fishing is essentially mobile, and to obtain the best possible results the angler should be prepared to cover as much water as he can, roaming in search of his fish rather than waiting for them to come to a fixed point. At times there are exceptions to this rule, such as reservoir fishing where rainbows patrol the margins – indeed, when reservoirs are crowded with anglers, early in the season, space to fish might be extremely limited and you might be forced to stay at one spot for some time. In sea-trout fishing, and sometimes salmon fishing too, there may well be days when the fish are on the move and it would be silly to forsake a favourable spot. However, let's consider mobility as the main 'state' of the game angler.

You'll find it impractical and tiring to carry either a lot of gear or numerous small packages and bags. Try to concentrate all that you do need in one bag or satchel, which should have a broad, comfortable shoulder strap. Your landing implement is the only item extra to rod and reel that should be ready for action while you are fishing, and here too it pays to have your net or tailer fitted with a lanyard to carry it over your shoulder, or with a clip to fasten it to your belt. A net with a long staff will, of course, have to be carried as a separate item.

You can if you wish take mobility a stage further than the satchel; there are on the market today some 'fishermen's vests' with handy pockets that will hold most of the essential gear such as fly boxes, scissors and so on (rods and tackle checklist §42).

§167 Approach

Trout: The trout of reservoirs are as demanding as river fish in a quiet, concealed approach to the water, but there is very often little that the angler can do to hide himself on clear reservoir banks. Where cover does exist, though, it is wise to use it, provided you are not hazarding your back-cast if you are fly fishing. Otherwise, keep footfalls light and make your movements deliberate and unhurried. If you are to wade in a reservoir, never neglect to cast and cover your swim before entering the water – many good trout are taken in this way, before the water is disturbed.

The same applies to river fish, for spinning, bait fishing or fly fishing. However, fly fishing does call for more concentration on approach than the other methods, and for very good reasons. To start with, it is always better to work your way upstream, rather than down. Whether you use a wet or dry fly, the trout you are after will be looking upstream for offerings to arrive on the current, and the angler stands a good chance of being spotted if he fishes downstream to his fish because the range of a fly line is comparatively short. Vibration from footfalls will also travel more quickly downstream than up, and muck from the bottom will be kicked up to travel down to the fish if the angler wades.

For dry-fly fishing in particular it is essential that the artificial fly travels at the same pace as the surface of the river; by casting upstream, a floating line is not generally retarded. Fished downstream, however, it would be very difficult to avoid dragging your fly.

Sea-trout: There are occasions when sea-trout show considerably less caution than brown trout, usually during evening feeding spells. When this happens it is sometimes quite practical to drag flies to make them more noticeable to the fish, and thus the necessity to fish upstream can be neglected.

Salmon: Fly fishing, and to some extent spinning for salmon, is an altogether different business from fishing for trout. The basic aim is to cast across or downstream so that the current sweeps the fly or lure in towards the angler's bank, fluttering and working as it goes. You can assume that a fish lying in a good, deep pool will have a range of some yards in which it is likely to move to, and take, a fly or lure (if it is in the mood), and that it will fail to move to a fly or lure seen well ahead outside this range. In between casts, therefore, it is best to move systematically downstream.

When salmon are not inclined to move much, especially in cold weather, the distance you move downstream can be a couple of yards at a time, but when fish are active ten or more yards at a time is realistic.

§168 Casting

Although approaches differ for trout, sea-trout and salmon, the casting techniques used are common to all. For bait fishing and spinning, the simple casting techniques used for coarse fishing are used (see Chapter fifteen).

Fly casting is not an easily-acquired skill. However, practice is the road to success and schooling at one of the many fly-casting schools can be used as a short-cut, or as a means of curing imperfections. Many people win through without any recourse to tutoring, but I do think that it helps if you practise with a friend, who can see more easily than you what your casting lacks – if you are letting your rod fall back too far on the back-cast, or applying power at the wrong stage and so on.

The fly-casting techniques described here are applicable to both single-handed and double-handed fly rods, although the double-

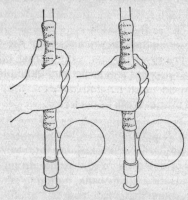

Fig. 166 (§168) The fly-rod butt is shaped for the palm, with the thumb held behind the rod (left). If you find the alternative grip (right) more comfortable, by all means use it – the biggest danger is that you might let the rod slope backwards too far when you are casting. Your thumb would naturally check this with the first grip.

haul takes some management with a large rod. The descriptions make the assumption that the angler is right-handed.

The overhead cast: Begin with short casts. Thread up rod, pulling out several yards of fly line by flexing the rod in the air above you between ten and two o'clock, making sure that the line straightens fully in front or behind you before beginning each flick ('false-casting'). Grip the butt of the rod lightly, using either the popular 'thumb-up' grasp, or letting the thumb overlap your index finger, whichever is the most comfortable (Fig. 166). The false-casting exercise will give you some idea of the principles behind fly casting, and a few switches will show that the line begins to pull the rod-tip after it as it extends on forward or back casts. You can now draw more line off your reel, and allow it to be pulled after the line in the air at the extended positions. With twelve or so yards of fly line in the air, allow it to drop onto the water before you, by lowering the rod-tip at the fully extended position on the forward flick – that, basically, is a cast, but ten to one the line crashed on the water and was far from straight and tidy. Now begin to brush up this technique so that you get more control and smoothness into the cast (Fig. 167). Stand facing the direction in which you want to cast, with the right foot a little forward. Make sure that your grip is comfortable, with the lower part of the butt lying along the underside of the forearm and the elbow tucked into your side. Raise the rod, starting slowly, so that the line begins to draw across the water towards you. Accelerate the pull until the rod is bending under the weight of the line lifting from the water and then apply a good hard flick to bring the rod to the upright position with your hand beside your cheek. Keeping the rod in this position, allow the line to straighten behind you. Don't let the backward pull of the line tug the rod and your wrist backwards – as soon as the line is straight, begin the forward cast, accelerating and finishing with a flick to bring the rod to an angle of forty-five degrees in front of you. Allow the line to straighten in front of you over the water before dropping the rod-tip gently to deposit the line on the water.

Shooting line: This is simply a means of extending the range on the forward cast. Begin the cast as before, drawing an extra length of line from the reel with your left hand as the back-cast extends.

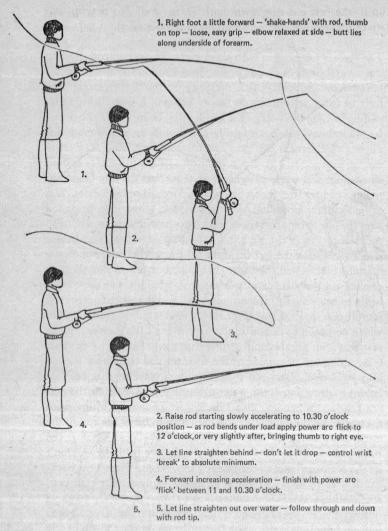

1. Right foot a little forward — 'shake-hands' with rod, thumb on top — loose, easy grip — elbow relaxed at side — butt lies along underside of forearm.

2. Raise rod starting slowly accelerating to 10.30 o'clock position — as rod bends under load apply power arc flick to 12 o'clock, or very slightly after, bringing thumb to right eye.

3. Let line straighten behind — don't let it drop — control wrist 'break' to absolute minimum.

4. Forward increasing acceleration — finish with power arc 'flick' between 11 and 10.30 o'clock.

5. Let line straighten out over water — follow through and down with rod tip.

Fig. 167 The overhead cast.

Hold the loop of line low to your left side as the forward cast begins, and deliver an extra-hard flick at the power stage. As the line straightens on the forward cast, bring the loop of line gently up to the first rod-ring with your left hand so that it is drawn after the extending line, and then lower the rod gently as before.

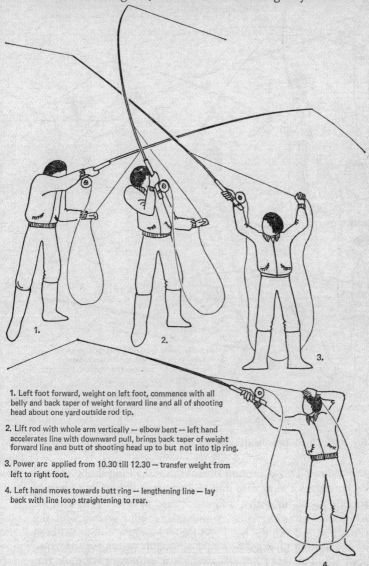

1. Left foot forward, weight on left foot, commence with all belly and back taper of weight forward line and all of shooting head about one yard outside rod tip.

2. Lift rod with whole arm vertically — elbow bent — left hand accelerates line with downward pull, brings back taper of weight forward line and butt of shooting head up to but not into tip ring.

3. Power arc applied from 10.30 till 12.30 — transfer weight from left to right foot.

4. Left hand moves towards butt ring — lengthening line — lay back with line loop straightening to rear.

Fig. 168a The double-haul back cast.

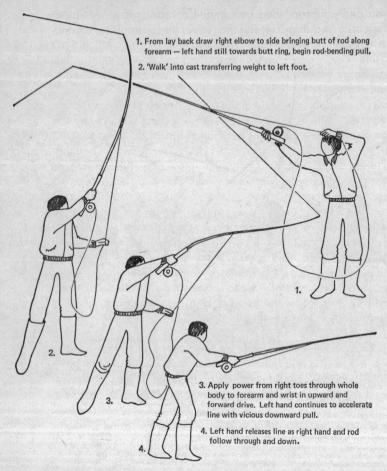

1. From lay back draw right elbow to side bringing butt of rod along forearm — left hand still towards butt ring, begin rod-bending pull.

2. 'Walk' into cast transferring weight to left foot.

3. Apply power from right toes through whole body to forearm and wrist in upward and forward drive. Left hand continues to accelerate line with vicious downward pull.

4. Left hand releases line as right hand and rod follow through and down.

Fig. 168b The double-haul forward cast.

Double-haul: This is a means of making really long shooting casts or punching a long cast into the wind; it is best used with a shooting head, or with a weight-forward fly line. Begin with the left foot forward (Fig. 168) and taking your weight. All the shooting head and the belly and back taper of a weight-forward fly line should be three to four feet outside the rod-tip. A large loop of line should be drawn off the reel, with the left hand holding the line close to the first rod-ring. Lift the rod vertically, using all your arm, accelerating and delivering a final, powerful, back-flick (which should take the rod slightly beyond the vertical), at the same time drawing down hard on the line with the left hand. This action compresses the rod and speeds up the line. Allow the back-cast to extend and draw your left hand back up to the first rod-ring before repeating the actions of the back cast – acceleration, flick, and sharp draw with the left hand – in the forward cast. When the forward cast shoots out across the water and extends, the loop of line or backing is released, to be drawn after it, and the rod-tip is lowered to drop the line as gently as possible. During the cast your weight should transfer from the left foot to the right at the extension of the back cast, and back to the left foot for the forward drive.

With both the overhead cast and the double-haul, some adaptions are necessary for wind; with a wind blowing into your face, you can begin the flick of the back-cast earlier than usual, and you should delay the forward flick as much as possible. Reverse these actions for a wind blowing from behind you. It is also advisable to shorten your leader and cast for fishing into the wind, while a long leader and cast can be managed much more easily with a following wind.

Roll cast: This is a very useful technique for short-range work or for use in situations where bankside vegetation etc. prohibits a long back-cast. Begin as if making an overhead cast, but omit backward flick and allow line to draw into a loop beside you (Fig. 169). When the line stops moving, begin a forward cast, delivering a powerful flick as late as possible. The loop of line should roll off the water and it will then begin to extend in front of you. Lower the rod-tip to let the extended line fall gently onto the water.

Common faults: Two of the most widely experienced difficulties are the line clouting the rod during casts, and the fly catching in the body of the fly line. Both can be caused by many factors, but the main fault is not allowing the cast to extend fully behind or to the fore before reversing direction. If you iron this out and still experience difficulties, you may be keeping your rod too straight during the cast – lean it away from you slightly to the right on the backward draw, bringing it closer to your head for the forward

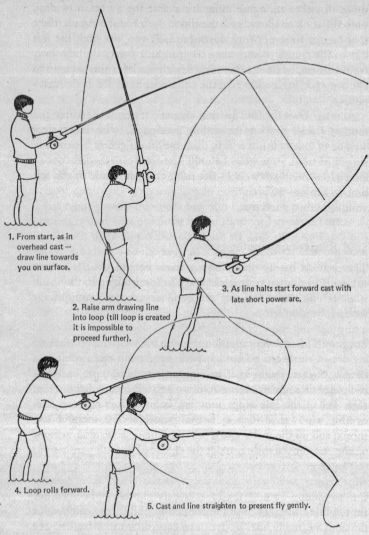

1. From start, as in overhead cast — draw line towards you on surface.

2. Raise arm drawing line into loop (till loop is created it is impossible to proceed further).

3. As line halts start forward cast with late short power arc.

4. Loop rolls forward.

5. Cast and line straighten to present fly gently.

Fig. 169 The roll cast.

drive. Another annoying difficulty is that the fly tends to drop onto the bank or the water behind you during casts. Again, there may be many reasons for this, but usually you will find that it is due to the failure to keep the rod upright, or only slightly away from vertical, while the line extends – the wrist is 'breaking' and allowing too great a slope in the rod under pressure of the cast's pull.

Another reason could be that you are trying to aerialize too much fly line, or that the rod is overloaded with the wrong weight of line – use the A.F.T.M. guide carefully. You might simply be tired, a situation I would suspect if casting goes wrong after a long period of trouble-free fishing. When this happens, it is time to explore the lunch bag or smoke a pipe – anything to give your rod-arm a good rest.

§169 Retrieves, stripping etc.

The reel can hardly play a less passive role than it does in fly fishing. Even when you are playing a fish, retrieving line by hand is more efficient than using the reel. Unless the reel is of the modern 'multiplier' geared type, its small diameter recovers such a tiny amount of line for every turn of the handle that you could not possibly keep up with fast, active fish such as trout and salmon running directly to you, and loss of contact will often mean loss of fish. For retrieving when your cast is fished out, too, it is best to loop the line by hand and keep it off the reel ready for the next cast. The other form of retrieve, withdrawing line to make a fly or lure 'work' in the water, is also best achieved by hand movements, and so is collecting the line which comes downstream towards you when dry-fly fishing.

The simplest form of retrieve or line-collection is 'stripping', which means pulling the line with the left hand and either holding it in large loops or allowing it to drop onto the water or into the boat. When stripping, the line is often hooked around the index finger of the rod hand (Fig. 170) so that it cannot slide back up the rod if released by the left hand. Stripping is also used to draw lures through the water in an attractive way – particularly large, fish-imitating lures.

For gentler retrieves, line can be collected by alternately gathering it around the little finger and index finger of the left

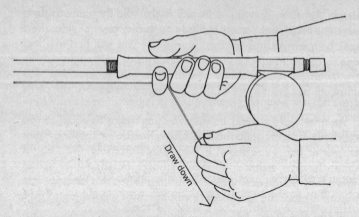

Fig. 170 (§169) Stripping – draw downwards on line until arm rests at thigh. Vary rate of retrieve.

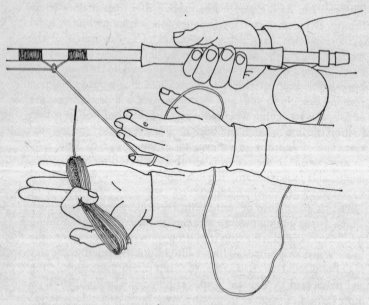

Fig. 171 Figure-of-eight retrieve – pick up line alternately with little finger and index finger and thumb, transferring coils to palm.

hand (Fig. 171). It can then be palmed to hold for the next cast. This method is also useful for working small flies.

§170 Colour of line, shadow

There is much controversy over the ideal colour for a fly line, some anglers favouring white, and others brown or green. However, the argument that white is less visible viewed from below just does not hold water – it throws just as much shadow as other colours, and the shadow is the really important factor. Having taken fish on lines of all colours, I'm inclined to think that it doesn't matter a great deal what colour is used, with the exception of deep-water fishing where white line might be a drawback because contrast makes it stand out too strongly.

A common experience with fly fishermen is that small coarse-fish, and sometimes salmon, leap over a moving line, and since this usually happens on a bright day the fish are probably experiencing a 'wall' of shadow that seems so solid that it must be

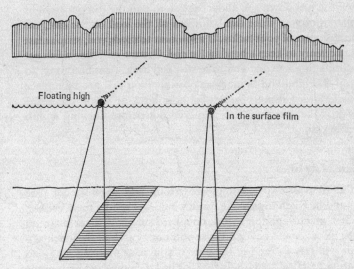

Fig. 172 (§170) Shadow created by floating, fly lines on a bright day – in certain conditions the shadow creates the impression of a solid wall, surface to bed, to the fish. They may surface and leap over the line to avoid it.

negotiated by hopping over the top. Thus, beware of putting a shadow wall too close to fish lies. With floating lines, those sitting on the surface throw a larger shadow on the bed than lines which float in the surface film (Fig. 172), and so surface-film lines are superior to high-floaters.

§171 Playing fish

Beginners to fly fishing are often surprised that trout in clear water make straight, fast runs and seem averse to tacking sideways. The reason for this is that the fly line has a large surface area and is easier to drag forwards than to either side. The fact that the line is exerting considerable drag on a running fish is important because it takes away the necessity for the angler to interfere too much with the run – the drag, plus the tension of the reel ratchet will generally tire a fish quickly enough. If the fish does head off sideways, so much the better – it will tire even more quickly. However, do maintain as close a contact as possible with your fish, keeping the rod well up. Don't, whatever you do, stop the reel down and allow the fish to pull the rod out straight in front of you, since this will place all the load on the cast, the weakest part of your tackle. If a fish runs towards you, strip as fast as necessary to keep a bend in the rod. Beware of letting a fish get near floating line that you have stripped back – it is best to try to drop it behind you as much as possible (you will not experience this hazard if fishing from a bank or boat, or if you use a line raft). Make sure your fish is played out before drawing it into netting range.

§172 Care of fly lines

Modern plastic-coated lines are strong and durable, but care should be taken to avoid damage which will render them useless. When practising, don't work on a hard surface – water is always best. You should never practise without a cast and fly attached – this will fray the end of the line. If you want to avoid snagging during practice, attach a fly that has had the point and barb of the hook removed. Don't use line flotants or line cleaners that the manufacturer of your line has not recommended; many of these preparations contain solvents which might weaken the plastic coating. Finally, before fishing, give your line a good stretch – not too hard (it will stand about 12 lb pull). This irons out the kinks and twirls formed on the reel.

§173 **Wading**

This is mainly a cautionary note, since it must be obvious that wading extends the scope of still-water and river anglers considerably. Rubber-soled waders are adequate for most clay-bottomed reservoirs with slightly sloping sides, but steeper banks, stony bottoms (particularly large stones which might rock under your weight) and swift rivers do make it necessary to have waders with nailed soles. Always avoid wading from very steep banks – it is wise to take the precaution of rolling down your waders to knee-level before stepping onto reservoir dams. It is very difficult to remove thigh waders if you fall into very deep water, but rolled-down waders can be kicked off. Use extra caution in murky water where you cannot see the bottom. A staff, or a long-handled landing net is useful for feeling for holes and ridges which might trap you. On the bank, avoid thorny areas which might puncture rubber waders. One of my worst experiences was walking over a piece of land where briars had just been cut, leaving short, dagger-like stems pointing from the ground. Through lack of caution I got two punctures and a cut shin, but I have learned to avoid cleared thickets since. It is a good idea to carry a cycle, puncture-repair outfit; on a warm day, rubber cement dries quickly enough to effect a repair in half an hour or so.

Fly fishing
Quick cross reference guide

Lines for casts, leaders, §11a, 11f.
Fly lines, §11d.
Hooks, §12.
Knots, §18c.
Rods tackle checklist, §42.
Preparations, §43.

Many salmon anglers of long standing will cringe at any attempt to condense the art into so short a passage, and I must therefore warn readers that the advice I am able to give can be extended greatly by experience and by reading the many excellent books on the subject – most of which make it clear that there is still much conjecture and controversy surrounding the salmon and the methods of fishing for it.

I should also advise you to take good heed of local advice, particularly regarding choice of fly patterns to suit individual waters. The salmon flies I have included here form only part of a huge list of patterns; nevertheless, they are a good basis on which to start a collection, and they are all tried and reputable takers-of-fish.

Because of the wide range of fly patterns and the fact that each of them is tied in a variety of sizes from $\frac{1}{2}$ in to 3 in or more, it is important to look at the laws governing choice of colour and size – hook size in this instance bearing no real relation to the size of fish you expect to catch, as it might in other forms of fishing. The next consideration is where they should be presented in the water – top, middle, or close to the bottom – and how fast they should move in order to encourage response from a fish.

The sizes of spinning lures also follow the basic rules for flies, with the exception that spinners, wobblers and plugs are generally slightly longer than the flies at all the stages in the tables below – add $\frac{1}{2}$ in to 1 in.

§174   Fly and lure sizes related to temperature

Some anglers stick to rigid water-temperature guides when selecting fly and lure sizes. The basic law works something like this:

Season	Temperature	Fly (lure) size
Spring	Below 42°	2½–3 in
Late spring	Around 48°	1½–2 in
Summer	50° and above	¾–1½ in
Autumn	50° and below	2–2½ in

As you can see, this shows fly or lure sizes decreasing as the temperature rises, and increasing when it begins to fall. However, there are a couple of spanners to throw into the works. First of these is the late spring arrivals, fresh-run and usually playful as they move upriver in a purposeful way. They will take the small flies normally associated with high temperatures and low water in summer. Secondly, there are the pool-locked, summer fish close to spawning which may well take large flies or lures, ignoring small patterns. Lastly there are the latest fish of all, the autumn travellers, which behave in much the same way as the late spring runners.

A more complex table emerges:

Season		Fly size
Spring	Fish in pools (disinclined to move)	2½–3 in
Late spring	Fish in pools (disinclined to move)	2–2½ in
	Travelling fish	1–1½ in
Summer and late summer	Fish in normal state	¾–1½ in
	Restless fish	2–2½
Autumn	Late stayers	2–2½
	Travelling fish	1–1½ in

§175 **Speed and depth at which to fish flies, lures**

Salmon in cold pools tend to take up station near the bottom, while travellers nearly always more close to the surface. Warm water increases activity, while the cold fish is largely inactive. You can relate the various moods of the salmon to the speed and depth at which the fly (and lure) sizes discussed above should be fished:

Season	Speed	Depth
Spring fish in pools (disinclined to move)	Slow, very slow	Low
Late spring fish in pools (disinclined to move)	Slow–moderate	Low–mid

Season	Speed	Depth
Late spring, travelling fish	Moderate	High–mid
Summer fish in normal state	Moderate	Varied (high if pool stale)
Summer fish, restless	Varied	Varied
Autumn, late stayers	Moderate–slow	Varied
Autumn, travelling fish	Moderate	High–mid

§176 Colour of flies and lures

'A bright fly for a bright day' is an old saying among salmon anglers, and this certainly seems to be borne out by results. Logically, brightness merely lightens dark objects, and they might thus be obscured from a fish's sight, whereas objects which are already bright are intensified. In contrast, black and dark-dressed flies are useful in murky water and poor light, when their dense colouration is further darkened. It can be assumed that the quieter fly-dressings will be quite noticeable outside the two states of brightness and poor light. This can be translated into fly patterns, forming a basic selection:

Bright: Garry, Torrish
Dark: Thunder and lightning, Stoat-tail, Jock Scott, Hairy Mary
Intermediate: Kate, March Brown

There is one further necessity for the collection – a flashy fly suitable for restricted areas and well-broken water, where the fish will have only a brief glimpse of the fly before it sweeps out of view. Such patterns as Stoat-tail silver and Silver Wilkinson fit the bill. Small, medium and large sizes should be obtained of at least one pattern of bright, dark, intermediate and flashy flies to cover most conditions.

With lures and spinners, silver, gold and yellow can be regarded as bright-weather choices, with bronzes and browns suitable for poor light. Green–yellow and brown–yellow finishes are suitable for a wide range of light conditions.

The effects of flood: Floods alter 'normal' salmon behaviour, and this in turn influences some of the rules discussed above. As rain freshens the river at the start of a spate, you can expect salmon to become more lively and they are often in a taking mood. However, as colour enters the rising river they may very well go decidedly 'off' spinners and flies. If high water is maintained over a period of days they will begin to take again, but otherwise it is best to fish when the river is fining down. During fining down, salmon will lie high in the water until the silt drops out of the lower levels of pools.

§177 Fly fishing – types of fly

There are two main types of salmon fly, the traditional fly, dressed on single or double hooks, and the tube fly (Fig. 173). The latter

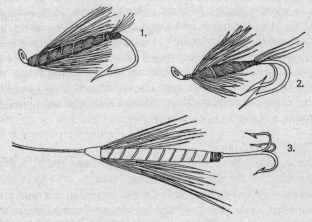

Fig. 173 (§177) Types of salmon fly: 1 – traditional fly tied on a large single hook; 2 – low-water fly on a double hook; 3 – tube fly, with a small treble hook.

is a fairly recent development, and it consists of dressings laid around a short length of tube, and a treble hook (sizes 12–8). The angler passes his cast through the tube, fastening on the treble, so that the body of the fly is free to travel up the line. This is important, because it means that a taking fish will nudge the body of the fly away from the comparatively short shank of the treble, and no leverage will be available to wrest the hook free – with the long shanks of the traditional flies, hard-jawed salmon might be lost if they roll and put pressure on the hook's shank. Many tube flies have a small brass cap at the head which weights them so that they swim attractively on an even keel.

§178 Sunk-line (traditional), fly fishing

The aim of sunk-line fly fishing is to use the current to take your fly to likely fish lies; it is a nice way of fishing pools of average depth, say to eight feet, and is unlike spinning in that the fly, sweeping clear of the river's bed, will usually avoid snags. It is most usefully employed when salmon are lying deep, and to re-capitulate on salmon moods, fly size and fishing speed of flies in the tables above, you can expect it to be rewarding to fish early in the year, with large flies, fished slowly, close to the bottom – and again in late summer and autumn. I wouldn't put this style out of court with one of the heavier reservoir trout rods, so long as a largish-capacity reel, capable of carrying over fifty yards of backing besides the fly line, is used. The longer, salmon, fly rods, however, have the important advantages of being able to throw longer lines, and of being better for controlling the move-ments of the line in the water. The modern, slow-sinking line comes closest to matching the traditional silk lines, and although spinning is better for pools deeper than the eight feet I suggested above, a fast-sinking line can be used for this deep water if fly fishing is mandatory.

Before looking at the actual technique of using the fly, a note about takes. At the times of year when the large, sunk fly is used, takes are slow and deliberate. For the bank angler, the usual for-mula when a take is felt is to move two or three paces down-stream, to make sure that the fly is firmly held, before tightening up on the fish (a good firm tug, not a line-whipping strike). For wading or fishing from a boat, a loop of line can be held in reserve in the left hand to release when the take is felt. It is not essential to have a combination of leader and cast exceeding six feet (10–12 lb breaking strain), from the point of the fly line to the fly, for this method. One fly is generally used, although two-fly casts are not uncommon. It is also worth mentioning that tube flies can be used in combinations of two or three to make up extra-long flies (Fig. 174).

Without visible signs of moving fish, and without any cir-cumstances to suggest that salmon might be stationed off the bottom (flood water, for example), you should begin at the head of the pool and work steadily with successive casts to the tail. The speed of your fly, while mainly dependent on the speed of the

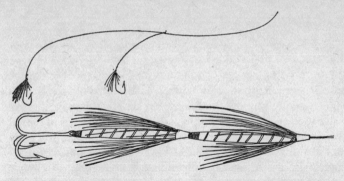

Fig. 174 (§178) Two-fly casts (above) or a single fly may be used. A large single tube fly can be made from two small tube flies (below).

current, can be controlled in its cross-river, underwater path by the angle at which you make your cast. In order to get it to travel at the fastest rate, a cast square across the river (Fig. 175) will have

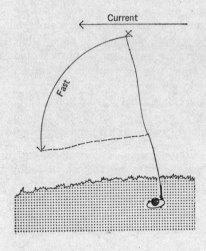

Fig. 175 The square cast will be swept at a fast rate in towards the angler.

the full force of the current driving against the side of the line. The more you angle the cast downstream, the slower it will go across the stream since the force of the current is dissipated in driving the line downstream (Fig. 176). An angle of about forty-five degrees downstream, and to the far bank, is the best cast for

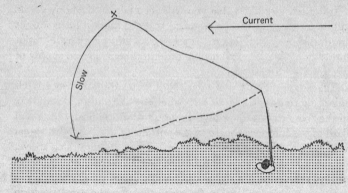

Fig. 176 An angled cast will work more slowly across the river to the angler's bank.

the slow, sunk fly. When the cast is made, a small amount of slack might be loosed to allow it to swim slightly downstream while sinking – it should be stopped, however, before the fly can sink entirely to the bottom and the line starts to double back on itself under the water. Then hold your rod before you, at an angle of forty-five degrees from the vertical, pointing it at the fly while the line works around and into your own bank. Your fly should now be swimming off the bottom, waving gently in the current (Fig. 177). You might be lucky enough to have a take first cast, but more often than not the first cast is a trial of the current speed, and if you feel that your fly is not moving sufficiently fast you can try drawing some line back slowly with your left hand (stripping) to speed it up.

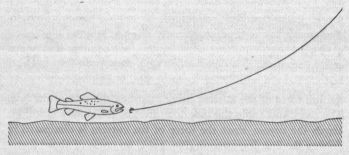

Fig. 177 The sunk fly in position.

It is also more likely that you will get a take in the body or the tail of the pool; it can be assumed that the salmon have sought an ideal spot or 'lie' where the amount of effort they have to put into staying in station is small in order to obtain a good supply of fresh, oxygenated water.

Takes are recognized in a variety of forms. Mostly they are felt as resistance on the line, or seen when the line within view falters in the cross-river path. However, you may occasionally see a dull flash as a fish moves square to the current to take, and this signal will come in advance of signals from the line. As suggested above, you should then give your fish time to grasp the fly firmly before setting the hook.

Some anglers will fish a fly twice through the same position before moving on, others make do with one cast at a time. If a fish moves to the fly without taking, however, it is generally worth having another try. In this instance some anglers will change to another fly pattern for the second attempt, while others will change the fly size, usually to a smaller size. I've taken fish without changing either, and many other anglers have had the same experience – the fly you are using, after all, has provoked some response from the salmon and there is no real reason why this should not be repeated. In all probability the fish misjudged the speed and direction of the fly first time around – the fish may be in quite an inactive mood. Whether or not you think such persistance worthwhile, the thrill of seeing a fish moving to your fly is tremendous.

At the end of each cast, when the fly is coming into your bank, draw it back smoothly, collecting line with the left hand, until you have a short enough line to lift from the water for the next cast. Don't become so engrossed in fishing down a pool that you forget about changing conditions, however – be prepared to change flies at any time, particularly if the light alters.

Moving into summer, with higher temperatures and more active fish, fly sizes should be dropped proportionately and can be fished more quickly by covering pools with a squarer cast; with small patterns, generally termed 'low-water' flies, fished in this manner, the sunk line need never be abandoned throughout the season. However, the alternative, fishing with a floating line, is in some instances superior and certainly more exciting.

§179 Floating line

The excitement inherent in this method is that the salmon actually 'rises' to a small fly pattern travelling no more than a matter of inches beneath the surface, and in doing so, frequently gives an indication of its size. It may, for instance, make a perfect 'head and tail' rise, displaying beautiful, porpoise-like elegance (Fig. 178). After interception, the fish will generally sink back to its

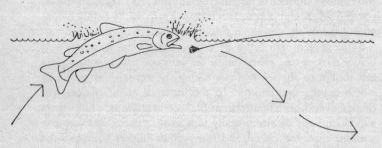

Fig. 178 (§179) The head-and-tail rise to a fly fished on a floating line – characteristic of a fish moving upriver.

lie holding the fly, and delay as in the above sunk-line method is advisable before the hook is set. However, it pays to be wary with a run of small salmon in the river – they have a tendency to spit out the fly.

The method of fishing the fly with a floating line is, however, quite unlike fishing for trout or sea-trout, and it seems critical that in order to be fully effective, the fly should travel no more than a few inches beneath the surface. At the times when a floating line is used, the fish are active and alert and you can assume that they will pick out suspicious objects such as the fly line; casts and leaders for this method should be 10–12 ft (9–12 lb breaking strain). The fly line is, of course, a floater, and the sink-tip is usually ruled out because it may take the fly too deep. All of the cast should be treated to make it sink. Although it seems logical to grease it to make it float to within a few inches of the fly, in practice, greasing like this will only make the fly rise quickly to the surface when the line is checked, while by checking a sinking cast you can easily bring your fly to the correct depth.

Otherwise, the fly should be made to work as would a fly on a sunk line – with the emphasis on making the fly pass briskly across likely lies by the use of squarish casts and some hand-drawing on the line. However, the drawback with a floating line fished downstream is that the surface movements of the water quickly put a bow in the line which can lessen control of the fly at a critical stage. It will be necessary to take in the line and create an upstream bow (Fig. 179) in order to combat this. I advised above that you

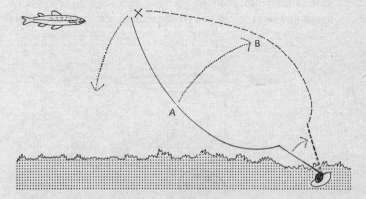

Fig. 179 With the line in position A the fly will swing too quickly into the bank, short of the fish – the floating line can be 'mended' with a flick upstream to keep the fly on a more acceptable path, although the manoeuvre is difficult and requires practice.

should move longer distances downstream between casts for the more alert fish; R. V. Righyni, in his book *Advanced Salmon Fishing* (Macdonald) describes the interesting reactions of salmon observed by somebody who was able to see fish, fly and the angler fishing for them in a pool. The salmon appeared to become aware of the surface activity of the fly when it was twenty yards upstream; they stiffened, and then resumed movement on a more rapid scale than before. If, after a couple of casts, the fly came in taking range, the salmon would generally rise. However, if the angler moved too slowly and made many casts before bringing his fly within taking-range of the fish, the fish seemed to be immune to its charms.

§180 **Spinning**

Spinning for salmon is roughly parallel to fly fishing, and the laws of fly size, colour and fishing speed apply equally to both styles. Anyone setting out to spin, therefore, should take note of the section on fly fishing above. In brief, one should try to fish large lures, deeply and slowly, early and late in the season, while in mid season the general practice is to fish small spinners and lures closer to the surface at a somewhat brisker pace.

Just as there are many fly patterns, there are many types of spinners and lures which will attract salmon, although only a few

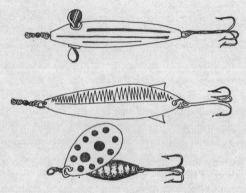

Fig. 180 (§180) Top, a metal Devon minnow; middle, the Toby lure; bottom, Mepps spinner.

tried and reliable designs need be carried (in a variety of lengths and colours to suit conditions). It is safe to say, however, that the slimmer-profile spinners and lures shown in Fig. 180 are regarded as best, while the large, broad spoons you might use for pike don't hold much attraction for salmon. Without a doubt the Devon minnow, produced in a variety of weights and materials as well as in several colours, is extremely popular, followed by the Toby lure which is a slim flutterer. The metal Devon's weight allows it to be used on an unweighted line, but a better, more level-swimming action will always be achieved with a plastic or wooden Devon and a line with a Wye lead (Fig. 181). Devons with weighted noses do work on their own, but not so well, I

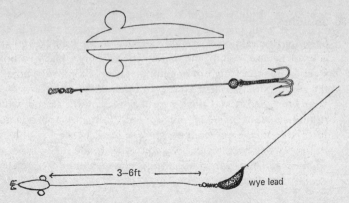

Fig. 181 Devons are made from a variety of materials, but all have a hollow interior and a swivelled, hook mount (top). Wooden and plastic Devons swim well on a weighted line (above).

think, as they can on a weighted line. Like the tube fly, the Devon is based on a hollow tube, and can slip off its mount and up the line when nudged by a taking fish – this avoids any leverage against the spinner's body forcing the hook free. Very light Devons, made of quill, are useful for light spinning in summer. The Toby, a bright metal lure, is extra useful in coloured water or poor light, when extra impact produced by its vibrationary, fluttering action is required.

Spinning does hold sway over fly fishing in the early and late parts of the season when heavy water virtually rules fly out. It is also a better alternative for the very big pools which may plunge to depths of twenty feet or more, and for the exploration of long, level stretches which would be tedious if fished with a fly.

In many places the current will work your spinner or lure much as it would a fly, and this is particularly true if you use the stouter, braided lines in place of nylon monofilament; however, in many more cases than in fly fishing the angler will have to impart sufficient action to the lure or spinner to make it work properly; in swift flows, this might amount to no more than a slow turning of the reel to keep in touch, but in sluggish water, especially with a nylon line, a more active retrieve will be necessary even with a square cast. A good dodge with light, summer spinning is to cast square, well above the fish's lie, with a light spinner on an unweighted, or slightly weighted line, and allow the current to accelerate it until, just above the fish, it is halted, to swing in a quick turn (Fig. 182).

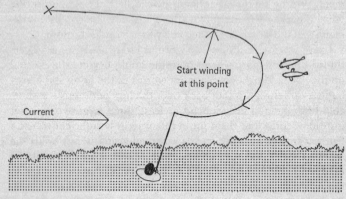

Start winding
at this point

Current

Fig. 182 U-turn spin.

An alternative to artificial spinners is a small deadbait – minnow, bleak, spratt – fished either on a spinning mount, or fished sink-and-draw (§151) with a tandem treble rig to ensure good hooking.

§181 Using the prawn, worms

Artificial or natural prawns (fished on a prawn mount – Fig. 183) are regarded by some anglers as a fool's choice, although they undoubtedly catch salmon that are in a dour mood and disinclined to accept anything else. They also have the power of scaring every fish out of a pool, as many anglers will testify.

Drilled bullet

swivel

5ft

Fig. 183 (§181) Rig for fishing prawn – an unweighted line may be used in low, clear water, but it is wise to retain the swivel in case the prawn spins.

Prawns can be used on a fly line, or on bait or spinning tackle – normally in summer and with somewhat stale conditions in the pools, although out of frustration many have been driven to try them at other points in the season, not always to their disappointment. Worms, on the other hand, are excellent at times, especially when the river is fining down after a spate. These conditions demand that the worms are fished fairly firmly on the bottom.

I say 'worms', because one worm is rarely used; some anglers thread three or more worms onto the hook, beyond the eye and up the line, adding a couple more worms to the hook and allowing the earlier ones to fall back over the new additions – a veritable festooning. I recommend at least three large worms, but instead of threading them up in this way, it is sufficient to use a baitholder sea-hook, which has a barbed shank which holds the worms clear of the bend and point. Hook sizes 2 or 4 should be used. As I said, this is normally fished (Fig. 184) on the bottom in heavy water periods. A lighter rig (Fig. 185) can be used satisfactorily in summer, allowed to swing through a pool much as a fly would, or dropped slowly downstream with small halts (a sort of sink-and-draw fashion, because the halts raise the bait in the water). Reactions to the take with baits are the same as for fly, with a delay to make sure that the hold is firm. Eels can be

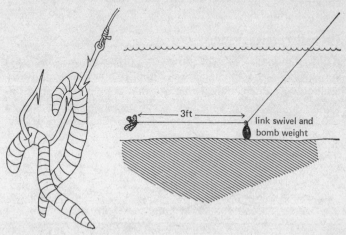

Fig. 184 Worms on 'baitholder' hook for salmon, and weighted leger rig.

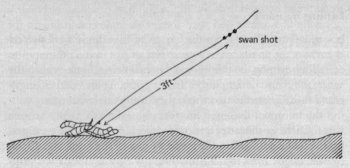

Fig. 185 Light worm-fishing rig.

troublesome at times with worm bait, and they may force a change to some other method.

Dropping-down: This can be achieved with either sunk-line flies, spinners or baits, and is used where salmon have taken up a station in a narrow neck where the flow is compressed into a fast chute. The fly, spinner or bait is allowed to drop gently downstream, with checks to keep it off the bottom, until it can be held working in the neck or dropped down further in case the salmon are lying below the obstruction. You should wait to give the fish a chance to see and inspect the lure (Fig. 186).

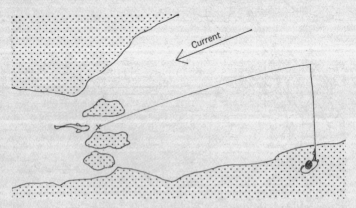

Fig. 186 Allow current to hold fly, bait or spinner in position when fish is stationed below restriction which creates fast water.

§182 **Tailing by hand**

It is quite possible to grasp the 'wrist' of the salmon's tail to land it without the assistance of a net, tailer or gaff, but a pre-requisite of tailing salmon is a firm, gently-shallowing bank where the angler will not be in danger from stooping low and lifting a heavy load. There are two ways of grasping the wrist; either with the thumb and forefinger towards the salmon's head, or vice versa. Of these, the latter is most secure. Not only is the strongest part of your grip around the end of the 'wedge' of the tail fin (which might force apart your hand with the alternative grip) but your arm is in the best position for coping with a heavy load – you can pull the fish up and draw it close to you, as opposed to drawing it out and away from you with the arm 'upside down' and in a walk lifting position (Fig. 187).

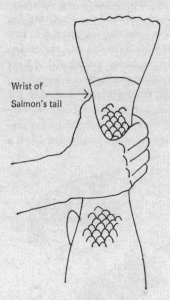

Wrist of
Salmon's tail

Fig. 187 (§182) Grasp with crook between thumb and forefinger facing tail when landing a salmon by hand. It gives a more secure hold and an easier lift.

§183 **Sea-trout fishing**

A curious mixture of salmon and trout in behaviour, the sea-trout is even called 'salmon-trout' in some areas. Driven by the urge to spawn, it foresakes sea feeding-grounds, running (sometimes in great numbers) up rivers to spawn. It is recognized that at least some fish are similar to the salmon when it comes to accepting flies, spinners and lures – i.e. they are fasting and motivated to snap at offerings for reasons other than feeding. However, many others (mainly summer-run fish) do feed, and pretty avidly at that, when the mood takes them.

Both salmon and trout anglers are likely to take sea-trout when they are present in the river, using either fly, spinners or bait, and it is fair to say that it takes no more than slight adaptations of trout or salmon styles to fish purposely for them, with the reservation that light trout-fly tackle is no match for a big sea-trout.

Otherwise the 'slight adaptations' are scaling down the salmon fly cast and leader, and the strength of the spinning line, while trout tackle should correspondingly be stepped up in strength to, ideally, the sort of gear one would use on reservoirs where large rainbows are present. In general, smaller spinners and lures than those used for salmon – $\frac{1}{2}$ in to 2 in – are used for sea-trout, but spinning in this instance differs from spinning for salmon in that the fish may well be actively hunting for food and will respond to the spinning styles developed for predatory coarse fish (§155) and trout. The sea-trout will also take worm, and I have even taken occasional fish in estuaries on lugworm intended for flounders. With fly fishing, however, a totally distinct range of fly patterns – mostly wet, i.e. sinking flies – has developed for sea-trout fishing. Many of the dressings are quite gaudy, although a

Fig. 188 (§183) Flies for sea-trout fishing – top left, Butcher; top right, Teal silver and blue; bottom, Jungle Cock Demon.

few are quiet, and it is wise to base a collection on the same principles discussed above for selecting salmon flies – brightish flies for strong light, darker dressings for dusk or dull conditions, and a flashy dressing for broken water. Like the salmon, the sea-trout's activity will increase with rising temperatures, and large, wet flies slowly will suit cold weather, while the smaller fly-patterns are best for summer.

Most of the moderate-to-small patterns are dressed on hook sizes 10–6, but the larger patterns – up to 2 in long – are frequently dressed on two or even three hooks tied in sequence (Fig. 188).

Suggestions for the basis of a collection of sea-trout flies are:

Bright: Dunkeld, Grouse and Orange
Dark: Grouse and Claret, Black Jay
Intermediate: Grouse and Green
Flashy: Teal Silver and Blue, Butcher, Bloody Butcher, Peter Ross, Blue Zulu

As can be seen, flashy patterns predominate, and this is because the flashy factor pays better when sea-trout are really 'on'; bright, dark and intermediate flies on hook sizes 6, 8 and 10 should be carried, and quite a large selection of flashy patterns in a variety of sizes. One or two large flies are always useful, such as the Peter Ross Tandem, or Blue Terror or Jungle Cock Demon (a long, black and white fly with a red tag) tied on three hooks in sequence.

Expect sea-trout to feed avidly, moving steadily upriver, at dusk, when the above flies should be employed with a sinking cast and either a floating or sink-tip line. The cast should be square, and, unlike salmon fishing, begin to work the fly (or flies) back with small regular movements by gathering line in the left hand. If this fails to meet with a response, faster stripping can be tried, with long swift draws of line gathered by the left hand. At other times, though, a fly allowed to fish salmon-fashion provokes a response. Sea-trout breaking the water is often a signal to prepare for action, and their boldness is quite considerable – they have been known to swim past wading anglers without fear, even brushing waders in passing.

Dry fly: Sea-trout seem less cautious about the types of dry fly offered than trout, and large patterns such as a Palmer are often quite acceptable. For dusk, darkness and dawn, when moths are on the water and sea-trout slash even at dragging flies which would put off trout, a fly with a predominance of white such as the Winged Coachman can be deadly. I include fishing in the dark because I've had some quite thrilling times in the West country, fishing for sea-trout with a large, white, dry fly after dark – summer night-light with a little bit of moonlight is quite sufficient to cast a fly somewhere onto the water, and at times that has been all that is necessary because the fish roam throughout the pools, right into the shallows where they wouldn't stray in the day-time.

Salmon and sea-trout fishing
Quick cross-reference guide

Fly casts, Spinning lines, §11a, 11f.
Fly lines, §11d.
Hooks, §12.
Weights, §16.
Knots, spinning, §18b.
Knots, fly fishing, §18c.
Rods, tackle checklists, §39, 42.
Preparations, §43.
Freshwater environments, §58–68.
Species, salmon, §160; sea-trout, §161.
Salmon and sea-trout runs, §166.
Approach, fly casting, wading, §167–173.

The trout feeds on almost any of the small creatures found in a river or lake, taking small fish, worms, snails, beetles and – perhaps most important of all from the angler's point of view – water-born flies at all stages of their development.

Leaving aside worming and spinning for the time being, it is the water-born fly which forms the basis of the fly fisherman's art, and although small fish, worms, beetles and so on can be, and are, represented by fly patterns, representations of natural water-born flies make up the main part of a huge list of imitative patterns. That these creatures also form the main part of the trout's diet cannot be doubted; there are times when trout are thoroughly preoccupied with a particular kind of fly (which one can suppose is available in such numbers that other food can safely be ignored, or is in some way tastier than alternatives) at one stage or another in its development.

It therefore becomes important to study the life cycle of winged, water-born flies in some detail. They begin life as an egg, either dropped in the water or laid beneath the surface on waterweed, stones or the bankside. After emerging from the egg, the grub or larva feeds on the bottom or among weed and debris, some species being active and able to swim, others crawling slowly and deliberately in search of food. It has been said that the larva of the mayfly spends around two years feeding in this fashion before starting its metamorphosis to an adult fly. Other species, such as olives, take less time, while some may take considerably more.

To continue the story: when the time comes, the larva (which has shucked several skins while it is growing) starts to make a hazardous journey to the surface, dropping downriver with the current as it does so. At this stage it probably forms the bulk of the trout's diet, and trout feeding on 'nymphs', as they are known to the angler, are quite noticeable, swinging two or so feet this way, and then that, across the current.

If the water is clear, you'll probably catch glimpses of white showing from inside the fishes' mouths as they intercept nymphs. When the nymphs are near the surface, you'll also notice that the fish are 'bulging', i.e. they disturb the surface without breaking through as they intercept the rising nymphs. Survivors struggle through the surface film, where the phenomenon known as a 'hatch' begins to take place. The skin of the nymph splits to allow a winged insect to crawl free and stand either on the shuck it has just left, or on the surface film, while its wings dry and harden. The winged insect is not yet an adult; it is known as a 'dun' by anglers. Wings hard, it lifts off the water and flies to land on bushes, grass or rushes where the final stage begins – the dun's skin is shed, just as it formerly shed the nymph shuck, and the adult flies off to join others of its kind and mate, usually in the air. Anglers call the mating fly a 'spinner'. The female spinner, after mating, flutters over the water dipping its abdomen into the surface to lay eggs, and it may settle momentarily to drop down a few feet with the current while it does so. Both sexes eventually drop on the water, exhausted, to die, when they are called 'spent flies'. At the dun, spinner and spent stages trout will rise to take the flies through the surface film. If there is a large hatch, the water-surface might boil with rising trout; at times in the mayfly season fish might become quite incautious, lying almost out of the water to drink in a plentiful supply of food like old topers slurping down pint after pint.

§184 Types of artificial fly

The artificial fly is created from scraps of feather, wool, silk and tinsel thread; naturally it cannot exactly resemble whatever it strives to imitate, but instead the aim is to give a fair representation of size, shape, density and colour, bearing in mind what the fish is expecting to see in the water (in the case of nymphs and wet flies) or on the water (dry flies). In the tying of patterns to represent the various stages of winged water-born flies described above, the most useful ingredients are feather 'herl', which is a single fibre from feathers such as the peacock's tail, which has small tufts of coloured filaments throughout its length (Fig. 189);

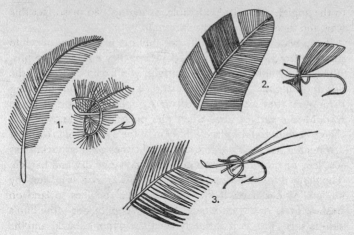

Fig. 189 (§184) Parts of feathers used for fly-tying: 1 – hackle, to make a ruffe of feathers when wound around hook; 2 – segment cut from feather to make a fly wing; 3 – individual fibres to make tail whisks.

'hackle', a single, small feather from the neck of a bird (hen hackles soft, cock's stiff); sections of larger feathers that can be cut to shape wings; and finally, individual small, smooth fibres which can represent tail whisks for tailed flies.

Fig. 190 shows the various stages of the natural fly and the imitations used to represent them. The first two stages, nymphs crawling or darting at the bottom, and nymphs rising to hatch, are dressed to sink and are largely constructed by winding herl, pipecleaner-like, around the shank of the hook (this gives a knobbly finish, resembling the many small gill-rakers running down the flanks of some nymphs), adding tail fibres where necessary. The characteristic humped forward end (head and thorax) of the nymph is created with a soft hackle, trimmed after being wound once or twice around the hook behind the eye. Sometimes copper wire is added to make these patterns sink.

The dun stage is dressed to create a fly that stands high on the water; all that the fish probably sees of the dun is interrupted water where the legs stand on the water film, and the silhouette above of the winged fly. Wings and tail are added if needed (the wings helping the artificial to fall right-way up, rather like a shuttlecock, when it is cast), but the most important part of the

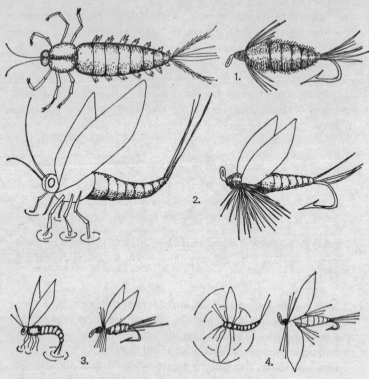

Fig. 190 The developing fly: 1 – underwater, nymph stage; 2 – the dun, just hatched from a nymph; 3 – the spinner, egg-laying; 4 – spent stage, fly dying on water.

fly is the forward hackle. This time a cock's hackle is usually chosen; this creates a fringe of hairy filaments behind the eye of the hook which trap air and allow the artificial to ride on the water (they also resemble the legs of the fly). In the spinner stage, the dressing of the fly may be concentrated at the head end, so that the hook bend and point rides on, or rests in, the water like the natural fly's abdomen, while the forward hackle keeps the head riding high. The final spent stage is dressed by using softer hen hackles and spreading the wings, and the artificial is used on or just in the surface film, like a drowning natural insect. Some fly patterns have no wings, relying on the hackle alone to produce a satisfactory representation of the natural fly.

Wet-fly patterns of natural, winged flies serve the purpose of representing drowned insects, and quite often they will be taken to be rising nymphs by the fish.

Leaving the winged flies aside, the wet-fly collection can be complemented with tyings that represent spiders, bottom creatures and small fish – the latter playing a big part in reservoir fishing – also the metamorphosis stages of other water flies such as the midge.

The dry-fly collection can include midges, spiders, gnats and so on, also tyings to represent moths, crane flies and midge pupae (fished in the surface film).

However, before the collection grows too large, it is wise to put a little thought into the selection of your flies. Beginning with nymphs, it is notable that most are fairly similar, in drab, brownish colouration. It would seem therefore that it matters more what size of nymph is fished, and how it is fished, than what it looks like. Therefore a basic, nymph pattern in a variety of sizes is the best choice.

With the floating and drowned stages of natural flies, silhouette is a more noticeable feature to the trout than exact colour, and you will therefore find it best to start with various sizes of light, intermediate and dark flies, tailed or tail-less, dressed in the dun, spinner and spent stages (omitting spinners if you can't manage a large collection). Thus, with dark flies appearing on the water, you would tie on a dark fly of the appropriate size, and for light flies you would choose a light pattern. I'll go no further than that, because trout can be in a devilish mood where even a slight alteration of pattern makes all the difference; you'll eventually collect a range of your own which will be influenced by the best taking patterns of the water you fish. However, here is a basis to start with:

Wet: Nymph pattern, Midge pupa, Orange Partridge, Yellow Partridge, Black Spider, March Brown, Red Ant (all small to medium sizes, hooks 1–10); Jersey Herd, Muddler Minnow, Worm Fly, Black Lure, Polystickle (large sizes 10–8 single hooks, tandem hooks – all are optional for rivers but valuable for reservoirs). Dunkeld and Butcher, in various sizes, are good standbys.

*

Dry: Alder, Black Gnat, Black Spider, Blue Upright, Blue Variant, Coch-y-Bondhu, Gold Ribbed Hare's Ear, Hackled Greenwell, Hackled Ginger Quill, Halford's Black Gnat, Iron Blue, Light Olive, March Brown, Orange Quill, Pheasant Tail, Silver Sedge, Tup, Wickham's Fancy. Mayfly patterns seem to be used by most anglers, although the season is really very short. The bushy Palmer dressing is a useful representation of a bee or a hairy caterpillar that has fallen into the water, while the white-winged Coachman can be deadly when there are moths on the water.

You can probably see that it is very useful to be able to tie your own flies; materials are readily available from tackle dealers or by post.

With the exception of the 'spent' stage, dry flies are dressed with wax or other flotants to make them water-resistant, but after fishing for a little while they will eventually become water-logged. You can temporarily put off changing to a new fly by false casting to swish the water out of a drowned dry fly. The 'spent' stage may be very slightly waxed to stop it sinking entirely, but the pattern is best fished well and truly in the surface film. When you do change waterlogged flies, however, avoid putting them straight back into your fly box – they might infect the whole collection with rust.

§185 **Lines, casts** (see §11d)

When talking of river fishing for trout, almost all styles of fly fishing are best served with a floating line; it should be the cast alone (or part of it) that sinks for wet-fly and nymph fishing – at least, that is true of most modestly deep trout rivers. In dry-fly fishing, while part of the cast may float, you should aim to get at least the last two feet above the fly to sink into the water, rather than lying upon it where it will be more visible. Casts may be greased with one of the excellent line flotants, and the parts that sink can be rubbed either with fuller's earth moistened with water to form a paste, a rag that has been soaked in washing-up liquid and water, or even a pinch of mud from the water margins.

The floating line is also useful on still waters, but here the angler's scope is widened by a sink-tip line and a sinking line, plus, for very deep water, a fast-sinking line. If you are unable to acquire all at once, the floating line will be found to be the most versatile beginner's choice.

Finally on the subject of casts and lines, a few points about tapers: the small, almost weightless artificials used by the trout angler need the assistance of a tapered cast which, unfurling and continuing the action of the unfurling fly line as it extends across the water, pushes the fly forward rather than letting it drop doubled-back on the cast. Shortish leaders and casts without any taper will just about achieve this action, and so will longer casts of level line providing a good stiff wind is blowing from behind – a situation which is rare enough to make tapered casts the only type of cast worth carrying. As for the fly line, untapered ones are usable only with a wind behind, or perhaps for very short-range work. The standard double-taper will, once casting becomes perfected, cover most small-to-moderate width rivers and will also be ideal for boat fishing. On large, still waters where you can wade a distance from the bank the double-taper will be quite useful, but longer casts will be achieved with the use of a shooting head or a weight-forward line ('long-belly forward' line is a variation).

§186 River fishing – wet fly

Leaving aside the interloping rainbow trout, the brown trout of flowing water and still water are the same species and alike in most respects, but there is a substantial behaviour change between the two locations. The trout of the river stations itself to intercept food, while the trout of the lake has to hunt for it. It is wise therefore to consider lake and river trout as two distinct problems, especially since there are also differences in the food supply for the two locations.

In turbulent, rapid water, and shallow, broken water, many water-flies, at all stages, drown. The trout inhabiting these regions, instead of rising to floating flies, are more likely to concentrate on nymphs and drowned flies, and so will station themselves conveniently where the press of the current is lessened, but where food is likely to come past in quantity. Large obstructions such as big boulders, creating a large area of slack, are inferior lies to the modest shelter provided by smaller, bottom stones where the fish has a good sight of what is coming towards it with the current.

Without the pointer of a rising fish to guide him, it is up to the wet-fly fisherman to spot likely trout lies, imagining himself in the place of the fish. He then has to cast an offering above such a lie in a manner which won't disturb the fish, which means that the fly line shouldn't drop over the lie, and that the fly should travel down with the current just as a natural fly would, without being pulled off course by the line or by the actions of the angler – the trout will cold-shoulder anything which behaves suspiciously.

Fig. 191 shows how approaches should be made with the wet

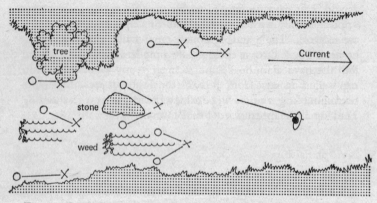

Fig. 191 (§186) Banks, weedbeds, submerged stones and boulders, and the water under overhanging trees and bushes are all good spots for trying wet fly if no rising fish are noticeable. Cast upstream and gather line to work the fly back to you – O = cast, X = likely fish.

fly to likely lies, and although the dragging effect of the line usually precludes fishing directly downstream, there may well be occasions when fishing across and down is quite feasible.

The entire cast (9–12 ft) should be treated to make it sink and the aim of the angler should be to make one or two passes over likely lies, collecting line as the fly line drifts back, withdrawing smoothly when the fly is well past the lie – quite often a trout will turn about and snap up a fly that has gone past, when you are beginning to believe it has been ignored. There is no reason why two, or even three, flies should not be used, the extra ones tied on to droppers spaced along the cast. However, it is best to choose your flies with an eye to whatever insect life is on the water at the time.

There are three main ways in which takes can be detected: the fish, turning to take your fly, might give off a flash that you can see, otherwise your fly line may halt in its downstream passage, or the tip (if visible) will dip or veer sideways. With the latter indications, you should react with a strike, but the flashing fish I believe needs a second or so to return to its lie unless there is a danger that the fly line will exert an instant drag.

There are occasions when wet fly may be used effectively on the clear even runs and pools of waters traditionally associated with dry-fly fishing – assuming, of course, that the method is allowed – and these occur when no appreciable hatch is taking place and the fish are feeding on bottom-swimming nymphs and larvae, or when flood water is trickling a supply of terrestrial creatures into the river. Patterns such as a small Jersey Herd give a fair representation of caddis, which trout take in quantity when bottom-feeding, and the wet dressing of the Spider is also useful. They should be fished close to the bottom.

§187 Nymph fishing

Nymph fishing is best regarded as an adjunct to dry-fly fishing, and the major difference between using a nymph and wet-fly fishing proper, is that you aim to catch fish that are visibly feeding on nymphs – i.e. fish stationed in mid-water, swinging from side to side to intercept food and, later in the hatch, bulging at the surface. It should be re-stated that the aim is to drop the offering ahead of the fish without laying the fly line on the fish's head or dragging the fly suspiciously. In general, it is helpful to land the sinking nymph as far as possible ahead of mid-water feeding fish, but four feet or so is sufficient for fish that are near the surface. Treat the cast to sink to the feeding depth of the fish, and grease the remainder – in the case of bulging fish, you can grease to within about a foot of the fly. Two nymph patterns may be used at once, and in view of the fact that the trout is ranging to either side of its lie this seems a good idea – however, many anglers would not contemplate the use of more than one fly, and I rarely use more than one. However, it is an extremely good idea to cast five or six times to the same fish when it seems clear that the plentiful supply of nymphs is the reason for your offering slipping past unnoticed. As in wet-fly fishing, let your offering drop well past the fish, before retrieving line for another throw.

§188 Dry-fly fishing

The visible, floating fly adds an exciting dimension to fly fishing, and the anticipation that builds up as the offering approaches a trout's lie often stops your breath.

The task of fishing a dry fly is basically similar to fishing wet flies and nymphs, and that means casting the fly so that it rides

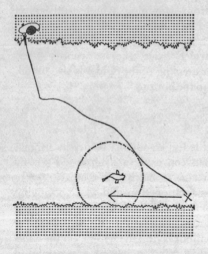

Fig. 192 (§188) Casting the dry fly to a rising fish – cast above the window area indicated by dotted line.

into the fish's vision in a natural fashion, making sure that it does not drag, and that the fly line is well out of the way. However, the closer the trout lies to the water surface, the smaller will be its 'window' of vision. You can, therefore, land your fly two feet or less in front of the fish and expect it to be taken (Fig. 192). The fish is unlikely to be weaving away from a set place in search of flies, and so long as your fly keeps to a path which passes over the last place the fish was seen to move, there is a good chance of provoking a rise – so long as your artificial pattern is acceptable in terms of colour, size and shape. During hatches, matching the natural flies that you can see in or on the water with a similar artificial is important. So is using your imagination, for instance, when you see a fish that is lying downstream of a weed patch and might well be feeding on the spent flies of the cloud of gnats hovering above the weed.

Assume, however, that you have a correctly matched pattern and that you have landed it correctly in front of your fish. If the fish rises and takes, you have done well, but if instead it starts to rise and shears off at the last moment, something has gone wrong. Suspect, first of all, your fly – making sure in particular that it is not too big. If the day is bright, then you might find that you are using a cast that tapers to too coarse a point – if it is too visible to the fish, you won't get a proper rise. The other cause could well be that you are dragging the fly, and however unnoticeable to you this may be, you can be sure that the fish is well aware of it.

This drag – the current moving the fly line so that it tows the cast and fly after it – is nearly always incurred when the current flows across the body of the river at different speeds. In casting your fly across a river that has a fast-flowing centre section, you might, with a straight line, only be able to gain two feet of uninterrupted travel for your fly – sometimes less. The trick in these circumstances is to lay either a crooked line, or a line with an upstream bow, across the water, which will have the effect of giving your fly a longer path of uninterrupted travel (Fig. 193). To make a crooked line – so easy when you begin fly fishing, but harder to achieve once you have polished up your casting – check the cast momentarily before it falls onto the water so that the whole business of line, cast and fly jerks backwards a little. Some practice is necessary to achieve this satisfactorily. Casting a bow into the line is more difficult, but it is not beyond the average caster prepared to practise. You merely lay the rod over to the side (according to which way you want the bow to form) once the cast is in motion, taking care to exert no check which will straighten the line out again. I'll repeat again that you'll need to practise, because it sounds much more easy than it really is. The bowed line is invaluable, too, when trying to cast to a fish rising against the bank you are fishing on (unless you can wade out to create a satisfactory angle and avoid covering the fish with your fly line).

Having covered your fish once or twice with no response, you

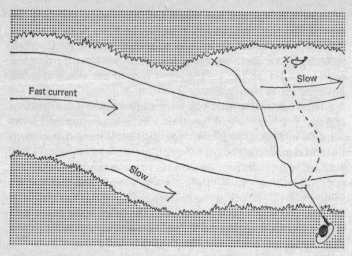

Fig. 193 With varied surface currents, a straight cast might draw the fly off course or make the fly move unnaturally when it is near the fish. A purposely bowed or crooked line will allow slack to be taken up while the fly stays on its path.

can either move on to a more willing riser or wait, allow the fish a couple more rises at natural flies, and try again. If you get half a rise and a refusal, however, you might find that it takes some time for the fish to begin rising with confidence again.

Unlike the other forms of fly fishing, you will know instantly when a fish has taken your offering, but a little caution is needed at this point. As soon as the fish's nose has broken surface and your fly is ingested, the fly is loosely held, together with a mouthful of water. My interpretation of what is happening is that the trout must have its gills closed, otherwise the prey could swish out through the rakers, and therefore if it closed its mouth in a hurry it would squirt out a mouthful of water together with the fly. Whatever, there is no doubt that too soon a strike cuts down your chance of hooking the fish. Some anglers count to three after the take before giving a firm tug to set the hook. I like to imagine the fish sinking a little, evening-up its keel and re-adjusting equilibrium – a mental picture sequence which usually allows sufficient time to elapse for the trout slowly to close its mouth and begin tasting the meal.

The dry-fly fishing day: Hatches of fly are related to water temperature and weather and might occur at most times of the day;
nevertheless, there is a pattern in the trout's feeding moods
throughout the day, and whenever a period of activity in the
trout coincides with a hatch of fly the best sport can be expected.
Early in the season, you can hear trout plopping as they take
hatching flies off the surface even before dawn, and dawn itself is a
period of widespread activity in the river. Before and after
summer (during summer there will be pronounced lulls both in
fly hatches and fish activity during the long, hot afternoons) there
are usually sporadic hatches of fly, to which some fish will always
respond, throughout the day, culminating in a brief but often
hectic evening rise, when, if you are fishing the right pattern, you
can expect brisk sport. It is possible to fish on into the dark,
when moth-like patterns of fly are a good bet, although by this
time the evening rise will be spent and fish will be rising only
intermittently. Because high summer has this noon slack in sport,
early and late season outings are best for spending an entire day
fishing, while early morning, before the sun has climbed too high,
and evening sessions are best during true summer weather. There
are interruptions to these feeding periods. Flood, for instance,
will freshen the river and get summer fish moving through the
day, and so will wind that gets a good chop going on the water.
Falling water temperatures, however – following a hail shower,
for instance – may put fish down even during the evening rise.
During the height of a flood it may be thoroughly impractical to
consider fly fishing, but when the water is fining down sport will
generally be brisk for a while.

§189 **Still-water fly methods**

In turning from running-water to still-water trout, we are turning
from fish that have their food delivered to fish that have to
actively hunt. It follows that the food that is animated by the
current in moving water will have no animation of its own in still
water, and movement must be imparted by the angler or, occasionally, by the wind.

The food to be imitated includes pupae, beetles, water boatmen
and small fish besides actual developing and hatched flies. In
still-water fishing generally there is a greater emphasis on wet-fly

methods than on dry flies, firstly, because you're not going to find many fish lying in one spot waiting for flies to conveniently appear above them and, secondly, because searching fish might miss out if they restrict themselves to a narrow, surface window.

Having made that statement, let me hastily add that occasions when a dry fly can be used do present themselves – usually in spots where the wind is conveniently depositing a good supply of insects on the surface. It is also strikingly noticeable that some trout will station themselves along the edge of an offshore ripple and take surface flies marginally into the calm water on the bankward side, and many's the time that a small, dry fly fished to the edge of a ripple where fish can be seen to be congregating pays off handsomely.

A fish that moves close to you while obviously intent on surface flies can sometimes be lured by giving a wet fly a good swishing in order to dry it sufficiently to make it float for a few seconds, after which it can be dropped lightly on the fish's nose. Trout feeding in this way will sometimes even turn about and lunge at a fly that has been misplaced behind them.

Turning to the wet fly, the action you give depends largely on what you are trying to imitate, which in turn can depend on nymphs, pupae or small fish that you see about you in the water. Without any noticeable guides from natural insects and the like, you can if you wish assume that they will be present and fish them according to their appearance. Pupae (green and black artificial patterns are useful) spend long periods dangling inertly near the surface, occasionally wriggling furiously into the surface film, and trout feeding on them will bulge rather like the nymphing river fish, sometimes making a head and tail rise to take a pupa near the surface. The aim here should be to induce occasional, small twitches to the artificial, and if there is wind you can cast and let the surface movement drift your pupa imitation while you twitch it – obviously it should not be allowed to sink far, which you can arrange by greasing part of the cast. Nymphs on their way to the surface, corixa, water boatmen and a wide range of creatures will move in small, fussy darts; they can be fished deeper and faster than the pupa with your left hand collecting short lengths of line. Small fish, represented by such patterns as the polystickle, can be fished swiftly with a stripping recovery, and bottom-living creatures, covered by such artificial creations as the Jersey Herd and

Worm Fly, can be allowed to sink and fished back erratically along the bed of the lake.

§190 Lines, casts for still water (see §11d)

As in river fly fishing, the tapered cast is the most useful type, level (untapered) casts being suitable mainly when a good wind is blowing from behind. However, it is true to say that you should try to use the longest cast allowed by conditions (twelve feet or more with a following wind) since the relatively straight throws made in still-water fishing mean that you will be drawing your flies back over ground that has been covered by the fly line. With a twelve-foot cast therefore your tail fly will travel twelve feet over ground covered by relatively invisible nylon before it begins to cover the path which the more noticeable fly line has been drawn over – and on days when fish are taking shyly, such a long cast will give you an important advantage. As for fly lines, the floating line will serve well for fishing flies near the surface and is especially useful in shallow, gently-shelving areas when you fish from the bank. The sink-tip is useful for fishing marginally deeper and it has the effect of sinking the cast quickly – a very good still-water line. For deeper regions such as steep-sided dam walls, and for fishing shallower regions along the bottom, the sinker can be used, perhaps even a heavy, fast sinker – with the latter two types of line, sinking is halted at the moment you begin to retrieve line, and with the foreknowledge of the depth of the water you can count down as the line sinks and begin to fish it, say, two feet clear of the bottom. As for colour, I am wary of using a white sinking line but brown or green lines don't appear to have any advantages over each other. I am sure that a floating line of any colour means much the same thing from the fish's point of view, but white does give the angler the ability to see the line for a good distance out and recognize the dips or veers that mean the fly has been taken.

Two or three flies may be fished at a time, and if you begin the day by using three different patterns on one cast you might be able to single out a fly that is more popular than others. However, three large, heavy flies might be difficult and dangerous to cast, and single large lures fished alone, or with two smaller flies (Fig. 194) are a better choice.

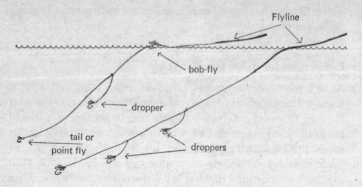

Fig. 194 (§190) Still-water wet-fly arrangements: top, loch rig with three small flies, the upper one kept 'bobbing' at the surface. The lower arrangement is more useful on water holding large brown trout and rainbows, and has two droppers and a larger tail fly.

§191 Shore and boat fly fishing

At the outset, the shore angler should regard the whole of the water before him, right up to the wavelets lapping on the shore, as capable of producing fish; the first casts, made in a fan-like fashion (if no fish are showing) should always be short ones made from the bankside before wading into the water is contemplated (waders increase your scope considerably and they are virtually a 'must' for still-water shore anglers). Entering the water, you can then move gradually outwards, casting as you go (Fig. 195).

If you are lucky, the water will be uncrowded and you will be able to choose points and bays, moving progressively from spot to spot. Bear in mind that a shore exposed to the wind is likely to contain more food matter for trout, but don't trust in this generalization so much that you overlook shallow, offshore banks and weedbeds where trout might congregate. However, if the water is crowded, and this is often true of the popular reservoirs early in the season, you might find all of the best points occupied, and you will have to look for what seems a good spot keeping at least forty yards away from any other angler. Whatever the situation, fish the water methodically and don't ignore the water to either side of you. It is a good idea to fish every cast right back to your feet, and even draw the line and flies past you

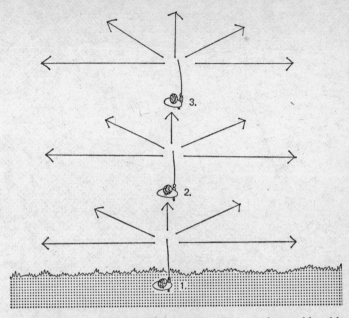

Fig. 195 (§191) In still-water fly fishing, search water thoroughly with a 'fan' of casts if no fish are showing, starting from the bank (1) and wading by stages into the water (2, 3).

– many times there will be a following fish which will take when it thinks its prey is going to run to cover in the bank. Long casts, of course, mean that your fly stays longer in the water, and this is why there is such an emphasis on long casting for still-water trout.

The most critical point of any cast is immediately after the fly has landed in the water, and this is when you should be particularly on guard to spot either the flash of a fish's flank or a 'boil' on the water, or a movement of the forward part of your fly line, that means a fish has taken. Concentrate especially on moving, steadily-rising fish, trying to ascertain their course and speed so that you can land a fly to intercept them – even when you are fishing out a cast it is sometimes valuable to lift the line quickly out of the water to cast to a riser.

You should usually give risers a moment to close their mouths on a fly before striking, but a movement of the line should always

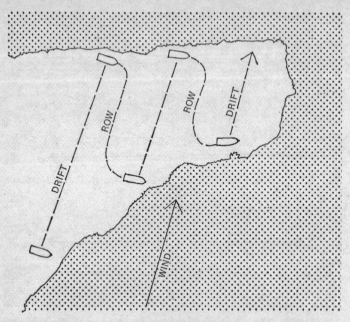

Fig. 196 Cast on the down-wind drifts, throwing fly on water before you as you go and working it back to the boat. At the far bank row or motor back to start new drift.

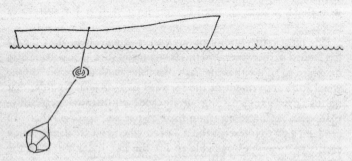

Fig. 197 The drogue, a sort of underwater parachute that can be attached to a rowlock, stops a boat from drifting too fast in a strong wind.

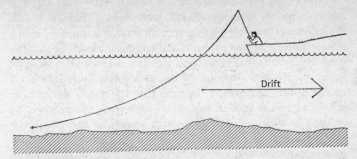

Fig. 198 Fly trolling is not allowed on some waters. Where it is, small, as well as large, flies may be used but a sinking line is essential. Hold the rod all the time or it may go overboard if a fish takes or the fly snags on weed.

be struck fairly quickly. When you are stripping in fast, however, a strike is often unnecessary since, nine times out of ten, the fish will hit the lure hard and hook itself.

A boat further increases your range on still water, and although you can if you wish anchor in one spot, the traditional method of boat fishing is drifting with the wind (Fig. 196) to quarter the water, casting before you as you go. If the drift is too fast, the boat may be slowed with a drogue or sea anchor (Fig. 197). Either a floating, sink-tip or sinking line may be used, depending on the depth you wish to fish, and it is usual to have a two-or-three-fly cast – traditionally, the upper, or 'bob', fly is kept riding at the surface. You can work your flies gently back to you, and the bottom of the boat is a convenient place to drop spare line as you collect it. Just as in bank fishing, there are underwater banks, weedbeds and so on that are worth extra concentration, and the edges of areas of wind ripple are especially productive. It is also worthwhile casting to rising fish.

Trolling, i.e. trailing a fly, is banned in many fisheries, but where it is allowed it is a good method of fishing extra large lures, very deep, for big fish (Fig. 198).

§192 Differences between brown and rainbow trout

The solitary nature of the brown trout and the more gregarious habits of the rainbow have already been described (§162, 163), but there are other characteristics of both species that deserve mention, mainly in relation to still-water fishing. First, although the still-water brownie has to search for food, it is much more of a stop-at-home than the rainbow, and large fish especially may become legendary inhabitants of particular territories. The rainbow is, by nature, the salvation of the reservoir bank angler on a crowded day, and many's the time that a formerly duff area is enlivened by the sudden appearance of a pack of rainbows. In fighting qualities, much can be said about the merits of each species, but it is most noticeable that the rainbow provides spectacular leaps and surface flurries, while the brownie fights doggedly and deep.

§193 Versatility of fly tackle

Fly tackle is extremely efficient as a casting mechanism, and fly patterns aside, it can be used to cast worms or small spinners (such as the traditional ½-inch fly spoon), so long as the rules of the fishery permit this. You can also use it to cast a small fish to a trout that is obviously intent on minnow-shoals (after catching a small bleak or dace by dabbling a tiny fly). You only need to replace the fly cast with a length of line and a bare hook or spinner.

Fly fishing should not be regarded as a method for trout, salmon and sea-trout alone – in fact, any game fisherman will tell you that he has caught many varieties of coarse fish while after trout or salmon. Dace and chub, and in the summer surface-feeding roach and rudd are good sport on fly tackle, and so is the grayling. Pike, sometimes quite large, and perch, will strike at wet flies.

§194 Spinning for trout

Both brown and rainbow trout are fish-eaters, and the latter species will sometimes gang up to herd shoals of small fish into restricted bays where they drive at them again and again, gorging themselves to bursting point. Spinning can be attempted with most small spoon, spinner and lure patterns, or with small dead-baits fished sink-and-draw or on a spinning flight. The methods employed are the same as those for predatory coarse fish (§155) and the tackle strength should be adjusted to the average size of

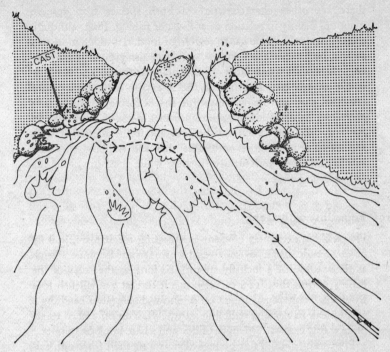

Fig. 199 (§194) Upstream spinning with a small Mepps spoon or a Devon minnow can be a very good way of taking trout on small rivers. Cast well into the white water below falls, letting the turbulence hold the spinner as long as possible.

the fish you expect to catch on a given water. Trout in large rivers have been known to respond to legered deadbaits, fished in spots such as the press of water under a weir. In small streams I like to use a method employed in the West country: the angler casts upstream into white, broken water under the lip of waterfalls, drawing a small spinner such as the tiniest possible Devon minnow through the tumble, out, and swiftly down the pool (Fig. 199). Although behaving unnaturally by swimming downstream, the bait is often followed swiftly out of the white water by a pursuing trout which endeavours to snaffle it before it escapes at the tail of the pool – altogether very exciting fishing.

§195 Bait fishing

Just as the trout fly fisherman will often pick up coarse fish, so the coarse bait angler will take trout on occasions, usually when fishing with lively baits such as maggots or worms. I recall one bright and bitterly cold day on the Usk when, together with a party of anglers, I was fishing for the shoals of very big dace which at the time were being contacted near the town of Usk itself. The six of us caught, if I remember, one dace between us – but nearly everybody had a brace or more of good brown trout around the pound mark.

We were trotting maggots with light float tackle, and, using very similar tackle, I've since had the same experience with trout on cold days, when fishing for grayling in north Yorkshire and fishing for roach in Hampshire. While bait fishing is unacceptable in many southern trout fisheries, in the north, trotting is quite widely used. However, for small upland brooks the technique of upstream worming is good fun. Basically, the angler works upstream from pool to pool, casting a worm to the head of each pool and allowing it to drift towards him as naturally as possible on the current. No float is used and there is rarely any need for weight on the line – perhaps a split shot or two to sink the bait if the current is heavy. Particular attention is paid to the sort of

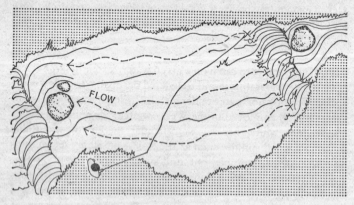

Fig. 200 (§195) Upstream worming – unweighted or slightly weighted worm is cast upstream and the line is gently retrieved as the bait swims back down to the angler with the current.

stony lies that would catch the eye of the wet-fly fisherman, and to undercut banks. As the bait comes back (Fig. 200), the angler collects his line gently, striving to keep in touch with the bait. A flash from the fish's flanks, a swirl at the surface, or simply a halt in the downstream passage of the line signals a bite, and the fish is given a moment to return to its lie before a strike is made. The worm may be cast on fly tackle, using a gentle, lobbing action so that the bait isn't thrown off the hook, but to my mind a better kit is a small bait-fishing or spinning rod with a fixed-spool reel and 2-lb line – the trout in these regions rarely run big. Just as wet flies used for salmon and trout rarely snag when they are in the play of the current, so the worm fished in this fashion usually steers clear of trouble. Were you to use weighted, float tackle instead, you might expect a different story.

§196 Methods for char

The limited distribution of the char means that it is largely overlooked in angling reference books. It is a deep-water feeder that

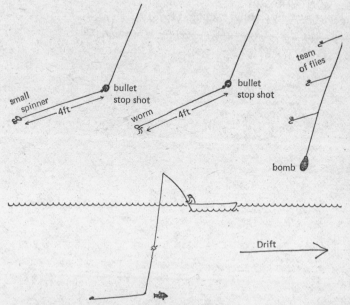

Fig. 201 (§196) Sunk-line methods for char.

will respond to all the methods used for trout with the proviso that offerings may have to be presented at depths of twenty feet or more. Trailing a weighted line with baited hooks (worms, maggots), artificial flies or a small spinner is recommended (Fig. 201).

Trout and char fishing
Quick cross-reference guide

Fly casts, spinning and bait fishing lines, §11a, 11f.
Fly lines, §11d.
Hooks, §12.
Weights, §16.
Knots, bait fishing and spinning, §18a, 18b.
Knots, fly fishing, §18c.
Rods, tackle checklists, §39, 42.
Preparations, §43.
Freshwater environments, §58–68.
Species, brown trout, §162; rainbow trout, §163; speckled trout §164; char, §165.
Approach, fly casting, wading, §167–173.

The most noticeable differences between summer and winter fishing for the sea angler will be the exchanges of cold- and warm-water species. The sea itself holds a vast range of differing terrains, each of which attracts certain species and precludes others; providing water temperature and food supply are equal in, say, reefs many miles apart, they might be expected to hold roughly the same range of fish species and can be approached with the same fishing methods.

§197 Effects of tide

Both shore and deep-water marks will either fish well or badly at particular states of the tide as it rises and falls twice daily in relation to the position of the moon to the earth. The tide rises, with a marked directional flow of current, until it is full. There is then a period of slack water before, current reversed, the level begins to drop. At the bottom of the tide there is a further slack before the rise begins again.

The times of the tides for your area, or for an area which you wish to visit, can be checked by the tables in most angling journals which list the predicted times of high-water at London Bridge, together with the number of hours and minutes which have to be added or subtracted from the London times for high-water at various stations surrounding the coast. There are other sources for this information such as the local newspapers in coastal towns.

Frequently, the height of the expected high tide is also given, from which you can gauge how much water will be covering marks of a given depth; the depths vary, like the times, from springs (the highest and the lowest water levels) to neaps (the

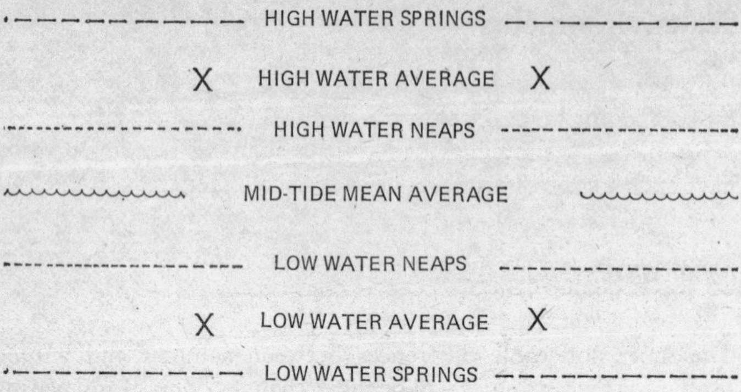

•—————————— HIGH WATER SPRINGS ——————————

X   HIGH WATER AVERAGE   X

•·····················•· HIGH WATER NEAPS ·····················•

∿∿∿∿∿∿∿∿∿∿∿∿∿∿ MID-TIDE MEAN AVERAGE ∿∿∿∿∿∿∿∿

·····················—— LOW WATER NEAPS ·····················—

X   LOW WATER AVERAGE   X

•—————————— LOW WATER SPRINGS ——————————

Fig. 202 Difference in spring and neap tides.

shortest range between high and low tide). Fig. 202 shows the water levels of springs and neaps, from which you could quite rightly deduce that springs might deprive a shallow harbour of sufficient water to leave or enter with a boat at the lowest point – a factor well worth considering if you plan a boat trip.

It is impossible to generalize about the best fishing times for various marks at different states of the tide, other than to say that rising tides are more often good than bad (particularly for shore fishing), and that both high and low slacks allow species such as conger and ling, which are not altogether happy in strong flows, to emerge from sheltering cover to feed. Falling tides in shallow water are often the signal for fish to leave to avoid stranding.

For the boat angler, a neap tide might allow fishing over a mark that would otherwise be covered by water too deep and strong-flowing to make fishing practical at high tide. The high-water of a spring tide, however, might attract deep-water fish to a mark they would normally avoid – the combinations are virtually endless. Good charter-boat skippers will undoubtedly know these quirks, but if you run your own boat you will have to learn them, exploring your area at various states of the tide, or pick up advice from the professionals.

The shore angler is particularly affected by tide since many of the places he fishes are dry and exposed at low tide – the intertidal areas known as the 'littoral zone'. Here, in sand, mud, rock and weed, there are large numbers of creatures not found in deep water. There are specialized burrowers, such as lugworm, razorfish and sandeels, browsers on rocks and weed such as limpets and barnacles, mussels, anemones, and also the growing fry of many fish species swimming freely about with shrimps and prawns and the scavenging crab. A very attractive area for hungry fish.

Steep, rocky shorelines and steeply shelving beaches do not have such a large intertidal zone as the shallower areas (Fig. 203).

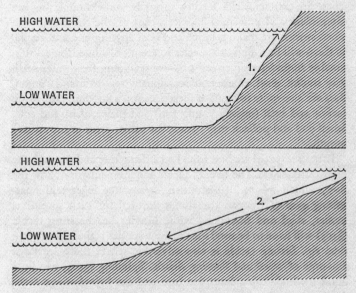

Fig. 203 The tide-rise covers a shorter distance on a steep beach (1) than on a gentler slope (2).

Some beaches and estuaries can have as much as a mile between high- and low-water marks, and in such areas the angler who begins to fish at low tide will have to move back gradually as the tide comes in. In this there is a certain measure of danger, since what appears to be a completely flat expanse of mud or sand is usually a series of low banks; unless the angler knows the area well he might find that the tide has raced up a valley behind him to cut him off. The speed that a rising tide has over shallow ground is phenomenal, and this makes fishing in fog or after dark especially risky. The rock angler is similarly at risk if he is working from a series of islets which might be cut off from the mainland.

Beaches with a moderate slope hold no such dangers, and here it is quite feasible to fish at night. But beware of storm waves, which make any exposed beach hazardous – it is best to stick to sheltered water during a blow.

§198 Estuaries and harbours

These are extremely rich feeding grounds, and although they are often bleak and inhospitable places, they can be havens of calm when storms are making beach and boat angling uncomfortable. In them will be found fish species tolerant of 'diluted' salt water, notably flounders, silver eels (mature sea-going freshwater eels), grey mullet, shad, smelt, and occasionally sea-trout and salmon. Bass are also quite tolerant of these areas on a flooding tide, as are turbot and brill (mainly young fish) and plaice, dabs and sole. Small cod and pollack may invade the saltier areas at the estuary mouth.

Estuaries (§299) are best fished on a rising tide and through the high-water slack. The overall tackle requirements must suit the flow, which means that stoutish, freshwater leger and float-fishing gear (§297) can sometimes be used for such species as mullet, shad and flounders, while heavier beachcasting tackle (§303) will have to be used for the same species if there is a strong tidal rip. Strong tackle is also advisable where there are large amounts of weed and floating debris. Spinning (§305) can be a good method, using lures for bass and the baited-spoon technique for flatfish. With a dinghy (provided you do not strand yourself well off the shore), trailed spinners and baited spoons are also useful – so is 'whiffing', which is trailing a line baited with strips of mackerel or some other fish bait.

In many respects harbours (§300) are like estuaries; many have muddy beds and are built about freshwater outlets. The same species encountered in estuaries are therefore often present. Like estuaries, harbours are also sheltered havens should it be stormy. Some contain permanent water, which is sometimes very deep, and so can attract pollack, cod and many other species. Harbours that are well-sheltered and unaffected by strong currents make light tackle possible for flounders and other flatfish, grey mullet and small pollack and codling, also wrasse – where large bass are present, though, stronger tackle is required. Float fishing is the best method, the main disadvantage of legering being that harbour beds are frequently a graveyard for old rope, cable and rusty chain. If you do leger, then the 'rotten bottom' described below for rock fishing is useful. Most harbours have a restricted entrance, and, since this is the only way in and out for fish as well as boats, it is usually a good fishing spot.

§199 Piers and jetties

These artificial promontaries (§302) enable anglers to walk out above deep water that normally could not be reached by casting from the shore. If the water reaches a good depth species such as conger, dogfish, monkfish, angler fish, rays and gurnard can be taken, with cod, bass, flatfish and bream in season. The rich food supply in the weeds, adhering to pier piles and jetty walls, will also attract browsing grey mullet and wrasse. Float fishing is useful on the down-tide side of piers, with a sliding float for deep water. Leger tackle for bottom species can be used either up-tide or down, but the down-tide side is better for keeping your tackle away from the danger of being swept around the piles and snagged. Often you will be fishing high above the water, and any fish that you catch will be well outside the range of a normal landing net or gaff. In these situations a drop net – a weighted net on a cord that can be lowered to the water from the pier deck – is most useful.

§200 Rocky shores

Rock fishing (§301) requires agility and modification of tackle and methods which take into account the high risk of snagging and losing tackle. It is also very useful to put in some survey work at low tide, before you start fishing, searching out such likely spots as sand-bottomed gullies between rocky walls.

It must be stressed that it is not worth casting leger tackle a long distance across rough ground because the likelihood of snags is high; instead, the aim should be to fish down into the rocks with a rotten-bottom tackle arrangement, or else hold the tackle well above snags with a float. Spinning can also be useful in rocky areas. Bass and pollack are likely to be taken on spinners and bait, while wrasse, congers and bream respond mainly to baits.

The 'rotten bottom' simply consists of a linking line between weight and main line which has a much weaker breaking strain than the rest of the tackle (§11g). The baited hook is fixed so that it fishes above snags, and the weight is usually some throw-away object – a rusty bolt, or a suitably heavy pebble. The weak line connecting the weight is sufficiently strong to hold the tackle in position, but should the weight snag during fishing a good hard pull will break the connection. The angler can then retrieve his tackle, or fish if he has one.

Fishing in pools and gullies among rocks calls for delicacy in placing the bait, and light, manageable tackle – a big beachcaster is much too unwieldy.

§201 Beaches

The generally accepted picture of beach fishing (§303, 304) is casting a line long enough to reach deep water and species such as cod, flatfish, rays, whiting and so on, and perhaps dogfish or even tope if there are good, deep gullies. It is for these long casts that the beach angler's long 'beachcaster' rod and tackle have been developed. However, beach angling is not all distance work, since bass and some flatfish species will often feed much closer to the shore than the hundred yards or so for which the long-caster strives. Bass will even feed among breaking waves, and here spinning (§305) or light legering with sandeel, peeler crab or worm bait is most effective.

For long-range beachcasting leger tackle is used – it is usually impossible to use a float with the tide sweeping along a beach.

Fig. 204 (§201) Sand or mud is scoured from one side of a groyne and banked on the other side. The scour is a good fish-holding area.

The terminal arrangement will either be a straight-through leger rig or some form of paternoster. When mackerel are about, a long cast with a set of feathers can be effective, and so can a heavy spinning lure.

Although, at a glance, most beaches seem to be featureless slopes, there is nearly always a deep gully or depression which will hold deeper water at high tide; as in rock fishing, low-tide exploration will enable you to pick spots worth concentrating on as the tide comes up. The gullies and banks that build around sand-holding groynes (Fig. 204) are often good fishing areas.

§202 Inshore boat marks

Between the shore angler's marks and the deep-sea, boat marks are areas best exploited with a small dinghy. These include all the shore marks previously mentioned, which can be approached without the need for long casts, and also large rocky areas, un-approachable from the shore, which can be tackled from clear water on the seaward side. The same methods used for shore fishing can be used in these places, particularly float fishing, light legering and spinning, and you can also troll through estuaries and along sandbars and reefs which are out of reach of the shore. Unless you know the area well, however, obtain an up-to-date chart to keep you out of trouble, and don't attempt to go out in your dinghy in rough weather or fog.

§203 Deep-sea marks

Moving out into the open sea, only a seasoned local boatman will be able to tell you what ground you are going over, judged by the shore features he can line up to place his position. If you go out with an experienced hand you will see that even when he reaches a given position, he will turn to an echo sounder to pinpoint the mark with more accuracy, and if he steers instead by dead-reckoning the sounder will play an even bigger part in the search for the mark. Pinpointing a relatively small object such as a coaster's wreck, going by its charted position, is so difficult for the in-experienced (even with a sounder) that it is wiser to cut your teeth on larger charted areas – reefs, sand and mud banks – if you are starting to pick up offshore angling on your own.

In recent years another invention (too expensive for most small boat anglers, unfortunately) has taken some of the guesswork out of navigation and position-fixing – the Decca Navigational System. It is installed nowadays on many of the top charter, fishing boats. It consists of a small receiver installed on the boat which is tuned to pick up shore-transmitted coordinates so that it can 'lock' onto the position it wants to reach. Using the system a skipper can steam straight to a mark, set down a 'dan' – a lightweight marker buoy – and his anglers can begin fishing.

The nature of the seabed – sand, shingle, mud, weed, rock or wreck – determines what sort of fish are likely to be present.

Sand or shingle banks: Turbot and plaice are attracted to this type of ground. Light to medium legering (§311), depending on the strength of tidal flow, is best for plaice, but turbot prefer a moving bait and will generally lie along the edges and in the deeper gullies in a bank to ambush such prey as sandeels and small fish. With a light lead it is possible to 'trot' a bait for turbot, lifting the weight periodically to allow the tide to bounce it along the bottom. Another approach is to drift the boat so that the bait is dragged along the bottom. Some rays are also found on this type of bank, the blonde ray in particular. Over well-mixed ground containing mud, weed and rock, besides sand and shingle, you can expect cod and whiting in winter. Legered baits, or jigged, baited feathers (§310) will take both species.

Mud banks: Flatfish of all types are quite common over mud, but in shallow water soles are likely to predominate. Mud is also attractive to thornbacks, dogfish and tope. Legered fish, squid, peeler crab and worm baits will take all these species – large tope preferring a whole fish. Expect cod and whiting in the winter.

Deep-water banks, gullies, pits: Monkfish, dogfish and the bigger species of skate can often be found on this type of mark, and the deep pits in particular might hold big conger, especially if they are weedy or rocky. For all these species it is best to anchor and fish firmly on the bottom (§311).

Reefs and wrecks: Because of the wide range of species they attract, and the chance of really big fish, reefs and wrecks are very popular marks for sea anglers. Conger eels, ling and other crevice-living species inhabit them in numbers, while there is usually abundant weed and small creatures to attract bream and wrasse. The many small fish seeking shelter in reefs and wrecks form the prey of pollack, coalfish, bass and cod, as well as species generally associated with more open ground – mackerel and gurnards in summer (year-round in the south-west), whiting in winter and flatfish, dogfish and rays throughout the year.

For congers and ling, stationary baits seem most attractive. Legering (§311) with a paternoster rig to keep clear of snags, or a running leger on very strong line will be the best approach for them.

For this, of course, it will be necessary to anchor. Stationary baits will also take the more active fish such as pollack, coalfish, cod and bass, but the alternative methods that can be tried for these species with an anchored boat are jigging with pirks and lures (§310) and bait fishing with a long flowing trace which streams out in the tidal flow.

In deep water with very strong tides it may be extremely hard to anchor; indeed, some skippers may refuse to anchor because of the risk of having to pull free under power – a process that involves chugging around in tight circles until something gives, that something usually being the rope, leaving the anchor and an expensive length of chain in Davy Jones's locker.

Drifting is then the only way of taking fish. The skipper will take his boat uptide of the wreck and allow it to move slowly over the ground. With favourable wind and tide conditions, he may be able to put out a sea anchor – a sort of underwater parachute – to play the wind against the current and slow the drift down greatly. Jigging while drifting is a good method and it will take pollack, coalfish, bass, cod, and occasionally ling. Pirks, lures or feathers can be used. You can fish baited lines well clear of snags by using a paternoster rig – good for bream – or a flowing trace kept above the wreck. Once the boat has passed well over the wreck, it is taken back uptide to cover the area again and again.

Large areas of rough ground swept by strong currents are usually fished on the drift, using the above rigs. Much of the water around the Shetlands is like this, and here haddock, cod and ling are taken, and there is also the chance of a very big halibut.

Open water: By this I mean the offshore areas well away from bottom-fishing grounds where the oceanic sharks and tunnies harry mackerel and herring shoals at the surface or in mid-water. Both sharks and tunnies are usually tackled with fish baits on float tackle, although the latter have been known to take trolled lures (§328–336).

The use of the term 'small to moderate' in the title of this chapter is to distinguish between those species which are the mainstay of the deep-sea and shore angler and those which are generally regarded as 'big game' – conger eels, halibut, the sharks and the shark-related tope, the large skates (common, long-nosed and white skate) and the tunny. Descriptions of all of these fish follow in the chapters on big-game fishing.

Size alone is no definition of the term 'big game', which implies some sort of adversary with powers beyond the normal – certainly true of the species just mentioned. You could argue, for instance, that the angler fish grows to a great size – but then again, a fish that merely sets a task described often as 'like hauling up a sack of rubbish' is scarcely an exciting proposition compared with battling with a fast-running tope or combating the vicious, sawing fight of a big conger.

Ling and cod also grow to great weights (and fight strongly too) but the average weight of these species is only around fifteen pounds except at such marks as the Gantocks, in the north, for cod, and the Eddystone Reef off the south-west coast for ling.

§204 **Angler fish** (frogfish)
Lophius piscatorius

A bottom dweller which, like the plaice, is able to assume the colour and pattern of its surroundings, the somewhat grotesque angler is widely distributed in fairly shallow water areas. Although specimens of 30 kg (66.1 lb) have been taken by anglers (caught, more often than not, by chance rather than design) some truly prodigious specimens have been noted – in October, 1970, Geoff Saunders, a Warwickshire angler, was fishing off Kinsale in Ireland when he came across a dying angler fish floating on the surface. The 7 ft 4 in fish was taken to Kinsale and weighed, turning the scales at 150 lb. The species is most likely to be taken with legered fish baits.

§205 **Bass** (small fish: schoolies, chequers)
Morone labrax

A silvery, dashing fighter of rocky coastal regions, beaches, estuaries and offshore reefs, the bass is extremely popular with anglers. It feeds in shoals, some of which may be quite large, taking worms, crustaceans, sandeels and small fish. Float-fishing, spinning and surf legering are the usual shore fishing methods, and over the reefs bass can be taken on pirks or bottom tackle – also trolled rubber sandeels are often used with good effect. Bass can be caught from June–November off the west and south coast of Ireland, and the south-west, Channel and eastern coasts of England, also off west Wales. The species is a slow grower and it is especially vital to return undersized fish to the water unharmed. Grows to about 8 kg (17.6 lb) but much larger fish are caught off Portugal and in the Mediterranean.

§206 **Black bream** (old wife)
Spondyliasoma cantharas

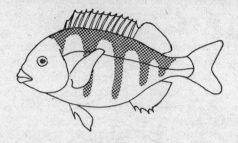

Found off the western and Channel coasts of England, also western Ireland and in the northern North Sea from June–October, the species favours reefs, wrecks and rocky shores. It has a distinctive, spiny dorsal fin and the silvery body is often crossed with dark vertical bars. Takes worm, feathers and fish baits, and is best approached with fairly light tackle on which it can be a dashing fighter. Shoals tend to feed above bottom, and you would normally lower your offering to the bed and retrieve five or six turns of line to suspend the tackle among the fish. A 1.3 kg specimen is a good fish. Very big bags of bream are taken when summer shoals arrive on the south coast reefs.

§207 **Rays bream**
Brama brama

Not closely related to the other sea breams, the rays bream has a steep-sloping forehead, yellow, sickle-shaped fins and brilliant silver flanks. It is present only in some warm years when it visits western coasts and may extend into the North Sea.

§208 Pandora bream
Pagellus erythrinus

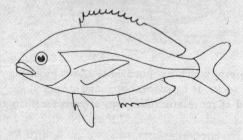

An occasional visitor to the south and west coasts of Britain and the North Sea, this fish resembles the red bream (see below) but has larger eyes and no spot on the shoulder.

§209 Red bream
Pagellus bogaraveo

A popular, reef fish like the black bream, the red bream is fairly common all around Britain in the summer. Colour varies from brownish red to silver-pink, and there is a distinguishing dark spot on each shoulder of the fish behind the head. Fishing baits and methods are as for black bream. All the breams are bony but quite palatable.

§210 **Bogue**
Boops boops

A small bream which has notched teeth for browsing on algae-encrusted rocks. It has dark, horizontal stripes along yellowish flanks and is more streamlined in appearance than the other breams.

§211 **Brill**
Scophthalmus rhombus

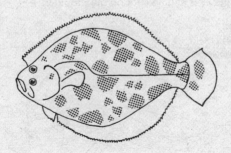

This flatfish likes shallowish banks of mud, sand or gravel like its larger relative, the turbot, but it is sometimes contacted close to reefs or wrecks. It feeds on small fish, particularly sandeels and sprats, and small crabs – sandeel or peeler crab make good baits fished on leger tackle. All the flatfish are strong fighters, making erratic, darting runs, and a characteristic vibration can be felt through the line and rod if one is hooked. Brill are found all around Britain in summer, but they migrate to deeper water in winter. They often keep company with turbot, with which species they are able to hybridize. A good eating fish, brill grow to about 5 kg (11 lb).

§212 **Coalfish** (saithe, coley)
Pollachius virens

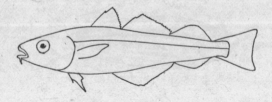

A relative of the cod, generally distributed around Britain. It is a fish of the reefs and wrecks, occasionally visiting rocky shores. The back is dun-coloured and the flanks are usually greenish, shading to a white underside. Coalfish are strong fighters and strongish tackle (lines of 7–11 kg – 15–25 lb breaking strain are recommended) and they will take legered fish and squid baits, pirks and feathers. The flesh is sold as 'coley'.

§213 **Cod** (small fish: codling)
Gadus morhua

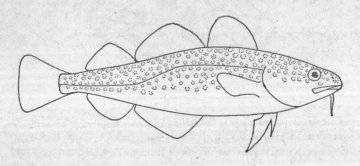

Our most important commercial fish, the cod is found all around Britain, with notable inshore populations on south and east coasts during the colder months, when it is a popular shore-fishing quarry. It has a catholic taste regarding the sort of ground it inhabits, and it will take a wide range of baits – fish, worms, squid, soft crab, mussel flesh – besides pirks and feather traces. Large baits and fairly heavy tackle should be used where big cod are expected. Fish up to 20 kg (44 lb) are taken on rod and line, with a fair number of 10 kg-plus fish every season. Fish of 50 kg or more have been taken by commercial fishermen.

§214 **Dab**
Limanda limanda

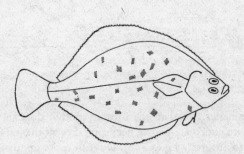

A small flatfish favouring inshore banks of mud, sand or gravel. It accepts worm baits fished on light tackle. Large catches may be taken if a feeding ground is discovered. Good to eat, especially if fried or grilled soon after catching.

§215 **Greater spotted dogfish** (bull huss, nursehound)
Scyliorhinus stellaris

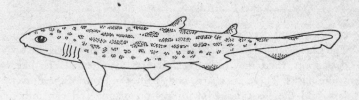

Dogfish and the tope are small members of the shark tribe, and their normal habit is to hunt in packs over banks and rough ground. They accept fish, squid, crab and worm bait, taking with a characteristic snap before moving purposefully off. The greater spotted dogfish, with a blotched, roughish hide, is usually found in deeper water than the lesser spotted dogfish (see below). It grows to around 9 kg (19.8 lb).

§216 **Lesser spotted dogfish** (common dogfish, rough hound)
Scyliorhinus raniculus

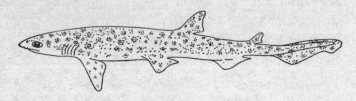

A much smaller fish than the greater spotted dogfish, liberally spotted with chocolate-brown flecks. It takes worm and fish baits, growing to around 2 kg (4.4 lb). Dogfish make good eating and are sold as 'rock-salmon'.

§217 **Spur dogfish**
Squalus acanthius

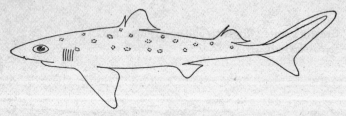

The spur dogfish has a steely-grey back and although there are no dark spots, there may occasionally be scattered, small, star-like, white flecks. There are sharp, bony spines in front of the dorsal fins, and these are linked with poison glands and can inflict painful wounds. Baits and methods are as for the other dogfish (see above). Spur dogfish grow to around 7 kg (15.4 lb).

§218 **Flounder** (fluke, butt)
Platichthys flesus

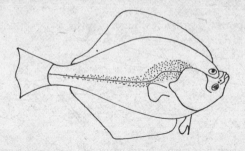

Common all around the British Isles, especially in creeks, harbours and estuaries where it will penetrate well upstream during winter spawning runs – often it is the mainstay of winter shore anglers. Worms or peeler crab fished on light tackle account for good fish and a baited spoon is very effective.

§219 **Greater forkbeard**
Phycis blennoides

A deep-water relative of the cod with a short 'beard' or barbel under the jaw and long, streaming pectoral fins. It migrates in winter to the Channel, parts of the North Sea, and Irish and Scottish waters. It is usually caught by chance rather than design, taking fish baits. It grows to about 2 kg (4.4 lb).

§220 **Lesser forkbeard** (tadpole fish)
Raniceps raninus

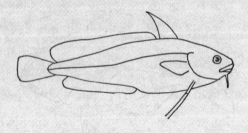

A small, dark fish with a large, rounded head and a small beard below the bottom jaw. Rarely caught. It grows to about 15 cm (6 in).

§221 **Garfish**
Belone belone

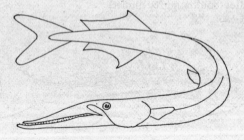

Arrives in the coastal waters of Britain in April–May (shortly before the main, summer, mackerel shoals) and leaves in late summer. It has a very distinctive long, toothed 'beak' and a green and silver eel-like body. It also has unusual green-coloured bones. Like the mackerel, it is fun to catch on light bait or spinning tackle, and it is quite good to eat. It grows to about 1 kg (2.2 lb).

§222 Gilt-head
Sparus aurata

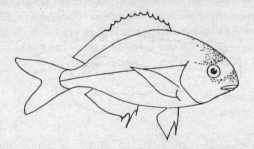

A relative of the breams but only an occasional visitor to Britain, the gilt-head has a distinctive spectacle-like patch of gold-coloured scales linking both eyes. It rarely grows to more than 0.5 kg (1.1 lb).

§223 Grey mullet (common grey mullet)
Mugil cephalus

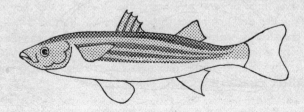

There are three grey mullets that visit British waters besides the common variety, and distinguishing between them takes some experience. Only the common mullet has a transparent eyelid. The thick-lipped grey mullet, *Crenemugil labrosus*, has a puffy upper lip which is sometimes warty (it is the only mullet found in Irish waters). The golden grey mullet, *Liza auratus*, is a smaller species with a yellowish patch of scales on the head not quite extending to the upper lip. The thin-lipped grey mullet, *Mugil capito*, has a similar patch of scales which do extend to the lip, rounded, rather than squared, pectoral fins, and often a black spot at the base of the pectorals. Mullet are popular shore, harbour and estuary fish, growing to around 4 kg (8.8 lb). They are extremely shy, and light, float tackle baited with worm or bread fragments is the usual approach. Freshwater tackle is often quite adequate, although the fish are strong fighters. They need to be played carefully because their lips are soft and a hook can easily pull free. Quite good to eat, but sometimes muddy-tasting.

§224 Grey gurnard
Eutrigla gurnardus

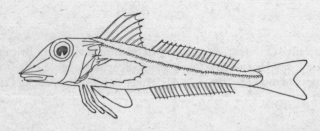

All the gurnards have wedge-shaped, armour-plated heads, spiny dorsal fins, and adaptations of some of the rays of their large pectoral fins into 'fingers' which feel the ground while they are hunting. Plentiful in summer, they feed on small, bottom-dwelling fish, crustaceans, worms and molluscs, and they can be caught on a variety of baits. The sombre-coloured grey gurnard grows to about only 0.5 kg (1.1 lb) and its relatives are much more colourful. All the gurnards grunt quite audibly.

§225 Red gurnard
Aspitrigla cuculus

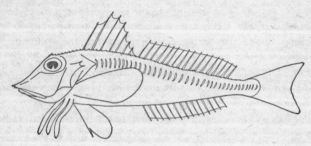

This is a handsome, orange-red fish, shading to pink on the underside, with prominently ribbed flanks. It grows to over 1 kg (2.2 lb) and makes good eating, but it should be baked – boiling spoils them.

§226 **Yellow gurnard** (tub)
Trigla lucerna

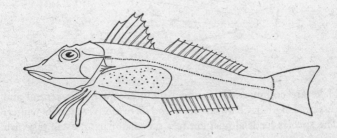

This is a large gurnard with a brilliant, blue edge to the pectoral fins (may be faded in older specimens). It is common around Ireland and in the Channel and parts of the North Sea. It grows to around 5 kg (11 lb) but is not normally eaten.

§227 **Haddock**
Melanogrammus aeglefinus

The haddock has a general distribution all around England but the greatest concentrations are in northern waters. It shoals over rough ground, feeding on small fish and crustaceans. There is a distinct, black spot on the lateral line behind the pectoral fin, and the first dorsal fin is tall and pointed. They will take feathers or pirks, as well as worm, soft crab and fish baits, on bottom tackle. Grows to about 4 kg (8.8 lb).

§228 Hake
Merluccius merluccius

Hake are common all around Britain except in the central and eastern English Channel. They move to deep water in winter. The species feeds almost entirely on small fish and will take fish baits or pirks. However, it is rarely caught on rod and line. It has a silvery appearance and the scales are much more noticeable than in many other members of the cod family.

§229 Herring
Clupea harengus

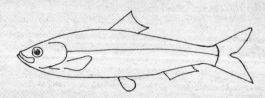

This is mentioned mainly because it makes a good bait for many species if fresh supplies can be obtained. A plankton feeder, it is sometimes taken on small baits and feather traces.

§230 **John Dory** (St Peter's fish)
Zeus faber

This species is common all around Britain in summer in rocky and weedy areas. A legend attributes the prominent purplish spot on the fish's broad, flat flank to thumb and finger marks left when St Peter picked up a John Dory. The fish also has long, trailing, bony dorsal and pectoral fins and a cantilevered mouth which it can shoot out to engulf shrimps and small fish. It grows to about 4 kg (8.8 lb) and makes good eating.

§231 **Lemon sole**
Microstumus kitt

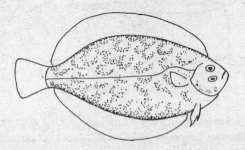

A longish flatfish, found all around Britain on muddy grounds, it does not feed in mid-winter but at other times may be taken on worm or soft-crab baits. Commercial boats have taken specimens up to 2 kg (4.4 lb) but not many large fish have been captured by anglers.

§232 Ling
Molva molva

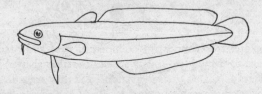

Found all around Britain but scarce in the central English Channel, the ling prefers rocky ground and wrecks where it can be taken on strongish tackle and fish or squid baits (pirks and feathers are sometimes taken). It moves to deep water in winter, although it may be present year-round in some localities (e.g. Eddystone reef). It grows to 20 kg (44 lb) or more and is good to eat.

§233 Lumpsucker (sea hen)
Cyclopterus lumpus

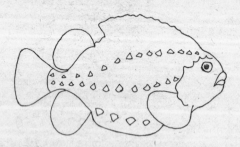

This is a scale-less fish with a box-like, dumpy appearance and knobbly flanks. A strong sucker on the underside, an adaption of the ventral fins, enables the fish to cling to rocks in strong flows. It takes worm, crab and fish baits and grows to about 6 kg (13.2 lb).

§234 **Mackerel** (small fish: joeys)
Scomber scombrus

The mackerel is an important commercial fish, and of no less importance to the angler – many species (notably sharks) follow the mackerel shoals on their migrations, and they are a fine bait – besides being fun to catch on light tackle. When required for bait they can often be taken in quantity with a 12–6 hook feather trace. Generally a surface fish, they tend to switch to bottom feeding late in the year and they may disappear from some areas such as the North Sea, but there are winter shoals in the Channel and off the south-west coast. Mackerel grow to about 2 kg (4.4 lb).

§235 **Megrim**
Lepidorhombus whiff-iagonis

A small, deep-water flatfish, sand-coloured and without spots, the megrim grows to about 1 kg (2.2 lb) and is occasionally taken on worm, mussel and soft-crab baits.

§236 **Monkfish** (angel fish)
Squatina squatina

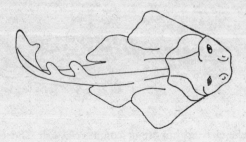

The monkfish is related to the sharks, and is occasionally taken in great numbers over skate grounds. It is a somewhat ugly fish, with four 'wings' and a broad, flat head with small eyes and a large mouth. It favours muddy ground where it feeds on small fish, crustacea and molluscs. It grows to around 30 kg (66 lb). There are mixed opinions about its fighting ability – the only one I ever caught, a 20-lb fish, did not give much of an account of itself. Monkfish are scarce in winter except in very deep water.

§237 **Norway pout**
Trisopterus esmarkii

A small, whiting-like fish, growing to about 20 cm (8 in), which is found off the north and west coasts of Britain and in the North Sea. It has a larger eye than the whiting and feeds mainly on small crustaceans.

§238 **Opah** (moonfish)
Lampris guttatus

This is a very colourful, tubby fish that occasionally drifts with warm water to Britain. It has rainbow-washed flanks spotted with white, and it feeds on small fish and crustaceans, growing quite large – a fish of 44 kg (97 lb) was found stranded quite recently. Moonfish are rarely caught on rod and line in Britain.

§239 **Pelamid** (short-finned tunny, belted bonito)
Sarda sarda

A small tunny with a streaked back, the pelamid is rare in Britain but common further south in the Atlantic and in the Mediterranean. It follows mackerel and pilchard shoals, growing to around 4 kg (8.8 lb).

§240 **Pilchard**
Sardina pilchardus

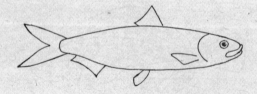

The pilchard is of interest to the angler because, like the mackerel, it draws such species as sharks close inshore. It makes a fine bait if fresh supplies can be obtained, and pilchard oil is also a good attractant taint for dipping such baits as fish strips before fishing. The visits of huge shoals of pilchards, mainly to western coastal areas, have diminished in recent years, but there are past records of shoals disappearing and reappearing some years later.

§241 **Piper**
Trigla lyra

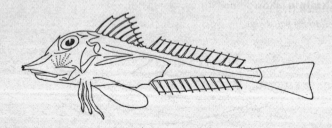

A gurnard which is occasionally caught off the south-west coast, the piper has similar colouration to the red gurnard, but is a stouter fish. It has a smooth lateral line, whereas the red gurnard's flanks are noticeably ribbed.

§242 **Plaice**
Pleuronectes platessa

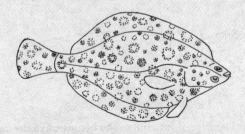

This is an important commercial flatfish and a favourite with anglers. It lives in fairly shallow water, generally near the coast, preferring sand and gravel grounds, where it feeds on worms, molluscs, crustaceans and small fish. It is renowned for being very able at changing colour and spot patterns to match its surroundings. It is best fished for with light, leger tackle, but has also been known to take small spinners, especially baited spoons intended for flounders. It grows to around 3 kg (6.6 lb).

§243 **Pollack** (lythe)
Pollachius pollachius

One of the most popular reef and wreck fish, pollack are very common off western coasts and on rocky shores and sea lochs in the north. Although good specimens are taken from the shore, the general run of shore fish are smaller than the specimens taken on offshore reefs. Pollack are hard fighters, accepting worm, squid and fish baits, as well as spinners and pirks – a moving bait fished off the bottom seems to attract them best. Shore methods are light legering, spinning and float fishing. They grow to more than 10 kg (22 lb).

§244 **Poor cod**
Trisopterus minutus

Aptly named, this small member of the cod family, which has large eyes and a silvery sheen, rarely attains more than 20 cm (8 in) in length. It is fairly common all around Britain.

§245 **Poutassou** (blue whiting)
Micromesistius poutassou

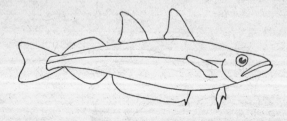

This is a shoaling, deep-sea member of the cod family, sometimes contacted off the Irish coast, and less commonly in the English Channel and Scottish waters. It grows to about the same size as the poor cod.

§246 **Pouting** (pout-whiting, bib)
Trisopterus luscus

Undoubtedly, more pouting are taken by sea anglers than any other species of fish. Pouting inhabit a variety of locales, greedily attacking any kind of offering – a characteristic tapping is transmitted through the line if small pouting are worrying a bait. They grow to about 2 kg (4.4 lb) and, although bony, they are quite good to eat.

§247 **Puffer fish**
Lagocephalus lagocephalus

Rarely attaining 0.5 kg (1.1 lb), the puffer fish is a squid-eating, warm-water species which sometimes drifts to south-west coasts. They have a prickly skin and are able to inflate suddenly with water so that they resemble a bristly football.

§248 **Rabbit fish** (rat fish)
Chimera monstrosa

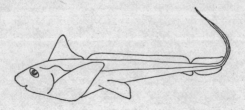

A weird, snub-nosed, deep-water fish with a long, whip-like tail, the rabbit fish belongs to a sub-class which separated from the sharks 410 million years ago. Like many of the cartilaginous fish, the male has 'claspers' used in the mating process. Very rarely caught by anglers, specimens up to 150 cm (5 ft) have been taken in trawls.

§249 **Blonde ray**
Raja brachyura

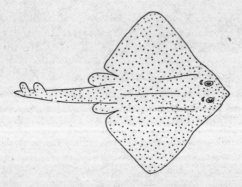

Rays inhabit a variety of locales but generally favour grounds of mud or sand, sometimes in quite shallow water. In still conditions it is possible to detect an initial pull as a ray descends on a bait. Then there is a pause as the fish tastes the bait before moving off – this is when the strike should be made. Rays feed on crustaceans, molluscs, worms and small fish. Care needs to be taken over identifying different species, which in some cases are quite similar in appearance – as with the blonde ray and the spotted ray. The blonde ray is scarce in the North Sea only. It has a brown or sand-coloured body or 'disc' peppered with small spots extending right to the margins of the wings. It grows to 16 kg (35.3 lb).

§250 **Cuckoo ray**
Raja naevus

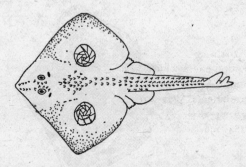

Among the smallest rays found in Britain, is the cuckoo ray caught all around the coast but is especially common in the south-west and off Ireland. It grows to about 2 kg (4.4 lb). It has a prominent, mottled blotch at the centre of each wing, and spines along the back ridge extending to the tail.

§251 **Sandy ray**
Raja circularis

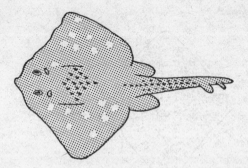

This species is occasionally caught in the Western Channel and off Ireland. The disc is covered with smaller spots than the blonde ray's disc, and, although the spots go right to the edge of the wings, there is usually an identifying handful of larger, lighter spots in the middle of each wing. It grows to about 2 kg (4.4 lb).

§252 **Small-eyed ray** (painted ray)
Raja microocellata

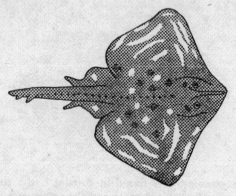

This ray is only rarely found outside the Devon and Cornwall coasts and off Ireland. The greyish back is patterned with light and dark circular spots, while there are short, dark stripes (like brush strokes) running parallel with the margins of the wings. Both back and underside are spiny. It grows to 6 kg (13.2 lb)

§253 **Spotted ray** (homelyn)
Raja montagui

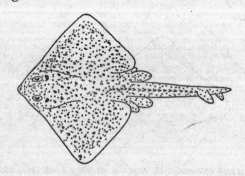

This is similar to the blonde ray, except that the spots stop 2–4 cm from the margins of the wings. There is also occasionally a light, circular blotch to the centre of each wing. Scarce in the North Sea, it grows to 7 kg (15.4 lb).

§254 **Thornback ray** (roker)
Raja clavata

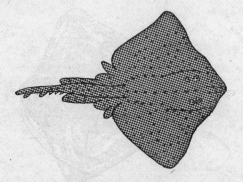

Our commonest ray (sold commercially as 'skate'), this fish prefers roughish ground or mud banks. Shoals will often consist of fish of a like sex and size (males have pointed teeth and the females flat, rounded ones). The greyish back is mottled with light and dark, irregular blotches and there are patches of spines on both wings and in a prominent ridge along the back and tail. It grows to 16 kg (35.2 lb).

§255 **Undulate ray**
Raja undulata

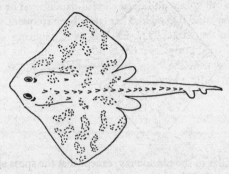

Rare outside southern English, and Irish coasts, this is a distinctive fish with an orange or yellow disc, marked with black or brown short, wavy stripes, looking rather like the peel in marmalade. It grows to about 8 kg (17.6 lb).

§256 Eagle ray
Myliobatis aquila

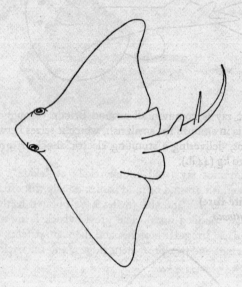

The eagle ray, stingray and electric ray belong to different families from the rays above. Both the eagle ray and the stingray have venomous tail spines and need careful handling. The eagle ray is caught all around Britain and has lately been frequently caught off Scotland in the winter. The fish has wide, tapering wings and a torpedo-shaped body. The tail is thin and whip-like and the poison spine is near the base. British specimens are mainly small, growing to about 3 kg (6.6 lb).

§257 Electric ray (crampfish)
Torpedo nobiliana

The electric ray is common all around Britain throughout the year. It waits in ambush for small fish, which it seizes between its rounded fins, delivering a stunning electric shock. It grows to more than 20 kg (44 lb).

§258 Stingray (fire-flare)
Dasyatis pastinaca

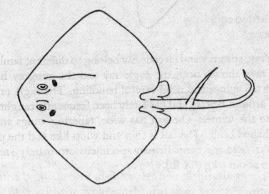

The stingray has rounded wings and is smooth-skinned save for the poisonous spine at the base of its long, whip-like tail. It appears to feed mainly on crustaceans, although many have been taken on fish baits. Specimens of more than 25 kg (55.1 lb) have been taken by anglers.

§259 Red mullet
Mullus surmuletus

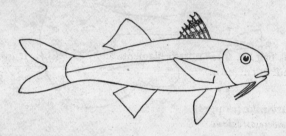

The red mullet has a distinctive sloping forehead and two long, streaming barbels under the lower jaw. The bronze flanks may be streaked with red, while sometimes a reddish colouration is uniform over the entire body. The fish is common off the south and south-west coasts of England and Ireland, and in the North Sea off Scotland. It feeds on squid, mussels and crustaceans, growing to about 1 kg (2.2 lb).

§260 Five-bearded rockling
Ciliata mustela

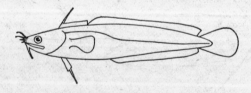

The rocklings are small, cod-related fish, resembling the ling in body shape. They get their name from the fleshy filaments which sprout from the head by the nostrils. The five-bearded rockling has four nostril filaments and one lower-jaw barbel. It grows to about 20 cm (8 in).

§261 **Four-bearded rockling**
Rhinonemus cumbrius

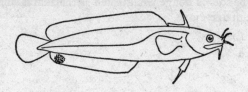

This fish has three nostril filaments and one barbel. It grows to about 25 cm (10 in).

§262 **Saury pike** (skipper)
Scomberesox saurus

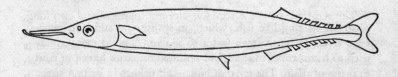

A sporadic visitor to south-west coasts, whose range may extend north to Scotland in some years. It is similar to the garfish but generally smaller, growing to about 45 cm (18 in), with a shorter 'beak'. It takes surface-fished baits or small spinners.

§263 **Scad** (horse mackerel)
Trachurus trachurus

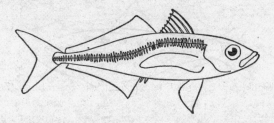

A mackerel-shaped fish, but with a prominent row of enlarged scales along the lateral line and disproportionately large eyes. It has similar habits to the mackerel, growing to about 1 kg (2.2 lb). Rare in the northern North Sea but common in summer elsewhere. The scad is not generally eaten as the skin is unpalatable and difficult to remove.

§264 Allis shad
Alosa alosa

Shad are herring-like fish, which, in spring and summer, penetrate rivers as far as fresh water to spawn. A good many rivers used to have 'runs' of shad, but polluted estuaries have put paid to many of them. The most famous shad fishery in Britain at the moment is the lower Severn, where the fish are taken on bait and small spinners. The allis shad has a small brown smudge on the lateral line, directly behind the gill covers. It grows to about 1 kg (2.2 lb).

§265 Twaite shad
Alosa fallax

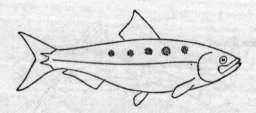

Can be distinguished from the allis shad by the row of five to seven dark smudges along the flank above the lateral line. It grows to about the same size as the allis shad.

§266 Smooth hound
Mustelus mustelus

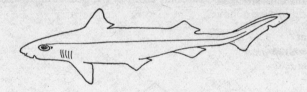

A largish dogfish growing to about 12 kg (26.4 lb), the smooth hound is caught fairly frequently off the south-west coast. It feeds mainly on crustaceans but will take small fish.

§267 Sole
Solea solea

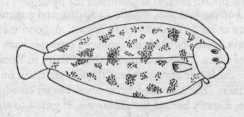

The sole's oval shape is unmistakable. It is common in the English Channel, the Irish Sea and the North Sea up as far as Scotland. It prefers muddy ground and shallow water, feeding on small crustaceans, worms and molluscs. It grows to about 1 kg (2.2 lb).

§268 Solenette
Buglossidium luteum

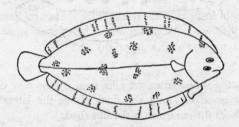

This is a small sole growing to about 12.5 cm (5 in) common in the English Channel and the southern North Sea. The fins are usually dark streaked.

§269 Sprat
Sprattus sprattus

Familiar to everyone, this small, silvery, coastal fish is present all around the British Isles. It is not fished for by anglers (a waste of time), but if fresh supplies can be obtained they do make fine baits.

§270 Stone bass (wreckfish)
Polyprion americanus

Rarely caught in Britain, the fish gets its alternative name from a habit of following floating wreckage. It feeds on small fish and can grow to weights of 45 kg (99.2 lb).

§271 **Sunfish**
Mola mola

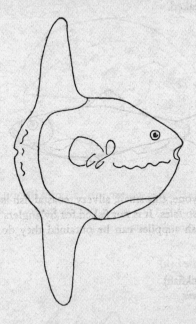

One of the weirdest fish to visit Britain, the deep, stout body and sail-and-keel, fin arrangements of the sunfish makes it look more like a space vehicle than a fish. Its distribution is world wide, but it has a preference for warm currents. Specimens up to 25 kg (55 lb) have been caught here, but huge specimens have been found in warmer seas – up to 997 kg (2,198 lb).

§272 Topknot
Zeugopterus punctatus

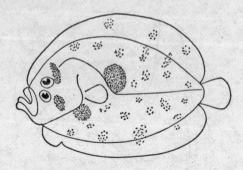

A small, rounded flatfish, common all around Britain, the topknot grows to about 25 cm (10 in). It prefers shallow water where it feeds mainly on small crustaceans.

§273 Trigger fish (file fish)
Balistes carolinensis

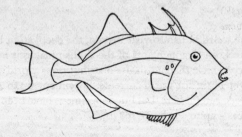

This is a tubby, box-like fish which gets its name from the sharp, erectile dorsal spines which lock into position and can be released by depressing the third and smallest spine. It inhabits rocky, shore areas, growing to about 1 kg (2.2 lb).

§274 **Turbot**
Scophthalmus maximus

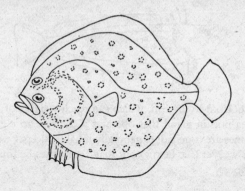

This large flatfish tends to lurk at the edge of sand and gravel banks where it ambushes sandeels and other small fish. Some very good fish have come from ground around wrecks in recent years. Small turbot are usually found in shallow, inshore water and may occasionally be caught in estuaries. It grows to 13 kg (28.7 lb).

§275 **Tusk** (torsk)
Brosme brosme

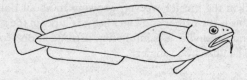

Occasionally caught off the north and north-west coasts of the British Isles, this member of the cod family tends to be solitary in habit. It feeds on squid and small fish, growing to about 5 kg (11 lb).

§276 **Greater weever**
Trachinus draco

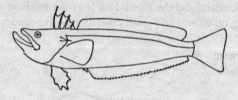

A small, bottom-living fish, which can reach weights of 1 kg (2.2 lb), with a poison gland that operates if the five to eight sharp dorsal spines are touched. It generally inhabits deeper water than the lesser weever (see below) but may sometimes be found quite close inshore.

§277 **Lesser weever**
Trachinus vipera

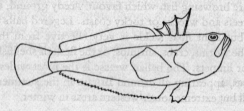

Smaller than the greater weever, growing to about only 11 cm (4.5 in), this is the bather's 'danger fish'. It lurks in the sand, half buried, and can inflict a painful sting if trodden on – or if it is carelessly handled by an angler!

§278 **Witch**
Glyptocephalus cynoglossus

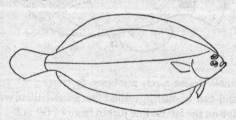

The witch is a small flatfish resembling an elongated dab, generally with no skin markings. It is common off the west of Ireland, in northern Scotland and the North Sea. It grows to about 30 cm (12 in), feeding on worms and small crustaceans over muddy ground.

§279 Ballan wrasse
Labrus bergylta

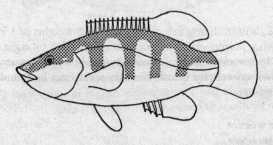

Wrasses are browsing fish which favour weedy ground, either on offshore reefs and wrecks or rocky coasts. Legered baits will take reef fish, but light float tackle is very effective from the shore. Baits can be worms, crabs, shrimps, or the flesh of shellfish such as mussels or limpets. The ballan wrasse is the most widespread of the wrasses, appearing all around Britain in the summer but departing all but extreme south-western areas in winter.

§280 Corkwing wrasse
Crenilabrus melops

This is a small wrasse rarely attaining 30 cm (12 in). It is rare in Scotland and can be distinguished from the ballan wrasse by a dark smudge on the lateral line just in front of the tail.

§281 Cuckoo wrasse
Labrus mixtus

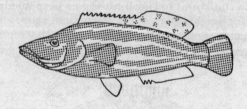

The male cuckoo wrasse has a red ground colour streaked with vivid blue, but in the female these stripes are absent. It is common in Irish waters and is occasionally caught in south-west England and in Scotland. It grows to about 30 cm (12 in).

§282 Rainbow wrasse
Coris julis

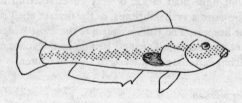

Distinguishable by a vivid multi-colour zig-zag pattern along the flanks, the rainbow wrasse is rare in British waters.

§283 Whiting
Merlangus merlangus

A commercially important member of the cod family, the whiting is fairly common in the English Channel, Bristol Channel, the Irish Sea and the North Sea. It feeds from mid-water to the bottom, on small fish, growing to around 2 kg (4.4 lb).

(N.B. The weights given in the descriptions above are for the average ceiling of fish taken by anglers – they do not represent the record weights for the various species, which are given elsewhere.)

Virtually all the small creatures of the sea are prey for fish, and the angler's choice is not confined entirely to the range given here. Nevertheless, some baits are more easily obtainable in quantity than others, which gives rise to their popularity. The best-known baits are the marine worms.

§284 Lugworm

This is a thickset, large worm, ranging in colour from yellowish to black, which can be dug from mud or sand between high- and low-water marks. It leaves a tell-tale 'cast', or squiggle of extruded sand, on the surface of the beach, close to which will be another depression or exit hole. The worm lies in a 'U'-shaped tunnel between these two marks, usually about a foot deep (Fig. 205). Collecting equipment is a bucket, and either a spade or a broad-tined, garden fork (thin tines will break the worms). Dig to the side of the two holes, throwing the first spit quickly away and looking for the worm in the second spit. By far the best method of keeping lugworm is to wrap them in a coil of newspaper. They can be preserved, but this makes them an inferior bait and they are best used as fresh as possible. The baitholder hook with a sliced shank (Fig. 206) is a good way of keeping lugworm on a hook – the point is inserted at the head (thick) end and passed some distance down through the body to emerge through the side. If the worm is to stand the shock of long casting, it is a good idea to double-up the remaining part of the body by passing the hook through once again. It makes a good bait for most species, but is especially famed for cod. With large cod about and a plentiful supply of worms, two or three, bunched onto a large hook will pay off.

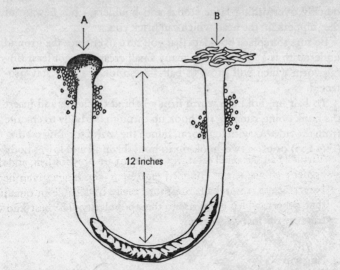

Fig. 205 (§284) To dig out lugworm, the spade or fork is thrust into the sand between and alongside the pit (A) and the cast (B). Normally it is necessary to go two spits deep, casting the first spadefuls quickly aside.

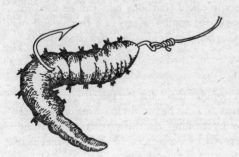

Fig. 206 A small lugworm on hook, which is threaded into the body starting at the head. The brittle sand-filled tail can be broken off.

§285 Ragworm

This is a worm with a compressed body and numerous centipede-like frills along its edges. It grows to over a foot in length, varying in colour from brown to yellow and rusty red. It inhabits mixed tidelines, preferring areas of thick, black ooze where it can be turned up with a thick-tined fork. It can also be collected by quickly overturning large stones and boulders – but beware of the 'nippers' in the head which can prick you.

Be sure to replace boulders that you turn over since the ground underneath is a 'nursery' for many small creatures, not least tiny ragworm which will grow to bait-size so long as they stay protected.

To bait up, hold the worm firmly behind the head, and insert the hook point, running the hook up through the body to emerge from the side. As with lugworm, bunch the worm for long casting (Fig. 207) or use a two-hook rig to hold the head and lower body

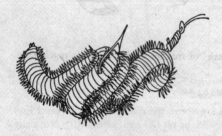

Fig. 207 (§285) Ragworm on hook.

of the worm. Ragworm make good bait for most species, but are especially good for bass, pollack, flounders and other flatfish. Small ragworms, generally called 'harbour rag' can be used individually on small hooks for mullet. Keep in a bucket full of muddy water and weed, or wrap individually in dry newspaper.

§286 Mackerel

This is one of the most popular fish baits because it is present all around Britain in summer and can be caught in quantity by using long feather traces, or by trolling on the way to the fishing ground. It can be preserved by deep-freezing, but this makes it much softer and less attractive than fresh fish.

The mackerel is either used whole for big fish, or can be cut into strips for smaller ones. To cut a large slice (which can be further divided into smaller strips) slit down into the fish just behind the pectoral fin (Fig. 208), going close to the backbone. Then turn the knife and slice cleanly towards the tail. A two-hook rig is useful for mackerel strips that are going to be thrown a long distance, or trailed through the water (Fig. 209).

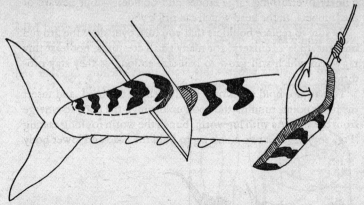

Fig. 208 (§286) Cutting a 'lask' of mackerel (above) and a mackerel-baited hook.

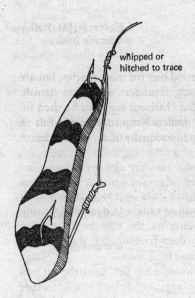

whipped or
hitched to trace

Fig. 209 Larger mackerel lask on a two-hook rig.

§287 Herring

This is obtainable from fishmongers at certain times of the year. Like the mackerel, it can be used whole for big fish, or sliced into pieces.

§288 Sprats

These tiny fish, obtainable from fishmongers, make good baits used singly for cod, dogfish, skate, bass and congers. If you have a deep-freeze, you can keep a stand-by supply, frozen in a coil of waxed or plastic paper – this stops them sticking together and tearing when you want to take them apart (Fig. 210).

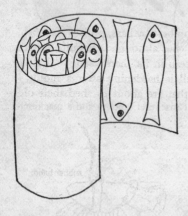

Fig. 210 (§288) Roll up spratts (or sandeels) in a strip of plastic paper for freezing.

§289 Sandeels

These small fish, which bury themselves in wet sand near the tideline, are unfortunately very localized and a 'sandeel beach' will have to be discovered if you want to dig them yourself (using a broad-tined fork). They are also the very dickens to keep alive, and for that reason professional fishermen who use them as bait, tow them in a wicker basket called a 'courge' behind the boat. If you are going to use sandeels immediately, it does not make much

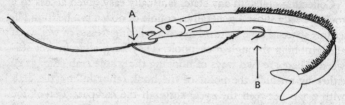

Fig. 211 (§289) Baiting with sandeel: A – small hook hitched onto the trace a few inches above the main hook, B.

difference if they expire, but if you need to keep a supply, the best method of preservation is deep-freezing (using the 'coil' wrapping, mentioned above for sprats). Frozen baits will be softer than fresh. The sandeel is best used on a two-hook rig (Fig. 211). They make an excellent bait for bass, pollack, coalfish, brill, turbot and big plaice.

§290 **Crabs**

Small crabs are taken in great numbers by bass, pollack, coalfish, dogfish, skates, turbot and brill, but although it is quite certain that these species all take the crab in its 'hard' state – that is, outside the time when the shell is hardening after a moult – anglers generally favour crabs that are about to shed their old

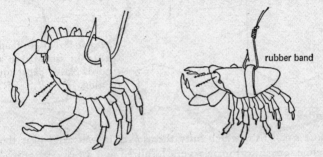

Fig. 212 (§290) Soft crabs can be hooked through body and carapace, or fished live with a rubber band securing the hook.

carapace (peelers) or the unprotected fresh-moulted animal (soft-backs). I think it is wrong to ignore the hardback as a bait, particularly for deep-sea legering.

Collecting crabs, in any state, is usually easy given access to a rocky, weedy shore – generally a couple of dozen can be found in a short space of time by turning stones, lifting tresses of wet weed and grubbing through rock pools. They keep alive in wet sea-weed. There are two ways of hooking the whole crab (Fig. 212), either by pushing the point of the hook (after killing the crab with a tap between the eyes) through the carapace out of the underside, and then back though again, or by slipping a small rubber band around the crab's body and passing the hook bend underneath it so that the crab dangles in a sort of sling. Halved or quartered crabs are useful for small fish such as dabs and flounders.

§291 Prawns

Like the crab, prawns are easily obtainable in most weedy areas. They can be caught with sweeps of a prawn net or by using a dropnet – a circular weighted net on a long cord – into which is tied an old mackerel or some other fish. They make fine baits for bass, wrasse and small pollack. They should be hooked through the tail (Fig. 213) and cast as gently as possible.

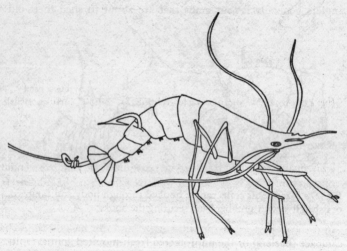

Fig. 213 (§291) A prawn should be hooked gently through the tail with a size 6 or 8 hook. Cast as gently as possible.

§292 Squid

Squid is now much more readily obtainable than of old, because much more is being eaten in Britain instead of being considered 'rubbish'. Sources are fishmongers as well as tackle shops. Even though fresh squid is best, it loses only a little of its appeal if deep frozen, and unlike fish, frozen squid stays tough. Whole, small squid can be used for cod, pollack, skate, dogfish and bass, but larger squid may be cut into strips or sections. A single tentacle presented on a small hook makes a fine flatfish bait (Fig. 214).

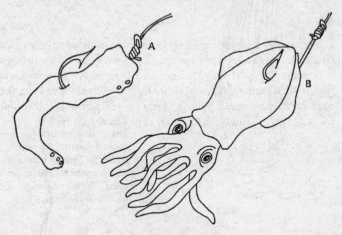

Fig. 214 (§292) A – squid tentacle on hook; B – whole, small cuttlefish.

§293 Razorfish

This small, elongated clam can be recognized as it squirts a spout of water into the air when you walk past its lair in the tideline. It is very quick to dig itself in, and needs some nifty spadework, but there is an alternative – if you drop a couple of pinches of salt into the hole it leaves, it will surface and can be grabbed. The whole of the fleshy interior (with the hook nicked through the tough 'foot' as in Fig. 215) makes a fine bait for many species.

§294 Mussels

Almost every rocky area has a colony of mussels clinging below the high-water mark. They can be pulled off the rock, but you need an old kitchen knife to force the shells apart. The whole of the flesh should be scooped out for bait, including the toughened parts which fasten the mussel inside its shell. These will give a more secure hold for your hook. On parts of the east coast, mussels are bunched onto a large hook and secured with a tie of

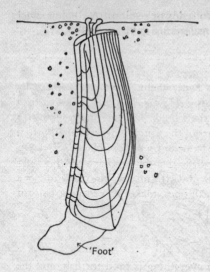

Fig. 215 (§293) The sand-burrowing razorfish, re-moved from its shell, makes a good bait for many species. The mus-cular foot provides a secure hook-hold.

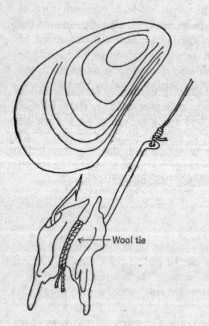

Fig. 216 (§294) The mus-sel is a good bait, but rather soft – a couple of turns of wool will help to keep shelled mussel on a hook.

wool (Fig. 216) as a cod bait. Mussel will attract many other species, and small pieces of the flesh are good for mullet.

§295 Limpets

These are readily available everywhere. If you take them by surprise, giving them a sharp, sideways tap with a stone or a knife, they fall easily from their hold. The interior resembles a snail without a shell, and part of the tough muscle at the bottom which holds the limpet to its stone or rock should be scooped out, along with the rest of the flesh, so that the bait has a secure hook-hold. Tiny bits of limpets are good for mullet, but the whole of a largish limpet, or several small ones, makes an excellent bait for big wrasse.

§296 Other baits

As I stated earlier, virtually everything is food for fish, and the diet will include the several other kinds of shellfish such as the slipper limpet, cockles, whelks, scallops, also shrimps and the hermit crab (found usually in vacated whelk shells). Small fish of every kind are worth a try, especially whitebait and brit (the small silvery fish which often scatter across the water in droves close to the shore when they are being hunted by bass or mackerel).

One fish deserves to be especially mentioned for its peculiar tastes, and that is the grey mullet. Bread, fished either as paste or flake, and even pieces of crust fished floating on the surface will take them. They have also been caught on pieces of bacon rind, and wads of cotton wool soaked in pilchard oil.

The very big range of sea-fish species means that you have to set out with a realistic target of one or two worthwhile species when you go fishing. What these 'worthwhile species' are, depends very much on where you go and when, but one thing is certain – you will invariably catch other species besides your target, some of which will be surprising, but rarely disappointing.

As a rough guide to targets, flounders (winter) and bass and mullet (summer) are worth going after in estuaries and harbours. Bass, wrasse, pollack, bream and mullet are the rock and pier angler's main objectives in summer, with 'bonus' mackerel and garfish, while in winter rocks and piers in some areas are worth trying for codling and whiting. Beach anglers can switch from winter fishing for cod, whiting and occasional thornbacks, to bass, plaice and other flatfish in the summer. The scope of the boat angler is wider, but the mainstay of winter fishing, except in the extreme south-west where summer species linger on, is the cod. Pollack, coalfish, ling, all manner of flatfish and rays, the 'big game' conger and shark, are all good summer targets, and some locations may attract sizeable populations of bream.

§297 Basic shore-fishing rigs

With the exception of open, tide-swept beaches, many areas of shore and estuary are suitable for float fishing. The hook-and-weight arrangement is the first consideration, and with the two-hook rig shown in Fig. 217 it is possible to use two different baits, and later change to the one of these which produces the most, or the best, fish. The amount of weight (which will affect the float size) depends on the strength of current; you will need more and more weight to take your bait to the chosen fishing level as

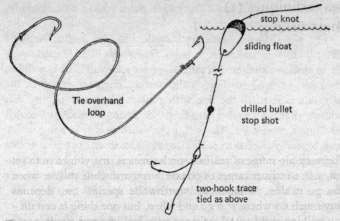

Fig. 217 (§297) A simple two-hook rig to use with float tackle.

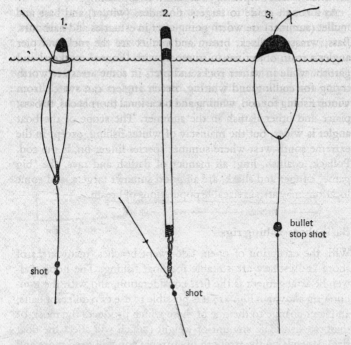

Fig. 218 Floats for sea work: 1 – large-bodied, balsa, freshwater float, for use in shallow, calm, sheltered spots; 2 – a peacock quill, a foot or more long, used here as a slider for deepish calm water; 3 – the sliding 'channel' float for use in heavier water conditions than the above two floats.

current increases. A small link swivel helps you to change ready-tied hooks and traces quickly.

Fig. 218 shows suitable types of float for sea work. The fixed float (in this instance a large, balsa, freshwater float) is used mainly in shallow, sheltered water. The peacock-quill float is a slider, and can be used for deep, calm water. The one shown in the diagram is fixed to the line with a sliding link swivel, and this allows floats of varied length to be changed easily to match changing conditions. The weight in this case is split shot, which can be easily altered to suit float size. The third float is a drilled balsa sea float (there are hollow plastic versions) which slides on the line to a stop knot. It will take heavier, drilled bullets to cock this float, which is more suitable than the other two floats for fast, deep water.

Turning to legering, the simple, straight-through rig (Fig. 219) is suitable only for smooth, snag-free ground. In all other circumstances it is best to use some kind of paternoster arrangement which keeps the baited hook – more likely to snag than the lead – away from entanglements. Various forms of paternoster are shown in Fig. 220 and of these, the simple, soft boom, with a loop tied into the line (swivel above), or a three-way swivel for attaching hook lengths, is the best rig for long casting. French booms and the like, which make the baited hook stand out from

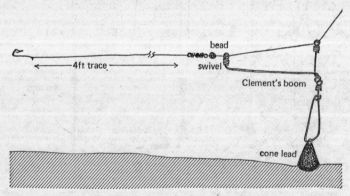

Fig. 219 Simple straight-through leger rig using a Clements boom and a conical lead.

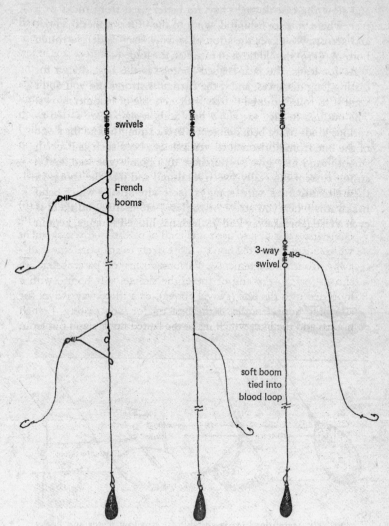

Fig. 220 Types of sea paternoster leger rigs.

the slipstream of the lead during a cast, will set up air resistance and slow the cast down. They are better used from rocks or a pier, where you are fishing down into the water, rather than out and across. Wherever the ground is truly snag-ridden, a rotten bottom (§119) should be used to attach the lead.

As for leads, the pear-shaped 'bomb' is the best design for casting long distances, and if the current is strong and you don't want it to roll, it can be flatted with a couple of hammer blows. The outlines in Fig. 221 show how weight shapes are suited to various kinds of sea bed, different current strengths and the slope of the line from horizontal to vertical. Sea beds such as packed, smooth sand may give no purchase to a bomb-type lead, and a strong current can easily sweep it around and into the shore. In these circumstances, wire 'spraggs' (soft wire bristles which bend backwards when you strike or retrieve) are useful, and there is even a lead ('breakaway lead') which has hinged spraggs, kept in

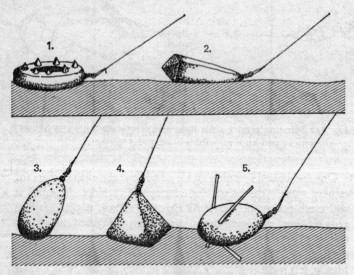

Fig. 221 The watch lead (1) is suitable for shallow water and heavy surf, but it is not a good casting shape and the flat-sided casting weight (2) is better. The bomb (3) suits many situations, but for fishing 'straight-down' into deep water pyramid leads (4), cone leads or Capta leads cannot be beaten. Where tides threaten to sweep a lead along over a soft bed, a casting weight with wire spraggs is useful (5).

position by a weak rubber band while you are fishing. Leads with spraggs are also suitable for fishing in heavy surf for bass, and so is the grip-type watch lead.

Spinning tackle for shore fish is the same, basically, as that employed for freshwater fishing (§155) with increases in line strength appropriate to the size of species sought. Spinners (and plugs) are of two types – those with sufficient weight to be cast on their own, and those which need extra lead on the line for casting. With the self-weighted spinner, an anti-kink vane and swivel should be incorporated in the tackle, while an anti-kink lead of the Wye type plus a swivel, is suitable for lighter lures (Fig. 222).

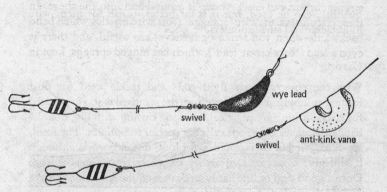

Fig. 222 Spinning rigs: 1 – for light spinners, a rig with a Wye lead; 2 – rig with an anti-kink vane for self-weighted spinners.

One specialized spinning tackle stands out above the others for estuary work – the baited flounder spoon (besides flounders it will catch plaice and bass). As Fig. 223 shows, it consists of a $1\frac{1}{2}$–3 in, slow, revolving spoon, trailing a 3–4 in trace and a hook baited, preferably, with ragworm or lugworm. Extra weight, in the form of a Wye lead, may be needed to cast this from the shore. Ideally, it is retrieved slowly, along a muddy or sandy bed, so that the spoon kicks up little puffs of debris as it moves. I don't really know what the attraction is, but it drives flatfish mad.

On occasions in the summer, mackerel shoals drive close enough to the coast for shore anglers to catch them. A six-hook feather trace, the same thing used by the boat angler to take mackerel in

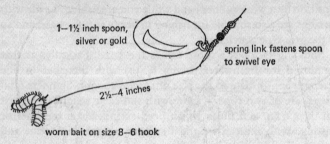

1–1½ inch spoon, silver or gold

spring link fastens spoon to swivel eye

2½–4 inches

worm bait on size 8–6 hook

Fig. 223 The flounder-spoon rig – it will need a drilled bullet or a Wye lead stopped 4 ft up the line for casting weight.

quantity, can be used, but it is far better to fish for them with light tackle and small spinners.

§298 Casting

With the comparatively light rods and tackle used for float fishing, spinning and light legering, the standard casts (§125) used for coarse fishing are practical, but long casting with big, double-handed, beachcasting rods calls for special techniques. The fixed-spool reel, first of all, is not ideal for long-distance work, although it will give a novice satisfactory distances from the word go. Once a good deal of line has been drawn off the spool it will have a hard job climbing over the spool lip.

The easiest way to use the fixed-spool reel is to exaggerate an overhead cast (§125), laying the rod well back over the shoulder to start with, and then pushing with the right hand and pulling down with the left (Fig. 224) to shoot the tackle up and forwards. The angler faces the direction he wants to cast.

With the ideal distance reel, the small, light-spooled multiplier, the 'lay back' cast gives the best results. The style was christened by Leslie Moncrieff, a well-known sea angler, who brought it to public notice by catching good bags of cod with extra-long casts from the shore. The angler begins by standing sideways to the water. The hook and weight should be only a couple or so feet from the tip of the rod, which is held, pointing away from the direction of the cast, with the right hand stopping the reel (set in the 'off' position and at this time underneath the rod) and the left hand grasping the lower butt grip (Fig. 225). The angler's

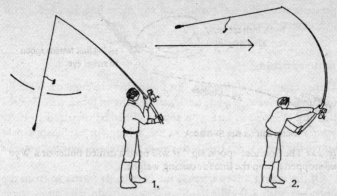

Fig. 224 (§298) Overhead cast for beach fishing with a fixed-spool reel. Space feet for balance. Swing tackle back, punch forward, and release line as rod comes well to the fore.

weight is on his right foot. The lead is swung gently away from the angler and the cast begins; the right hand lifts the rod to eye level and drives forward, while the left hand draws sideways across the body from right to left, finishing at groin level. This sweeps the rod in a leaning arc across the angler's body, compressing it sharply into a tight bow, while the angler's weight shifts from the right foot to the left. He finishes up facing in the direction of the cast. The reel spool is released from thumb pressure as the rod uncoils and shoots the lead upwards and forwards. Gentle pressure is applied at the zenith of the lead's trajectory to slow the reel, which by now is on the top of the rod. Firmer

Fig. 225 The 'lay back' style of casting for use with a multiplier reel.

pressure stops the reel turning off any more line, just before the lead enters the water.

§299 **Estuary fishing**

Estuaries are not all muddy, but those that are demand Wellington boots at least. Waders are ideal. Bearing in mind, too, that the tide might come in fast, you should either be prepared to carry your tackle and bait while you are fishing, or establish a base above the high-water to which you can retreat as the water comes up.

Of the main estuary species, the bass tends to run in from the open sea with a flooding tide, retreating soon after high-water slack. Such runs are often predictable in course, and in the times they begin, after the tide starts making. The fish move quite quickly because of the limited time they are going to stay, and they thoroughly investigate worm-producing flats, and gullies filling with water. In summer, their main food is shrimp and prawns – the main concentrations of these creatures will be at the head of the estuary, feeding on river debris.

If the estuary banks are uncomplicated the angler's best approach is to wait until bass begin moving, and then to move on upwards, casting to the shoal as it forages its way to the feeding grounds. When the tide turns and begins falling, the bass will usually make for the main channel and, providing this can be reached with a comfortable cast, the angler can work downstream with the shoal, retracing his steps.

Spinning is the best method for following a shoal of bass, since the simple tackle does away with the need to carry too much gear. Although the fish are concentrating mainly on worms, shrimp and the like, a small spinner put across their noses time after time often goads them into an aggressive take. Legered worms and, if the current is not too strong, float-fished baits, can also be used. If you do find out the feeding grounds of the bass at the top of the tide, you can often have a hectic hour's sport with legered or float-fished baits, and spinning.

I've known flounders to be present in an estuary at all states of the tide, although it is probably best to try for them when the tide is rising and they begin to move into side gullies which hold only a trickle of a stream at low water. Flounders are bottom feeders and by far the best baits are worms and small crabs, which should be legered on light tackle. The flounder-spoon tackle described above is an excellent way to fish for them; move along the bank as you cast, drawing the spoon back slowly so that you feel it dragging the bed. When you catch a fish, move a few yards on before casting again in case you have taken the tail-ender of a shoal. When the tide starts dropping, flounders don't seem unduly worried in water as shallow as six inches; in fact, they frequently become stranded in shallow pools until the next tide releases them.

Two basic flounder leger rigs are shown in Fig. 226. They should be used where the bottom is smooth (mud, sand). Weed or rocks demand a paternoster rig because of the possibility of snagging. One possibility is a rolling arrangement (with a drilled bullet) which enables you to pace along the bank with your tackle as it is driven by a rising or falling tide.

Like the flounder, the mullet is present at all states of the tide and, although it never appears to get stranded, it is happy in very shallow water at low tide. Fishing for surface-feeding mullet is very exciting – you can see the fish moving near to your bait, and there is a heart-stopping moment when you wonder if it is going

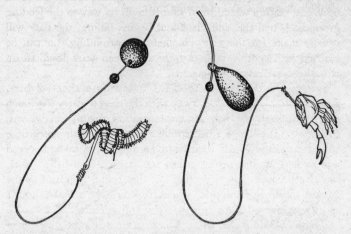

Fig. 226 (§299) Simple, leger rigs for estuary flounders – the top rig can be allowed to roll with the current in search of fish. Lugworms, small harbour ragworms, and pieces of soft crab are good baits.

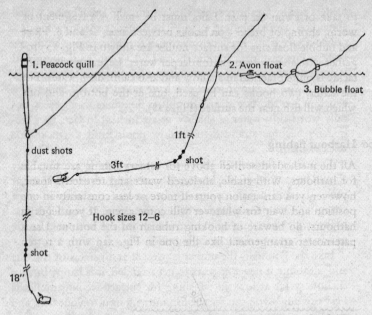

Fig. 227 Some mullet float arrangements: 1 – quill float rig for fishing medium-depth, calm water; 2 – surface-fishing rig; 3 – half-filled bubble-float and a piece of floating crust.

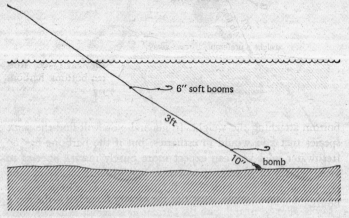

Fig. 228 Mullet legering rig.

to take or swim on past. Baits must be small – a fragment of worm, shrimp or bread – on hooks between sizes 12 and 6. Float and bubble-float rigs for surface mullet are shown in Fig. 227 together with an arrangement for deeper water. Legering with light tackle is quite practical in shallow and also calm, deep water. For the latter, two hooks can be used, one at the bottom and one which will fish near the surface (Fig. 228).

§300 **Harbour fishing**

All the methods described above for estuary fishing are suitable for harbours. With stable, sheltered water and restricted space, however, you can station yourself more or less constantly in one position and wait for whatever will come along. If you leger in harbours, do beware of hooking rubbish on the bottom. Use a paternoster arrangement like the one in Fig. 229 with a rotten

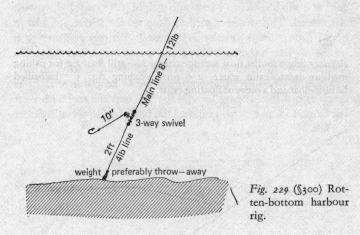

Fig. 229 (§300) Rotten-bottom harbour rig.

bottom attaching the weight. In general, you will find the same species that you would in estuaries, but if the harbour has no freshwater inlet you can expect more purely marine species to visit: wrasse in summer (sometimes garfish and mackerel) and codling and whiting in winter. Pouting are present in many harbours.

§301 Rock fishing

Fishing from rough, weed-covered rocks demands agility on your part, and light, wieldy, portable tackle. Boots with cleated soles are useful for rock-scrambling and they will save you from slips on wet weed.

Float fishing is quite practical from many rocky vantage points, and is a good method for wrasse, pollack and bass. Small, fixed floats can be used in rocky gullies, and the angler can work over a large area dropping a bait here and there until fish are found. Another good method is to scramble out to the outer edge of a rock bed where the use of the large, sliding float is recommended. Sometimes (Fig. 230) you can find a projection of rock which will allow you to drop the float where the current will 'trot' it along the rock face.

Legering in narrow gullies calls for special skill in placing the bait out of harm's way; it is best to use extremely sensitive gear, such as a 7 lb line with a $\frac{3}{4}$ oz bomb weight (flattened slightly with a hammer). This can be aimed to drop on the surface of a large boulder, or perhaps a clear patch of sand. At times you may even be able to watch the dark shape of a wrasse or pollack leave the shelter of weed cover, making across the clearing to your bait; this means, of course, that you must try to keep out of sight as much as possible. It pays to hold the line near the reel with your left hand, too, so that you can feel the bite of a fish – you'll detect

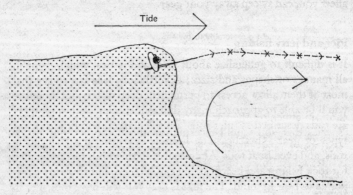

Fig. 230 (§301) Along-shore tidal flows can help you 'trot' float tackle from rock promontaries.

nibbles which the rod-tip won't show, especially if it is windy and the rod is waving about.

Although mainly a summer pursuit, rock fishing for cod and whiting can be attempted in winter. Normally, these fish will be taken by fishing out from rocks rather than among them, although there are places in the north of England where anglers fish down from cliffs, which may be a hundred feet or so high, into boiling, turbulent, rocky water for cod. Not a game for anyone who suffers from vertigo!

I've found that one of the beauties of summer rock fishing is that you don't have to take bait with you: in rock pools and among the weeds you will find more than you need as you go along. Limpets can be gleaned from rocks, and so can mussels. There will be sheltering crabs in plenty, and prawns – you can catch them by hand in pools, but a simple prawn net is easier.

Bait methods are not the only way of tackling rocky areas. From the outer edges you can cast spinners or feather traces for mackerel, while spinning for bass and pollack can be tried along the rock faces and in the larger gullies.

Do make sure that wherever you fish among rocks, you will have easy access to whatever fish you catch – many a large bass has been hooked, played out, and then lost, because the angler cannot get his landing net near it. Also try to be constantly aware of the rising tide and your escape route, and keep an eye open for extra-large waves and heavy boat washes which, if they don't affect you, can sweep away your gear.

§302 Pier and jetty fishing

It is difficult to generalize about piers and jetties, which come in all manner of shapes and sizes; nevertheless, it is fair to say that most of them allow access to permanent deep water, and therefore you'll be able to approach many different species. Although there are rods described as 'pier rods' on the market, you can use most types of gear – beachcasters, lighter, float-fishing and legering rods, and even boat rods. Almost all of the methods recommended for rock fishing and beachcasting can be tried, but there are a few points to bear in mind. The first is that you will have difficulty in winching up large fish on light lines, and a drop-net is useful if the pier deck is some way above the water surface. Secondly, you will have to be extremely careful about casting, especially if the pier is crowded. You need to watch out for obstructions such as strings of pier lights as well as nearby people.

If you fish uptide from a pier with leger tackle, you should be on guard for slack-line bites – i.e. the line will fall slack as the fish moves the weight back towards you. On the other side of the pier, it will be possible to trot a small weight a considerable distance away from you by raising it gently off the bottom so that the current pushes it along (Fig. 231). You can also trot float tackle.

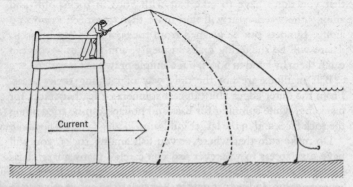

Current

Fig. 231 (§302) From a pier, raising a light weight off the bottom will 'trot' the bait down-tide.

§303 Beach fishing

The main targets of the beach angler are cod (winter) and bass, and so by concentrating on these two species the main techniques of beach fishing can be explored. They can be adapted for other species such as rays and flatfish.

Cod fishing tends to be slack during warmish, calm spells, and a winter storm accompanied by cold weather tends to draw the fish well inshore. Although they might come into the breaking waves, the cod usually wait in the deeper water, well out, sorting through the debris that the waves draw out. In these situations, long casting pays handsome dividends. The normal approach on the east and south coasts of Britain is to seek out beach depressions at low tide, which might well have concentrations of cod when they fill with water. The angler casts to these regions, lets his tackle settle, and moves gradually back as the tide comes in. Baits for cod are legion, but by far the most attractive one is a lugworm, or several lugworm if they can be obtained in quantity. The fresher the worm, the better it will stay on the hook. To ensure that soft baits stand the shock of long casting, a small piece of squid, which is tough, is often added to the hook after the worm has been bunched on a 'baitholder' shank (Fig. 232).

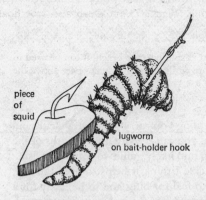

piece of squid

lugworm on bait-holder hook

Fig. 232 (§303) A piece of tough squid will hold soft lugworm on hook during cast.

If the bait is fished on static leger tackle, the angler can set up camp around his rod, moving the whole lot back as the tide rises; on the steeper beaches, this might not be necessary at all, but on shallow beaches an angler might expect to move as much as five hundred yards on a rising tide.

You should aim to cast only when necessary; constantly withdrawing the line to check the bait is only going to lose ground. If you leave your tackle in for long enough, you can walk back with the tide, releasing more line as you go, and you might finish with the bait a hundred and fifty yards or so out in good, deep water.

Another good method, useful only on certain beaches where the current flows from side to side and slanting waves create an outward push or 'undertow' (Fig. 233) is 'walking the lead'. A weight which will just trundle along the bottom is chosen. The tackle is thrown well out, allowed to sink and, as the current starts to push it along, the angler moves to keep pace with it on the shore. If the beach is small or if your distance is restricted by other anglers you can fish for some distance and then return to

Fig. 233 Where the tide runs at an angle to the beach, it can be used to push a light lead along the shore while the angler keeps pace above the tideline ('walking the lead').

start again; otherwise, providing you carry your extra tackle and bait slung on your shoulder, you can explore great lengths of the shore with your bait dipping into likely gullies to search out fish.

Even with static leger tackle I think it helps to hold the rod, or at least part of the line, to feel for bites and to be ready for a snatch take – you can if you wish put the rod on a rest to watch the rod-tip, but if you stray some way from the rod and have to sprint to it when a bite develops, you will lose some fish. If you hold the rod all the time you will find it less tiring to face away from the water and put your rod at a comfortable 'slope arms' position over your shoulder

Whether you hold or watch, you will soon come to recognize the pattern of regular tugs which the waves impart to the line; any interruption of this pattern is likely to be a take. However, you will find that there is usually a bow in your line formed by the push of the current, and you will also find that the considerable stretch in long lengths of nylon saps the power of your strike. At any indication of a bite, make a good sweeping strike that draws the rod well back over your shoulder, and back quickly up the beach away from the fish, striking as you go, until you are certain that you have firm contact. You can then hold the fish steady while you walk back down to the waterline, retrieving line as you go. Unless the fish runs strongly, in which case you will have to fight it to a standstill before drawing it in, you can repeat the walk up the beach and back again to retrieve, or you can pump the

fish from the tideline, raising the rod to draw the fish towards you
and then dropping it while you retrieve line. Landing in surf is
tricky; try, if you can, to hold the fish out of the surf until a
good-sized wave is coming in, and then draw the fish steadily
back with the wave so that it does the work for you. As soon as it
is close enough, you can go into shallow water to meet it and
bring a net or gaff into play. You might even be able to beach it,
high and dry, when the wave retreats, and you can then grab the
fish firmly with your hand under its gills to take it to safety.

The bass is a somewhat different proposition, mainly because it
is a surf feeder. The main requirement of surf tackle is that you
either root your leger in the furthest of the breakers, or walk the
lead (see above). Unless the breakers begin a good way off shore,
bass are often in reach of the less-able beachcasters. Worms are a
good bait, but sandeels are best for most beaches. Fish strips or
crab will substitute if sandeels are unavailable. Bass are unlikely
to stay in one position, and you ought to be prepared to follow a
feeding shoal along the beach.

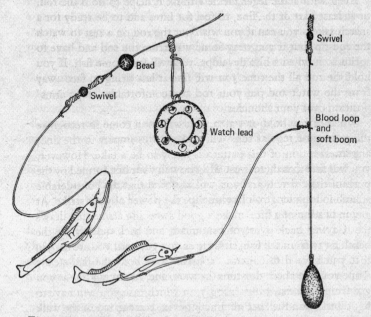

Fig. 234 Bass end-rigs using sandeel bait.

A sign of feeding bass is leaping whitebait, and bass may actually jump out of water as they pursue such shoals of small fish. With a simple leger rig (Fig. 234) you can keep abreast of your quarry, casting ahead of them as you go. This demands a light tackle-and-bait bag with a shoulder strap, and it is also a good idea to fix a cord shoulder sling to your landing net or gaff.

Summer beach fishing in the south and south-west also offers turbot, plaice and other flatfish (use a two- or three-hook paternoster and cast well out) while the east coast offers thornbacks and even tope, for which fish baits are best.

As a final note on long casting: a pair of waders will add many yards to your cast – you can follow out a falling wave, cast, and retreat before another one sweeps in. Waders will also be useful when it comes to landing a fish.

§304 Night fishing

It is wise to settle for static fishing at night, whether you are after winter cod or bass. You will need a good strong lamp – pressure lamps are best, and there is now a very good gas lamp, fed by cartridges, which keeps going for a long time. You can also keep your hands warm with a flame lamp, unlike an electric one.

For safety's sake don't arrive in the dark to fish a beach which you do not know. Try to pick a beach with a good slope so that there is absolutely no chance of the water sneaking round behind you in the dark to cut you off. Keep an eye on the encroaching tide and move back well before it threatens to swamp your gear.

For bite detection, you will normally be able to see your rod against the sky, but you can paint the last six inches or so with luminous paint if you like. A clip-on bell will also give an indication of a shaking tip.

Having made a lot of cautionary noises, I can tell you that fishing in the dark is exciting and that you are much more likely to catch good fish – cod or bass – than during the day. Both species lose their day-time caution and move much closer in during the dark.

Dusk, and the first glimmers of dawn are good taking times, and it is wise to arrange to fish a tide which reaches its highest point at dawn. Practise your casting well before you attempt night fishing, where you won't see the lead enter the water.

§305 Spinning

In all the locations mentioned in this chapter on shore fishing, it is worthwhile spinning. The rewards might be winter cod (for which you need a heavy lure that can be cast a good distance) or bass and pollack in summer. Spinning in the sea is much the same as spinning in freshwater, i.e. you should spin in gulleys and near fish-harbouring rocks, making your lure behave as erratically and attractively as possible.

Spoons and flutterers such as the Toby are good bass and pollack lures, and you can try heavier pirks in deep water, working them with a jigging action as you retrieve (Fig. 235). For mackerel, small flutterers and spoons are also very good, but if you want quantity, rather than sport, a set of feathers with a heavy, terminal weight can be used. If a mackerel shoal is spotted, you can then move along the shore keeping pace with it while you cast and draw the feathers through them. Plugs are very good, especially if used in rocky gullies for pollack and bass. Spinning at night is rarely satisfactory.

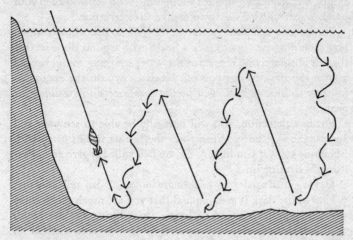

Fig. 235 Jigs or pirks may be used from deep-water shores – the rod is raised smartly and then dropped to make them work. Retrieve line during lifts.

Shore fishing
Quick cross-reference guide

Although the various forms of shore fishing have a growing
following, to many thousands of anglers 'sea fishing' means 'boat
fishing'. Looking through the angling press it isn't hard to find
combinations of skipper and boat that; time and time again, hit
the headlines with superb catches; such skippers have a reputation
to maintain and are likely to work hard for their anglers. Although
they can rarely guarantee fantastic catches on every trip, they
will do their level best to find a good mark and advise on the best
ways to tackle it.

It is easy to charter a boat, although it must be said that the
most renowned of boats are likely to be booked solid, at least
through the summer. You either find a party large enough to chip
in for a whole outing, or, as an individual, you put yourself forward as wishing to make up a boatload. Either way, you contact a
skipper, find a date on which he is free to book you in, and send
off a securing deposit. Having said that, I had better warn you
that the skipper's word is law if he cancels the trip through bad
weather – you'll get your money back, though.

A deep-sea trip on a large charter boat is not, of course, the
only form of boat fishing. You might hire a dinghy for inshore
fishing, and we'll turn our attention to this first of all.

No angler should set out in a small boat without a buoyancy
jacket, and this particularly applies to children. Even if the sea is
calm there is the off-chance that you might get run down by a
bigger boat – don't trust to luck.

A dinghy opens up many shore areas which are inaccessible to
the shorebound angler – e.g. the outer edges of sea-swept rocks.
All of the methods mentioned in the preceding chapter – float
fishing, legering, spinning – can be used where appropriate. The
dinghy angler can also explore deeper water, well out, where the

main techniques for deep-sea fishing, discussed later in this chapter, are valuable.

But it is perhaps in the field of trolling that dinghy anglers have a great advantage. With a trailed, baited line, or a spinner, it is possible to thoroughly work over large areas, exploring long reefs, weedbeds and sandbars, either by rowing or under low power from an outboard.

With an outboard it is not advisable to fish a moving bait on your own – you cannot hope to concentrate on minding the engine, keeping your course and playing a fish at the same time. Even with rowing, it is hard to ship the oars and spring to your rod when you get a take – for safety's sake the oars and the rod ought to be secured to the boat with lanyards. With two anglers, one can mind the rods, while the other rows or tends the engine and steers.

Trolled, spinning baits and lures (Fig. 236) usually need to be weighted to keep them at fishing level, and the best arrangement is a Wye lead, with swivels, as used in conventional spinning arrangements. However, it is advisable to have quite a good length between weight and lure – about ten feet. Generally this means using a longish rod – again ten feet or more – and with two such rods you can arrange them in the stern so that the lures are swimming well away from one another (Fig. 237). As in conventional spinning, the variation of the lure's movement makes it more attractive to fish, and actions can be induced by frequently changing the boat's speed (to make your lure swim slow and deep, or high and fast) and by swerving the boat – but not too abruptly, or you will foul either the lures or the propeller if you are under engine power. A moderate burst of speed

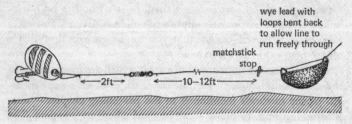

Fig. 236 Basic trolling rig.

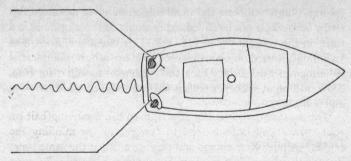

Fig. 237 Space rods in the stern when trolling so that lures swim well away from each other.

can be used now and then, slowing to a crawl – high speeds, if they are maintained, will only draw the lures to the surface, and anyway they will probably be travelling too fast for the fish to take. You will find that you have to let off anything between twenty-five to fifty yards of line to keep your lure at an acceptable depth.

As well as conventional spinners, baits and lures – rubber eels,

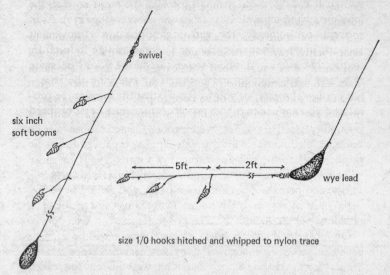

Fig. 238 Two arrangements for 'whiffing' or trolling with baited lines.

spoons, plugs, wobblers and small fish on spinning mounts – fish strips or sandeels can be fished either singly or three or more at a time on the rigs shown in Fig. 238. This technique, known as 'whiffing', is used on a much larger scale by inshore, commercial fishermen to work slowly back and forth over sandbars for bass. Slow trolling over deeper reefs is also a good method for coalfish and pollack.

§306 Deep-sea fishing

Any beginner who wants to try sea fishing in a deep-sea boat without taking the plunge and equipping himself with gear, could scarcely do better than taking one of the short angling trips offered at most resorts through the summer; gear will be provided and, although you are unlikely to make a headline-hitting catch, you'll at least get a taste of this exciting form of fishing.

For those already converted, it is clear that more than one set of gear – a medium and a light boat rod, perhaps even a heavy one too – expands your enjoyment. Instead of deadening the actions of a small, sporting fish such as the black bream with a rod that is far too heavy, you can change to light gear if such species are about (Checklists §46).

A few points are worth consideration before you step into your boat. Firstly, it will be twice as windy, twice as cold, and the sea will be twice as rough when you leave the shelter of the land. Take anti-seasickness pills if you feel you will need them. Even on a calm, warm day you often need to pull on an extra sweater on the way out – so take plenty of warm gear and, if rain is a possibility, good heavy-duty waterproofs. Cleated rubber soles on boots or Wellingtons will stop you slipping on a wet deck – no skipper will thank you for using any form of nails or metal 'Blakeys' on your footwear, since this will scratch his decking. Lastly, and perhaps most important of all, you should have prepared most of your traces at home. Tying hooks and the like in a pitching boat is difficult.

On most good charter boats, this equipment will be carried: adequate safety aids such as buoyancy jackets, life-savers or life-raft for the entire complement of anglers and crew (governed by Board of Trade regulations), plus first-aid equipment and distress flares; landing nets and gaffs; fish boxes for keeping your catch; and a stout board and sharp knife for cutting up bait (plus a bucket for calls of nature). There may be a galley for cooking up coffee.

The skipper will tell you what sort of mark he is going to, and what sort of gear and baits will pay off, although you can of course apply your own judgement on those scores. The skipper's choice of mark will usually be one that offers the best sport, taking the season, weather conditions and state of the tide into account, but if you wish, you may, providing the majority of anglers on the boat agree with you, ask to be taken to some other spot. Always arrange things by a consensus of opinions, tempered by the skipper's advice, once a trip has started. He might himself advise a move to some other mark if his first choice offers poor sport.

Normally you would bring your own bait, unless you have arranged beforehand with the skipper to supply you with some. In summer, however, most trips will begin with a spell of fishing for mackerel to be used for fresh bait, and every sea angler's tackle ought to include a mackerel feather trace. This is simply a six-foot length of line, weighted at one end and with a swivel at the other, which has three to six feathered hooks, spaced on short lengths of line along it. The boat may be stopped to drift only a short distance offshore while enough mackerel for the trip are caught; rods are set up, the feather traces are tied on, and over the side they go. The art of using the traces is simple. From the moment they go in the water, you begin to 'jig' them, raising the tip of the rod with a smart lift and then dropping it to let the feathers sink (Fig. 239). You might strike mackerel at any depth, and with sufficiently sensitive gear you will feel them hitting the feathers and making the line 'lighter' because they are holding up the weight. Begin jigging near the surface, and if nothing happens, start to let off line, short lengths at a time, until you hit bottom. Ideally, you should 'measure' the length of line you let out by using the rod as a rough fathom guide (Fig. 240). Keeping the weight just under the surface, take the stop off your reel and allow sufficient line out, under gentle control, to bring the tip of the rod up to about eleven o'clock. Stop the reel, lower the rod-tip to the water's surface, and you will have lowered roughly a fathom. The usefulness of this is that once you have lowered to contact with a shoal of mackerel you can easily find them again and you

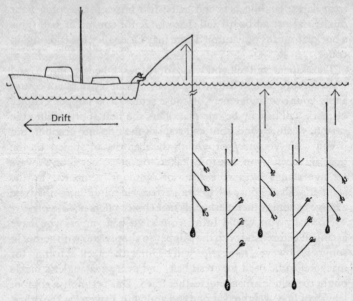

Fig. 239 (§306) Rod is alternately raised and lowered to work mackerel feathers. They can be used from a stationary or a drifting boat.

can shout to your companions on the boat 'six down' or whatever the depth is, and they can begin to catch without having to search the water themselves.

You will find it quite easy to judge that you are keeping the weight at a steady level in the water while you are bringing the rod to the 'up' position and letting out line under control.

If you are lucky, the mackerel will come pouring in. As you pull a trace-full to the surface, keep them well away from the outside of the boat hull so that they do not kick against it and fly off the hooks. Lift them gently inboard, unhook them, and give them a tap on the head before consigning them to the bait box.

Whatever fishing style you are going to use when you reach your mark proper, you should be considerate about the other anglers in the boat. First of all, you should all arrange yourselves with equal space between you. For example, six people would sit with one at each side of the stern, two amidships, and one each

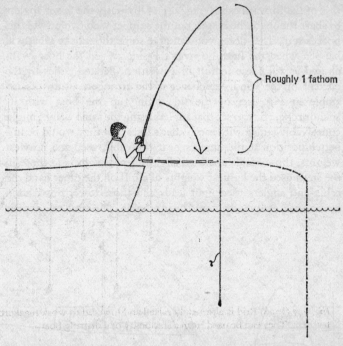

Roughly 1 fathom

Fig. 240 Most boat rods are around a fathom's length – as a rough guide to the depth of water in fathoms, hold the lead steady and let line slip from the reel while you raise the rod to an upright position. Stop the reel here and lower the rod (one fathom's depth) and repeat.

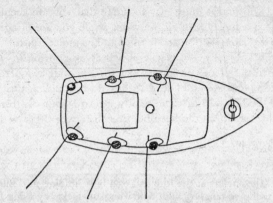

Fig. 241 Share space in a boat so that you are out of each others' way

side of the forward cabin (Fig. 241). Obviously the fewer anglers to share the space the better, but the skipper who overcrowds his boat is rare. That done, you can give some thought to what will happen when the lines go over the side. When the boat is anchored it will come to rest in a position dictated either by the current or the wind, whichever is the stronger. Using the example in Fig. 242 of the tide lining up the boat with its anchor rope, you can see that anglers using the same weight might conceivably tangle with each other's lines, but they would be in a better position if the anglers near the cabin used the heaviest weights, those amidships used slightly less weight, and those in the stern used the lightest weights of all. If on the other hand the cabin-end anglers used light leads and those lower down used heavy ones, everybody would be in trouble. The same rule applies

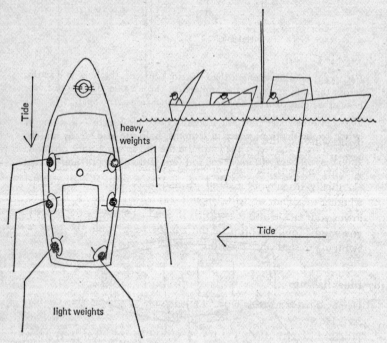

Fig. 242 The anglers at the fore end of a boat heading into the tidal current will save tangling with fellow anglers' tackle by using heavy weights.

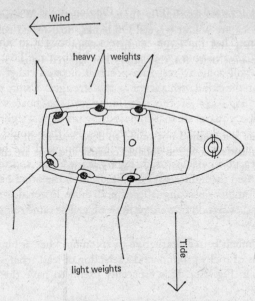

Fig. 243 If wind is stronger than the tidal current, the boat will settle across the tide and here the anglers on the up-tide side should use heavier weights than the anglers on the other side of the boat.

if the wind lies the boat across the current (Fig. 243), in which case it is best for the anglers on the uptide side to use heavy weights and the downtide anglers to use light weights. When you eventually reach your fishing ground, the skipper will decide whether to anchor or drift. He will also tell you when it is safe to lower your tackle into the water – if you lower away prematurely you might foul the prop or the anchor rope while the boat is swinging to settle into position.

§307 Float fishing

Using a float is scarcely worthwhile in depths greater than twenty feet. However, float fishing is an excellent method for reefs that jut close to the surface and for shallower banks. On the former, using a rig incorporating a sliding float, you can trot baits a fair distance with the current. In summer you might expect to catch pollack, coalfish, bream and bass in this fashion, keeping the baited hook or hooks slightly above obstructions. Whiting, cod and haddock are winter targets. On banks, float-fished baits will take dogfish and the larger flatfish, turbot and brill (sandeels being the best baits for the latter) but legered baits are more useful for rays.

§308 Spinning

Again, this is a method not suited to deep water, but it will pay off on shallow reefs where pollack, coalfish and bass are the main targets. Tackle is the same as you would use for shore fishing (§305).

§309 Trolling

This is a much better alternative to spinning when fishing over large areas of rocky ground, and a selection of lead arrangements is shown in Fig. 244. It is especially useful to have the lure –

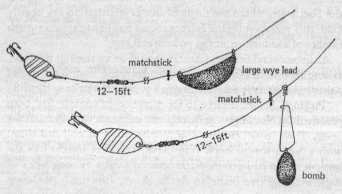

Fig. 244 (§309) Arrangements for deep trolling – there should be at least one swivel between spinner and weight.

artificial sandeels, spinners or small fish on spinning mounts – about fifteen feet from the lead, and bearing in mind that with a fixed lead you will only be able to reel back until the lead reaches the rod-tip, the arrangement using a matchstick which breaks on the strike is best. By trailing under low power, with the lures swimming fifty yards or more behind the boat, great areas can be worked over thoroughly. However, this method is unsuitable for more than, say, four rods, spaced at the stern, and a great deal of caution is needed to avoid lines tangling when the boat turns.

§310 Feathering, pirking

A set of mackerel-fishing feathers, tipped with pieces of mackerel, makes an excellent rig for many reef species, taking bream, pollack, coalfish, whiting and cod (you can if you wish obtain a cod feather trace, on which the feathered hooks are somewhat larger than those used for mackerel).

This is also an extremely good method for fishing on the drift over rough ground. Fish might be contacted at any level, but normally pollack, coalfish and cod will be near the bottom, while bream and whiting might be at mid-water or above. Paul Cartwright, an angler who is frequently among the winners in the Southern Television Sea Angling Championships, ties his own traces, using large salmon flies in place of feathered hooks: fished on the drift over rough ground in northern venues such as the Shetlands, where the finals of this championship are usually held, this variation on the feather theme has brought him superb catches of haddock, whiting, pollack and ling.

As in mackerel fishing, feathers should be worked all the time, raising the rod to lift them, and then dropping it so that they fall – they must actually seem like a small group of prawns to the fish.

'Pirking', before it came to the attention of anglers, had been practised by Norwegian and Icelandic commercial fishermen for years. Their 'pirk' consisted of a hefty lump of polished metal with a large, spread hook (Fig. 245). This was lowered to the bottom in the cod grounds and worked with a vicious series of tugs, the objective being to foulhook any fish that came close enough to investigate. This is far from the effect that the angler wants, and the angling lures also shown in Fig. 245 are taken by fish much as spinners would be. Self-weighted, the pirk needs no extra lead on the line – several different weights are manufactured so that the angler can be equipped for strong or slight currents. They can be used over almost any ground. Lower the pirk to the bottom and then wind it back a few turns if there is any danger of it snagging. Then begin to work it, drawing it swiftly upwards

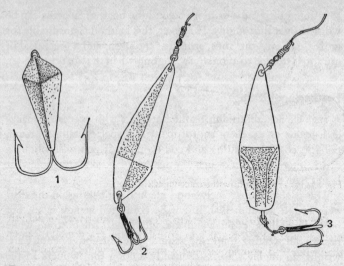

Fig. 245 (§310) 1 – the rip-hook, forerunner of the angling pirks (2, 3).

and then allowing it to drop, fluttering, before drawing up again. The upward action should be similar to a strike and, as you might expect, a fish hooked in this fashion does not need an extra strike to be sure the hook will hold.

§311 Legered baits

Since there are only two basic rigs for legering – the straight-through leger and the paternoster – it is best to discuss them only briefly and then to look at ways to adapt them for various species.

For either style, the amount of lead you use should be the lightest you can possibly get away with, since this helps bite detection. In a few places you may need as much as a pound of lead to keep your bait down, but even so, you will generally find a couple of ounces sufficient when slack water arrives. Therefore, it is a good idea to carry a range of leads, and to make sure that you incorporate some means of changing leads quickly in the tackle-rig. The other thing worth remembering is that you need a swivel between your hooks and the main line for all rigs, to accommodate the twisting of a fish as you draw it upwards.

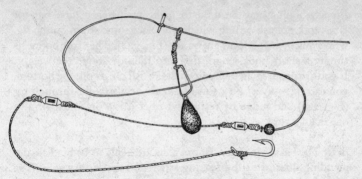

Fig. 246 (§311) Long flowing-trace leger rig.

The straight-through leger rig (Fig. 246) can have any length of trace you desire, but if you do fish with a trace much longer than your rod you should use a matchstick weight-stop which breaks on the strike. Unless held clear of the bottom, this rig is likely to snag in rough ground and the long-trace paternoster shown in Fig. 247 is a better choice. The paternoster, kept above the bottom, is also good for drifting. For small fish such as bream

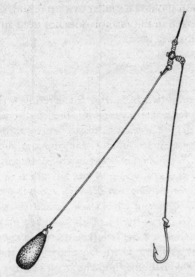

Fig. 247 Simple paternoster leger rig.

French booms may be used to make up paternosters, but for large cod, pollack or ling which will place some strain on the rig, wire arms or soft booms are better (Fig. 248). The 'soft boom' is simply a short hook-length tied into the line above the weight. If you are unsure whether you will take fish on, or off, the bottom, you can tie a 'flyer' on a soft boom above a straight-through rig (Fig. 249) and judge by results whether it is worth changing to one main style.

(a) *Bass:* The bass (§205) of offshore reefs are likely to be big fish, demanding lines of 15 lb breaking strain and up. Hooks should be related to the size of the bait, i.e. worms, size 1–4/0; sandeels and fish strips, around 4/0. The latter baits can be fished on the trolling rig described above, or on a straight-through rig with a long, flowing trace (suitable for drifting if held clear of the bottom).

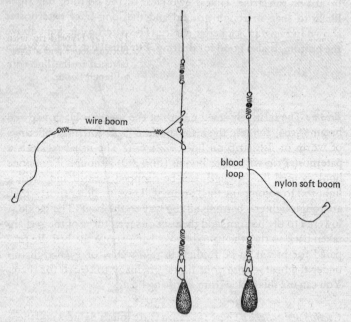

Fig. 248 Alternative paternoster rigs.

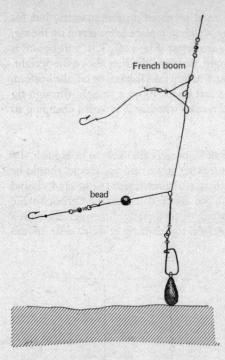

French boom

bead

Fig. 249 Hybrid rig with bottom leger and a 'flyer' fastened to the line with a French boom.

(b) *Bream:* The relatively small mouth of the bream – black and red bream (§206, 209) are the main species – calls for small offerings of worm or fish strip on hook-sizes 6–1. The usual tackle is a paternoster rig with three booms (Fig. 250) although if only one hook is used line strength can be dropped to 8 lb and, with a light rod to accompany this, bream will give thrilling sport – they are tough fighters, battling all the way to the boat. The tackle is lowered to the bottom, and then six or seven turns of the reel are taken back so that the baited hooks hang above the bed. Be prepared for bream to be feeding in mid-water, or even right up under the boat – raise your tackle gradually to search for them. You can use this tackle from a drifting boat.

(c) *Coalfish and pollack:* These (§212, 243) are tough fighters and there is always the chance of a really big fish. Lines of less than 18 lb breaking strain are not recommended. As for bass, hook size

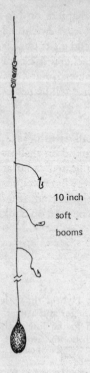

10 inch

soft

booms

Fig. 250 Three-hook rig
for bream.

should relate to the baits used, which can be worms or, for pre-ference, sandeels and fish strips. The long, flowing trace is the best tackle, and it can be used for trolling or drifting besides legering on the bottom, so that the bait streams towards the flank of a reef or wreck.

(d) *Cod:* Lines between 20 and 25 lb breaking strain are adequate for the average run of cod (§213). The straight-through leger with a 4–5 ft trace is suitable, also a paternoster with 18 in soft booms (two booms is the most I would recommend). The latter, with a rotten bottom, is suitable for fishing over rough ground, and can also be trailed from a drifting boat. As for hooks (again, size is related to bait size) the cod has a huge mouth and can take bunched worms, fish strips, squid or crab on size 8/o hooks.

(e) *Ling:* A large predator, the ling (§232) is rather conger-like in behaviour (for conger methods see following chapters on big-game fishing) living in crevices in reefs and wrecks. Anchored baits with strong, straight-through, leger tackle and a 3 ft trace is best. Large fish baits, such as the whole of a mackerel flank, or whole, small squid, should be offered on hook sizes 8/0 and up. Where big fish are known to be present a 30 lb line will be necessary.

(f)   *Plaice and dabs:* With both of these relatively small flatfish (§214, 242), light tackle can be used. Both are usually found on shallow sand, gravel and mud banks, which are uncomplicated as far as snagging goes, and it is therefore possible to use very light weights which you can allow the current to trot along the bottom (Fig. 251). Pieces of worm, crab or small fish strips can be used on hook sizes 6–1 for plaice and 10–6 for dabs.

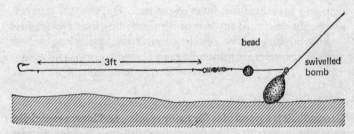

bead

3ft

swivelled bomb

Fig. 251 Simple light-leger rig for plaice, dabs etc.

(g)   *Rays:* lines of 15 lb breaking strain are adequate for thornbacks and most other rays (§249–55), although where big blonde rays are present a 20 lb line might be needed. The rig is a relatively simple, straight-through leger with a 3 ft trace, and hook sizes 1–6/0 are baited with worms, crab, or fish-strip.

(h)   *Turbot:* The turbot (§274) and the smaller brill (§211) usually lie at the edge of mud and shingle banks, rising from the bottom, where they are camouflaged, to ambush unwary sandeels and small fish. A straight-through leger with a long, flowing trace can be placed so that the bait – sandeel or a fish strip – waves attractively in the current, across gullies and bank edges. With a light lead you can let the current trot your tackle over a large area, and drifting, with the same rig dragging the bottom, is also effective. A 15 lb line is usually adequate, although if you fish at the fringes of wrecks, which have produced some giant turbot in recent years, a 20 lb line will be safer.

(i) *Whiting, haddock:* Both these smallish fish (§227, 283) are present on a variety of grounds and might be contacted at almost any depth. A paternoster with three short booms is the usual tackle, and this is suitable either for legering or drifting with the weight clear of the bottom. Both species will take disproportionately large baits, but fish strip, squid or worm on size 1 or 2/o hooks is ideal.

(j) *Other species:* The short résumé above does, I know, miss out many species, but by using the rigs mentioned you'll take more than you bargained for, most of the time. Dogfish, for instance, are caught on almost any sort of rig – including mackerel feathers – while pouting will be a pest or a salvation, depending on how well other species are responding.

§312 Groundbaiting at sea

Groundbait is a good idea for many species, and bream especially. Because the currents encountered in sea fishing will quickly sweep away any objects simply thrown into the water, the usual method of groundbaiting is to fill a loose-weave sack or net bag with mashed-up fish heads, guts, bones and old mackerel into which can be stirred a liberal quantity of pilchard, or cod-liver, oil. This is tied to the anchor rope before it is lowered, and when in position the oils and small pieces of fish will trickle out to attract and hold a shoal of fish.

Boat fishing
Quick cross-reference guide

Main lines, §11a, 11b, 11c.
Traces etc. §11g, 11h, 11i.

Hooks, §12.
Weights, §16.
Booms, §17.
Knots, §19b.
Rods, equipment checklist, §46.
Preparations, §47.
Sea environments, §202, 203.
Baits, §284–296.
Species, §204–283 (see also big game species, §313–327).

The small number of species counted in this category and the fact that most of them belong to two main 'groups' in the biological sense – the sharks and the skates – enables me to be more specific when describing fishing methods than for the huge range of small-to-medium fishes covered in the preceding chapters. The methods follow these brief introductory descriptions.

§313 Broad-billed swordfish
Xiphias gladius

This is mentioned mainly because it is from time to time present in British waters. Despite the fact that there are no records of swordfish being taken on rod and line in Britain, it does seem on the cards that someone, somewhere, will one day find himself up against this formidable adversary. Elsewhere in the world the species is a popular, big-game fish.

§314 **Conger eel**
Conger conger

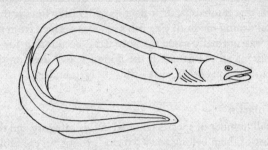

Rare in the central, southern North Sea, the conger is otherwise widely distributed in the warmer months. Large specimens favour reefs and wrecks, where fish baits and strong tackle are used to take them, often in great numbers at a time. Fish up to 25 kg (55.1 lb) are often taken on offshore marks while shore fish tend to run smaller. Some very large fish have been found dead after cold weather – one of 72 kg (158.7 lb) was recorded in 1904. At the time of writing, the record (rod-caught) weight for this species is 46.5 kg (102.5 lb).

§315 **Halibut**
Hippoglossus hippoglossus

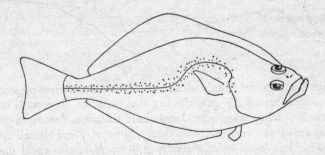

Until fairly recently, this giant among flatfish (commercial boats have taken specimens of up to 300 kg – 661 lb) was never tackled on rod and line, but now many anglers travel to Scottish and

Northern Irish waters to fish for them. Fish of 50 kg (110 lb) and more have been taken. An arctic, deep-water fish, the halibut feeds on flatfish, haddock and lobsters. In the current-swept rocky grounds that it inhabits, drift-fishing with heavy lines is the most practical fishing method. The fish's name is derived from the fact that it was normally eaten on holy days (accounting for 'hali', and 'butt' is an old name for the flounder, still used on the east coasts and in some other parts – thus 'holy flounder').

§316 White marlin
Tetrapturus albidus

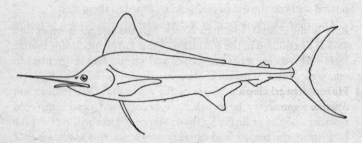

A species which, like the swordfish, has yet to appear in British angling records despite many sightings, mostly in the Channel and south-western waters. A legendary big-game fish.

§317 Blue shark
Prionace glauca

It is not often realized that sharks (counting all species) are very widespread and can be fished all around Britain's coast in the summer. Wherever regular concentrations of mackerel are to be found, some shark are likely to be present. Latterly a few more angling centres have begun to fish for shark in Wales, Ireland and off the south coast of England – before, the main recognized, shark centre was in Looe, Cornwall, where the Shark Angling Club of Great Britain is still based. Playing a very big shark can be an exciting business, but it is also likely to be tiring. Strong tackle is a necessity, and a butt pad and harness ought to be used. The well-equipped shark boats of the West country also have a 'game chair' able to swivel in any direction, into which an angler playing a good fish can be strapped. Despite their reputation for ferocity, it is utterly senseless to kill every shark taken. Small fish may be boated without the use of gaffs and returned to the water.

The blue shark is one of the smaller sharks, and a summer visitor to western coasts in particular. They can grow to about 90 kg (198.4 lb).

§318 Hammerhead shark
Sphyrna zygaena

Unmistakable because of the wide, flat head with eyes at the outer extremities, this shark is fairly uncommon in Britain. It grows to about 400 kg (881.8 lb).

§319 Mako shark
Isurus oxyrhincus

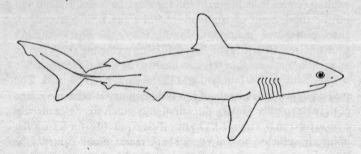

This is a large, strong shark which provides a spectacular fight, sometimes leaping entirely clear of the water. I haven't been able to verify accounts that hooked makos have leaped into a boat to attack the angler playing them! Makos have sometimes been confused with porbeagles (see below). The porbeagle's height, belly to back, in the region of the pectoral fin is about a sixth of the total length, while in the mako the height is about a ninth. Makos grow to around 220 kg (485 lb).

§320 Porbeagle shark
Lamna nasus

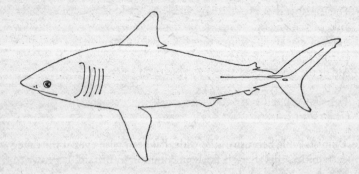

A stouter shark than the mako, the porbeagle is common all around Britain during summer. It grows to around 195 kg (429.9 lb).

§321 **Six-gilled shark**
Hexanchus griseus

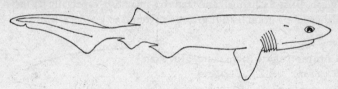

This is a rare visitor sometimes contacted in south-western waters and off Ireland. It has six gill slits immediately in front of the pectoral fin, and a sickle-like tail fin without a lower lobe (but shorter than the thresher's tail fin). It grows to about 70 kg (154.3 lb).

§322 **Thresher shark**
Alopias vulpinus

The thresher is easily distinguishable by the long, tapering, upper lobe of the tail fin, which is used to thrash the water around a shoal of mackerel, compacting them before making a strike. It is usually found off western coasts but has been caught at the eastern end of the Channel. It grows to about 120 kg (264.5 lb).

§323 **Tope** (sweet william)
Galeorhinus galeus

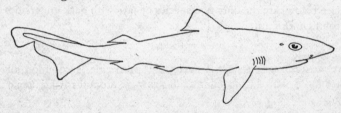

Widely distributed around Britain, this small shark prefers open, and somewhat shallow, ground over mud or shingle (e.g. The Wash, Bristol Channel) and feeds on small fish, especially flatfish – dabs make a good bait. It grows to around 30 kg (66.1 lb).

§324 **Common skate** (blue skate, grey skate)
Raja batis

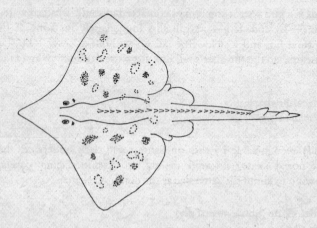

Our skates are more commonly found in deeper water than their relatives, the smaller rays, although their habits are similar. Because of the great weights they attain, very strong tackle must be used, and a harness and butt pad is useful. The common skate is fairly widespread in Irish and Scottish waters and it may, in fact, be quite generally distributed elsewhere, although it is rarely fished for outside recognized, skate-fishing centres (e.g. Kinsale, Ullapool). They eat fish and crustaceans, growing to well over 150 kg (330 lb) although the present record (rod-caught) is somewhat smaller. The common skate and the long-nosed skate (see below) are the only two species of rays with dark undersides found in Britain.

§325 **Long-nosed skate**
Raja oxyrhinchus

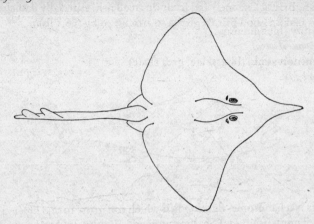

Easily recognizable by the long snout and dark underside, the long-nosed skate is found mainly on Atlantic-facing coasts, growing to about the same size as the common skate.

§326 **White skate** (bottle-nosed ray)
Raja alba

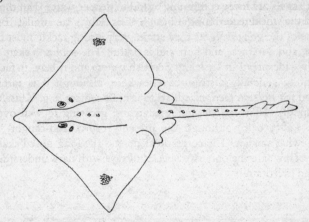

Distinguished from the long-nosed skate by the white underside, the white skate is found in the western part of the Channel and in

Irish waters. It grows to around 200 kg (440 lb) although, like the other skates, the rod-caught record is much smaller.

§327 **Tunny** (blue-fin tuna)
Thunnus thunnus

This is a handsome, fighting fish which can grow to 700 kg (1543 lb). Tunny fishing off Scarborough and Whitby used to be much more actively pursued before the last war, and among the reasons for its decline are the dwindling shoals of herring on which it preys and the sheer cost of chartering an angling boat to follow the herring shoals until tunny show. There are undoubtedly still many tunny to be caught off Britain, particularly over the Dogger Bank. The British record rod-caught tunny, a fish of nearly 386 kg (851 lb) which was taken off Whitby in 1933, at one time also held the world record for the species.

Setting out to catch large fish demands careful selection of appropriately strong tackle as well as some 'extras' to assist you in what might be a long, exhausting struggle. The most useful extra is a butt pad (variously known as tuna belts, tarpon belts, groin protectors and butt rests). It consists of a stout leather belt which is buckled about the waist, with a padded 'sporran' that has a metal socket to hold the butt of the rod (Fig. 252). A rod harness, a belt

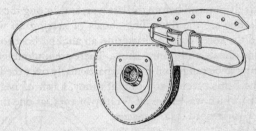

Fig. 252 The butt pad (groin protector).

arrangement which passes around the angler's back and fastens onto lugs on the reel (taking the strain off the arms and transmitting it to the shoulders) is not widely used in Britain. A person with average strength can certainly beat such fish as tope, conger and blue shark without one, but where larger shark and some of the giant skates and the halibut are concerned, the harness would be very useful.

§328 Hooks, traces

The strongest hooks for big fish are forged steel; drawn wire hooks have a tendency to straighten under stress. Since the hooks are large (conger, 6/0–10/0; skate and halibut, 6/0–12/0; tope, 6/0–10/0; tunny, sharks, etc. 10/0 and up) they will have to be kept extremely sharp, as big blunt hooks require such a powerful strike as to make them useless.

With formidable teeth and strong jaws to contend with, big-game hooks should be attached to a length of stranded wire (three feet giving a good safety margin) which is at least as strong as the main line. It is essential that the wire trace incorporates a large, stout swivel even if you use the type of hook that has a swivel eye (Fig. 253). With sharks in particular a further length of wire

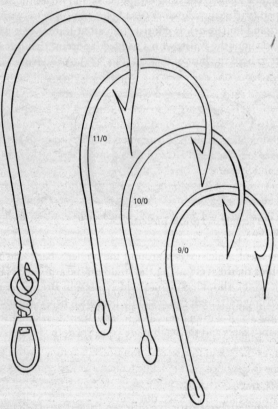

Fig. 253 (§328) Heavy forged hooks for large fish – the so-called 'conger' hook on the left has a swivelled eye.

or strong line (stronger than the main line, and six to ten feet long) connects the wire trace to the main line – this is so that the fraying effect of the shark's rough skin is avoided (generally called a 'rubbing trace'). Again, it is wise to incorporate a further swivel at the angler's end of this trace.

It is recommended that the knots and whippings used in wire to join hooks, swivels and so on are finished with solder.

§329 Rod and landing gear

Most angling boats chartering for big-game fishing will already be equipped with the appropriate gaffs, fighting seat and so on, and some will even provide full kits of tackle for hire (obviously you should check this beforehand if you do not intend taking your own gear). If you attempt big-game fishing with your own boat, it is advisable firstly that you take a friend – you won't be able to manage the boat at the same time as playing and gaffing a big fish – and secondly that you take two really stout gaffs of the lash-on type (gaff heads with a screw-attachment for fastening the pole can easily become wrenched undone). Your rod should be in the 50-lb-line class and up. Recommended line-strengths for various species are discussed later in the chapter (see §46, 47, 48 Check-lists and preparations).

In some areas, it is quite possible to fish for blue shark, tope, and even porbeagles, mako and thresher shark from the shore. If you do so, you will need a stout beachcaster in place of the strong, boat rod.

§330 Conger fishing

The tackle rig for conger (§314) must be simple and, for safety's sake, it should not incorporate such items as three-way swivels, or wire booms, both of which will flex and break under extreme pulls. Pulling, after all, is what this game becomes, for with the conger there is no powerful, long distance run. Instead, as soon as the fish is hooked it must be hauled away from its lair and from other snags, with a do-or-die effort. If it gets any sort of hold with its strong tail, you'll have the devil's own job to shift it. The top rig in Fig. 254 has a 'rotten bottom' connecting the lead, and it should be used in extremely snaggy areas. Over less rough but

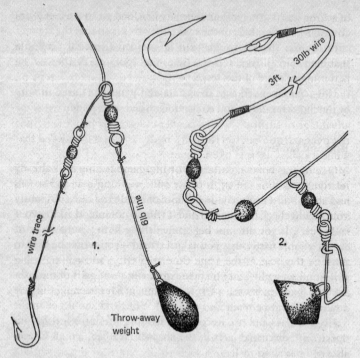

Fig. 254 (§330) Rigs for conger – the more usual rig (2) can be replaced with a rotten-bottom paternoster rig (1).

weedy ground the lower rig can be used, relying on the strength of the tackle to pull clear of weed snags. At least one barrel swivel must be used.

The bait most widely used for conger is mackerel, either whole or part of the fish. A whole fish is traditionally fixed upside-down on the hook (tail pointing up the line) so that the conger may take it head first.

If no mackerel are available, other fish (herring, spratts, small pouting or flatfish) will substitute.

As for line strength, there is absolutely no sense in fishing light in the hope of only small congers. You must always be prepared for a really big one – and, of course, even the smaller ones will place a considerable strain on the line if they have to be hauled out of a stronghold. This means that the main line must be somewhere around the 70 lb mark.

For such a formidable fish, the take of the conger is so gentle that many are missed. There is first of all a slight vibration as the bait is inspected, followed by a gentle – and often short – draw on the line. This is the time to strike, and the strike and the beginning of the haul should be one continuous movement to give you the advantage of surprise. With a conger clear of the bed, the fight is not over and you can feel the fish's body lashing this way and that while it shakes its head like a terrier.

One of the worst experiences I had when playing a conger – a relatively small one of 25 lb taken off Looe – came when the fish had almost surfaced. The main hook pulled straight and lost its hold, but as the fish turned to dive a 'flier' – a small, baited hook I had fastened into the line well above the weight, in the hope of bream if sport with congers was slow – caught the eel's tough skin three or four inches from the tip of the tail. The dive was then almost unstoppable, and it was many tiring minutes before I got the fish back up to the gaff. Since then I have never used any other hooks on a conger line.

Even when your conger is safely aboard, it deserves respect – the strong jaws can crush a gumboot heel. If there is no fish-hold aboard, it is wise to have a sack to put your eel in, which will keep it quiet while you decide what to do with it – if the hook cannot be seen to unhook it with long-handled pliers, cut the trace rather than risking your hand close to the mouth.

The really big year for conger fishing was 1970, when some huge hauls were taken, including fish of 70 lb (several), 80 lb and 93 lb (the record was broken twice) by boats working out of the Devon port of Brixham – *Our Unity* and *Girl Allison*. The current record conger was taken on a Mevagissey boat.

§331 Halibut fishing

Although more and more halibut (§315) are being taken by anglers (the main fisheries being the north of Scotland, Shetlands, Faroes, the northern North Sea and Northern Ireland) the species does not yet have a big enough following to establish a set pattern of behaviour, and no set 'halibut tackle' has been developed. However Mike Pritchard, a much-travelled angling photographer, tells me that he's seen anglers in the northern islands of Japan troll for smallish halibut with a large baited spoon. Bearing in mind that normally there is rough ground in the sort of areas where the fish are found, some sort of trolling, or perhaps even pirking, might pay off. Most of the halibut so far have been caught on fish baits, legered at great depth or fished on the drift with modified conger tackle – a sliding lead, wire trace and fish-baited hook. On a visit to the Shetlands some time back, I tried the rig in Fig. 255 since it seems that there is no need for a

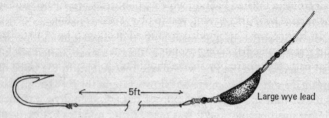

Fig. 255 (§331) Drift-rig for halibut.

sliding lead when fishing on the drift. However, I was fishing out of the halibut season and caught only ling.

One thing is certain: line to hold such monster weights as those that the halibut reaches must be very strong. Something in the order of 60 lb breaking strain seems about the lightest you should go.

§332 Shark fishing

The strength of line in shark fishing can be related to the size of species (§317–322) expected, which means that for the average runs of blue shark in the south-west lines of 50 lb are adequate, while at the other end of the scale, lines of 120 lb breaking strain and up will be needed for big makos. Generally one can rely on skippers of charter boats that go after shark regularly to have the proper tackle on board.

The sharks, although they have good eyesight, detect their prey in the first instance by an extremely acute sense of smell – by far the biggest part of their brains is taken up with smell-detecting equipment. A shark trip begins by steaming out to the grounds and then switching off the engine to drift. A string bag full of minced fishheads, guts and pilchard oil is slung overboard on a rope so that it begins to lay a long scent trail up which, one hopes, shark will begin to swim.

The anglers' lines are made up, baited, and set overboard to wait for the shark. Usually, they will be set at varied depths from six feet to fifteen feet or so, in order to spread the chances of contacting a fish. Shark floats of the large, cork, 'bung' type are now largely ignored (being pegged to the line they sap the force of a strike and also impede playing a fish) and it is usual to suspend the bait from an inflated balloon which will burst when rushed under the surface by shark, leaving you to play it on a free line.

In baiting up I am guided by the advice given by Australian surf guards who have long experience of sharks: they recommend that bathers bothered by sharks should try to keep a level keel in

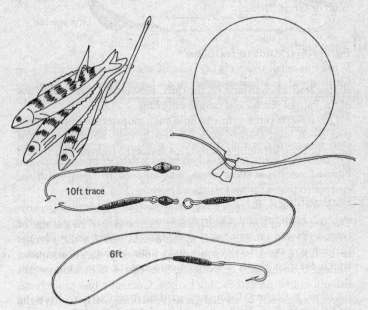

10ft trace

6ft

Fig. 256 (§332) Parts of shark rig – above, balloon hitched to main line; below, hook tied in to a chomping trace of 250 lb wire, ending in a strong split-ring to connect to a rubbing trace of 100–150 lb wire. All knots and joins are covered with wire whippings finished with solder.

the water. To a shark, they say, anything that is lying perpendicularly in the water is either dead or in trouble, and therefore easy game. The bait can be anything from one to four mackerel, suspended by hooking through either the head or tail (Fig. 256).

When a shark takes, ignore the preliminary bobs and dips of the float until it begins to move off purposefully. Thumb-down hard on the reel and lean well into the fish with hand on the star-drag ready to loosen off to let the fish run if it is a very big one.

When a good fish is contacted, it is usual for the other anglers fishing in the boat to draw in their lines until the fight is over: don't ever ignore the skipper's advice in this matter, or in fact in any other matter if you are a novice – he will have seen most of the situations that develop in sharking, many times over.

Catching a shark of 75 lb or over from a boat operating out of a British port qualifies you for membership of the Shark Angling Club of Great Britain.

§333 Tope fishing

What this small shark (§322) lacks in size it more than makes up for in speed. It is not essential to go higher than 30 lb breaking strain for a line, but it is vital that your reel holds at least 150 yards of line.

Tope move into relatively shallow ground (six feet to thirty feet) in summer, mainly to pursue small fish, especially flatfish. Provided it is calm, a float-fished bait – a dab for preference – can be used on the shallow areas, and allowed to 'trot' with the current so that it swims just above bottom (Fig. 257).

As with shark fishing, a bag of attractant offal (called 'rubby-dubby') is useful, and if more than one angler is fishing from the boat, baits can be set at varied depths. The float should be the smallest you can get away with, and should have a central channel which the line passes through freely until a stop knot arrests it.

Deeper water and stronger currents demand that a free-running leger is used, and to allay suspicions on the part of the tope the best rig is a Kilmore of Clements boom attaching the lead, stopped anything from ten to fifteen yards away from the bait by a matchstick, clove-hitched into the mainline (Fig. 258). The matchstick will usually break on the strike. Dabs, of course, are

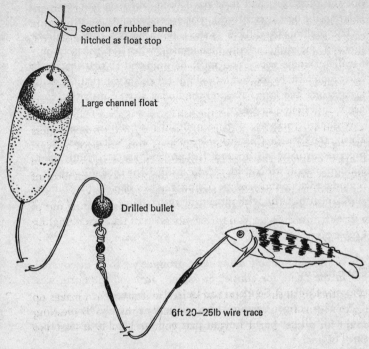

Section of rubber band
hitched as float stop

Large channel float

Drilled bullet

6ft 20—25lb wire trace

Fig. 257 (§333) Tope float rig.

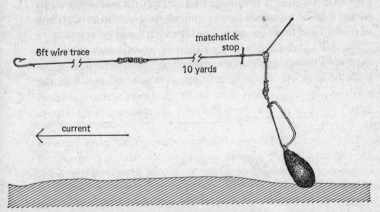

6ft wire trace

matchstick
stop

10 yards

current

Fig. 258 Tope leger rig with a long flowing trace.

not the only bait, and tope have been taken on mackerel and herring (the best alternatives), worms, crab and squid bait.

The preliminary dithers as the tope inspects a bait should be ignored, the strike usually being made when the fish sets off – usually at some pace. You must be prepared at that instant to allow your fish to run, under a slight check – a run that is usually fast, strong and long. To stop the line at any point with a fresh fish would spell disaster.

Although there are well recognized tope fishing areas – the Wash, the Bristol Channel, Herne Bay, the Solent – they are present virtually all around Britain and are frequently close enough inshore to consider shore fishing for them. Again, it is essential that a good yardage of line is used when shore fishing to allow the fish to run without getting into trouble.

§334 Skate fishing

There are undoubtably many skate grounds yet to be discovered, but in the main, for consistent fishing, areas off the north-west coasts of England, Scotland and Ireland are best.

As with conger fishing, the rig is comparatively simple (Fig. 259) and bait can be a whole or part of a mackerel or some other small fish.

Skate (§324, 325, 326) are truly weighty fish, although they are not likely to make the runs associated with shark or tope, and they have the added advantage of a large surface-area which, in strong tidal flows, makes them a difficult proposition to haul clear of the bed and up to the boat. Line strength could be as low as 70 lb breaking strain but wherever there is heavy water 100 lb, or even 120 lb breaking strain will give a bigger safety margin.

Skate hunt by 'flying' gently over the sea bed and flopping

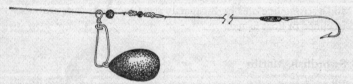

Fig. 259 (§334) Simple rig for skate. The hook-length must be wire to stand up to a skate's teeth.

suddenly on their prey; they then continue to flop about on it until, presumably, it is too stunned to make a getaway and can be engulfed. You can often detect the initial flop as a short tug on the line, followed by a series of small tugs. Once the skate starts pulling steadily, you can strike. Virtually useless for anything but fertilizer, it is a good idea to return your fish alive to the water wherever possible – this goes for most sharks and tope as well as skate, although the porbeagle and the conger eel are quite good to eat.

§335 Tunny fishing

During the great spell of tunny fishing in the North Sea between the wars, anglers would set out for the herring fishing grounds in a well-found large boat carrying a smaller craft in davits which could be lowered once the fishing began. They would search out a drifter hauling nets regularly, every three or four hours, and tag along until the nets were being drawn. Weather permitting, the small fishing boat with the anglers aboard would be lowered and they would then cast baits – herrings usually – to the boil surrounding the nets, where tunny are attracted by stunned fish and the shower of loosened scales.

Considering the fact that nowadays most angling boats are too small to venture to the herring grounds (from fifteen or so miles offshore) because of the unpredictable North Sea weather, and the cost of hiring the sort of boat the early tunny fishers used, it is hardly surprising that the pursuit declined. Despite the fact that the herring shoals – and presumably the numbers of tunny following them – have declined, they are still there. Our tunny fishery was once, and for all we know still is, among the best in the world. A good discovery for its revival would be to find some place where the tunny (§327) run fairly close inshore. A heavy rod and a strong line on a high-capacity reel is needed. Baits are either freelined or float fished.

§336 Swordfish, Marlin

I'll repeat an earlier statement: someone, somewhere is going to contact fish like the swordfish (§313) and marlin (§316), and whoever does will have a great tale to tell. In the established marlin and swordfish angling centres of the world they are taken on bait, like the tunny, or on trolled lures spread out from the sides of a powered boat on outriggers – long poles with quick-release line clips.

Big-game fishing
Quick cross-reference guide

Main lines, §11a, 11b, 11c.
Traces etc., §11g, 11h, 11i.
Hooks, §12.
Weights, §16.
Knots, §19b.
Rods, checklist, preparation, §46, 47, 48.
Sea environments, §202, 203.
Main bait fish, §286, 287.
Species, §313–327.

Neither 'match fishing' nor 'specimen hunting' necessarily implies fishing for reward in material terms; with the exception of the bigger 'opens' (see below) most matchmen fish at club level for cups and trophies which change hands over the years, while specimen-hunting enthusiasts might not even like the term 'competition' to be associated with them – they are happy, having set themselves a target of, say, a big carp, with achieving that objective. Specimen hunters can, however, enter their catches in big-fish competitions (for either certificates, medals or prizes) and even without this there's an element of competitiveness in their make-up.

Like drinking, competition is one of those things that most people can take or leave, while others pursue it with such dedication that virtually everything else in life is excluded. Happily, though, a keen competitive angler isn't likely to harm himself through his pursuit, other than that he might suffer complaints about absence from family life for much of his spare time.

Fishing matches and specimen-fish competitions all have a wide coverage in the angling press (a calendar of forthcoming events, sea and freshwater, is given in both *Angling Times* and *Anglers' Mail*, together with a thorough results service).

§337 Freshwater match fishing

It is fair to say that you get results from match fishing in proportion to the amount of effort you put in, and that this effort begins with preparation. It is valuable, for instance, to put in some practice on the water where the match is to be fished, and you might have to do this some time ahead of the match because the water can be closed to anglers for up to a week so that it is 'fresh' on match day. From such practice you can ascertain what baits and methods are likely to be best on the day. On the night before the match you should pay attention to tackle, bait and groundbait.

You will need enough groundbait for the length of time over which the match is to be fished, and perhaps a little to spare (if you accidentally kick over a tin of maggots you'll be glad of a reserve supply). If the match rules state that you shouldn't break the water (i.e. touch it in any way) before the starting whistle or maroon, you might consider getting your groundbait partially dampened overnight, adding more water in the morning before you set out – you can then begin fishing from the whistle without having to mix up on the bank. Make sure that you have enough spare hooks to make up for losses or blunting. I usually sleep better if I've done all this!

Freshwater matches are fished on a 'pegged' or 'roving' basis, mostly the former. With pegged matches, you arrive at the match H.Q., pass over your ticket or pay your entry fee, and draw 'blind' from an old sock or a hat for peg numbers – these numbers are written on wooden pegs set at regular spaces along the river bank, and on some popular waters there are even permanent, numbered, concrete posts. In roving matches, numbers are drawn as above, but all anglers wait until the last number is drawn and then set out, at intervals of a few minutes, starting with number one and working to the highest number (sometimes vice-versa) who leaves last. Thus the first off has a choice of any swim (and if he knows the river well he will make for the best swim). The last man will have to fit himself in wherever he finds a space.

Pools: Sweepstakes are often run in big matches, and by contributing you stand to win a cut of the total if you finish among the winners – they usually pay first, second and third places. There may be separate pools for different amounts, e.g. 25p, 50p, £1, and you can enter either one or all of them. Obviously if you really think you have a winning chance you will enter them all, but it is wise for beginners to risk only the smallest pool to begin with. Team matches: Some matches are open to teams of four, or some other number, besides individuals, with separate pools and prizes for teams.

Size-limit and all-in matches: Some matches are fished to the size-limits for takeable fish enforced by the organizing club or the local water authority, which means that only sizeable fish are eligible to be weighed-in. It also means in many cases that you might be disqualified for keeping fish that are too small in your keepnet.

The all-in match on the other hand means that you may weigh undersized fish so long as they are returned unharmed to the water after the match.

Matchmanship: Whether you fish as an individual or team member, from the start of the match you must have the will to win, and usually you can count success in terms of beating your neighbours on either side. The stretch you are fishing might not be capable of producing the overall winning weight – beat those around you, though, and you can congratulate yourself on fishing well.

Matchmanship begins before the starting whistle, and besides wetting your groundbait, suggested above, for matches where a 'don't-break-the-water' rule applies, you can arrange your tackle and make yourself comfortable, and you can place rod-rests in position and perch your dry keepnet on top of its pole so that when the whistle does go you simply drop it into the water. That done you can, seconds before the start, bait your hook and roll some throwing-sized balls of groundbait. This gives you a 'flyer' to start with – while other anglers hurry these last preparations after the whistle you can get both hook and groundbait into the water.

During the match, you'll have to go for the best that's offering itself, perhaps a shoal of bream or, with nothing else offered, bleak (bleak, pike and eels are not counted in some matches). Whatever, there's one prime factor to concentrate on – speed. The more time your baited hook spends in the water, the more chance you have of taking fish, and so it is important that you brush up unhooking, rebaiting and casting, and changing hooks and other tackles as quickly and smoothly as possible. Don't let this advice lead you into hurrying a big fish in too fast though – be ruled by common sense.

I think it is a good idea to ignore any rumours, that come 'down the line' or from bystanders, about 'some chap pulling 'em in one after the other' around the corner – this leads to unnecessary panic. Very often the rumours, like many stories that have passed too many lips, are completely untrue.

All fishing, unless you are landing a fish hooked before the finish, must stop on the whistle. Pack up your tackle and wait for the weighmaster (in some roving matches you might have to take your fish to a central weighing-in point).

Supervise the weighing of your fish, making sure that the result is entered correctly in the steward's list, against your name – occasionally there are slips. Also make a note of the result yourself. With the weighing complete, everybody usually congregates at the H.Q. while officials work out the placings. Your catch may be assessed on points as well as aggregate weight – a point per fish is the usual system.

To sample the world of match fishing the beginner can't do better than enter matches at local club level. Such matches might be small, with twenty or so entries, and the rewards not great – cups, trophies, and perhaps a pheasant or a bottle of Scotch at the annual 'fur-and-feather', Christmas match. But you can enjoy camaraderie and very friendly rivalry. With greater confidence you can try open matches – matches thrown open to anglers who don't belong to the organizing club, or sometimes organized by individual sponsors. These are much bigger affairs, and both the match winnings and pools can be high.

If you stay at club level, though, you can compete in inter-club leagues, and if you are lucky you might fish your way into a 'National' squad. The National Championships, now in three divisions, are the high spots of the match calendar – clubs put forward their best teams to fish for national glory in these National Federation of Anglers events. And from the best of the anglers in these events Britain's squad for international matches is picked. All you need to do to start on the bottom rung of the ladder is join a club, and start fishing in club matches.

N.B. It is essential to be covered with an appropriate water authority rod licence for all freshwater matches – if you travel to a match outside your area, it is usually possible to obtain a day rod licence.

§338 Sea matches

Unlike freshwater fishing, the majority of sea matches are roving matches (shore or boat) within defined geographical limits, and the onus is usually on the angler to get back to a central weighing point at a certain time. That said, you should be at least as practical as the freshwater matchman in your approach to a competition, making sure that your bait, tackle and preparations give you the best possible chance of winning.

There is usually a wide range of classes in sea matches, with separate prizes for shore and boat aggregate weights and specimen fish. Most of these matches are run under National Federation of Sea Anglers rules which, among other things, lay down minimum acceptable size limits for various species (copies obtainable from the Secretary of the N.F.S.A., address in Chapter 36). Besides individual matches there are week-long sea angling festivals with prizes both for each day's winners and for overall winners. There are also competitions based purely on one species, such as tope and conger, which are organized by specialist clubs.

§339 Specimen hunting

It is impossible to advise on the approach to specimen hunting, sea or freshwater, other than to say that preparation is as demanding as preparation for match fishing, if the game is followed in a dedicated way – as well as selecting the bait and tackle appropriate to the species sought, the true specimen hunter must spend many hours actually seeking out places where fish of known specimen-quality exist.

What the freelance specimen hunter does with his catch is very much up to him. With a record fish, of course, the wisest action is to follow the procedure for entering it in the British record list (Chapter 35), but there are also prize competitions for good fish (*Angling Times*, *Anglers' Mail* and other newspapers) besides awards sponsored by other sources. Many clubs also run small competitions for fish caught in local waters.

§340 Casting competition

The remaining competitive field in angling is casting, and annual casting championships are staged in Britain by the British Casting Association under International Casting Federation rules. Events are open to casters of amateur and professional status, and the main contests are: Trout-fly accuracy; Fly accuracy and distance; fly distance (single handed); Fly distance (double-handed); Bait accuracy (5/8 oz); Bait accuracy (3/8 oz); Bait distance (5/8 oz); Bait distance (3/8 oz.); Bait distance (single-handed, 5/8 oz); Bait distance (double-handed, 30 gramme); Bait distance (4 oz, restricted line); Bait distance (2 oz, restricted line); Bait distance (6 oz, unrestricted).

The term 'unrestricted line' means that a shock leader and very light reel-line may be used, 'restricted line' being a level line with no shock leader.

At the end of this round-up of current British angling methods and activities, I want to try to answer a question often asked: 'What makes a good angler?'

It is all too plain that the questioner usually means to ask what makes a notable, or even a famous angler, and taken on that level the answers are easily come by – commonsense, good judgement, a measure of experience, and sound gear, maintained in good order. It is clear that that gives us all the potential of becoming notable anglers, given time and a proportion of luck. Enough said.

The word 'good' though has deeper implications than the bubble reputation, and if I seem to be urging that everybody who uses a fishing rod strives to be 'good' in this deeper sense I hope that I don't drive people off with what looks like preaching. A good angler, to me, is a person aware of the consequences of his actions as they affect fish, the environment in which he follows his sport, and the outside world.

Fish, first of all, are vital, thrilling creatures – to learn about them is to love them as such, and it should become second nature to treat them with respect, care, and mercy. That means that once a fish is landed it should be handled with gentleness, unhooked as tenderly as possible and placed – not thrown – into a comfortably large keepnet, or back in the water from which it came. If the fish is going to be kept, then it has earned a quick, merciful despatch, and not a lingering death gasping and drying, out of its element.

Turning to environment, it is clear that the many generations of good anglers who have preceded us have left us a precious legacy – the respect of landlords and others for our careful and responsible ways. We keep this only by maintaining high standards, by shutting farm gates after us and by not disturbing crops or stock, by avoiding litter-dropping and by trying to make sure that the spots in which we fish return to peace when we go, as if we had never visited...

The outside world probably doesn't realize or even care what angling and anglers have done for it. Down through the ages, who but anglers have worried deeply if fish, or at least the fish we catch, exist? I'd ask that question again if I didn't have a limit on space, for I want its impact to be felt. It has been a long, long time since freshwater fish, coarse especially, and even the fish of inshore coastal waters, have been considered as significant sources of food. They are rarely seen even, and so cannot be regarded as visually attractive in anything but an aquarium. So, truthfully, who would know if they were not about their business in the dreamy, dusky depths of a river, or darting among the coastal breakers? I'm talking about pollution, of course. Almost every major river and many parts of the coast of this country have been threatened by that scourge of industrial life. It is still going on, but I'd be greatly worried about that if there were no anglers, no watchdogs.

You might argue that everybody would be up in arms over a smelly river. Would they, I wonder, if it was treated with a hefty dose of chemical deodorant? That's not beyond the cunning of commercial interests. Look what a mess they've made of the Rhine, the great spine river of Europe – chemical stew.

I firmly believe it to be true that anglers, more than any other section of the community, have ambitiously and vociferously combated pollution. And yet when I say, in the next breath, that there are actually enemies of angling in the outside world, I cannot, and will not, put that forward as an argument for our case even after a summer such as 1976 when our limited resources of pure water were highlighted so vividly. Against the specific charge of cruelty it simply becomes no argument at all.

It is silly to ignore opposition, to sweep it under the carpet. That won't make it go away. Opposition to angling, a misjudgement of the angler's character by well-intentioned people, took a firm direction in 1976 when the R.S.P.C.A. announced that it was going to study allegations of cruelty to fish. A clear conscience is as good a defence as any against that, and there I'd let the subject rest but for the fact that evidence of cruelty will be found, and the unsupervised young and inexperienced will provide it. Each and every one of us has to be aware of that, and our task is clear: we must foster the right attitudes and spirit in those to whom we hope to leave our sport for safe keeping into the future.

I would hate to see any change that would deny future generations the joy of casting to trout in a spring meadow, waiting in hushed excitement for daylight on the misty bank of a tench lake in midsummer, or the contained anxiety on a darkened, wave-swept beach when the rod-tip dithers, a signal that the far-off bait is being investigated . . . I could go on, but it would take several books. In this last respect of being good anglers, then – our relationships with the outside world – it behoves us to make even the very youngest of our numbers as good as we are.

We also have a duty to support, as fully as possible, all the organizations that work for angling, especially the National Anglers' Council and the Anglers' Cooperative Association (which is enabled to fight pollution cases only by voluntary contributions and deserves a generous dip from everybody). They don't just serve us individually, they also give us a united voice. They enable every one of us, if necessary, to put his foot down in unison with fellow anglers. And with four million anglers in the country, that's bound to make a lasting impression.

Part Three

Nobody can fail to be impressed by the sheer variety of fishing offered in England, Scotland, Ireland and Wales, but this brief section takes account of the fact that adventure draws many to explore fishing further afield, and that many more have to travel to far places for business and other reasons. The frustration of finding yourself without tackle beside some tempting piece of water in a foreign place is great, so much so that I've taken to carrying at least one rod wherever I go – it takes up little space in a car, caravan or hotel room, and adds hardly any weight to airline baggage quotas. Odds and ends which you might need, such as weights, lines, hooks and bait, are obtainable almost everywhere in the world.

It should be made clear that British tackle and fishing methods are useful everywhere, even though the gear and styles used by the native populations appear to be radically different. For instance, consider how successful we are in using our coarse-fishing styles in European international matches against the almost universal use of the roach-pole style on the Continent.

Europe probably offers the most people a chance of fishing overseas, although I'm also led to give sources of information on fishing in Ireland for the benefit of English people who don't realize what superb fishing exists at the end of a short boat or air trip, in a land where English is spoken and the Guinness is so good!

With one or two additions, the fish species encountered in Britain can be caught. The quality of the fishing varies though, and by and large it is best to aim for areas that offer excellence if you take a trip with only fishing in mind. For the coarse fisherman that could well mean the comparatively underfished rivers of Denmark, while the game angler cannot fail to be attracted by

Scandinavia's salmon and trout fishing. The sea angler has a wide choice, extending from the cod, pollack and coalfish grounds of Iceland to the Mediterranean and its quota of exotic game fish. Wherever you go, though, you'll make the delightful discovery that you are welcomed by the anglers of that country. But be warned that many countries have fishing regulations just as we do – make sure you comply with them.

Andorra: Mainly trout fishing. Permits from: Sindicat d'Iniciativa, Plaza Princep Benlloch, Andorra la Vieja. Information from Andorra Information Office, 49 Wentworth Road, London NW11.

Austria: Excellent trout fishing and some good coarse fishing. A state rod licence is necessary, plus local permits. Booklet *Fishing in Austria* from the Austrian State Tourist Department, 16 Conduit Street, London W1.

Belgium: Mostly very good coarse fishing, with trout fishing in the streams of the Ardennes. Some waters are free of restrictions but for most, an annual rod licence is necessary, together with local permits. There is a trout-fishing close season from 1 October to the fourth Sunday in March, and a coarse-fish close season from the Monday following the fourth Sunday of March to the second Sunday of June. There is good sea fishing along the forty-odd miles of coastline. Leaflet *Fresh and Salt-water Fishing in Belgium* from Belgian National Tourist Office, 66 Haymarket, London SW1.

Czechoslovakia: Very good game and coarse fishing. Visitors must take out a territorial fishing licence and a local permit issued for various watersheds. Salmon caught in the Danube have to be surrendered or paid for at a rate per kilo, but all other fish remain the angler's property. Further information from the Czechoslovak Travel Bureau, Cedok (London) Ltd, 17–18 Old Bond Street, London W1.

Denmark: All Danish rivers are well-stocked and most contain salmon, sea-trout, trout and coarse fish. There is also some good shore fishing. In many places a local-fishing-association permit is all that is needed. Pamphlets available from the Danish Tourist Board, Sceptre House, 169–73 Regent Street, London w1. Details of coarse-fishing holidays from Abbeygate Travel Ltd, 12 Midgate, Peterborough, and Castle Holidays Group (Management) Ltd, 521 Royal Exchange, Manchester. The tourist board also provides information on fishing in Greenland.

Finland: Excellent game and coarse fishing in the many lakes and rivers, some of which are extremely isolated. Best time to fish is June in the north of the country, and throughout summer and autumn in the south. Most waters owned by the State Board of Forestry, who supply permits. Information from Finland House, 56 Haymarket, London sw1.

France: Such a large country as France offers practically everything the angler wants, from the salmon of the Pyrenees and trout and char in the ice-cold waters of the Alps, and a huge number of coarse-fishing waters, to sea fishing on Atlantic and Mediterranean coasts. A map of the country and an information sheet *Fishing in France* is supplied by the French Tourist Office, 178 Piccadilly, London w1. It explains licence requirements and close seasons thoroughly.

Germany: The wilder parts of Germany are especially good for game and coarse fishing, although many waters in industrial areas are heavily polluted. An explanatory leaflet *Angling in Germany* is available from the German Tourist Information Bureau, 61 Conduit Street, London w1.

Gibraltar: Superb Mediterranean sea fishing, and the shark fishing is particularly good. Leaflet *Fishing in Gibraltar* from the Gibraltar Tourist Office, 15 Grand Buildings, Trafalgar Square, London wc2.

Hungary: Good coarse fishing, particularly in the large Lake Balaton, and also trout fishing. Details from the Hungarian Travel Centre, 10 Vigo Street, London w1.

Iceland: Especially notable for its excellent sea fishing and the annual sea-fishing festival fished from Reykjavik, Iceland also has some superb salmon, sea-trout, trout and char fishing. Details from the Iceland Tour Information Bureau, 73 Grosvenor Street, London W1.

Ireland: Ireland, north and south, offers excellent sea and fresh-water fishing and is still largely uncrowded, except for main centres in the tourist season. There are some particularly good sea-fishing festivals during the season, and a big attraction to many English anglers is the absence of a coarse-fishing close season. Full details on all angling waters and activities can be obtained from the Irish Tourist Board, PO box 273, 63–7 Upper Stephen Street, Dublin 8, and the Northern Ireland Tourist Board, River House, High Street, Belfast.

Italy: Fair coarse fishing in most regions, with trout fishing in mountainous areas. For freshwater fishing a permit must be obtained from the local police. Good sea fishing. Details on fishing are included in the booklet *Italy – Travellers' Handbook* obtainable from the Italian Tourist Office, 201 Regent Street, London W1.

Luxembourg: Good, mixed, freshwater fishing. Details of permit requirements and regulations given in the booklet *Grand Duchy of Luxembourg* obtainable from the Luxembourg National Tourist Office, 66 Haymarket, London SW1.

Netherlands: Good coarse fishing, and virtually no game fishing. Details included in *Holland – Water Sports Paradise* from the Netherlands National Tourist Office, 143 New Bond Street, London W1.

Norway: To the game fisherman, Norway's excellent salmon and trout rivers must be a big attraction, but the excellent sea fishing, offshore and in the numerous tidal inlets should not be ignored. An extremely comprehensive booklet, *Angling in Norway* has from time to time been out of print and if a copy can be found the angler will quickly realize that it is invaluable. Otherwise, information on fishing in the country can be obtained from the Norway National Tourist Office, 20 Pall Mall, London SW1.

Portugal: Although there is some good coarse fishing and even salmon fishing in the north of the country, by far the biggest attraction in Portugal is sea fishing, which in the south provides swordfish, marlin, tunny, bonito, amberjack and sharks. Boat fishing is particularly well organized. Full details in the booklet *Line Fishing in Portuguese Waters* from the Portuguese National Tourist Office, 20 Regent Street, London SW1.

Spain: There is very good coarse and game fishing in Spain, although in the south many waters can dry to a polluted trickle in summer. The sea fishing is also very good. A comprehensive booklet, *Spain: Hunting and Fishing,* is obtainable from the Spanish National Tourist Office, 67 Jermyn Street, London SW1.

Sweden: This country has an enormous number of rivers and lakes offering a range of coarse and game fishing. Private owner-ship of sea-angling areas can extend well out from the shore, and you might have to pay for sea fishing, which can be good. The various counties organize their own tourist information, which can be obtained through the Swedish Embassy at 23 North Row, London W1.

Switzerland: Coarse and game fishing. Full details are given in the booklet *With Rod and Line in Switzerland* which is expected to be produced in a new edition at the time of writing. It is obtainable from the Swiss National Tourist Office, Swiss Centre, 1 New Coventry Street, London W1.

Yugoslavia: It is said that still there are rivers here rarely, if ever, fished. Even the popular angling waters, offering coarse fish and game fish, are good by our standards. The Adriatic offers good sea fishing. Explanatory notes are obtainable from the Yugoslav National Tourist Office, 143 Regent Street, London W1.

U.S.S.R.: Visits to Russia are now very easy and some excellent fishing is available through the national tourist body, Intourist. Information can be obtained from the U.S.S.R. Embassy Infor-mation Department, 13 Kensington Palace Gardens, London W8.

It is not only the sea angler who finds his scope widened abroad
with exciting fish such as marlin, bonefish and barracuda – the
freshwater fish of many countries are also different, and in many
cases extremely challenging. Take the mighty masheer of India,
a species which can run to over 100 lb, or the truly gigantic Nile
perch.

Unfortunately, it is not possible to list the world's fishes in this
book, although the guides supplied through various tourist
boards will make a fairly thorough job of listing the species
worth going after.

It is necessary to warn that political upheavals in some
countries might alter the structure of tourist facilities, and all
visitors ought to check the situation for themselves at the time of
departure for the less stable areas of the world. As in Britain and
Europe, many countries also have fishing regulations which must
be complied with, besides entry regulations and health requirements.

Argentina: Good sea-trout fishing, also dorado. Booklet *Fishing
dorado, salmontrout* through Argentinian Embassy, 9 Wilton
Crescent, London sw1.

Australia: Although largely arid, Australia has some good freshwater fishing for trout and local species. The sea fishing, particularly on the Barrier Reef, is superb. Details of fishing from the
tourism bodies of individual states: New South Wales, 56 The
Strand, London wc2; Queensland, 392–3 The Strand, wc2;
South Australia, 50 The Strand, wc2; Tasmania, 457 The Strand,
wc2; Victoria, Victoria House, Melbourne Place, The Strand,
wc2; Western Australia, 115 The Strand, wc2.

Bahamas: Superb, well-organized, sea fishing. Send for *Fact Finder, Fishing* to Bahama Islands Tourist Office, 23 Old Bond Street, London W1.

Bermuda: Excellent shore fishing and well organized boat fishing, particularly big-game fishing. Booklet *Bermuda Fishing* from Bermuda Department of Tourism, Trevor House, 58 Grosvenor Street, London W1.

Canada: Really good game fishing with specialities such as steelhead and pacific salmon, and excellent fishing for freshwater species such as bass, pike and northern pike. Sea fishing superb on either coast. Province-by-province guide *Canada, Fisherman's Paradise* through Canadian High Commission, Canada House, Trafalgar Square, London SW1.

Cyprus: Inshore waters overfished, but good big-game fishing well offshore. Inquire through Cyprus Trade and Tourist Centre, 213 Regent Street, London W1.

Greece: Some good inland trout and coarse fishing in lakes and rivers, also offshore sea fishing. Explanatory notes *River and Lake Fishing in Greece* through the Greek State Tourist Office, 195–7 Regent Street, London W1.

Israel: Inland fishing in the Sea of Galilee and rivers, good shore fishing in Mediterranean and at Eilat on the Red Sea. Notes from the Israel Tourist Office, 59 St James's Street, London SW1.

India: Trout and masheer fishing, also good sea fishing especially in Indian Ocean. Details through the Government of India Tourist Office, 21 New Bond Street, London W1.

Jamaica: Good sea fishing. Booklet *Jamaica Watersports* from Jamaica Tourist Board, 6–10 Bruton Street, London W1.

Japan: Notes in *Your Guide to Japan* from the Japan National Tourist Organization, 167 Regent Street, London W1.

Kenya: Good freshwater fishing in Lake Victoria and Lake Rudolf, also rivers, where Nile perch may be taken. Excellent sea fishing.

Booklet *Kenya – The Big Fish Country* from the Kenya Tourist Office, 318 Grand Buildings, Trafalgar Square, London WC2.

Malawi: Good freshwater fishing for trout, lake salmon and tiger fish, particularly in Lake Malawi. Details from Malawi Angling Society, PO box 744, Blantyre, and through Malawi High Commission, 47 Great Cumberland Place, London W1.

Malaysia: Good freshwater fishing for, among others, the kelah or Malaysian masheer, especially away from iron-ore workings which have muddied some rivers. Excellent sea fishing. Details through the Malaysia High Commission, Information Department, 45 Belgrave Square, London SW1.

Mauritius: Particularly good big-game fishing, Details from the Government Tourist Office, Chaussee, Port Louis, or Le Morne Anglers' Club, Black River, Mauritius.

Morocco: Excellent boat, shore and inland river fishing. Ask for booklet *Morocco Tourism, No. 63 – Fishing* from Morocco Tourist Office, c/o 49 Queens Gate Gardens, London SW7.

New Zealand: Really superb game fishing (in places you can cook your catch in hot springs) besides good sea fishing. Leaflet *Fishing in New Zealand* from the Information Officer, New Zealand High Commission, New Zealand House, Haymarket, London SW1.

Nicaragua: Organized shore fishing, and fishing in the vast Lake Nicaragua. Notes through the Nicaraguan Embassy, 8 Gloucester Road, London SW7.

Panama: Organized big-game fishing. Leaflets through the Panama Embassy, 29 Wellington Court, 116 Knightsbridge, London SW1.

South Africa: Well-organized freshwater and sea fishing of all kinds. Notes on regulations etc. from the South African Tourist Corporation, 13 Regent Street, London SW1.

Tunisia: Good sea fishing. Details through the Tunisia National Tourist Office, 7A Stafford Street, London W1.

Part Four

All anglers ought to be able to swim, but many cannot. Swimming lessons are cheap for something so valuable as your life. Fortunately, accidents are rare, but it is a good idea to take every precaution, particularly at sea in your own boat or dinghy, against drownings – that means carrying lifesaving gear and wearing life-jackets. It is also extremely useful, in both sea and freshwater fishing, to have instruction in lifesaving and basic first aid. You might never need it – I hope you don't.

I cannot hope to give a lifesaving and first-aid course in this book, but I can point out the most useful areas.

First, though, a word about sea rescues: carry flares besides rescue gear, and don't have them packed in the bottom of a box of other gear or under piles of old rope in the bulkhead. Let off flares as you are able if you capsize and, unless you are extremely close to the shore, try to keep all the ship's company together and near the capsized boat, unless it is obviously sinking fast. This will give rescue teams a marker.

Besides flares and lifesaving gear in the boat it is essential to carry:

(a) A compass – when you are fishing, you should always take a note of the compass direction back to port in case you have to make your way in fog.
(b) A loud whistle, large bell or hooter to give regular signals for other shipping when anchored or making way in fog. If there is a danger of grounding on reefs, post a bows lookout with a rope tied about his waist for security.

Make sure that both aids can be easily found.

Do use the Coastguard Service card-system, leaving details of

SOUTH EAST ICELAND

FAROES

BAILEY

FAIR ISLE

VIKING

HEBRIDES

1. CROMARTY

FORTIES

ROCKALL

12. MALIN

2. FORTH

11.

FISHER

TYNE

DOGGER

GERMAN BIGHT

10.

IRISH SEA

HUMBER

SHANNON

3.

9.

4. THAMES

FASTNET

6. 5. DOVER

7. WIGHT

8. PLYMOUTH PORTLAND

STATION REPORTS:

SOLE

1. WICK
2. BELL ROCK
3. DOWSING
4. NORTH HINDER
5. VARNE
6. ROYAL SOVEREIGN
7. PORTLAND BILL
8. SCILLY
9. VALENTIA
10. RONALDSWAY
11. PRESTWICK
12. TIREE

FINISTERRE

BISCAY

Fig. 260 Weather-report areas.

number of crew, boat's name, and estimated time of return to port. Your local coastguard will tell you all about it.

A small transistor radio is useful for weather reports, given on the hour by BBC Radio 4, long wave only. The areas covered in the reports are shown in Fig. 260.

Finally, if you haven't capsized yourself, but you notice flares or anything suspicious (1) report immediately to the coastguard if you are able and (2) go to assistance no matter what else you are doing. Shore-bound anglers should also report any suspicious lights or sightings.

Mouth-to-mouth resuscitation, or mouth-to-nose resuscitation should be used for people who have stopped breathing. The latter is best for patients while floating in the sea since the mouth may be blocked or closed. Continue mouth-to-mouth when ashore if necessary, and make sure a doctor is called. If patient doesn't seem to be responding, continue resuscitation until the doctor advises you to stop. With large wounds, get medical help immediately. If afloat, put into shore with haste. Other wounds can be cleaned and dressed with elastoplast of the waterproof variety. Don't use river water for washing broken skin of any kind, since it might carry infections. Sea water is fairly safe.

Hooks in any place but the eye may be removed by the methods shown in Fig. 261, but for eye injuries medical help must be obtained immediately.

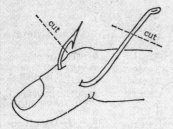

Fig. 261 Hooks caught in skin etc. should not be pulled free without cutting off barbed point or part of shank and eye.

Cover all concussed or obviously shocked persons with plenty of warm clothing. This also applies to people with broken limbs etc., in whom shock might develop some time later.

Don't be brave about sea-sickness if it gets too much for you. Tell the skipper, who'll try to do what's best for you, even if that means going back to port. Forty winks in the cabin, stretched out, usually works wonders.

As with most people who spend a great deal of the time out of doors, anglers usually develop good weather sense – intuitive weather forecasting pays off time and time again!

For anglers visiting areas away from home, however, the telephone forecasting service can be extremely useful, particularly for sea anglers planning an offshore trip, where winds above force 6 (Beaufort Scale) will usually mean the cancellation of the trip unless there are signs of a rapid improvement.

The Beaufort Scale, so far as most mariners are concerned, is as follows:

Scale No.	Wind force	M.P.H.	Knots
0	Calm	1	1
1	Light air	1–3	1–3
2	Slight breeze	4–7	4–6
3	Gentle breeze	8–12	7–10
4	Moderate breeze	13–18	11–16
5	Fresh breeze	19–24	17–21
6	Strong breeze	25–31	22–27
7	High wind	32–38	28–33
8	Gale	39–46	34–40
9	Strong gale	47–54	41–47

Telephone numbers of the regional weather forecasts are given in the next chapter.

The greatest effect of the weather can be felt in clothing, and the warning that extra warmth and protection for offshore trips is essential should not go unheeded. Nevertheless, there are other considerations in choosing weatherproof clothing. For the freshwater fisherman, the choice of clothing should be tempered with the fact that you might be seen by the fish you are out to catch.

Quiet colours, merging with the terrain, are logical – a bright white shirt on sunny days might spell disaster. The same applies to rock fishing on the sea-shore. At sea, in a boat, such precautions need not be taken.

As well as weatherproofing, for which the overlap system works best (Fig. 262) you do need to make sure that your clothing gives you freedom of movement.

Fig. 262 Weatherproofing is easy if you remember the overlap principle – nothing is worse than having a jacket which channels water into your boots!

The ratification of British record fish is undertaken by a committee, meeting regularly throughout the year to assess claims. The full title of this body is 'The British Record (rod-caught) Fish Committee of the National Anglers' Council'. They are based at 5 Cowgate, Peterborough (Tel. Peterborough 54084), to where all claims should be directed.

To avoid disappointment if you catch what you believe to be a record fish, here is an extract of the Committee's rules of procedure:

(1) The claimant should contact the Committee secretary. Advice will then be given on preservation of the fish and identification.

(2) Claims should be made in writing to the secretary stating the species of the fish and the weight; the date and place of capture and the tackle used, and whether shore or boat caught in the case of sea fish; the names and addresses of reliable witnesses to both capture and weight of fish (without witnesses a claimant must verify capture by affidavit).

(3) No claim will be accepted unless the Committee is satisfied as to species, method of capture and weight. The Committee reserves the right to reject any claim.

(5) Fish caught at sea will be eligible if the boat has set out from a port in England, Wales, Scotland, Northern Ireland, the Isle of Man or the Channel Islands and returns to the same port without having called at any port outside the United Kingdom. Fish caught in the territorial waters of other countries will not be eligible.

(4) To ensure correct identification it is essential that claimants should retain the fish and immediately contact the secretary, who will advise where to present the fish for inspection; no claim will

be considered unless the fish is in its natural state, dead or alive, when presented for inspection (after weighing and securing witnesses, fish may be preserved by freezing or in a formalin solution – chemists will advise).

(6) The fish must be weighed as soon as possible after capture on scales or steelyards which can be tested on behalf of the Committee. Small fish should be weighed on finely graduated scales, and the weight claimed should be to a division of weight (ounce, gramme, dram) not less than the smallest division shown on the scales. For fish of less than one pound, the weight should be submitted to the Committee in grammes. A Weights and Measures certificate must be produced certifying the accuracy of the scales used indicating testing at the claimed weight.

World record fish

World record marine game fishes are dealt with by the International Game Fish Association, Holiday Inn Arcade, 3000 E. Las Olas Boulevard, Fort Lauderdale, Florida 33316, USA. World record claims in respect of sharks should be made through the Shark Angling Club of Great Britain, Looe, Cornwall.

Irish record fish

Claims for fish caught in Northern Ireland are dealt with by the British Record (rod-caught) Fish Committee. Claims for fish caught in Eire should be made to the Irish Specimen Fish Committee, Balnagowan, Mobhi Boreen, Glasnevin, Dublin 9.

British Record Freshwater Fish List

Species & Scientific Name	lbs	ozs	Weight drms	kilos	gms	Date	Captor & Location
Barbel *Barbus barbus*	13	12	— :	6	237	1962	J.Day, Royalty Fishery, Hants.
Bleak *Alburnus alburnus*	—	3	15 :	—	111	1971	D. Pollard, Staythorpe Pond, Nr Newark, Notts.
Bream (Common, Bronze) *Abramis brama*	13	8	— :	6	123	1977	A.R. Heslop, private water, Staffs.
Carp *Cyprinus carpio*	44	—	— :	19	957	1952	R. Walker, Redmire Pool.
Carp, Crucian *Carassius carassius*	5	10	8 :	2	565	1976	G. Halls, at lakes Nr. King's Lynn, Norfolk.

Species & Scientific Name	lbs	ozs	drms	:	kilos	gms	Date	Captor & Location
Catfish (Wels) *Silurus glanis*	43	3	—	:	19	730	1970	R.J. Bray, Wilstone Reservoir, Tring, Herts.
Char *Salvelinus alpinus*	1	12	4	:	—	801	1974	C. Imperiale, Loch Insh, Inverness-shire.
Brook Char (Brook Trout) *Salvelinus fontinalis*	4	5	—	:	1	956	1978	K. Crawford, Loch in Perthshire
Chub *Leuciscus cephalus*	7	6	—	:	3	345	1957	W.L. Warren, Royalty Fishery, Hampshire, Avon.
Dace *Leuciscus leuciscus*	1	4	4	:	—	574	1960	J.L. Gasson, Little Ouse, Thetford, Norfolk.
Eel *Anguilla anguilla*	8	10	—	:	3	912	1969	A. Dart, Hunstrete Lake.
Gudgeon *Gobio gobio*	—	4	4	:	—	120	1977	M.J. Bowen, Fish Pond, Ebbw Vale, Gwent, Wales.
Gwyniad (Whitefish) *Coregonus lavaretus*	1	4	—	:	—	567	1965	J.R. Williams, Llyn Tegid, Wales.
Loch Lomond Powan *Coregonus albula*	1	7	—	:	—	652	1972	J.M. Ryder, Loch Lomond, Scotland.
Orfe, Golden *Leuciscus idus*	4	3	—	:	1	899	1976	B.T. Mills, River Test, Hampshire.
Perch *Perca fluviatilis*	4	12	—	:	2	154	1962	S.F. Baker, Oulton Broad, Suffolk.
Pike *Esox lucius*	40	—	—	:	18	143	1967	P.D. Hancock, Horsey Mere, Norfolk.
Pike–perch (Walleye) *Stizostedion vitreum*	11	12	—	:	5	329	1934	F. Adams, The Delph, Welney, Norfolk.
Pike–perch (Zander) *Stizostedion lucioperca*	17	4	—	:	7	824	1977	D. Litton, Great Ouse Relief Channel.
Pumpkinseed *Lepomis gibbosus*	—	2	10	:	—	074	1977	A. Baverstock, G.L.C. Highgate Pond, London.
Roach *Rutilus rutilus*	4	1	—	:	1	842	1975	R.G. Jones, Notts. Gravel Pit.
Rudd *Scardinius erythrophthalmus*	4	8	—	:	2	041	1933	Rev. E.C. Alston, Thetford, Norfolk.
Ruffe *Gymnocephalus cernua*	—	5	—	:	—	141	1977	P. Barrowcliffe, River Bure, St. Benets Abbey, Norfolk.
Salmon *Salmo salar*	64	—	—	:	29	029	1922	Miss G.W. Ballantyne, River Tay, Scotland.
Schelly (Skelly) *Coregonus albula*	1	10	—	:	—	737	1976	W. Wainwright, Ullswater, Cumbria.
Tench *Tinca tinca*	10	1	2	:	5	567	1975	L.W. Brown, Peterborough Brick Pit.
Trout, American Brook *Salvelinus fontinalis*	2	9	—	:	1	162	1973	M. Forbes, Loch in Perthshire, Scotland.
Trout, Brown *Salmo trutta*	19	4	8	:	8	745	1974	T. Chartres, Lower Loch Erne, Northern Ireland.
Trout, Rainbow *Salmo gairdneri*	19	8	—	:	8	844	1977	A. Pearson, Avington Fishery, Hants.

Species open for Freshwater Fish Claims

Species		lbs	ozs	drms	:	kilos	gms
				Minimum Qualifying Weight			
Grayling *Thymallus thymallus*		3	—	—	:	1	361
Sea Trout *Salmo trutta*		20	—	—	:	9	071
Silver Bream *Blicca bjoernka*		1	8	—	:	—	680

NOTE:— The above qualifying weights are subject to revision by the Committee if necessary.

British Record Sea Fish List

Boat and Shore

Species & Scientific Name		lbs	ozs	drms	:	kilos	gms	Date	Captor & Location
Angler Fish *Lophius piscatorius*	B	82	12	—	:	37	533	1977	K. Ponsford, off Mevagissey, Cornwall.
	S	68	2	—	:	30	899	1967	H.G.T. Legerton, Canvey Island.
Bass *Morone labrax*	B	18	6	—	:	8	334	1975	R.G. Slater, off Eddystone Reef.
	S	18	2	—	:	8	220	1943	F.C. Borley, Felixstowe.
Black-fish *Centrolophus niger*	B	3	10	8	:	1	658	1972	James Semple off Heads of Ayr.
	S	2	—	—	:	—	907		Qualifying weight.
Bluemouth *Helicolenus dactylopterus*	B	3	2	8	:	1	431	1976	Anne Lyngholm, Loch Shell, Stornoway, Scotland.
	S	2	—	—	:	—	907		Qualifying weight.
Bogue *Boops boops*	B	1	10	—	:	—	737	1975	D.R. Northam, Plymouth Devon.
	S	1	9	14	:	—	733	1968	Mrs. S. O'Brien, Sorel Point, Jersey.
Bream, Black *Spondyliosoma cantharus*	B	6	14	4	:	3	125	1977	J.A. Garlick, over wreck off Devon coast.
	S	4	14	4	:	2	218	1977	R.J. Holloway, off Admiralty Pier, Dover, Kent.
Bream, Gilthead *Sparus aurata*	B	4	13	—	:	2	182	1975	M.J. Bryant, Salcombe, Devon.
	S	6	15	—	:	3	146	1977	H. Solomons, Salcombe Estuary, Devon.
Bream, Ray's *Brama brama*	B	5	—	—	:	2	268		Qualifying weight.
	S	7	15	12	:	3	621	1967	G. Walker, Crimdon Beach, Hartlepool.
Bream, Red *Pagellus bogaraveo*	B	9	8	12	:	4	330	1974	B.H. Reynolds, off Mevagissey, Cornwall.
	S	3	—	—	:	1	360	1976	D.J. Berry, Alderney, C.I.
Brill *Scophthalmus rhombus*	B	16	—	—	:	7	257	1950	A.H. Fisher, Isle of Man.
	S	5	12	4	:	2	615	1976	M. Freeman, Chesil Beach, Dorset.
Bull Huss *Scyliorhinus stellaris*	B	21	3	—	:	9	610	1955	J. Holmes, Looe, Cornwall
	S	17	15	—	:	8	136	1977	M. Roberts, Trefusis Point, Flushing, Falmouth, Cornwall.

Species & Scientific Name		lbs	ozs	Weight drms	:	kilos	gms	Date	Captor & Location
Catfish *Anarhichas lupus*	B	12	12	8	:	5	923	1978	G.M. Taylor, Stonehaven, Scotland.
	S	6	1	8	:	2	763	1977	J.H. Reay, South of Eyemouth, Berwickshire.
Coalfish *Pollachius virens*	B	30	12	—	:	13	947	1973	A.F. Harris, Eddystone.
	S	16	8	8	:	7	497	1977	N.T. Randall, at Rusty Anchor, Plymouth, Devon.
Coho Salmon *Oncorhynchus kitsutch*		1	8	—	:	1	870	1977	R.J. McCracken, Petit Port, Guernsey.
Cod *Gadus morhua*	B	53	—	—	:	24	039	1972	G. Martin, Start Point, Devon.
	S	44	8	—	:	20	183	1966	B. Jones, Toms Point, Barry, Glamorgan, Wales.
Comber *Serranus cabrilla*	B	1	13	—	:	—	822	1977	Master B. Phillips, off Mounts Bay, Cornwall.
	S	1	—	—	:	—	454		Qualifying weight.
Common Skate *Raja batis*	B	226	8	—	:	102	733	1970	R.S. Macpherson, Duny Voe, Shetland.
	S	150	—	—	:	68	036		Qualifying weight.
Conger *Conger conger*	B	109	6	—	:	49	609	1976	R.W. Potter, S.E. of Eddystone.
	S	67	1	—	:	30	417	1967	A.W. Lander, at Natural Arch Rock End, Torquay.
Dab *Limanda limanda*	B	2	12	4	:	1	254	1975	R. Islip, Gairloch, Wester Ross, Scotland.
	S	2	9	8	:	1	176	1936	M.L. Watts, Port Talbot, Glamorgan, Wales.
Dogfish, Black-mouthed *Galeus melastomus*	B	2	13	8	:	1	288	1977	J.H. Anderson, N.W. Poll Point, Loch Fyne, Scotland.
	S	1	—	—	:	—	454		Qualifying weight.
Dogfish, Lesser Spotted *Scyliorhinus raniculus*	B	4	1	13	:	1	865	1976	B.J. Solomon, off Newquay, Cornwall.
	S	4	8	—	:	2	040	1969	J. Beattie, off Ayr Pier, Scotland.
Flounder *Platichthys flesus*	B	5	11	8	:	2	593	1956	A.G.L. Cobbledick, Fowey, Cornwall
	S	4	7	—	:	2	012	1976	M. King, off Seaford Beach, Nr. Newhaven.
Forkbeard, Greater *Phycis blennoides*	B	4	11	4	:	2	133	1969	Miss M. Woodgate, Falmouth Bay, Cornwall.
	S	2	—	—	:	—	907		Qualifying weight.
Garfish *Belone belone*	B	2	13	14	:	1	300	1971	S. Claeskens, off Newton Ferrers, Devon.
	S	2	8	—	:	1	33	1977	S. Lester, Pembroke Bay, Guernsey.
Greater Weaver *Trachinus draco*	B	2	4	—	:	1	020	1927	P. Ainslie, Brighton, Sussex.
	S	2	—	—	:	—	907		Qualifying weight.
Gurnard, Grey *Eutrigla gurnardus*	B	2	7	—	:	1	105	1976	D. Swinbanks, Caliach Point, Mull, Scotland.
	S	1	8	—	:	—	680	1977	S. Quine, off Peel Breakwater, Isle of Man.
Gurnard, Red *Aspitrigla cuculus*	B	5	—	—	:	2	268	1973	B.D. Critchley, 3 miles off Rhyl, Wales.

Species & Scientific Name		lbs	ozs	drms		kilos	gms	Date	Captor & Location
	S	2	10	11	:	1	209	1976	D. Johns, Helford River Glebe Cove, Cornwall.
Gurnard, Streaked	B	1	—	—	:	—	454	Qualifying weight.	
Trigloporus lastoviza	S	1	6	8	:	—	637	1971	H. Livingstone Smith, Loch Goil, Firth of Clyde, Scotland.
Gurnard, Yellow or	B	11	7	4	:	5	195	1952	C.W. King, Wallasey.
Tubfish	S	12	3	—	:	5	528	1976	G.J. Reynolds, Langland Bay, Wales.
Trigla lucerna									
Haddock	B	12	10	1	:	5	727	1975	Sub Lt. K.P. White, Manacles Area, Falmouth Bay, Cornwall.
Melanogrammus aeglefinus	S	6	12	—	:	3	061	1976	G.B. Stevenson, Loch Goil, Scotland.
Haddock, Norway	B	13	11	4	:	6	908	1978	G. Bones, Falmouth, Cornwall.
Sebastes viviparus	S	1	3	—	:	—	538	1973	F.P. Fawke, Southend Pier, Essex.
Hake	B	25	5	8	:	11	494	1962	H.W. Steele, Belfast Lough, N. Ireland.
Merluccius merluccius	S	5	—	—	:	2	268	Qualifying weight.	
Halibut	B	212	4	—	:	96	270	1975	J.A. Hewitt, off Dunnet Head, Scotland.
Hippoglossus hippoglossus	S	14	—	—	:	6	350	Qualifying weight.	
Herring	B	1	1	—	:	—	481	1973	Brett Barden, off Bexhill-on-Sea, Sussex.
Clupea harengus	S	1	—	—	:	—	454	Qualifying weight.	
John Dory (St. Peter's fish)	B	11	14	—	:	5	386	1977	J. Johnson, off New-haven, E. Sussex.
Zeus faber	S	4	—	—	:	1	814	Qualifying weight.	
Ling	B	57	2	8	:	25	924	1975	H. Solomons, off Mevagissey, Cornwall.
Molva molva	S	15	5	11	:	6	965	1976	P. Sanders, Porthleven Beach, Cornwall.
Lumpsucker	B	6	3	4	:	2	813	1968	F. Harrison, Redcar, Nth. Yorkshire.
Cyclopterus lumpus	S	14	3	—	:	6	435	1970	W.J. Burgess, off Felix-stowe Beach, Suffolk.
Mackerel	B	5	6	8	:	2	452	1969	S. Beasley, north of Eddystone Light.
Scomber scombrus	S	4	—	8	:	1	828	1952	Sqn. Ldr. P. Porter, Breakwater, Peel, Isle of Man.
Megrim	B	3	12	8	:	1	715	1973	Master Paul Christie, Loch Gairloch, Scotland.
Lepidorhombus whiff-iagonis	S	2	—	—	:	—	907	Qualifying weight.	
Monkfish	B	66	—	—	:	29	936	1965	C.G. Chalk, Shoreham, Sussex.
Squatina squatina	S	50	—	—	:	22	679	1974	R.S. Brown, Monknash Beach, Wales.
Mullet, Golden Grey	B	1	—	8	:	—	467	1977	R.A. Andrews, Southampton Water
Liza aurata	S	2	10	—	:	1	190	1976	R.J. Hopkins, Burry Port, Nr. Llanelli, Wales.
Mullet, Red	B	3	8	—	:	1	587	Qualifying weight.	
Mullus surmuletus	S	3	10	—	:	1	644	1967	J.E. Martel, Guernsey,C.I.

Species & Scientific Name		lbs	ozs	drms		kilos	gms	Date	Captors & Location
Mullet, Thick-lipped	B	10	1	—	:	4	564	1952	P.C. Libby, Portland,
Chelon labrosus	S	10	—	12	:	4	745	1978	R. Gifford, Lagoon Leys, Aberthaw, Glamorgan
Mullet, Thin-lipped	B	4	—	—	:	1	814	Qualifying weight.	
Liza ramada	S	5	11	—	:	2	579	1975	D.E. Knowles, River Rother, Sussex.
Opah	B	128	—	—	:	58	057	1973	A.R. Blewett, Mounts Bay, Penzance, Cornwall.
Lampris guttatus	S	40	—	—	:	18	143	Qualifying weight.	
Pelamid, (Bonito)	B	8	13	4	:	4	004	1969	J. Parnell, Torbay, Devon.
Sarda sarda	S	4	—	—	:	1	814	Qualifying weight.	
Perch, Dusky	B	28	—	—	:	12	700	1973	D. Cope, off Durlston Head, Dorset.
Epinephelus guaza	S	14	—	—	:	6	350	Qualifying weight.	
Plaice	B	10	3	8	:	4	635	1974	Master H. Gardiner, Longa Sound, Scotland.
Pleuronectes platessa	S	8	1	4	:	3	664	1976	Master N. Mills, East Point, Southend Pier, Essex.
Pollack	B	25	—	—	:	11	339	1972	R.J. Hosking, off Eddystone Light.
Pollachius pollachius	S	16	—	—	:	7	257	1977	B. Raybould, Portland Bill, Dorset.
Poutassou		1	12	—	:	—	793	1977	J.H. Anderson, Loch Fyne, Scotland.
Micromesistius poutassou									
Pouting, (Bib, Pout)	B	5	8	—	:	2	494	1969	R.S. Armstrong, off Berry Head.
Trisopterus luscus	S	3	—	—	:	1	361	Qualifying weight.	
Ray, Blonde	B	37	12	—	:	17	122	1973	H.T. Pout, off Start Point, Devon.
Raja brachyura	S	25	4	—	:	11	453	1975	S.B. Sangan, Greve de Lecq Pier, Jersey, C.I.
Ray, Bottle-nosed	B	76	—	—	:	34	471	1970	R. Bulpitt, off The Needles, Isle of Wight.
Raja alba	S	30	—	—	:	13	607	Qualifying weight.	
Ray, Cuckoo	B	5	11	—	:	2	579	1975	V. Morrison, off the Causeway Coast, N. Ireland.
Raja naevus	S	4	8	—	:	2	040	Qualifying weight.	
Ray, Eagle	B	52	8	—	:	23	812	1972	R.J. Smith, off Nab Tower, Isle of Wight.
Myliobatis aquila	S	25	—	—	:	11	339	Qualifying weight.	
Ray, Electric	B	96	1	—	:	43	571	1975	N.J. Cowley, off Dodman Point, Cornwall.
Torpedo nobiliana	S	47	8	—	:	21	544	1971	R.J.F. Pearce, from Long Quarry, Torquay, Devon.
Ray, Sandy	B	4	—	—	:	1	814	Qualifying weight.	
Raja circularis	S	4	—	—	:	1	814	Qualifying weight.	
Ray, Small-eyed	B	16	4	—	:	7	370	1973	H. T. Pout, Salcombe, Devon.
Raja microocellata	S	13	8	15	:	6	149	1976	A. Jones, off Trevose Head, Cornwall.
Ray, Spotted	B	6	3	4	:	2	813	1977	P.J. England, off Caliach Point, Isle of Mull, Scotland.
Raja montagui									

Species & Scientific Name		lbs	ozs	Weight drms		kilos	gms	Date	Captor & Location
	S	7	12	—	:	3	515	1977	P.R. Dower, in Stoke Beach Area, Plymouth, Devon.
Ray, Sting *Dasyatis pastinaca*	B	59	—	—	:	26	761	1952	J.M. Buckley, Clacton, Essex.
	S	51	4	—	:	23	245	1975	A.L. Stevens, Sowley Beach, Hampshire.
Ray, Thornback *Raja clavata*	B	38	—	—	:	17	236	1935	J. Patterson, Rustington, Sussex.
	S	19	—	—	:	8	618	1976	A.K. Paterson, Mull of Galloway, Scotland.
Ray, Undulate *Raja undulata*	B	19	6	13	:	8	811	1970	L.R. Le Page, Herm, Channel Islands.
	S	10	10	4	:	4	826	1968	G.S. Robert, Port Soif Bay, Guernsey.
Rockling, 3-bearded *Gaidropsarus vulgaris*	B	3	2	—	:	1	417	1976	N. Docksey, off Portland Breakwater, Dorset.
	S	2	14	8	:	1	318	1976	N.S. Burt, from a cliff at Portland, Dorset.
Rockling, Shore *Gaidropsarus mediterraneus*	B	1	—	—	:	—	454		Qualifying weight.
	S	1	13	10	:	—	992	1978	E.R. Jones, Holyhead Breakwater.
Sea Scorpion, Short-spined *Myoxocephalus scorpius*	B	2	3	—	:	—	992	1973	R. Stephenson, Grt. Cumbrae Island, Scotland
	S	2	2	8	:	—	977	1972	R.W. Tarn, off Roker South Pier, Sunderland.
Scad, (Horse Mackerel) *Trachurus trachurus*	B	3	5	3	:	2	102	1978	M.A. Atkins, Torbay, Devon.
	S	2	5	13	:	1	071	1977	W.K. Rail, at North Cliffs, Cornwall.
Shad, Allis *Alosa alosa*	B	3	—	—	:	1	361		Qualifying weight.
	S	4	12	7	:	2	166	1977	P.B. Gerrard, off Chesil Beach, Dorset.
Shad, Twaite *Alsoa fallax*	B	3	2	—	:	1	417	1949	T. Hayward, Deal, Kent.
	B	3	2	—	:	1	417	1954	S. Jenkins, Torbay, Devon.
	S	2	12	—	:	1	247	1978	J.W. Martin, Garlieston, Wigtownshire.
Shark, Blue *Prionace glauca*	B	218	—	—	:	98	878	1959	N. Sutcliffe, Looe, Cornwall.
	S	75	—	—	:	34	018		Qualifying weight.
Shark, Mako *Isurus oxyrinchus*	B	500	—	—	:	226	786	1971	Mrs. J.M. Yallop, off Eddystone Light.
	S	75	—	—	:	34	018		Qualifying weight.
Shark, Porbeagle *Lamna nasus*	B	465	—	—	:	210	910	1976	J. Potier, off Padstow, Cornwall.
	S	75	—	—	:	34	018		Qualifying weight.
Shark, Six-gilled *Hexanchus griseus*	B	9	8	—	:	4	309	1976	F.E. Beeton, south of Penlee Point, Plymouth, Devon.
	S				NO MINIMUM QUALIFYING WEIGHT				
Shark, Thresher *Alopias vulpinus*	B	280	—	—	:	127	—	1933	H.A. Kelly, Dungeness.
	S	75	—	—	:	34	018		Qualifying weight.
Smoothhound, Starry *Mustelus asterias*	B	20	—	—	:	9	071		Qualifying weight.
	S	23	2	—	:	10	488	1972	D. Carpenter, Beach at Bradwell-on-Sea, Essex.

Species & Scientific Name		lbs	ozs	drms		kilos	gms	Date	Captor & Location
Smoothhound	B	28	—	—	:	12	700	1969	A.T. Chilvers, Heacham, Norfolk.
Mustelus mustelus	S	14	14	12	:	6	768	1977	A.J. Peacock, at St. Donats, Glamorgan Wales.
Sole	B	4	—	—	:	1	814		Qualifying weight.
Solea solea	S	4	3	8	:	1	913	1974	R. Wells, Redcliffe Beach, Dorset.
Sole, Lemon	B	2	2	—	:	—	963	1976	J. Gordon, at Loch Goil Head, off Loch Long, Firth of Clyde, Scotland.
Microstomus kitt	S	2	2	15	:	—	990	1971	D.R. Duke, Victoria Pier, Douglas, Isle of Man.
Spanish Mackerel	B	1	—	6	:	—	464	1972	P. Jones, off Guernsey, C.I.
Scomber japonicus	S	1	—	—	:	—	454		Qualifying weight.
Spurdog	B	21	3	7	:	9	622	1977	P.R. Barrett, off Porthleven, Cornwall.
Squalus acanthias	S	16	12	8	:	7	611	1964	R. Legg, Chesil Beach, Dorset.
Sunfish	B	108	—	—	:	48	986	1976	T.F. Sisson, off Saundersfoot, Wales.
Mola mola	S	49	4	—	:	22	338	1976	M.G.H. Merry, Fisherman's Cove, North Cliffs, Cornwall.
Tadpole-fish	B	1	—	—	:	—	454		Qualifying weight.
Raniceps raninus	S	1	3	12	:	—	559	1977	D.A. Higgins, Browns Bay, Whitley Bay, Tyne & Wear.
Tope	B	74	11	—	:	33	876	1964	A.B. Harries, Caldy Is.
Galeorhinus galeus	S	54	4	—	:	24	606	1975	D. Hastings, Loch Ryan, Wigtownshire, Scotland.
Torsk	B	12	1	—	:	5	471	1968	D. Pottinger, Shetland.
Brosme brosme	S	5	—	—	:	2	268		Qualifying weight.
Trigger Fish	B	4	9	5	:	2	077	1975	E. Montacute, Weybay, Dorset.
Balistes carolinensis	S	4	6	—	:	1	984	1975	M.J. Blew, Bossington Beach, Somerset.
Tunny	B	851	—	—	:	385	989	1933	L. Mitchell Henry, Whitby Yorks.
Thunnus thunnus	S	100	—	—	:	45	357		Qualifying weight.
Turbot	B	32	3	—	:	14	599	1976	D. Dyer, off Plymouth, Devon.
Scophthalmus maximus	S	28	8	—	:	12	926	1973	J.D. Dorling, Dunwich Beach, East Suffolk.
Witch	B	1	—	—	:	—	454		Qualifying weight.
Glyptocephalus cynoglossus	S	1	2	13	:	—	533	1967	T.J. Barathy, Colwyn Bay, Wales.
Whiting	B	6	4	—	:	2	834	1977	S. Dearman, West Bay, Bridport, Dorset.
Merlangus merlangus	S	3	2	—	:	1	417	1976	C.T. Kochevar, off Dungeness Beach, Kent.
Wrasse, Ballan	B	7	8	5	:	3	410	1975	M.B. Hale, north of Herm, C.I
Labrus bergylta	S	8	6	6	:	3	808	1976	R.W. Le Page, Bordeaux Beach, Guernsey, C.I.

Species & Scientific Name		Weight							
		lbs	ozs	drms		kilos	gms	Date	Captor & Location
Wrasse, Cuckoo	B	2	—	8	:	—	921	1973	A.M. Foley, off Plymouth, Devon.
Labrus mixtus	S	1	4	8	:	—	581	1973	R. Newton, Holyhead Breakwater, Wales.
Wreckfish	B	7	10	—	:	3	458	1974	Cdr. E. St. John Holt, Looe, Cornwall.
Polyprion americanus	S	2	—	—	:	—	907		Qualifying weight.

British Record Sea Fish List

Mini Records – Weight up to 1 lb

Species & Scientific Name		Weight		Date	Captor & Location
	ozs	dms	gms		
Argentine *Argentina sphyraena*	5	3	: 147	1978	I. Millar, Arrochar, Loch Long.
Blenny, Tonipot *Parablennius gattorugine*	5	2	: 145	1977	J. Hughes, Portland Bill, Dorset.
Blenny, Viviparous *Zoarces viviparus*	11	3	: 317	1975	D. Ramsey, at Craigendoran, Scotland.
Dab, Long Rough *Hippoglossoides platessoides*	5	8	: 155	1975	I. McGrath, at Coulport, Loch Long, Scotland.
Dragonet *Callionymus lyra*	4	12	: 134	1976	R.P. Jones, in Rye Bay, Sussex.
Goby, Black *Gobius niger*	1	8	: 042	1975	P.J. Whippy, 1 mile out from Pevensey Bay, Sussex.
Goby, Giant *Gobius cobitis*	6	10	: 187	1974	P.A. Cadogan, Herm Island, Near Guernsey, C.I.
Goby Rock *Gobius cobitis*	—	14	: 024	1977	C.L. Phillips, Menai Straits.
Pilchard *Sardina pilchardus*	7	—	: 198	1976	K.W. Jarrett, at Littlehampton. Sussex.
Poor-cod *Trisopterus minutus*	10	5	: 294	1976	H. Livingstone Smith, in the Gantock area, Scotland.
Red Band-fish *Cepola rubescens*	13	8	: 382	1975	K. Bradbury, off Paignton, Devon.
Rockling, Five-bearded *Ciliata mustela*	9	4	: 262	1968	P.R. Winder, Lancing Beach.
Sandeel, Corbin's *Hyperoplus immaculatus*	4	6	: 124	1975	M.J. Priaulx, off Plymouth, Devon.
Sandeel, Greater *Hyperoplus lanceolatus*	7	12	: 219	1977	P.E. Lucas, at Amfroque Bank, East of Herm, C.I.
Sea Scorpion, long spined *Taurulus bubalis*	8	—	: 226	1978	W. Crone, Royal William Yard, Plymouth.
Shanny *Lipophyrs pholis*	2	5	: 065	1977	Master K. Woolfe, at St. Martins Point, Guernsey, C.I.
Smelt *Osmerus eperlanus*	5	9	: 158	1978	C. Wyganowski, Southend Pier, Essex.
Smelt, Sand *Atherina presbyter*	2	9	: 072	1975	Master A.D. Laws, at New Jetty, St. Peter Port, Guernsey, C.I.
Stickleback, Sea *Spinachia spinachia*	—	4	: 7.818	1978	Master Kevin Pilley, Poole Harbour, Dorset.

Species & Scientific Name	ozs	drms	gms	Date	Captor & Location
Topknot, Common *Zeugopterus punctatus*	11	2 :	315	1972	P. Andrews, St. Catherines, Jersey.
Weever, Lesser *Trachinus vipera*	2	2 :	060	1976	M. Nickolls, at Schole Bank, ten miles N.E. Guernsey. C.I.
Wrasse, Corkwing *Crenilabrus melops*	11	4 :	318	1974	T.R. Woodman, off Portland Bill, Dorset.
Wrasse, Goldsinny *Cetnolabrus rupestris*	2	9 :	072	1977	R. Lambert, at Portland Bill, Dorset.
Wrasse, Rock Cook *Centrolabrus exoletus*	2	9 :	072	1977	A.L.C. de Guerin, at St. Peter Port Breakwater, Guernsey, C.I.

General

Weather forecasts:

Bedford area	– (01) 8099
Belfast area	– (0232) 8091
Birmingham	– (021) 246 8091
Bristol	– (0272) 8091
Cardiff area	– (0222) 8091
Central Lancs	– (0254) 8091
Edinburgh	– (031) 246 8091
Essex coast	– (01) 246 8096
Glasgow	– (041) 246 8091
Kent coast	– (01) 246 8098
Lancs coast	– (061) 246 8092
Leeds area	– (0532) 8091
London area	– (01) 8091
Norfolk and Suffolk	– (0473) 8091
N. Lincs	– (0472) 8091
N. Wales	– (061) 246 8093
Notts Leics and Derby	– (0602) 8091
Sheffield	– (0742) 8091
Devon, Cornwall	– (0752) 8091
S. Hants	– (0703) 8091
S. Lancs	– (051) 246 8091
S. W. Midlands	– (0452) 8091
Sussex coast	– (01) 246 8097
Thames valley	– (01) 246 8090
Tyne-Tees	– (0632) 8091

National Anglers' Council: 17 Queen Street, Peterborough.
British Record (rod-caught) Fish Committee: 17 Queen Street, Peterborough.

Anglers' Cooperative Association: Midland Bank Chambers, Westgate, Grantham, Lincs.

Freshwater

The British Waterways Board, Melbury House, Melbury Terrace, London NW1.

The Freshwater Biological Association, Windermere Laboratory, The Ferry House, Ambleside, Cumbria

The Salmon and Trout Association, Fishmongers' Hall, London EC4.

The British Carp Study Group, Newhaven, Marsh Lane, Easton-in-Gordano, Bristol.

The National Association of Specimen Groups, 22 Peveril Street, Alfreton Road, Nottingham.

The Tenchfishers, 90 Bures Road, Great Cornard, Sudbury, Suffolk.

The National Federation of Anglers, Haig House, 87 Green Lane, Derby.

The London Anglers' Association, 183 Hoe Street, Walthamstow, London E17.

The Birmingham Anglers' Association, 40 Thorp Street, Birmingham 5.

Water authorities

Anglian Water Authority, Diploma House, Grammar School Walk, Huntingdon.

Northumbrian Water Authority, Eldon House, Regent Centre, Gosforth, Newcastle upon Tyne.

North West Water Authority, Dawson House, Great Sankey, Warrington.

Severn–Trent Water Authority, Abelson House, 2297 Coventry Road, Sheldon, Birmingham.

Southern Water Authority, Guildborne House, Worthing, Sussex. (Free booklet on fishing)

South West Water Authority, 3–5 Barnfield Road, Exeter. (Booklets on fishing)

Thames Water Authority, New River Head, Rosebery Avenue, London EC1.

Wessex Water Authority, Techno House, Redcliffe Way, Bristol 1. (Booklets on fishing)

Welsh National Water Development Authority, The Barracks, Brecon, Breconshire.

Yorkshire Water Authority, West Riding House, 67 Albion Street, Leeds.

Sea

National Federation of Sea Anglers, 26 Downs View Crescent, Uckfield, Sussex.

Northern Federation of Sea Angling Societies, 8 Gainsborough Square, Grindon, Sunderland, Tyne and Wear.

Tope Angling Club of Great Britain, The George and Dragon, Castle Street, Conway, Wales.

The European Federation of Sea Anglers, 81 Longwood Gardens, Clayhall, Ilford, Essex.

The Shark Angling Club of Great Britain, The Quay, East Looe, Cornwall.

The British Conger Club, Plymouth Sea Angling Centre, Sutton Jetty, Barbican, Plymouth.

Welsh Federation of Sea Anglers, 21 Glasfryn Dasen, Llanelli.

Scottish Federation of Sea Anglers, 11 Rutland Street, Edinburgh.

The Marine Biological Association of the United Kingdom, The Laboratory, Citadel Hill, Plymouth.

Annuals

Where to Fish (The Field).

An extremely useful guide to river- and sea-fishing waters in Britain, including extensive notes on fishing abroad.

Woodbine Angling Yearbook (Queen Anne Press).

Complete updated British and world match and specimen, record lists, plus digest of the year's big fishing matches, casting tournaments etc.

Periodicals

Anglers' Mail, weekly (54 Stamford Street, London SE1. Tel. (01) 634 4444).

Full news coverage of the week's angling events, coarse, game, and sea. Advance notices of matches, match reports, and a specimen-fish competition.

Angling Times, weekly (E.M.A.P., Oundle Road, Peterborough. Tel. Peterborough 61471).

Full news coverage, articles on all fields of angling, match guides and reports, specimen-fish competition.

Angling, monthly (30–34 Langham Street, London W1).

Articles on all fields of angling.

Sea Angler, monthly (E.M.A.P., Oundle Road, Peterborough).

Sea-angling news, articles on sea-angling techniques.

Trout and Salmon, monthly (E.M.A.P., 21 Church Walk, Peterborough).

Game-fishing articles. Reports on condition of major game-fishing waters.

Books, general

Edwards, Capt. T. L., and Horsfall Turner, E.,
The Angler's Cast (Herbert Jenkins, 1960).

Howes, Bill,
English Reservoirs (Benn, 1967).

Pratt, Mary M.
Better Angling with Simple Science (Fishing News (Books) Ltd, 1975).

Sosin, Mark, and Clark, John,
Through the Fish's Eye (André Deutsch, 1976).

Coarse-fishing books

Bartles, Bill,
Coarse Fishing (A. & C. Black, 1973).

Birch, Eric,
The Management of Coarse Fishing Waters (John Baker, 1964).

Burrell, Leonard F. G.,
Beginners' Guide to Home Coarse Tackle Making (Pelham, 1972).

Forsberg, Ray,
Coarse Fishing (Arthur Barker, 1972).

Gay, Martin,
Beginners' Guide to Pike Fishing (Pelham, 1975).

Hilton, Jack,
Quest for Carp (Pelham, 1972).

Lane, Billy, and Graham, Colin,
Freshwater Fish and How to Catch 'em (Pelham, 1975).

Macan, T. T., and Worthington, E. B.,
Life in Lakes and Rivers (Fontana, 1972).

Marks, Ivan, and Goodwin, John,
Ivan Marks on Match Fishing (Pelham, 1975).

Righyni, R. V.,
Grayling (Macdonald, 1968).

Stone, Peter,
Come Fishing With Me (Pelham, 1973).

Walker, Richard,
Still Water Angling (David and Charles, 1975).

Webb, Ray, and Rickards, Barrie,
Fishing for Big Pike (A. & C. Black, 1971).

Game fishing books

Bridges, Anthony,
Modern Salmon Fishing (A. & C. Black, 1969).

Dutton, T. E.,
Salmon and Sea-trout Fishing (Faber and Faber, 1972).

Falkus, Hugh,
Sea-trout Fishing (Wetherby, 1975).

Gingrigh, Arnold,
The Joys of Trout (Crown Publishers New York, 1973).

Goddard, John,
Trout Flies of Still Water (A. & C. Black, 1975).

Harris, Brian,
Stillwater Trout (Osprey, 1974).

Kite, Oliver,
Nymph Fishing in Practice (Herbert Jenkins, 1969).

Lawrie, W. H.,
Scottish Trout Flies (Frederick Muller, 1966).

Mansfield, Ken (editor),
Trout and How to Catch Them (Barrie and Jenkins, 1970).

Righyni, R. V.,
Advanced Salmon Fishing (Macdonald, 1973).

Stewart, Tom,
Fifty Popular Flies series on tying instructions (Benn).

Taverner, Eric, and Scott, Jock,
Salmon Fishing (Seeley and Service, 1972).

Turling, H. D.,
Trout Fishing (A. & C. Black, 1961).

Walker, Richard,
Fly Dressing Innovations (Benn, 1974).

Sea fishing books

Carl Forbes, David,
Successful Sea Angling (David and Charles, 1971).
Big Game Fishing in British Waters (David and Charles, 1972).

Lythgoe, John and Gillian,
Fishes of the Sea (Blandford, 1971).

Stoker, Hugh,
Complete Guide to Sea Fishing (Benn, 1968).
The Modern Sea Angler (Robert Hale, 1971).

Fish Index

(First entries in bold type shows main reference.)

Freshwater fish

Sea fish

General Index